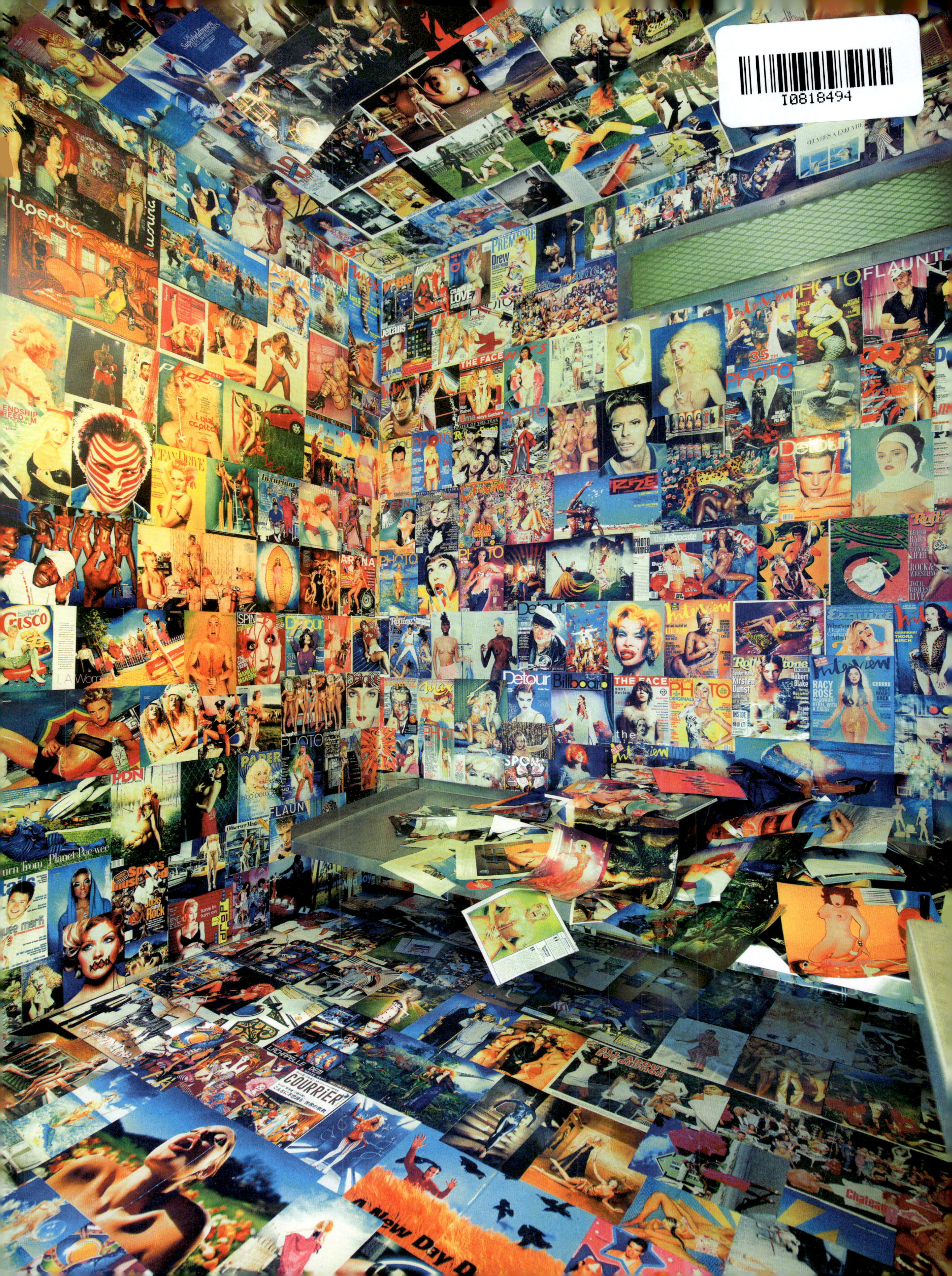
THE FACE
Detour
Billboard
SPIN
COURRIER
A New Day D

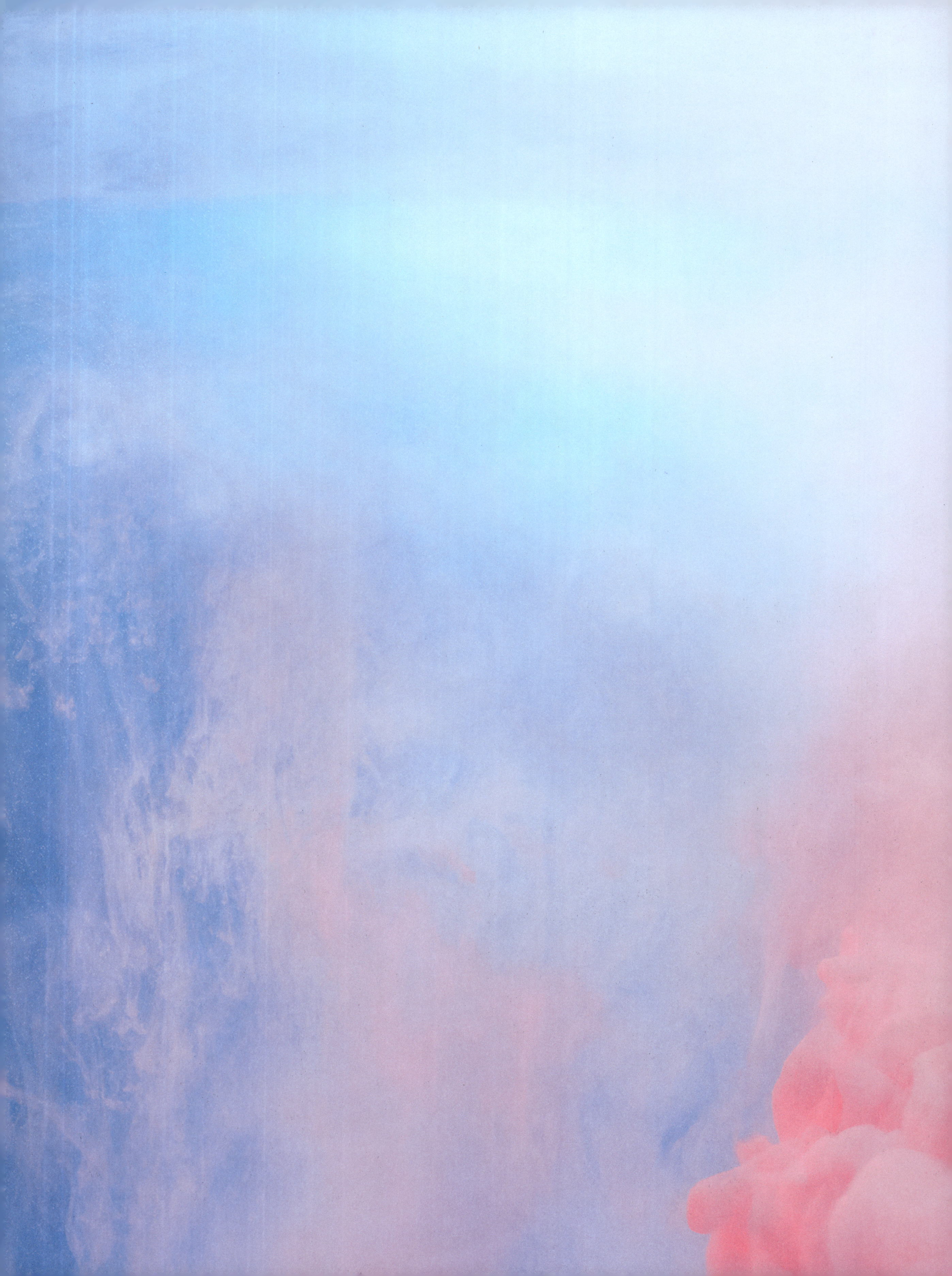

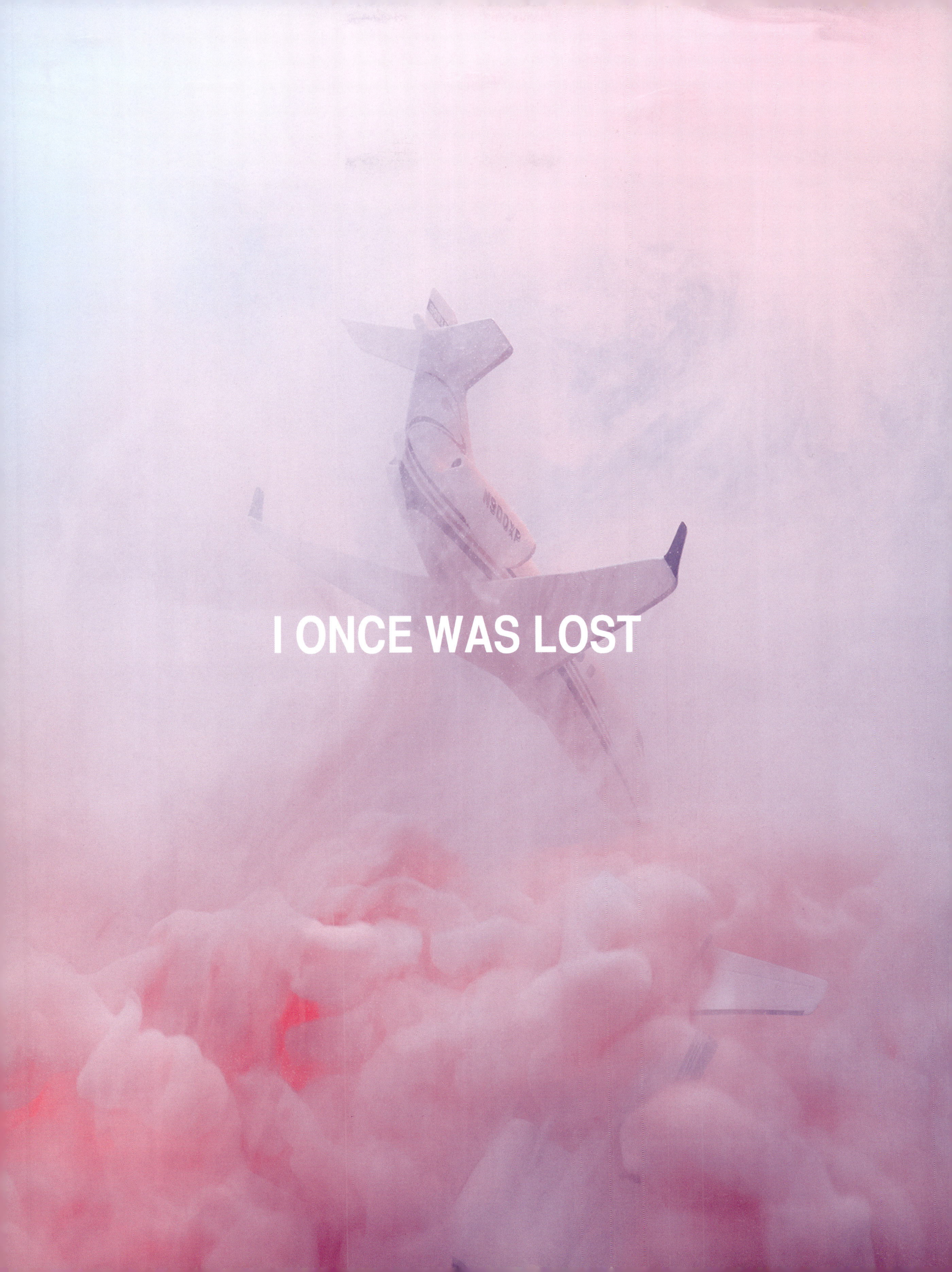

I ONCE WAS LOST

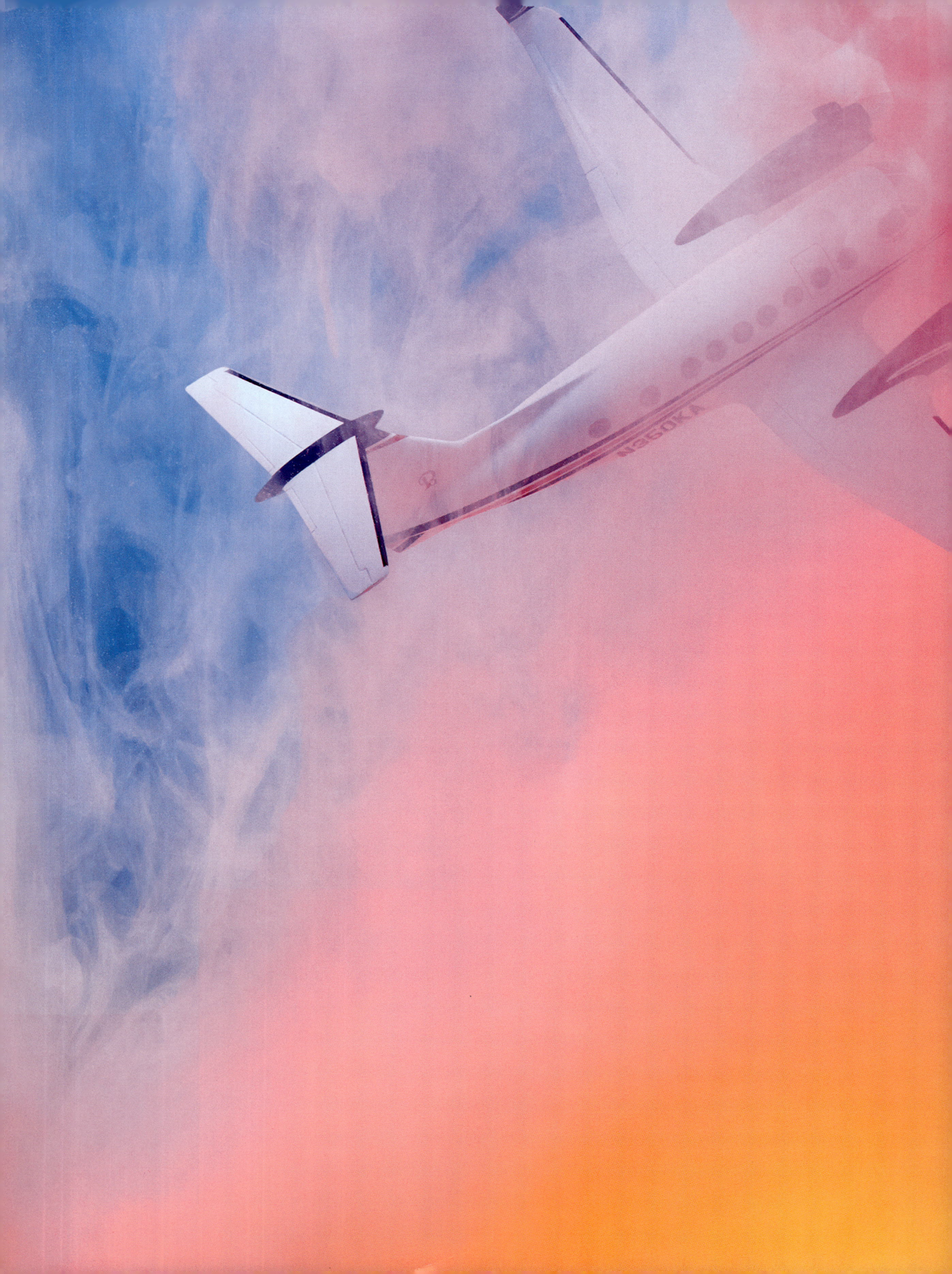
N360KA

DAVID LACHAPELLE LOST + FOUND

TASCHEN

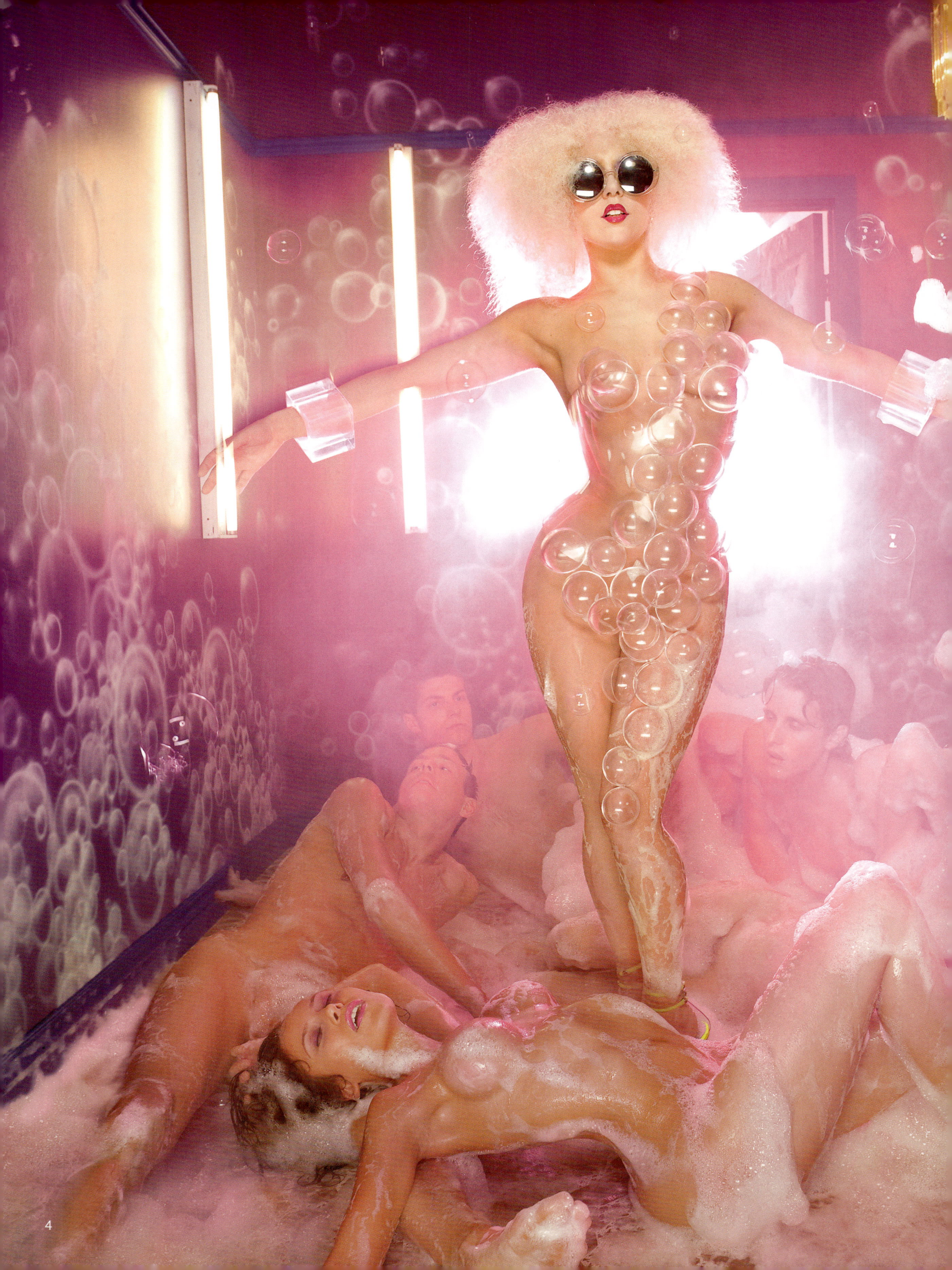

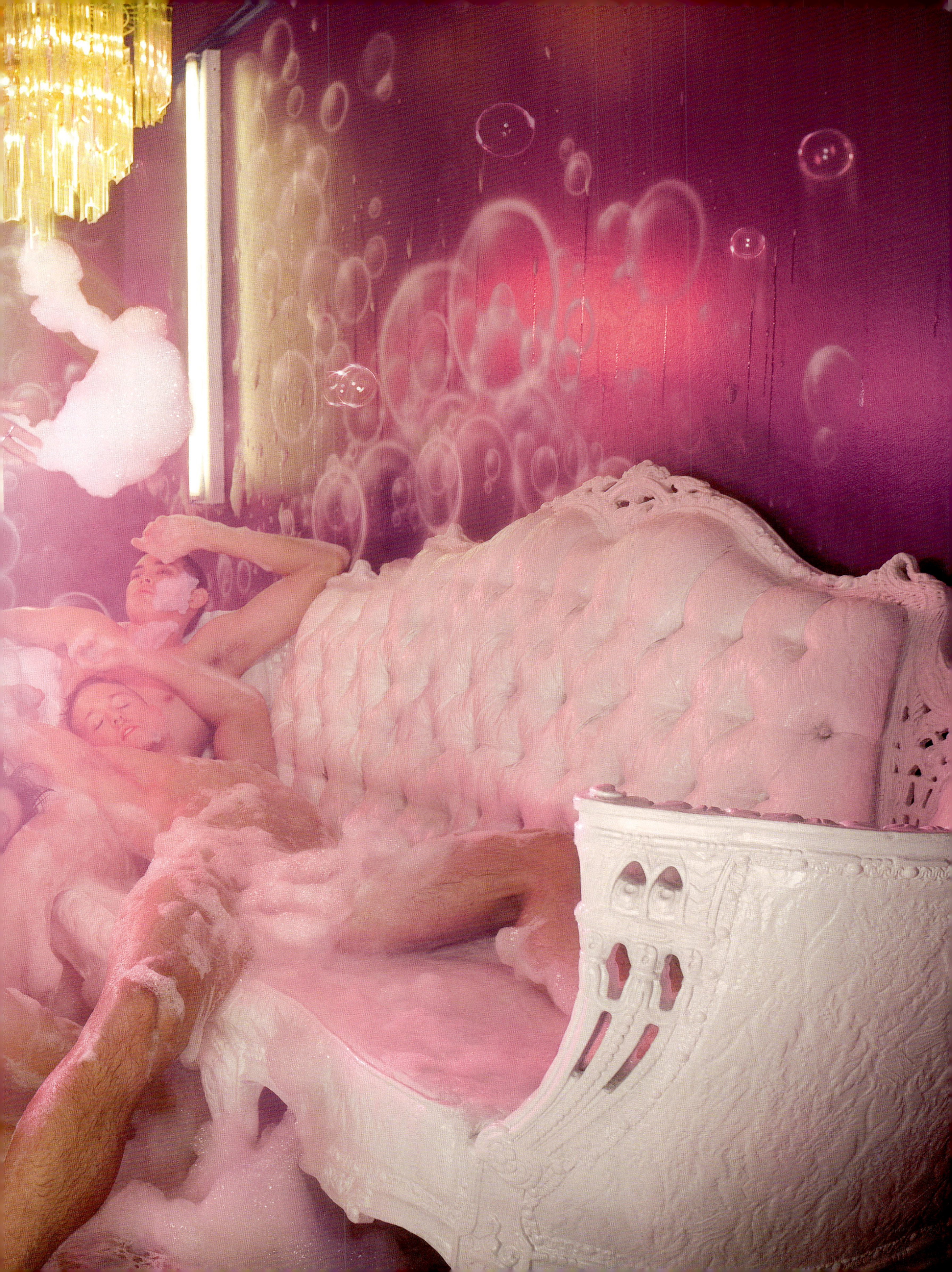

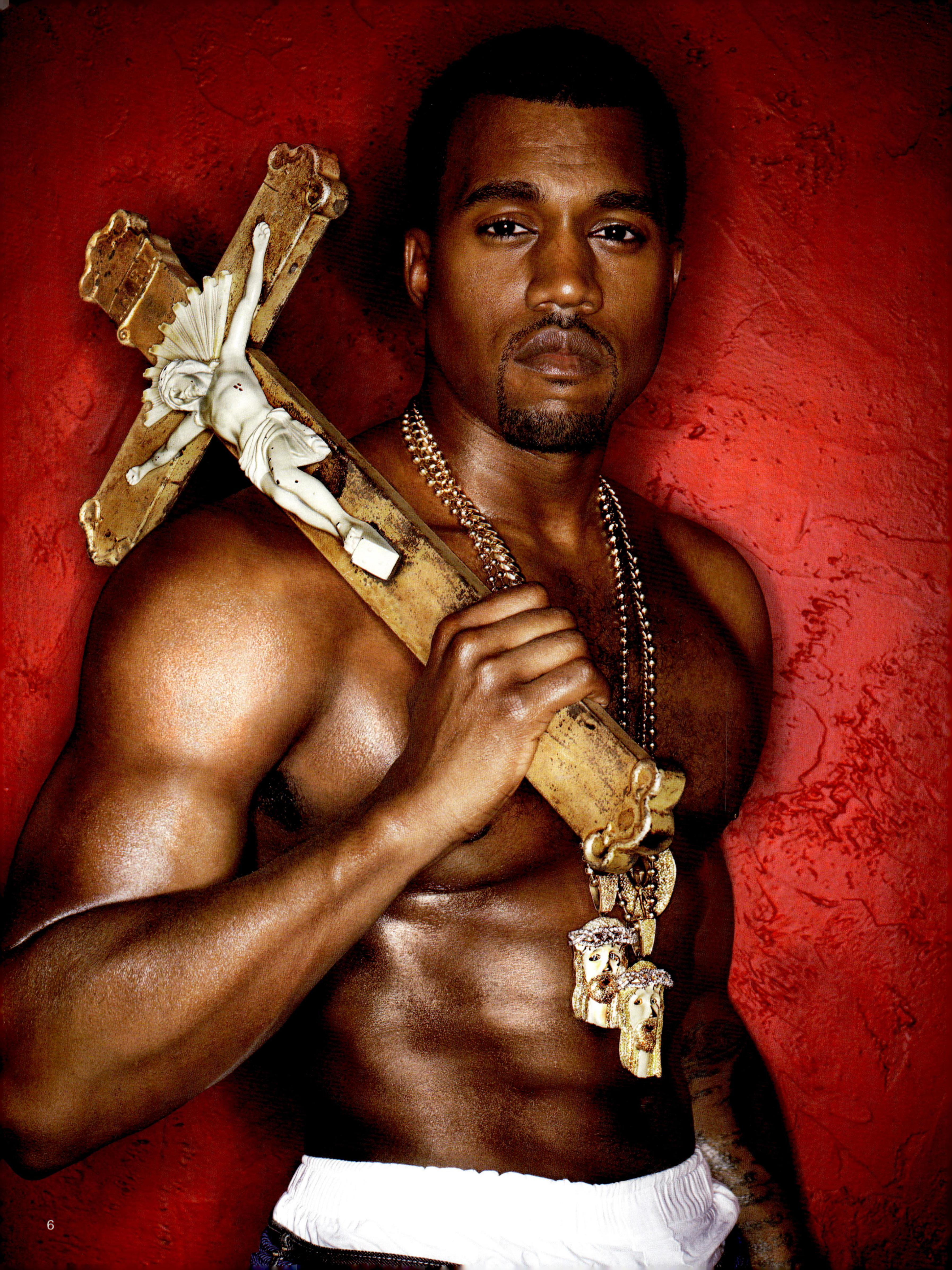

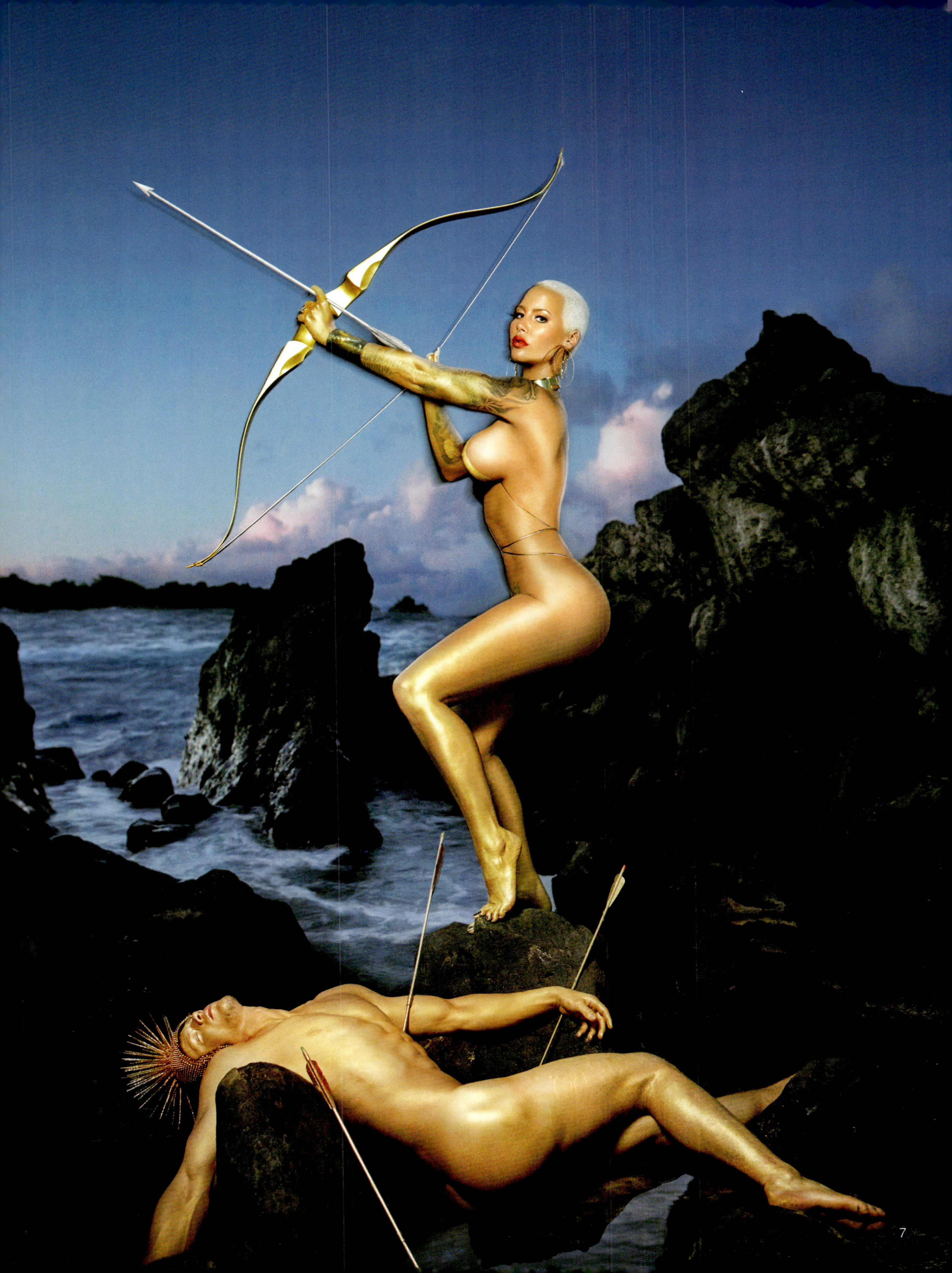

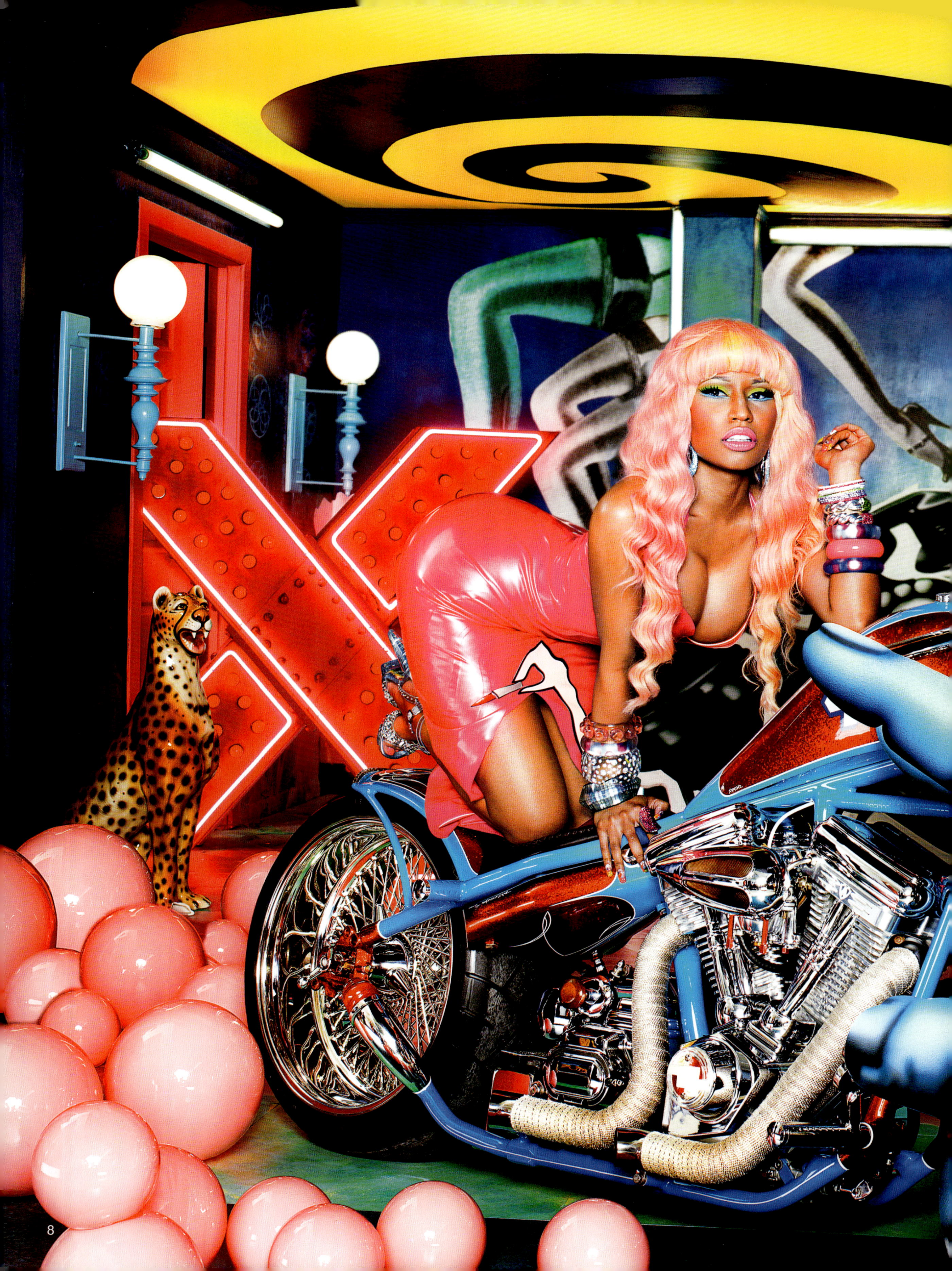

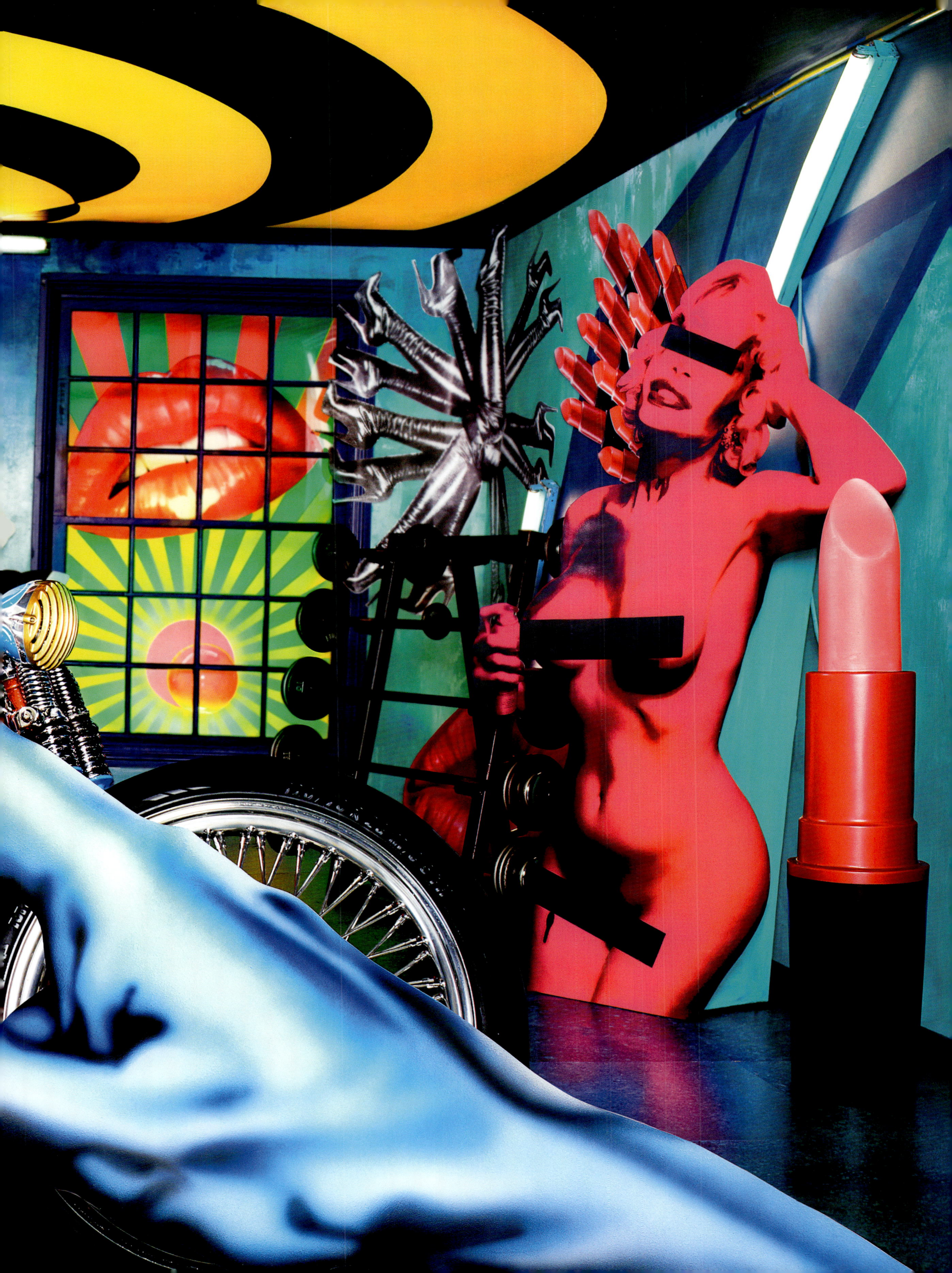

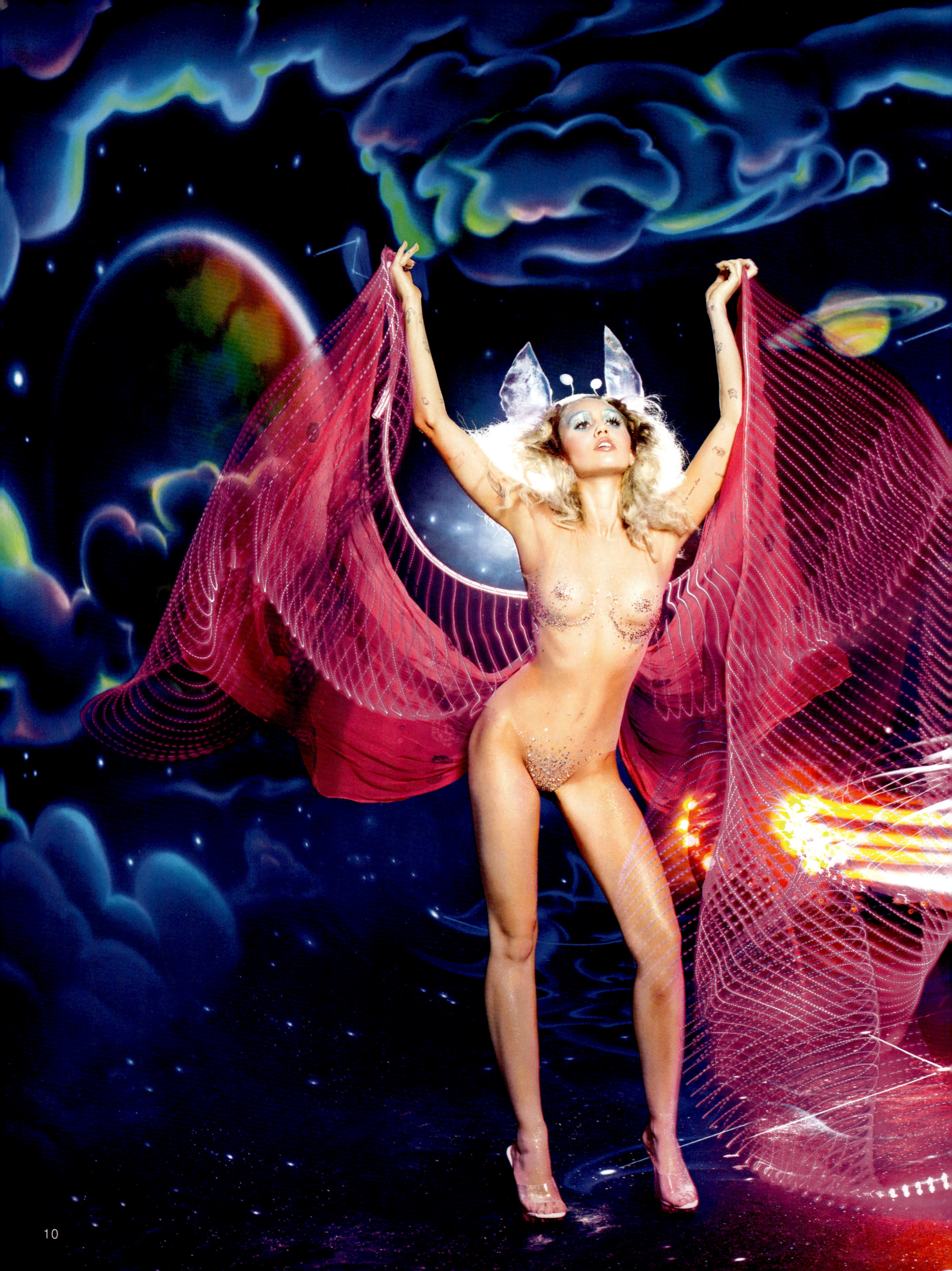

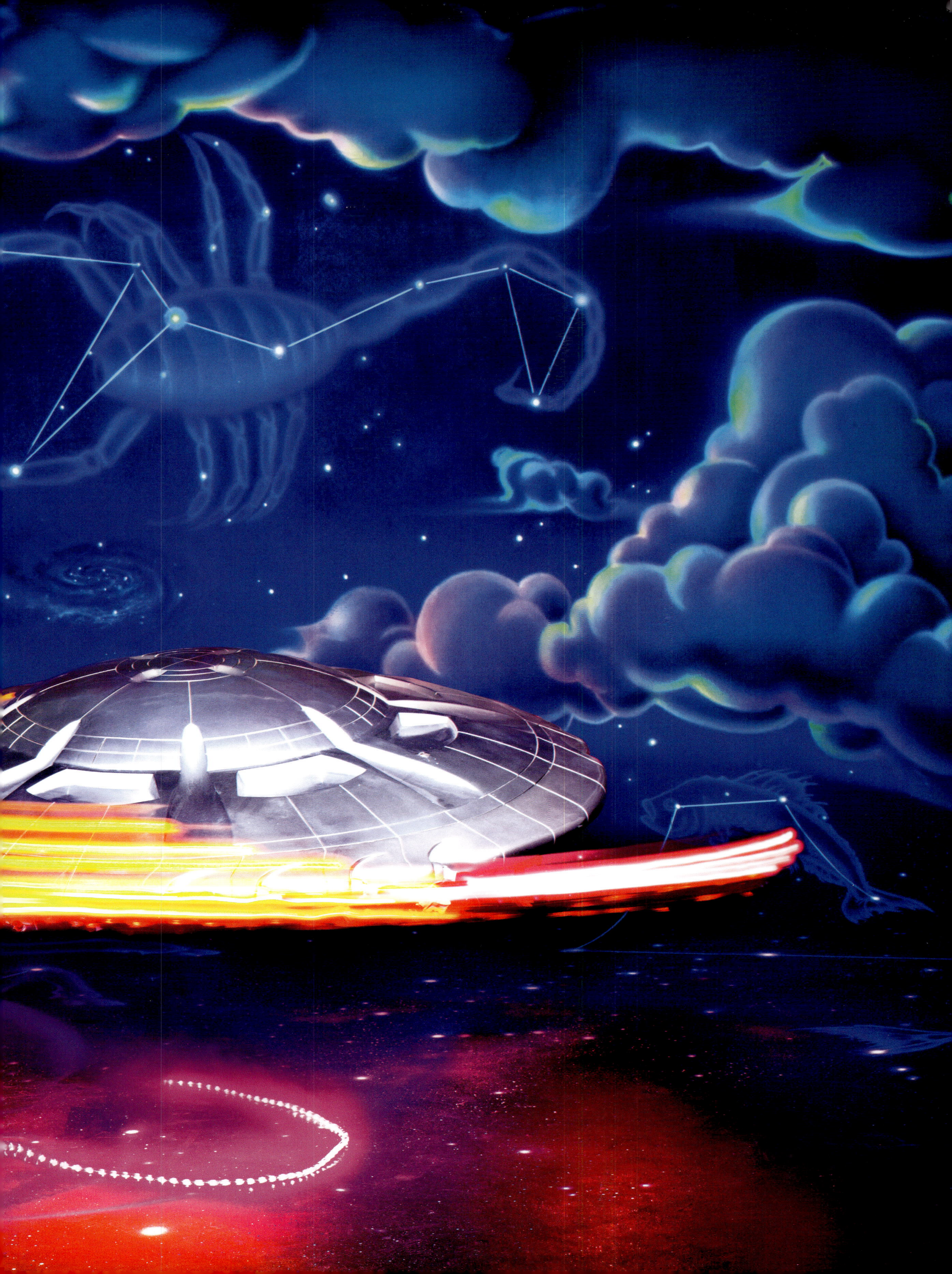

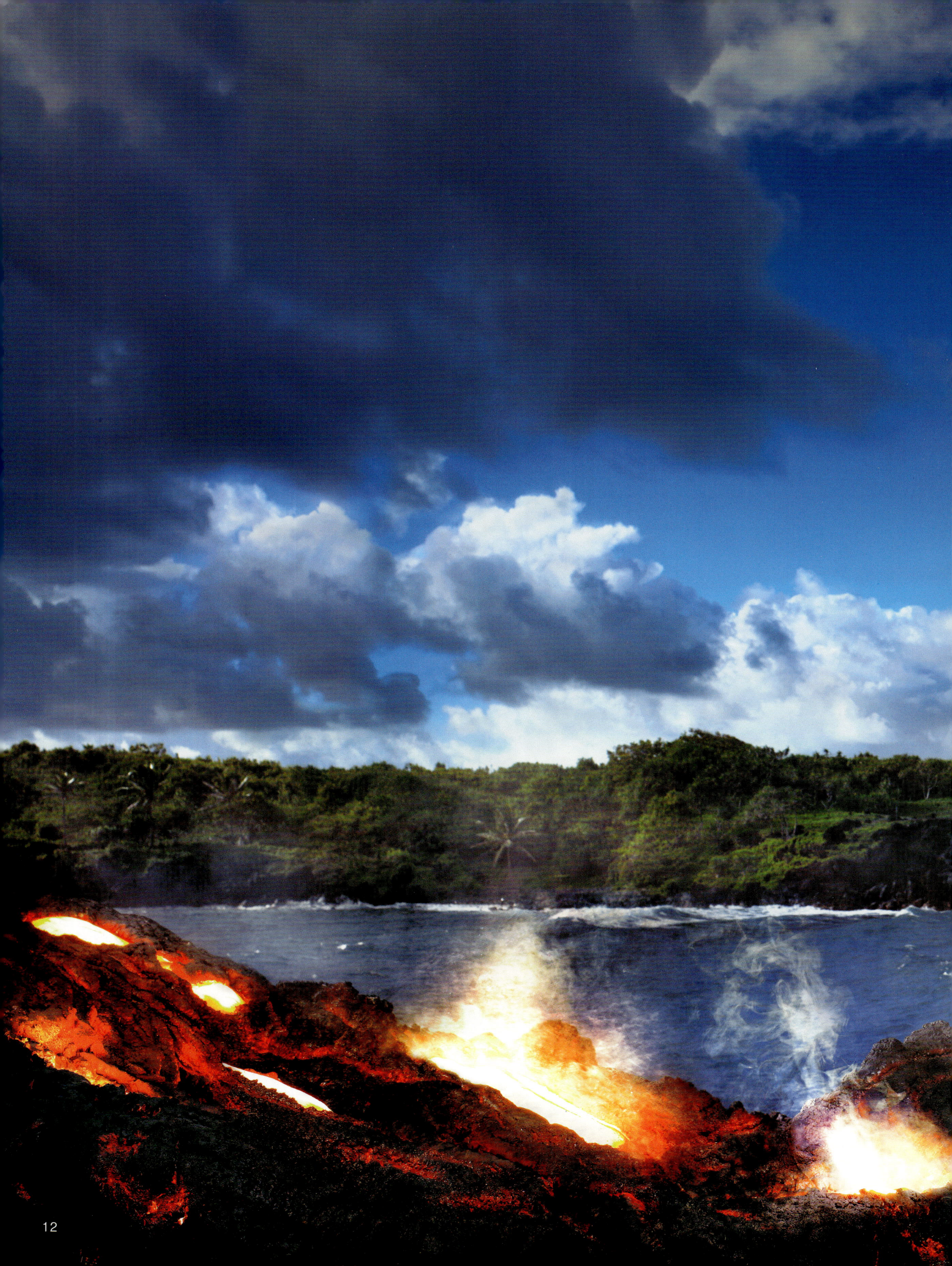

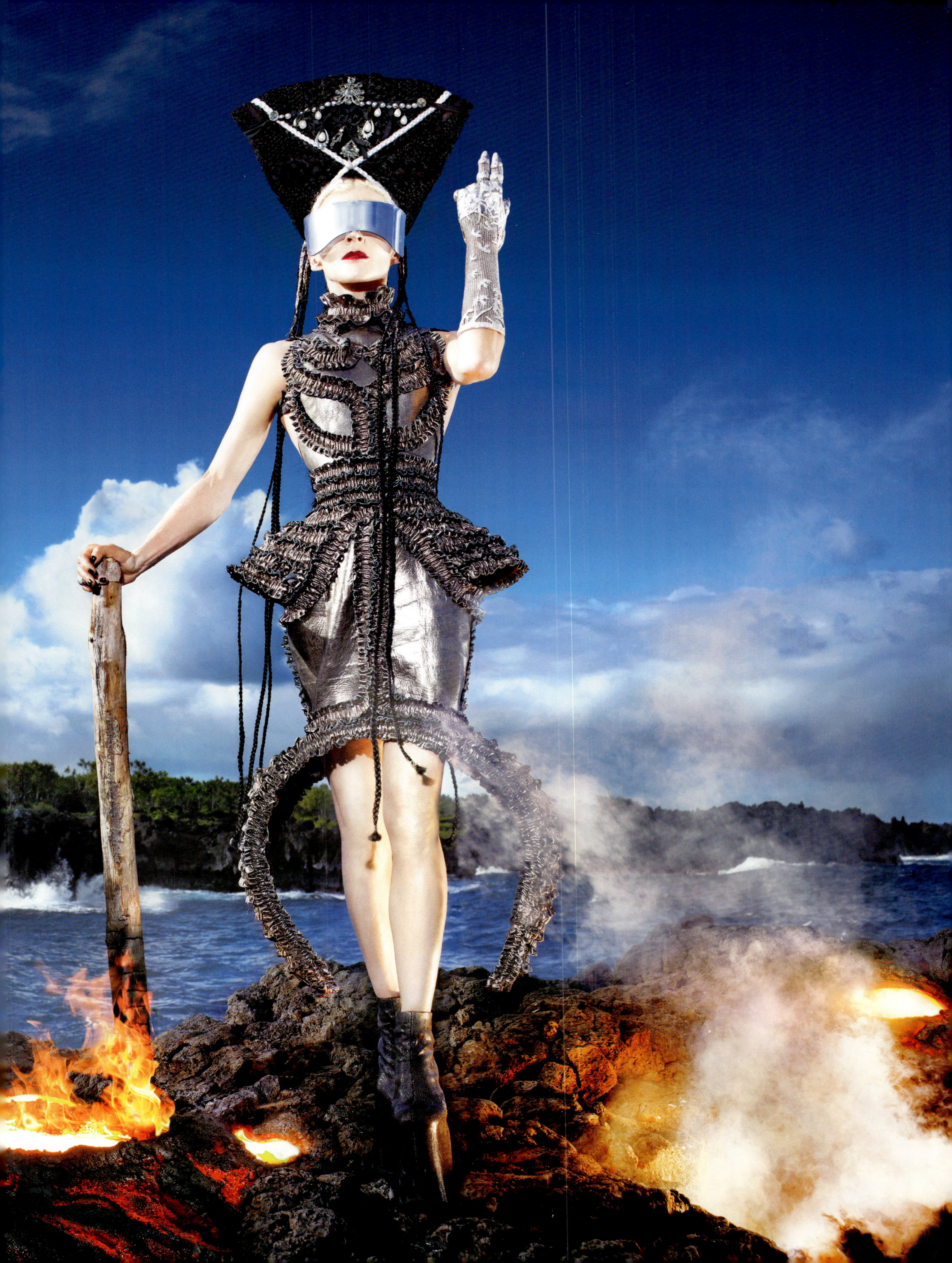

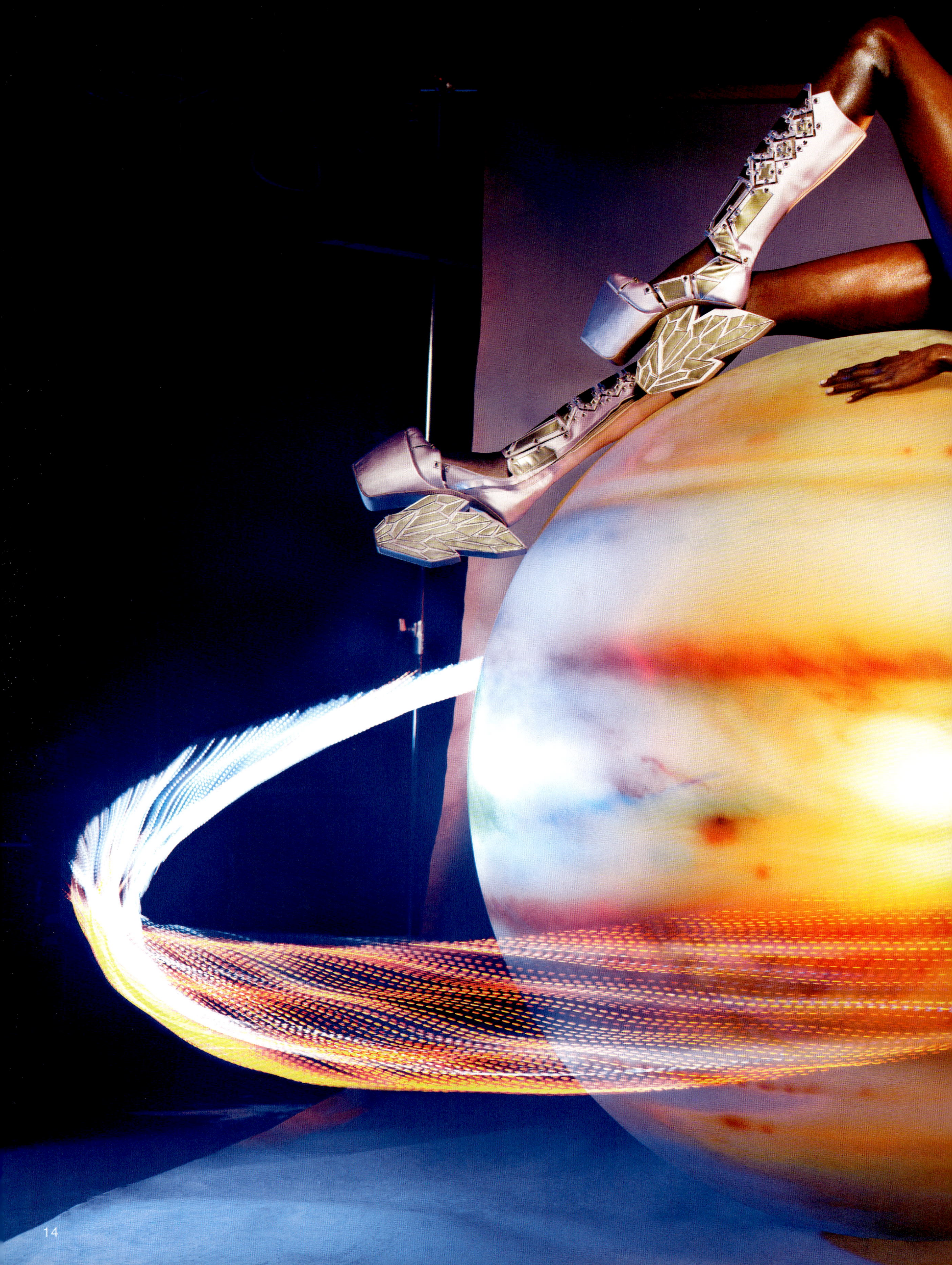

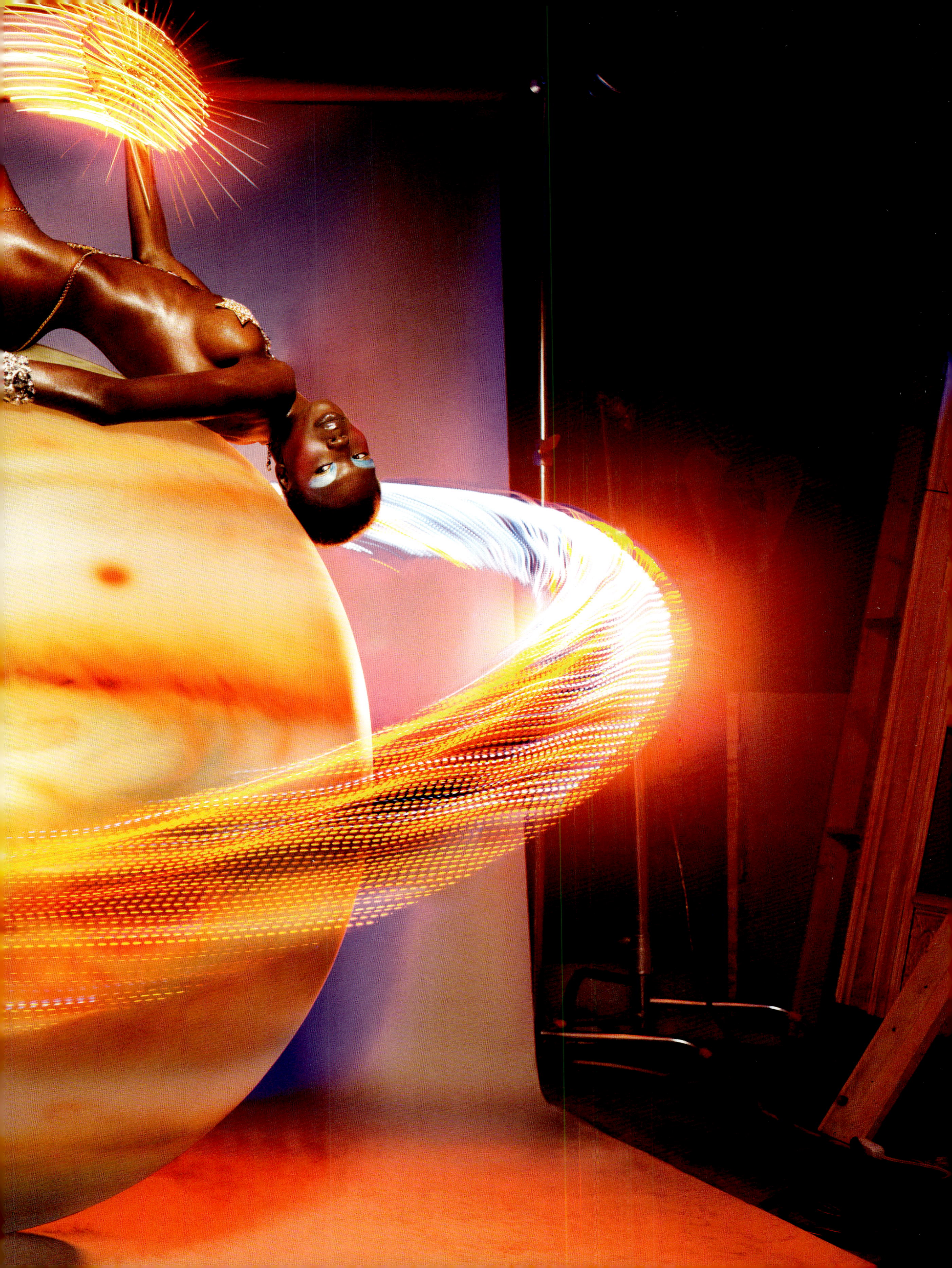

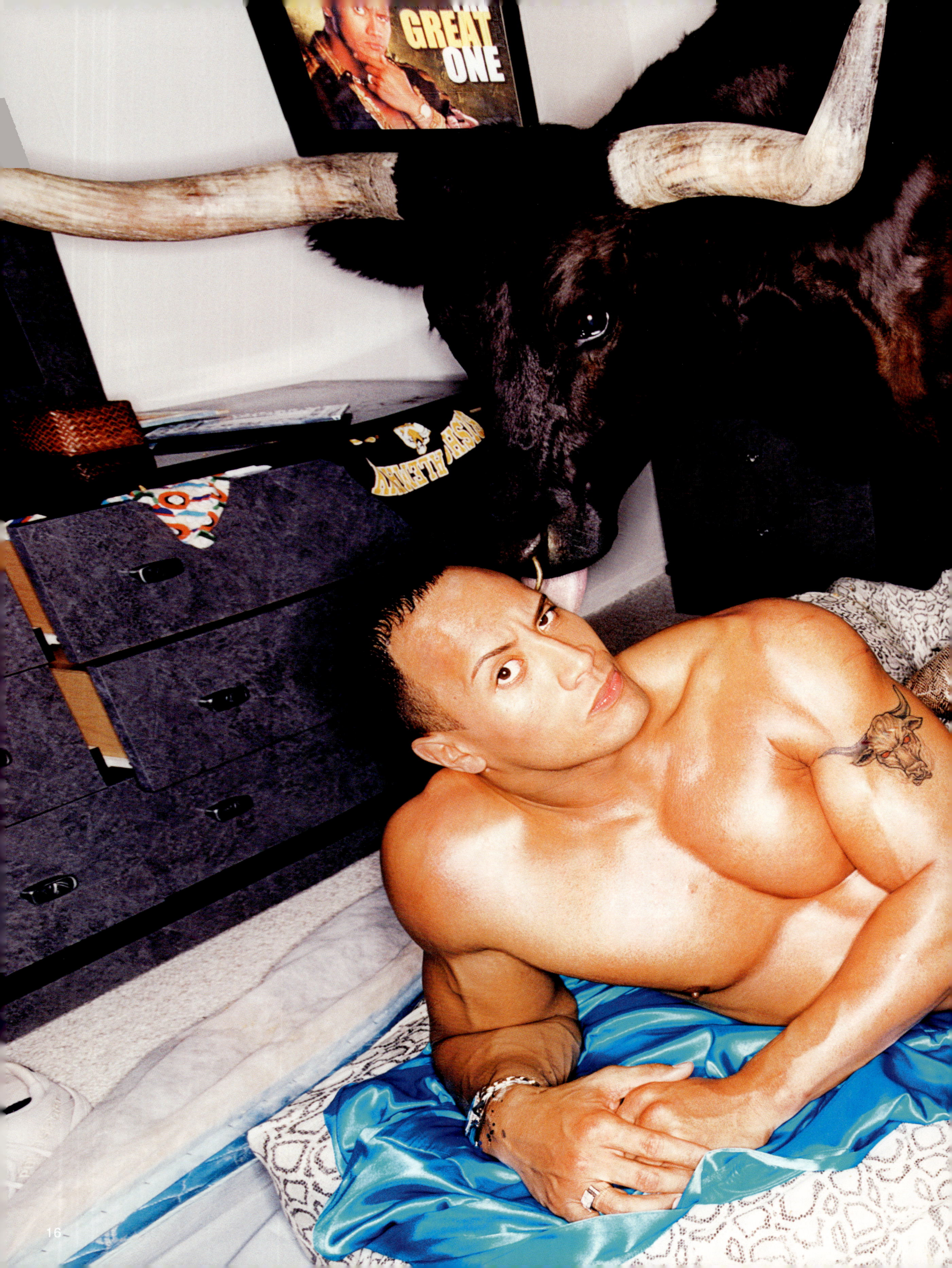
GREAT
ONE

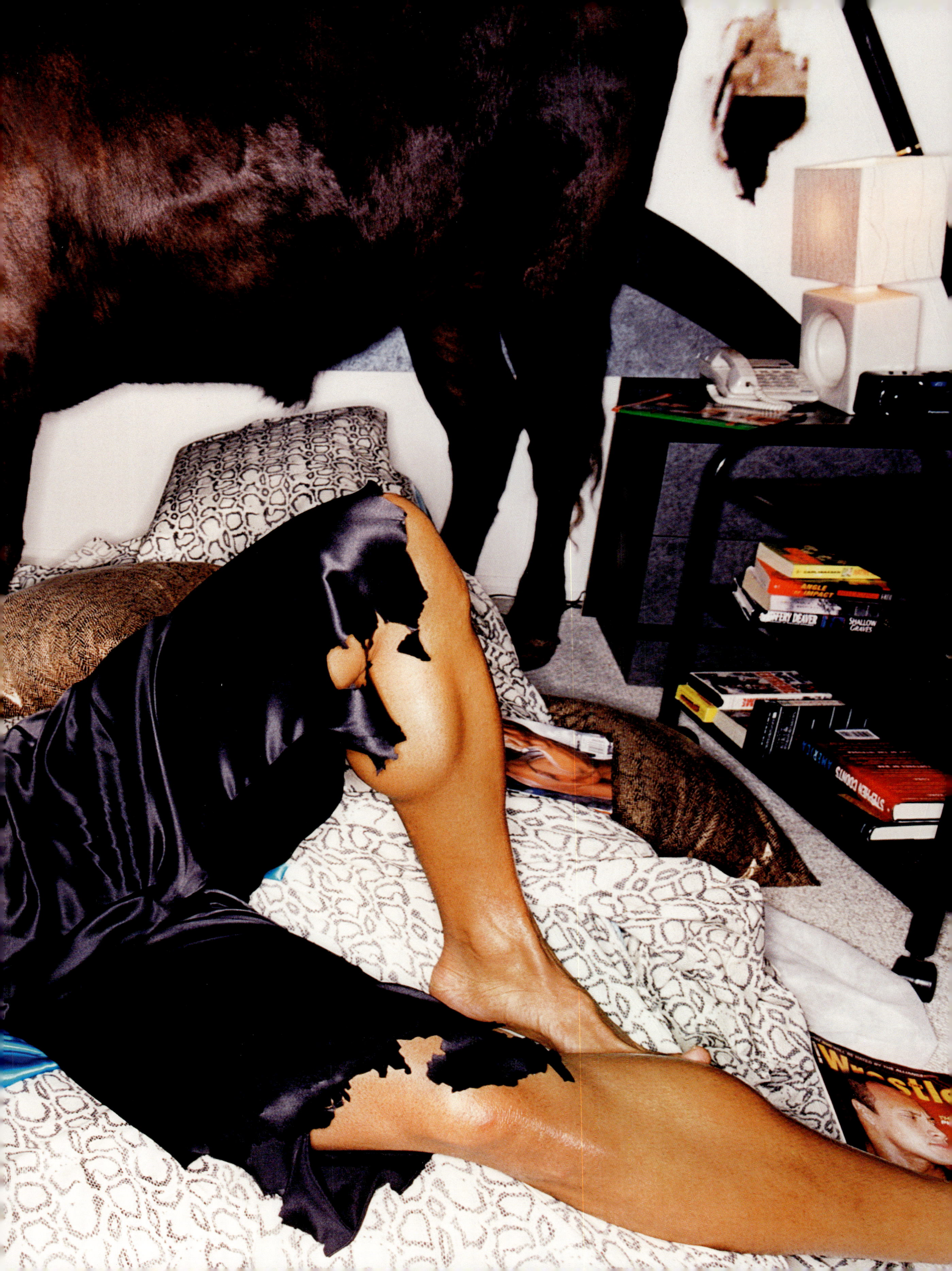

ANGLE
IMPACT
DEAVER
SHALLOW GRAVES
STEPHEN COONTS
AMERICA

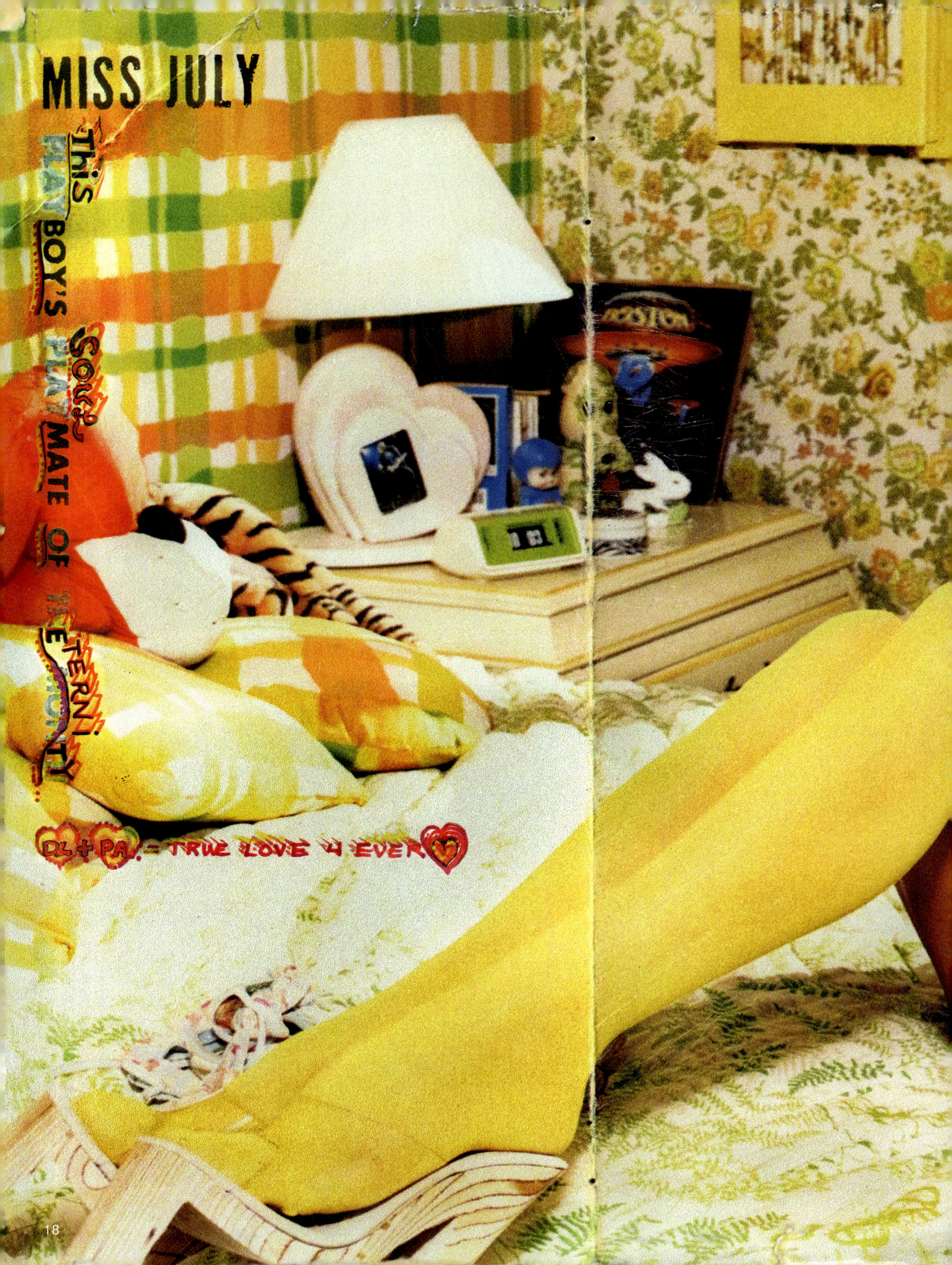
MISS JULY
This BOY'S SOUL MATE OF ETERNITY
DL + PA = TRUE LOVE 4 EVER

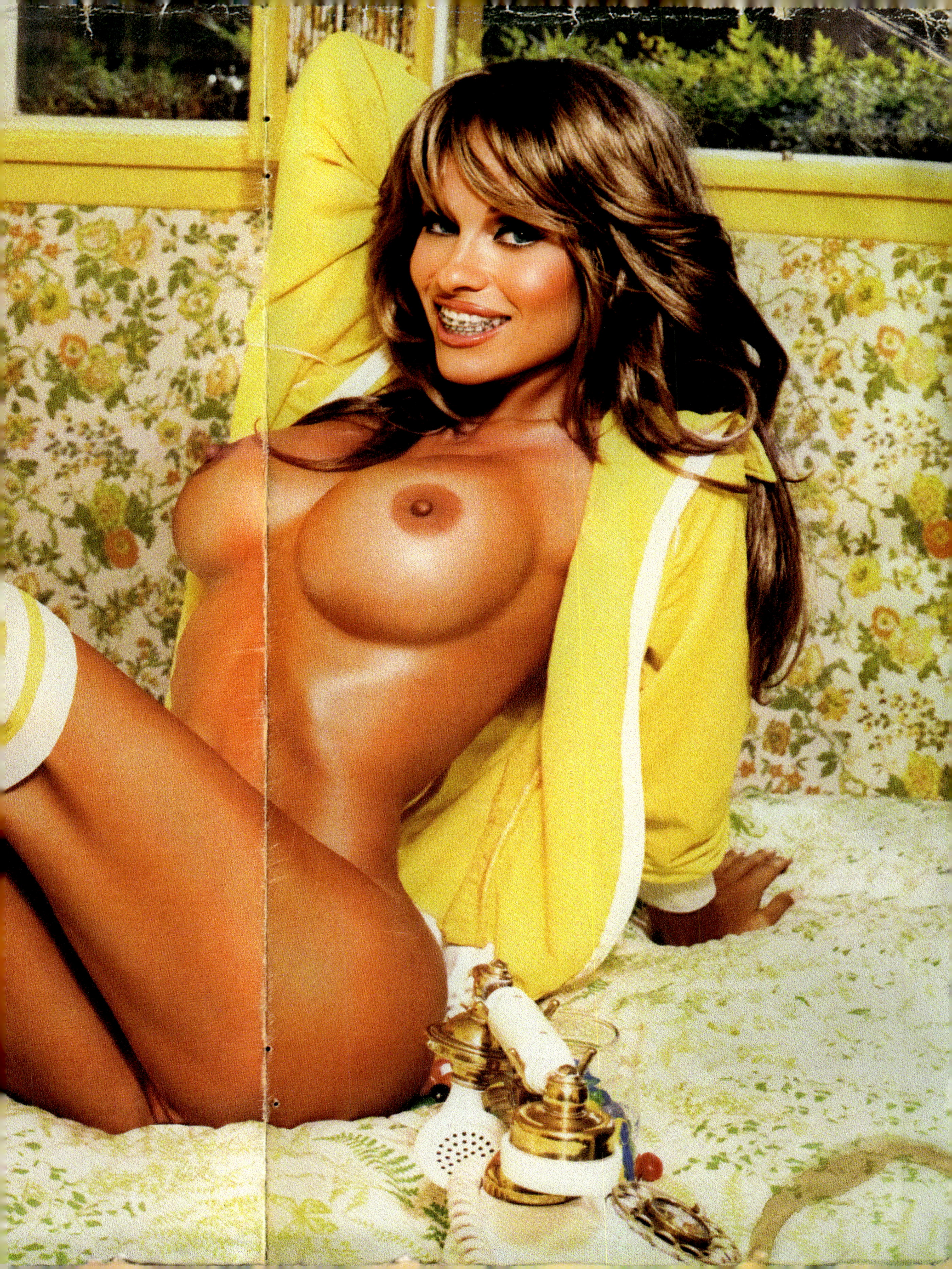

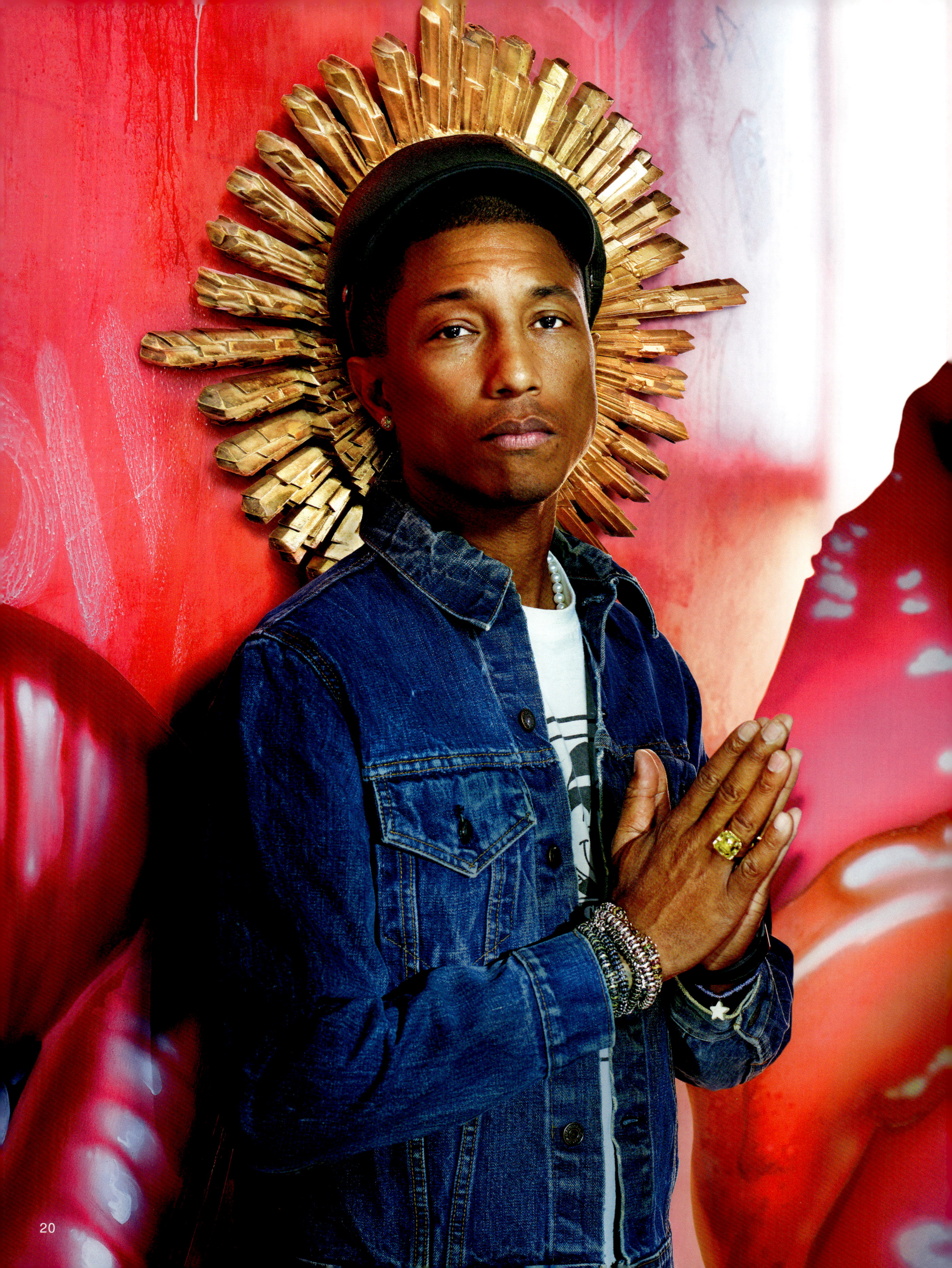

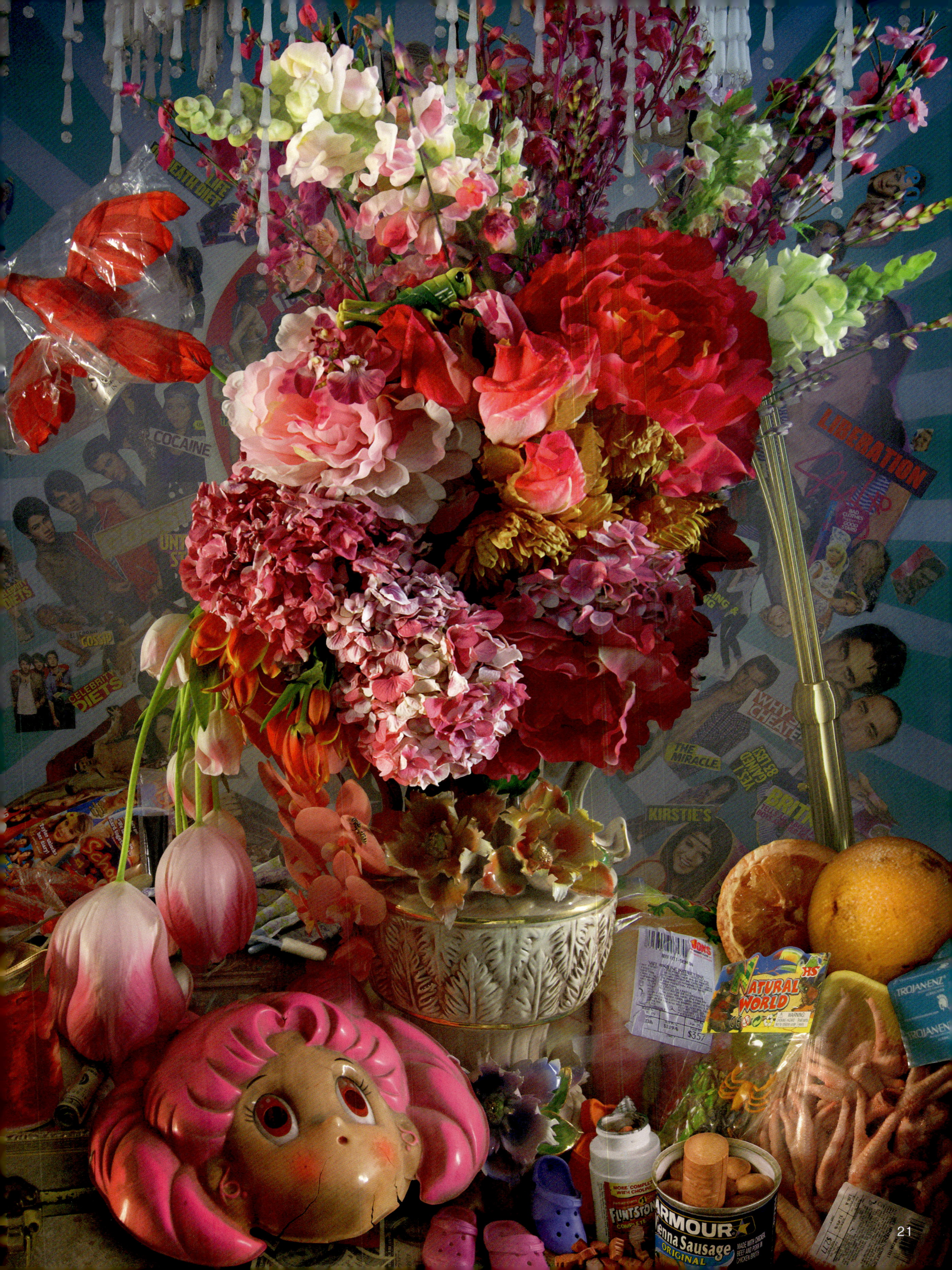
COCAINE
CELEBRITY DIETS
GOSSIP
LIBERATION
THE MIRACLE
KIRSTIE'S
NATURAL WORLD
ARMOUR
Vienna Sausage
ORIGINAL

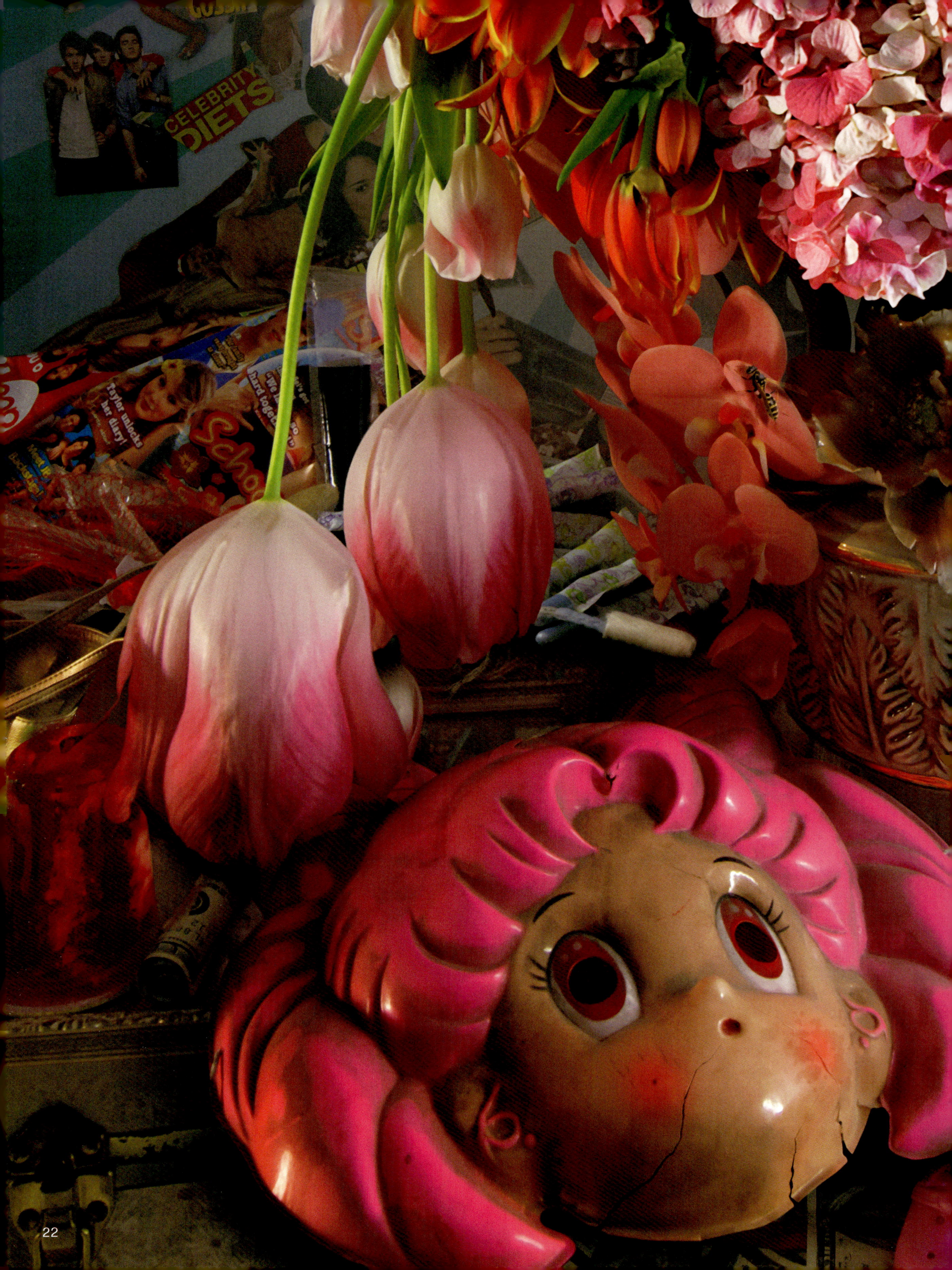
CELEBRITY
DIETS
Taylor unlocks
her diary!

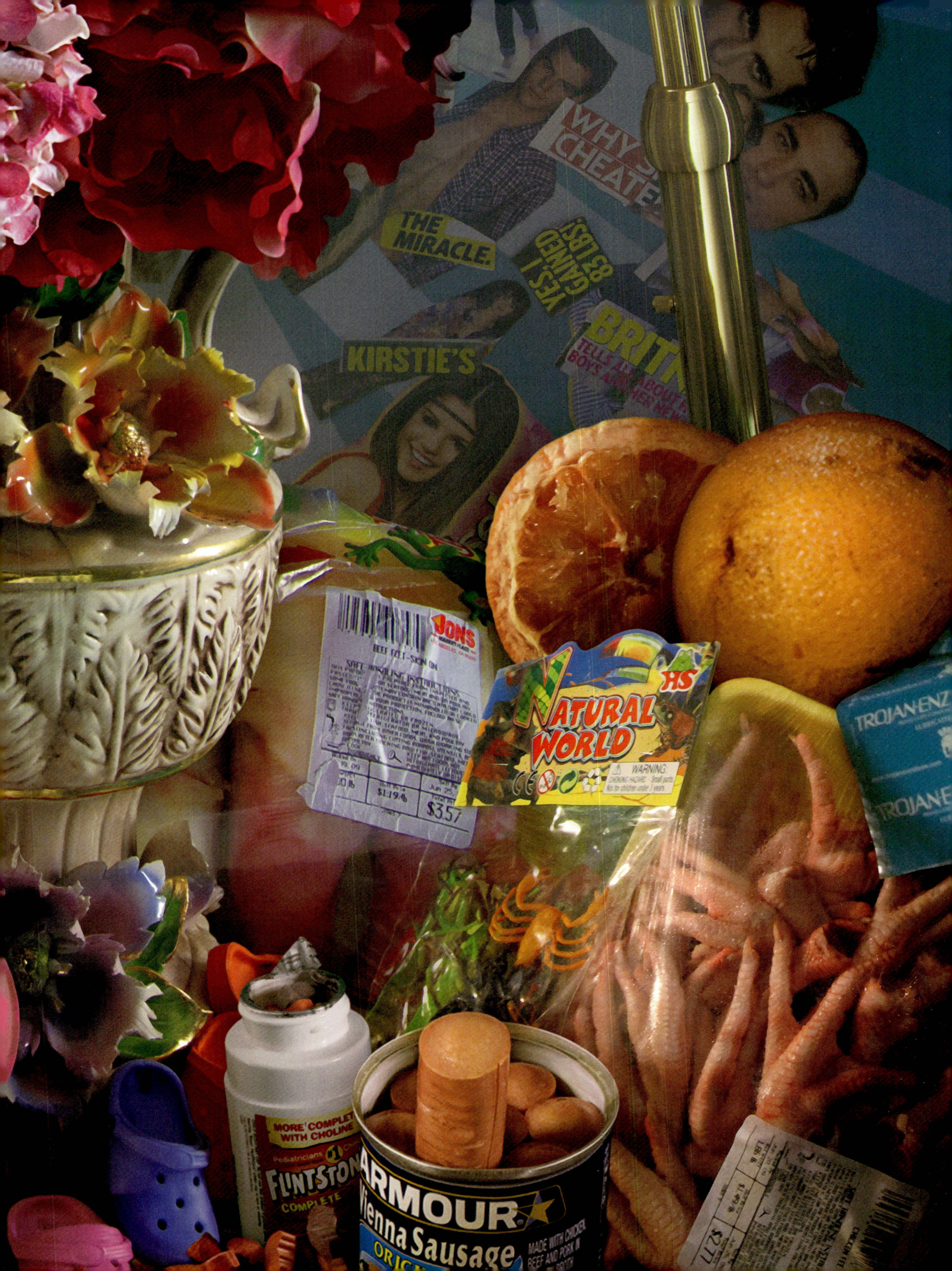

THE MIRACLE.
YES! I GAINED 83 LBS!
KIRSTIE'S
JONS
$3.57
NATURAL WORLD
HS
WARNING
ARMOUR
Vienna Sausage

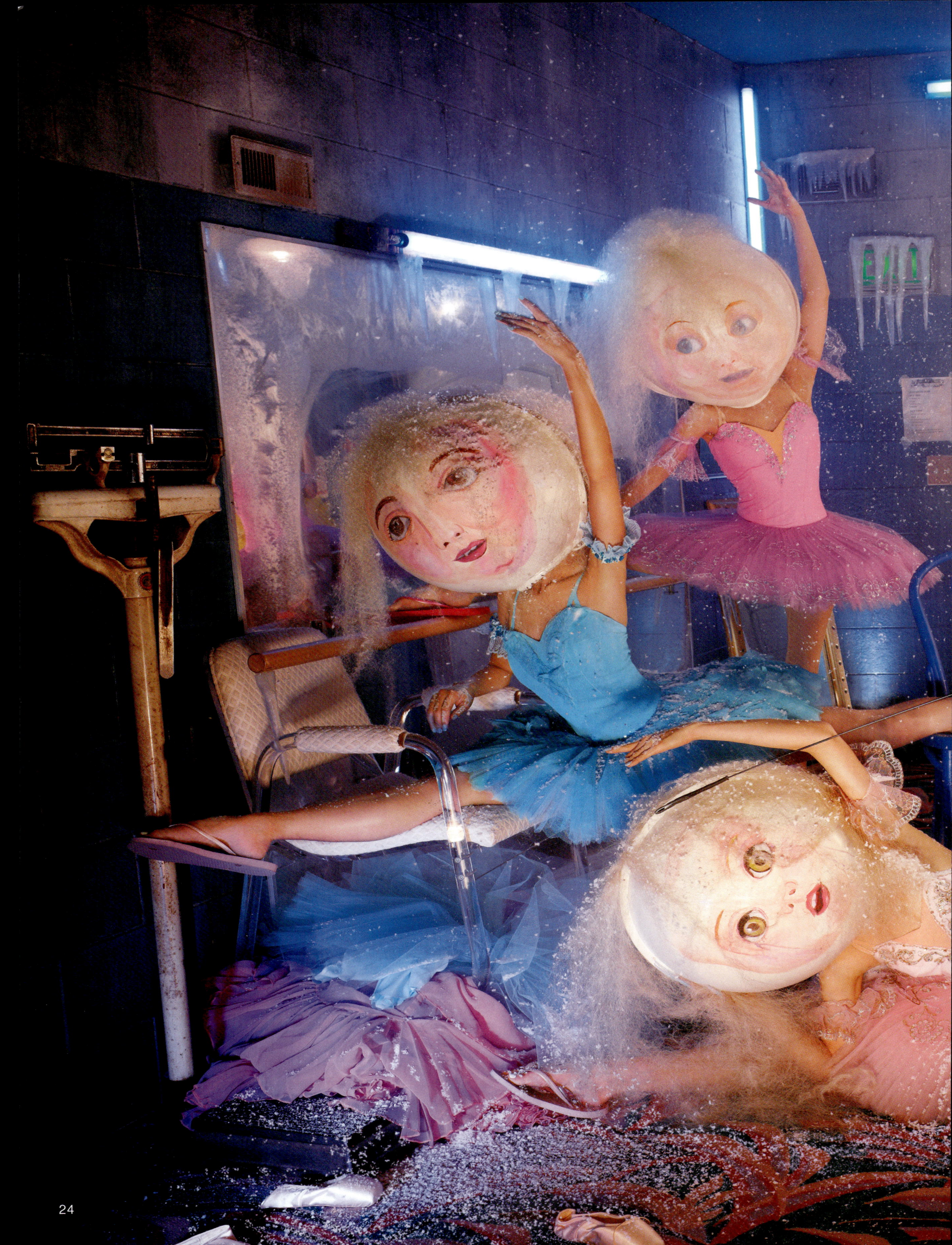

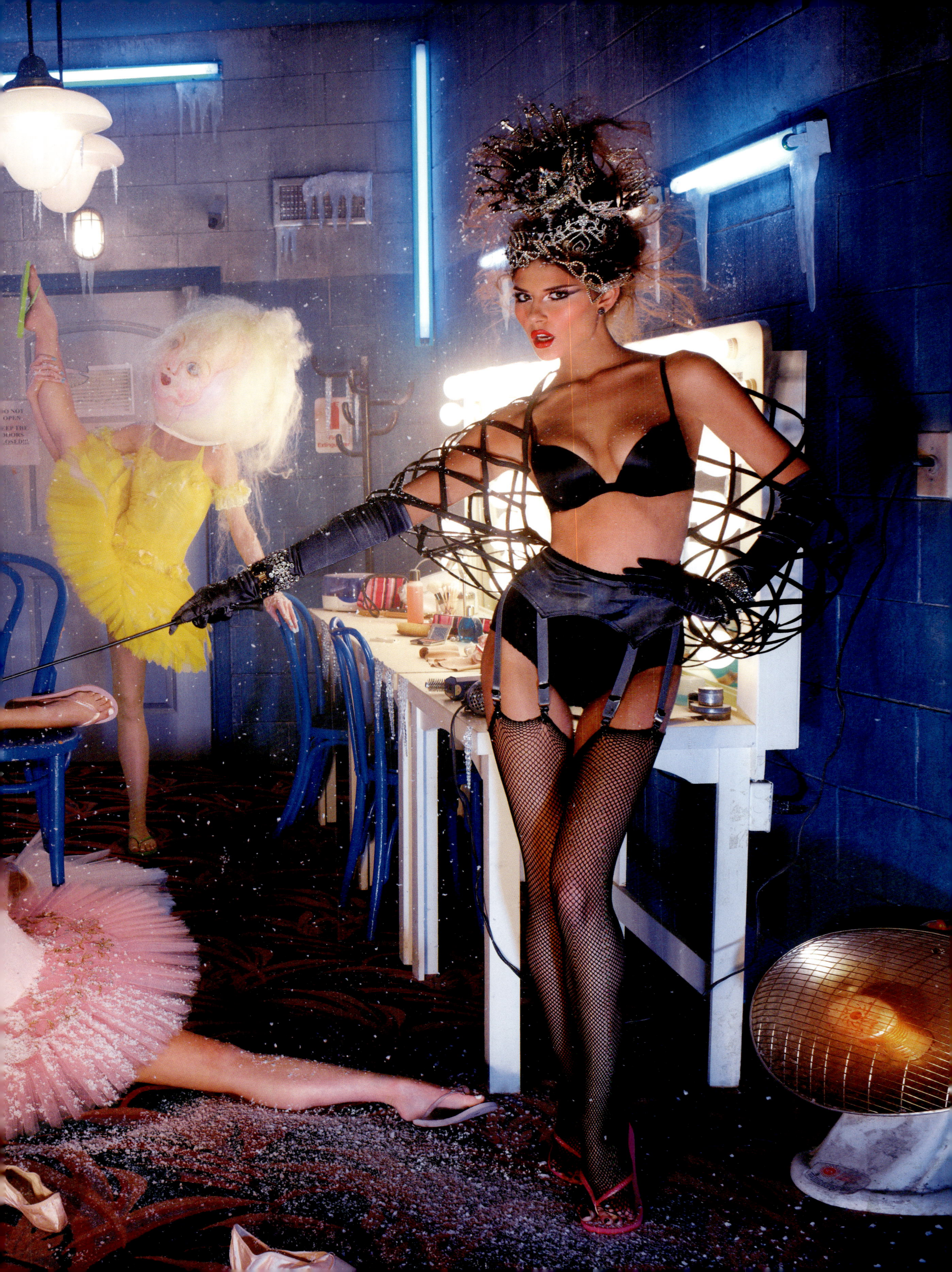

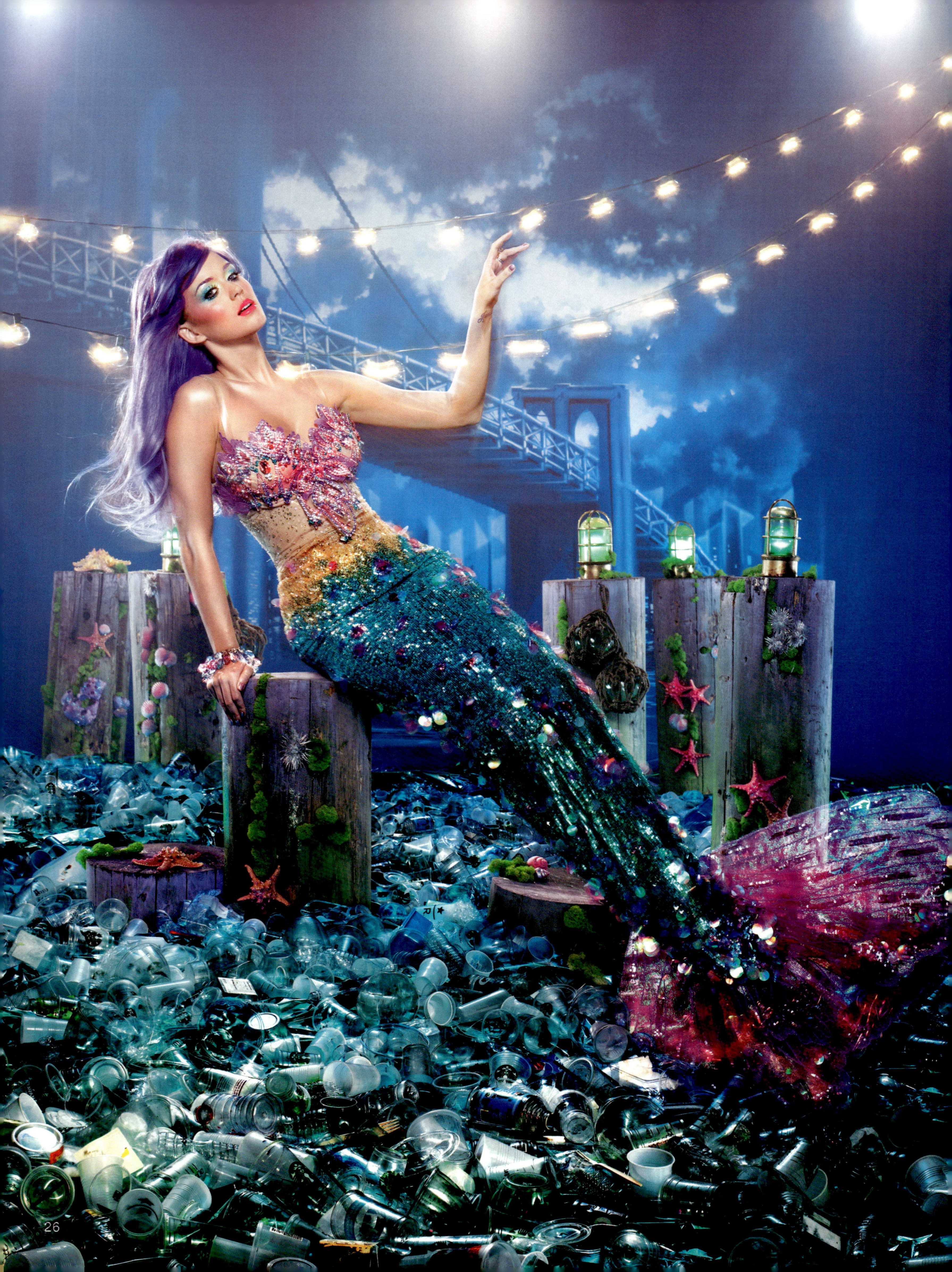

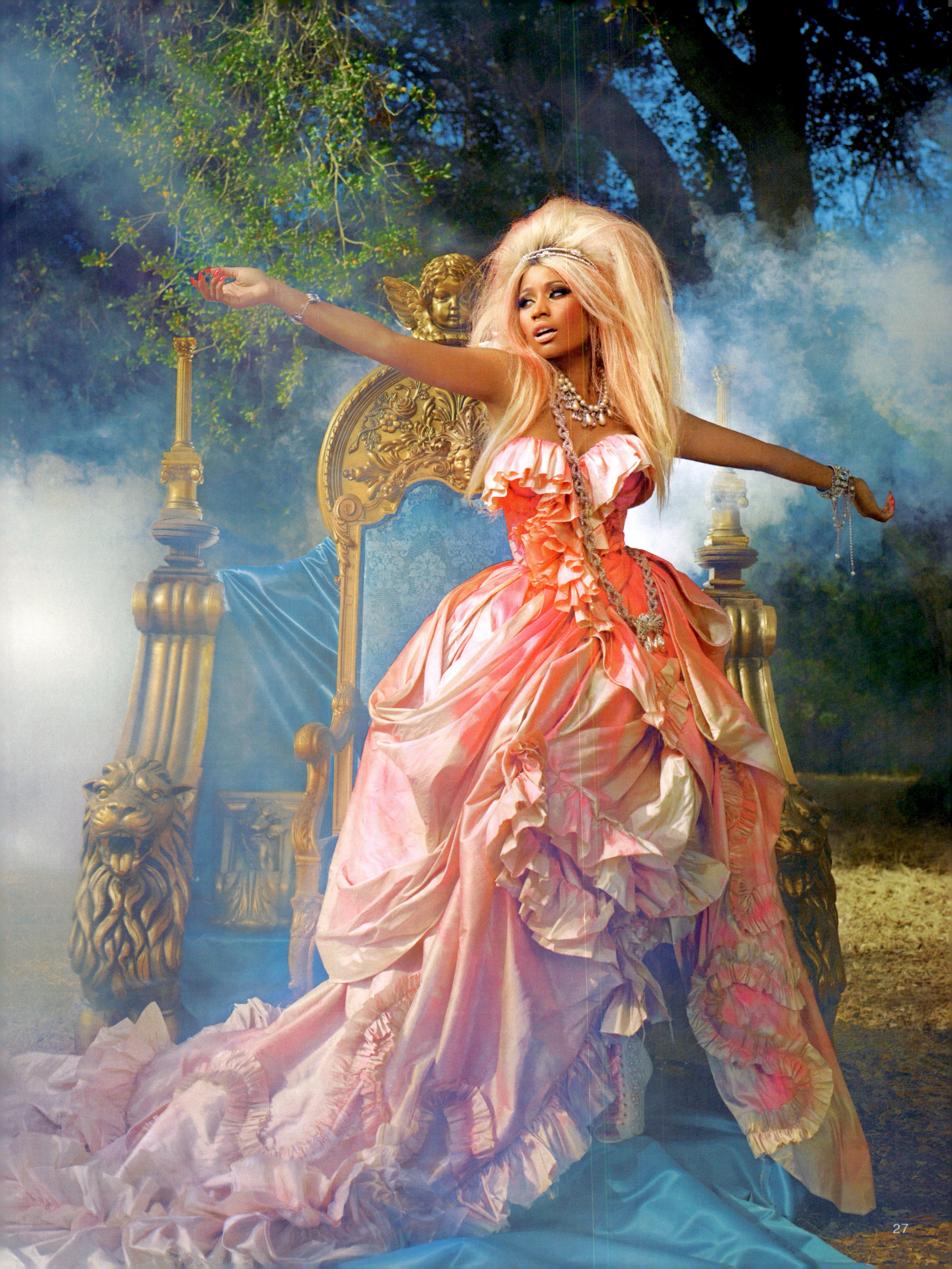

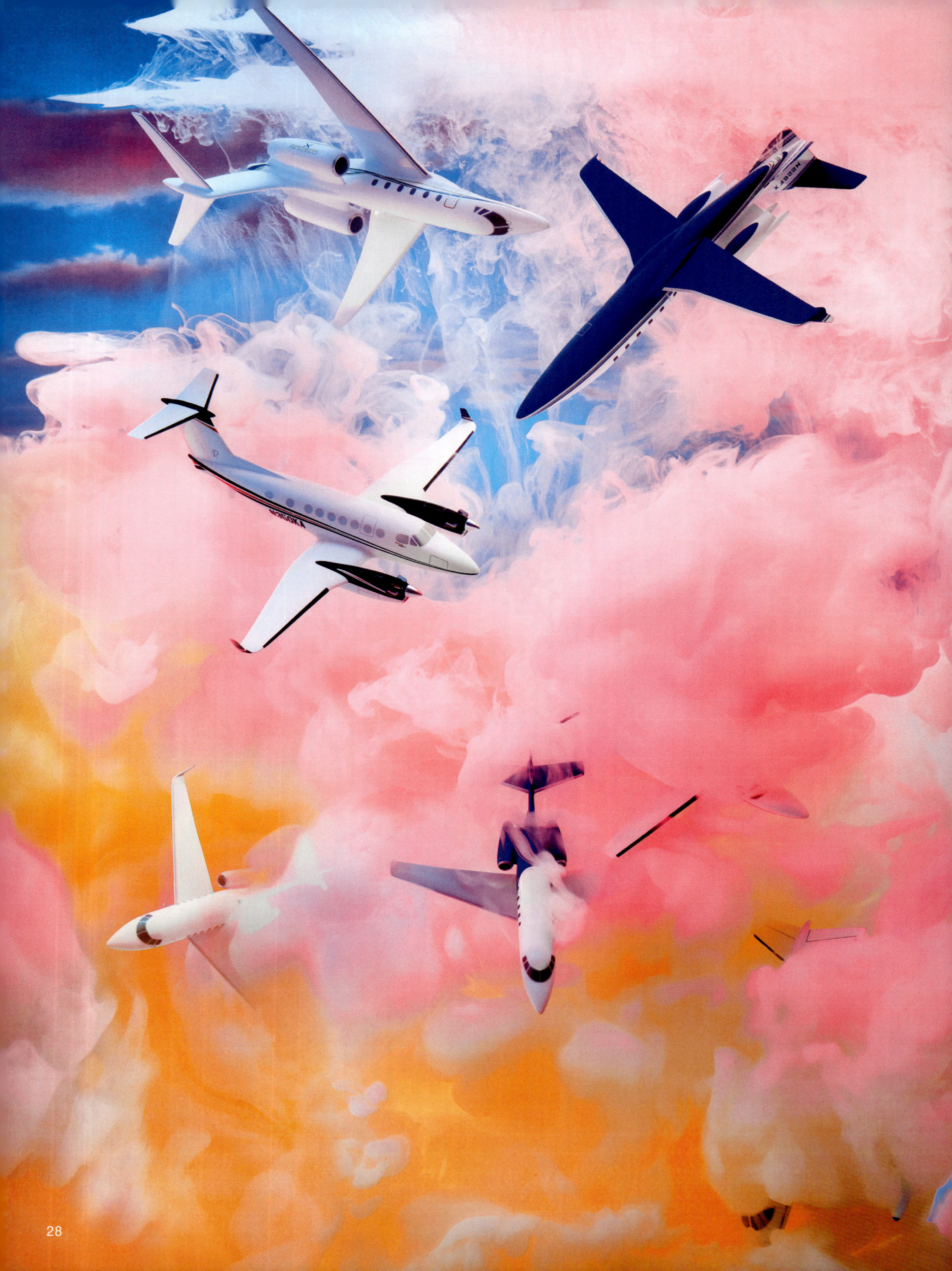
N350KA

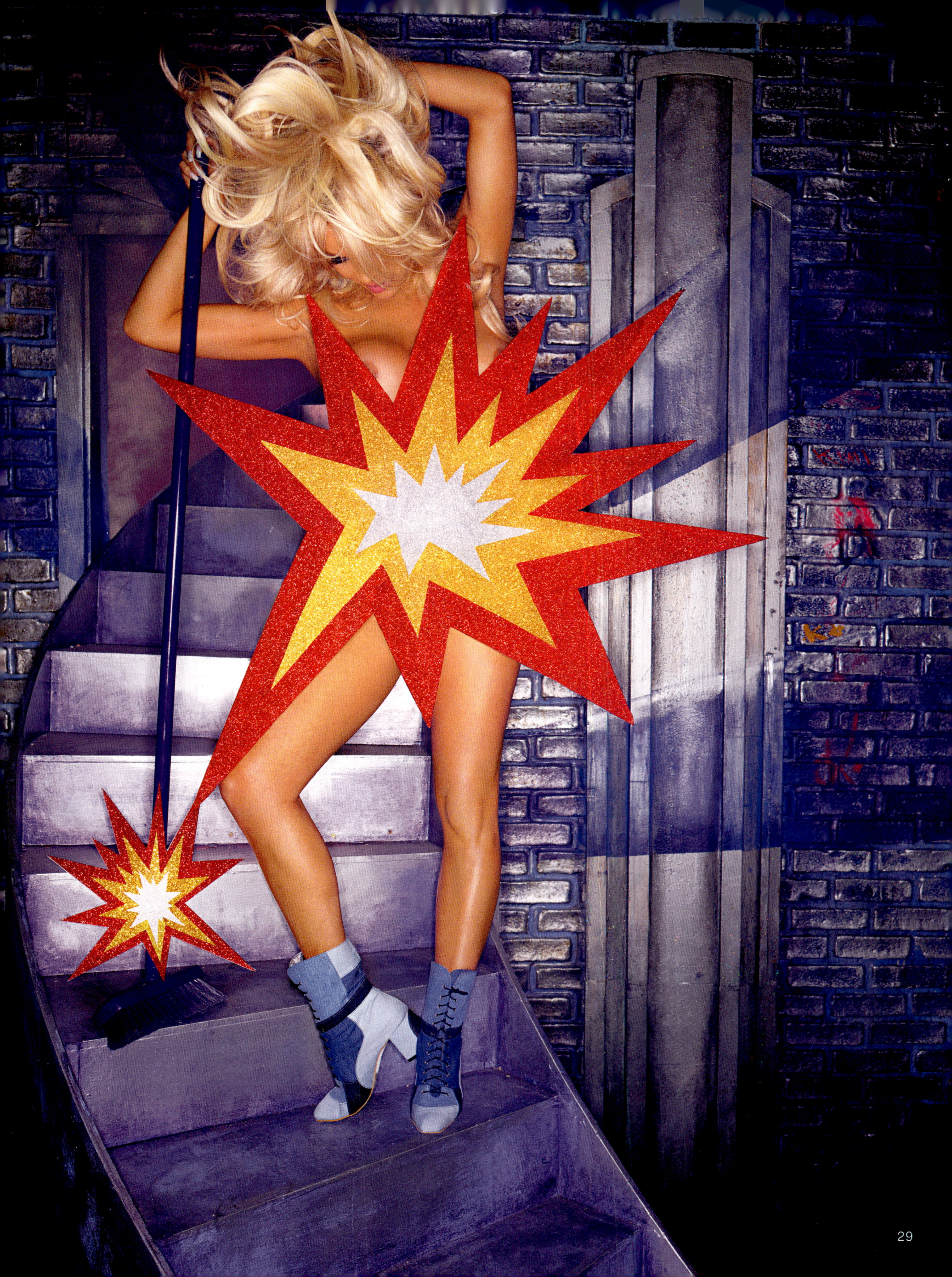

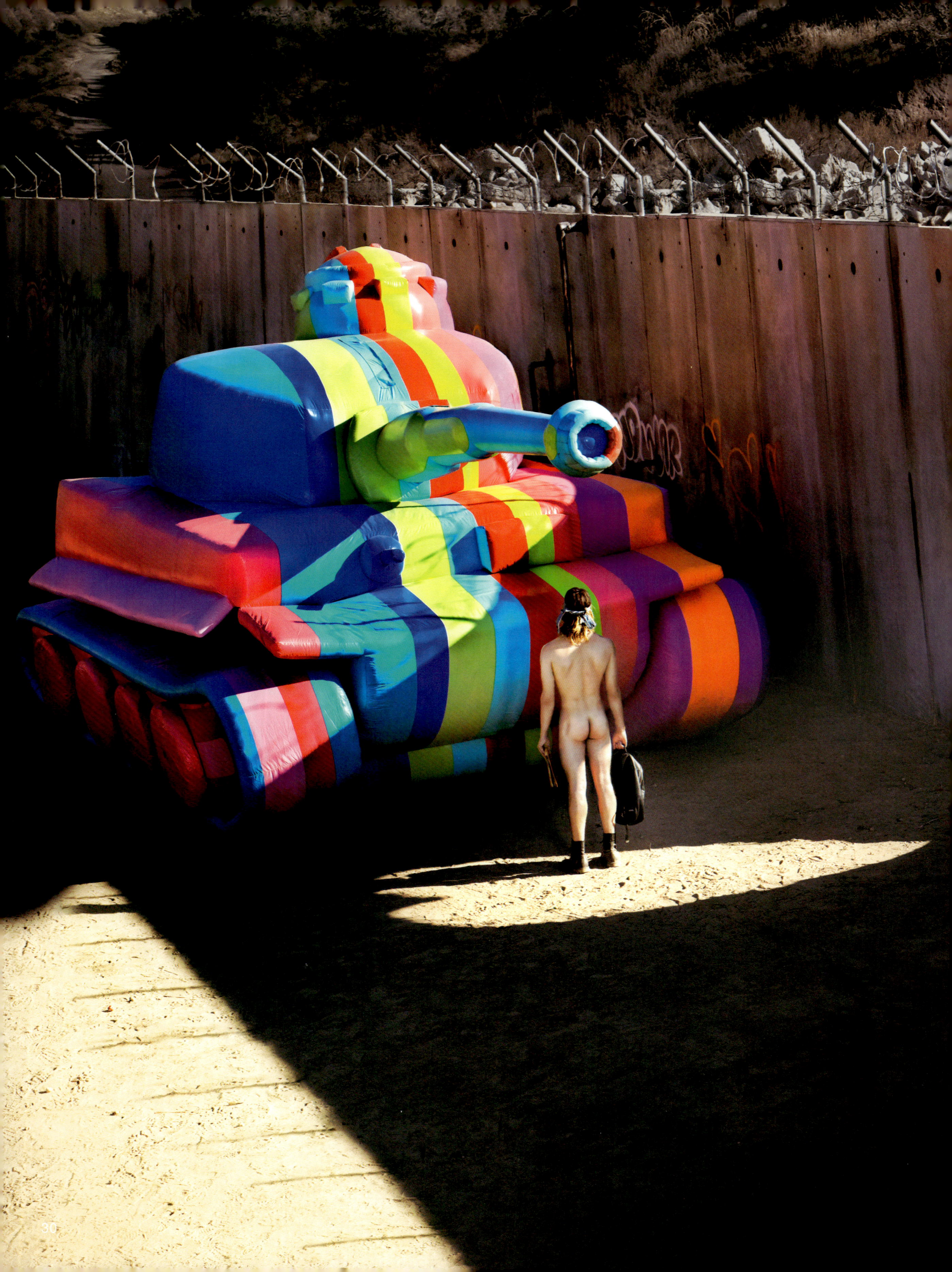

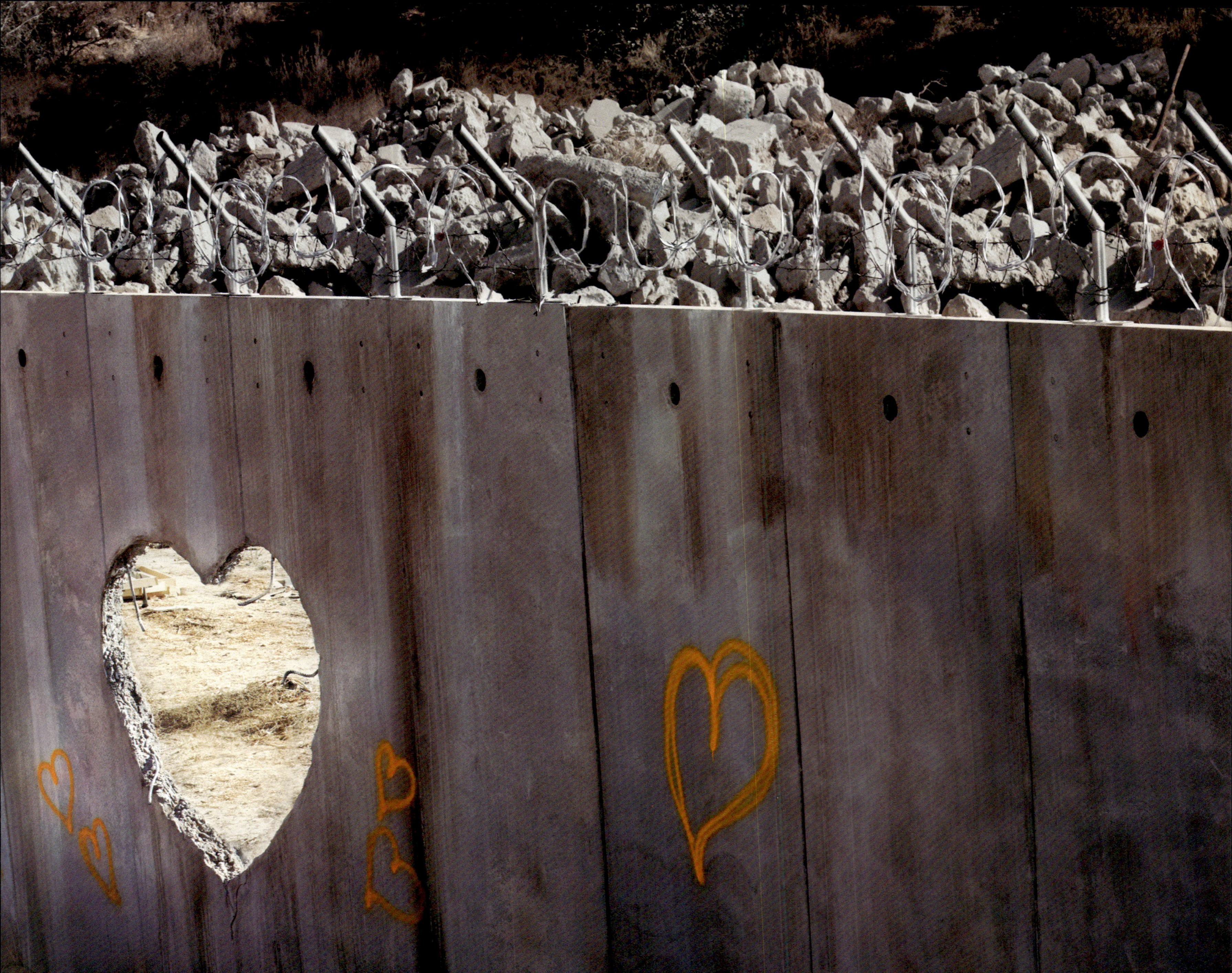

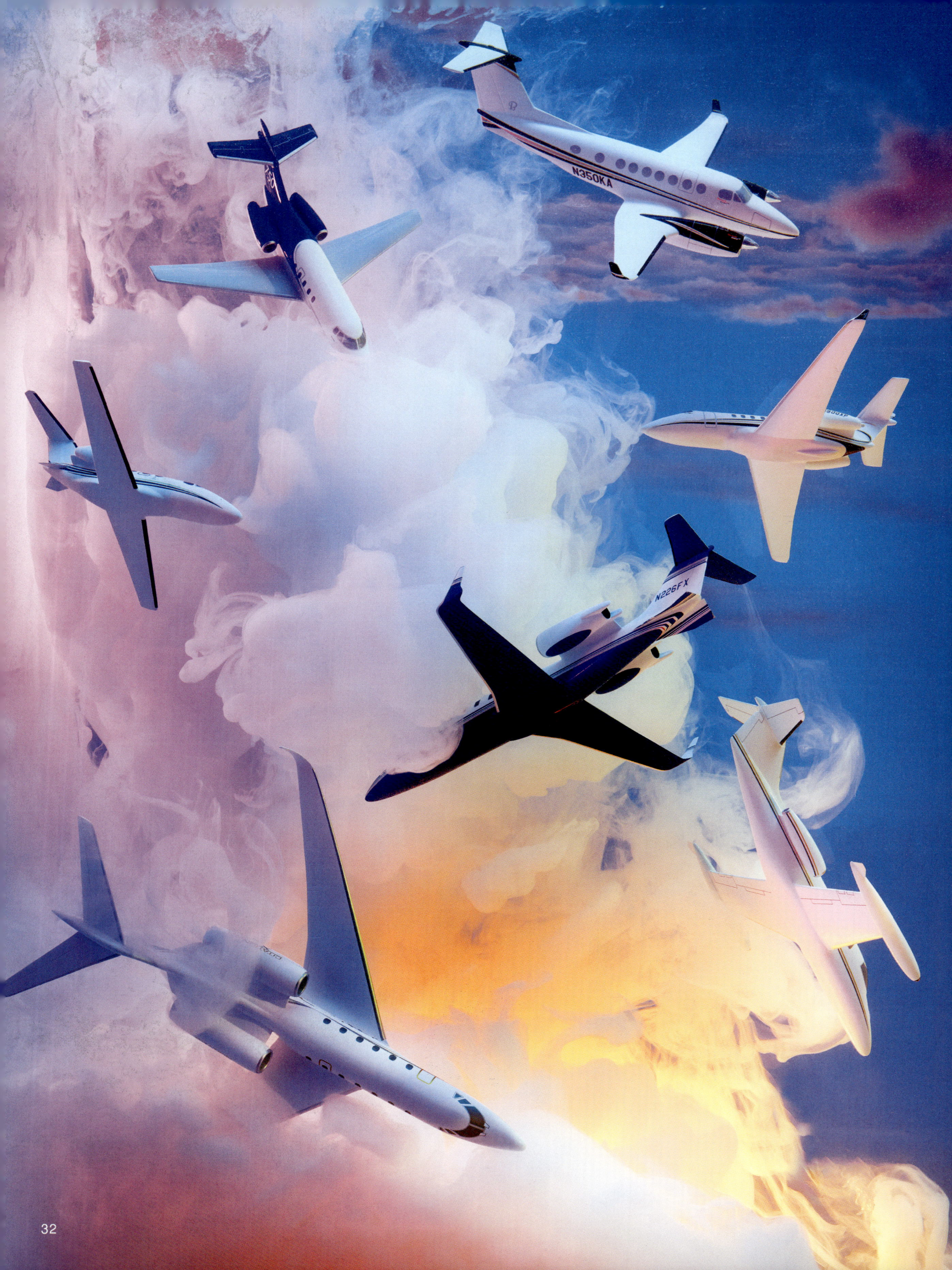
N350KA
N226FX

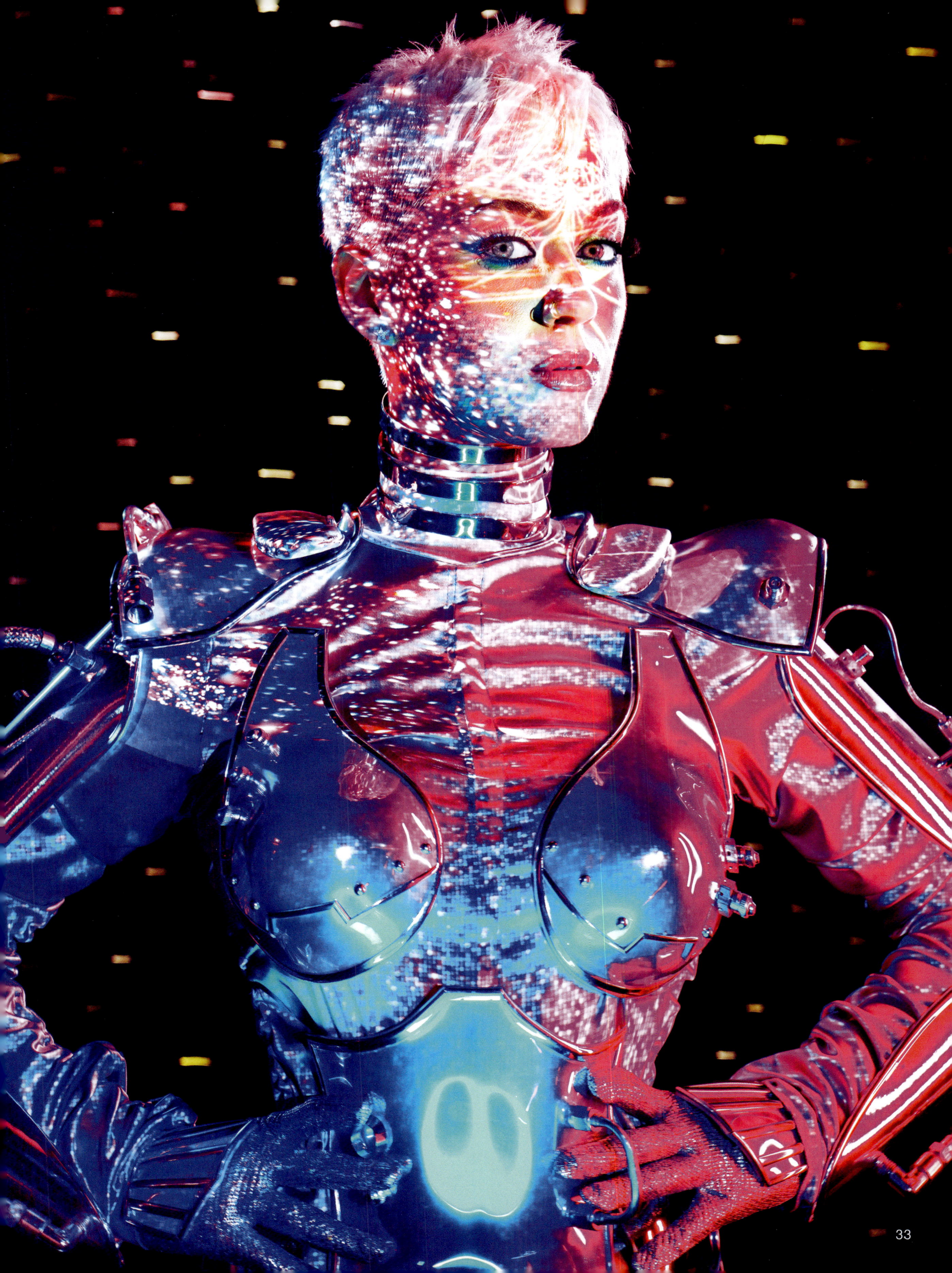

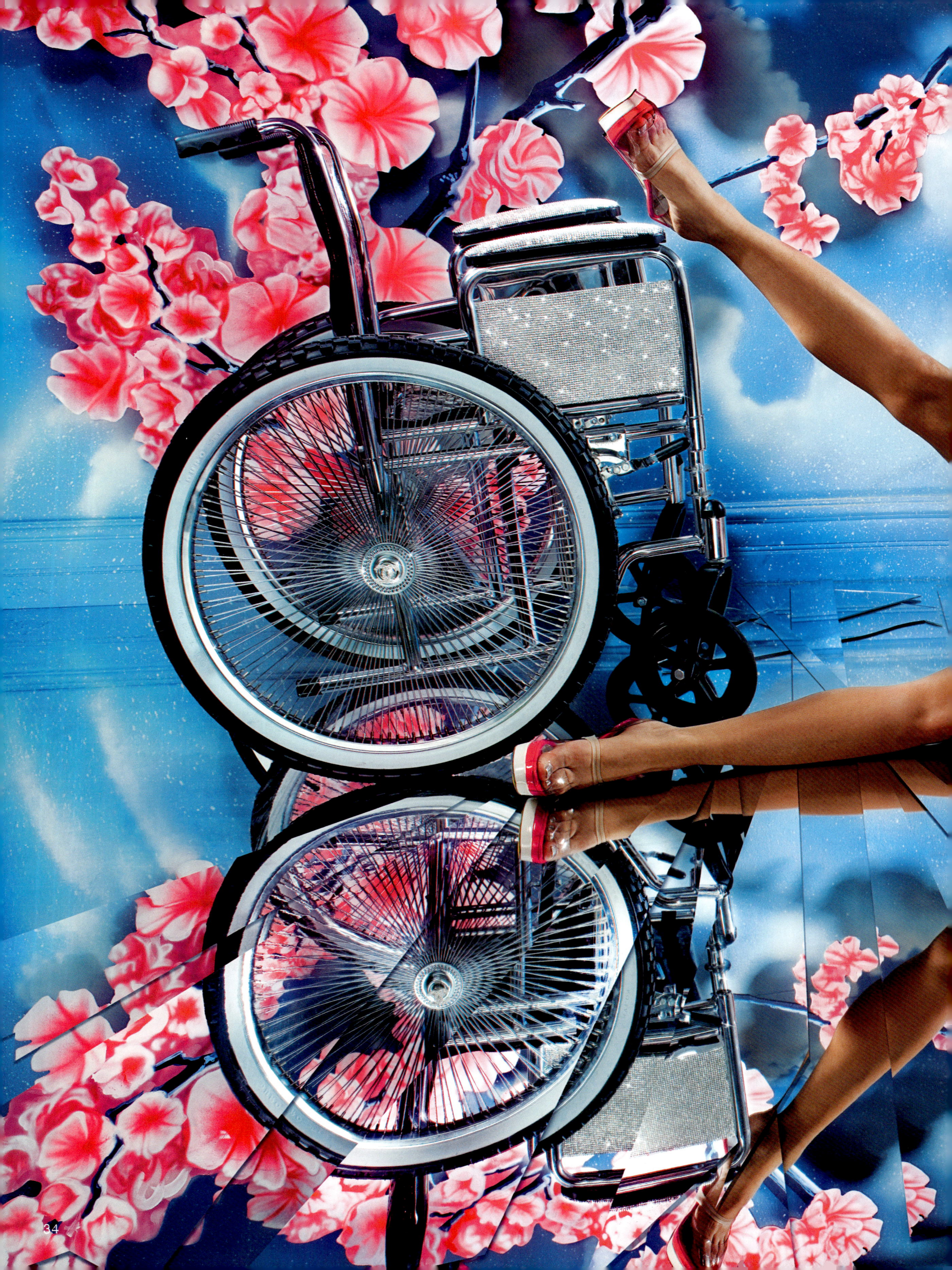

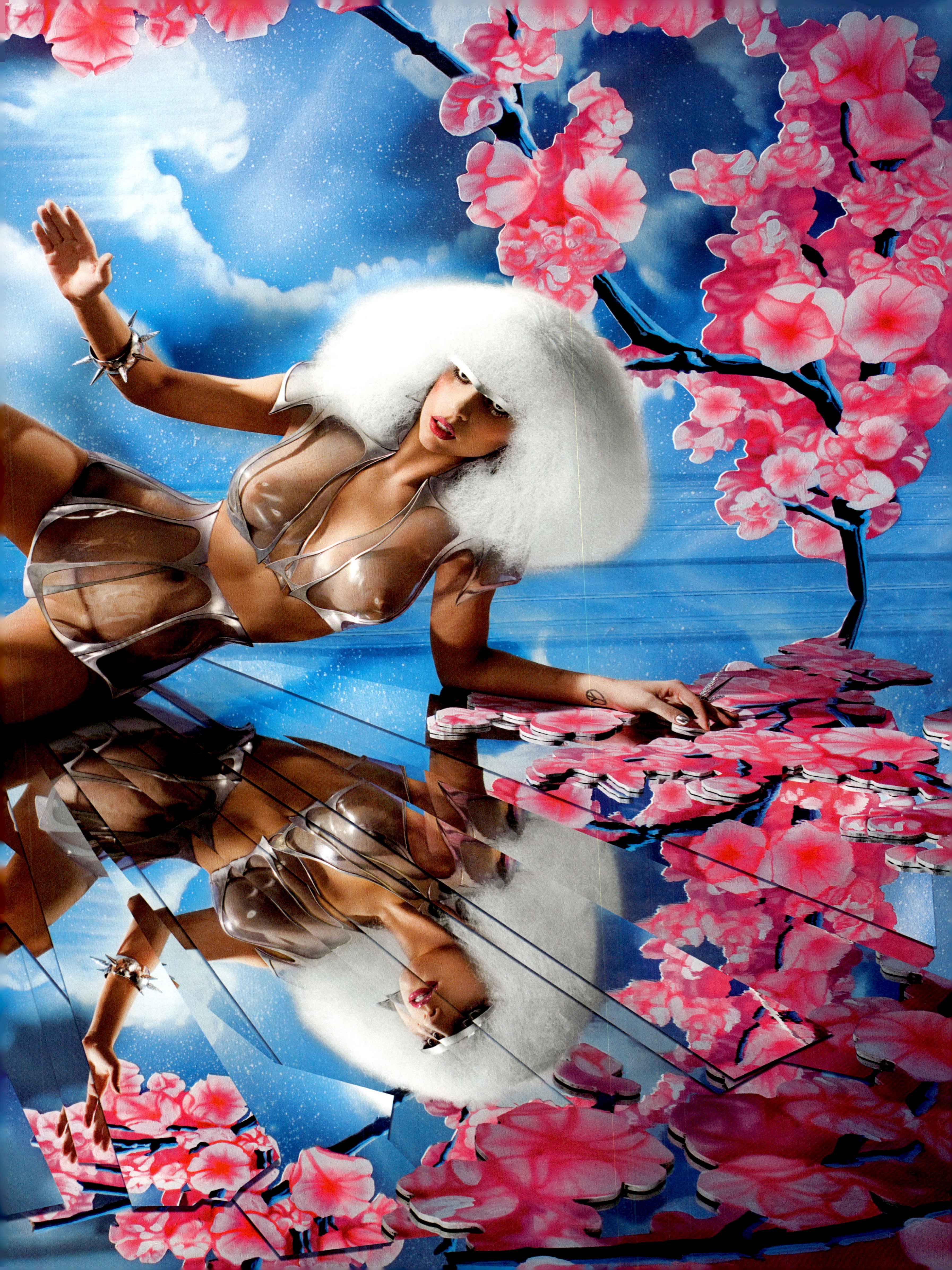

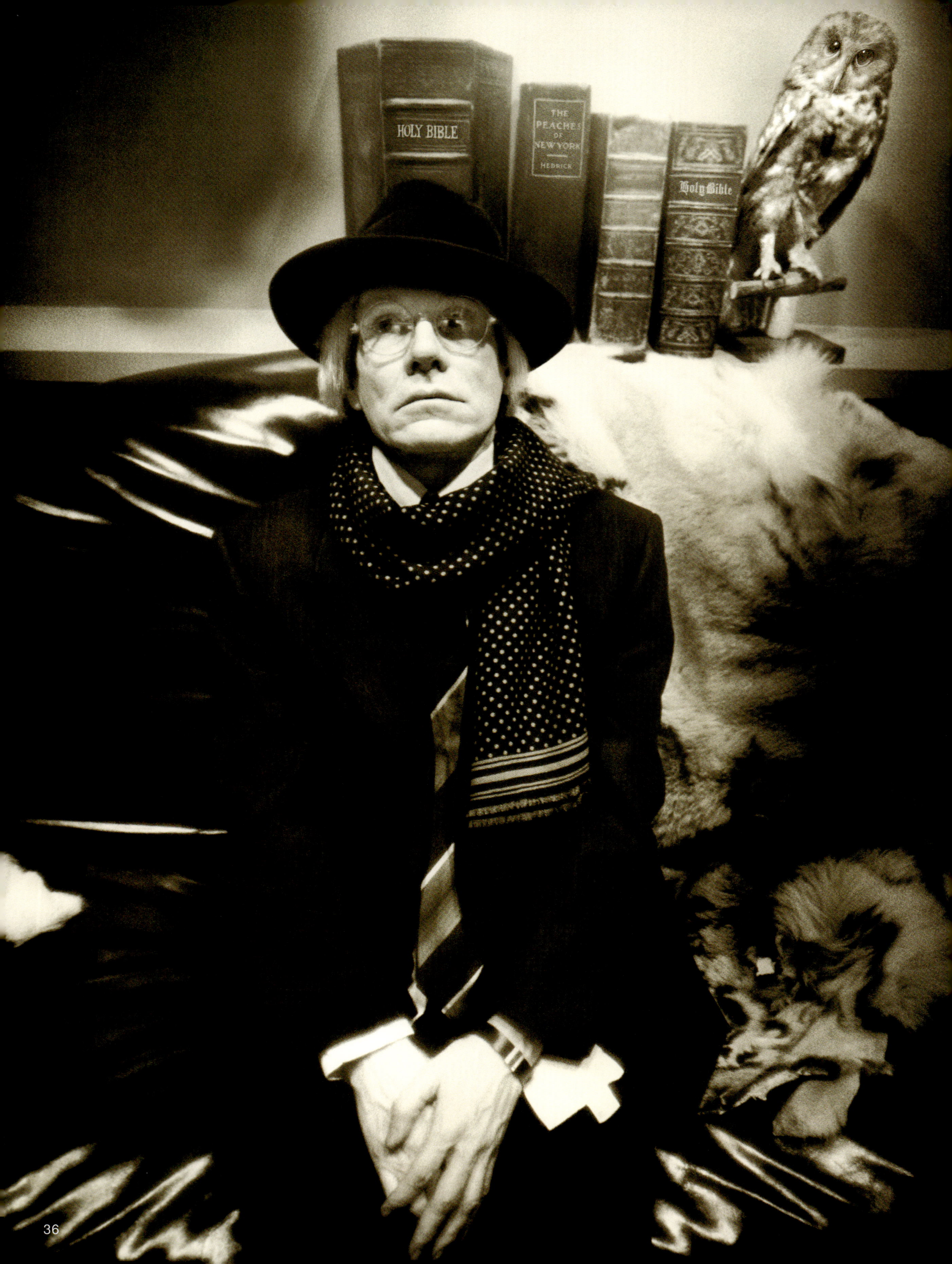
HOLY BIBLE
THE PEACHES OF NEW YORK
HEDRICK
Holy Bible

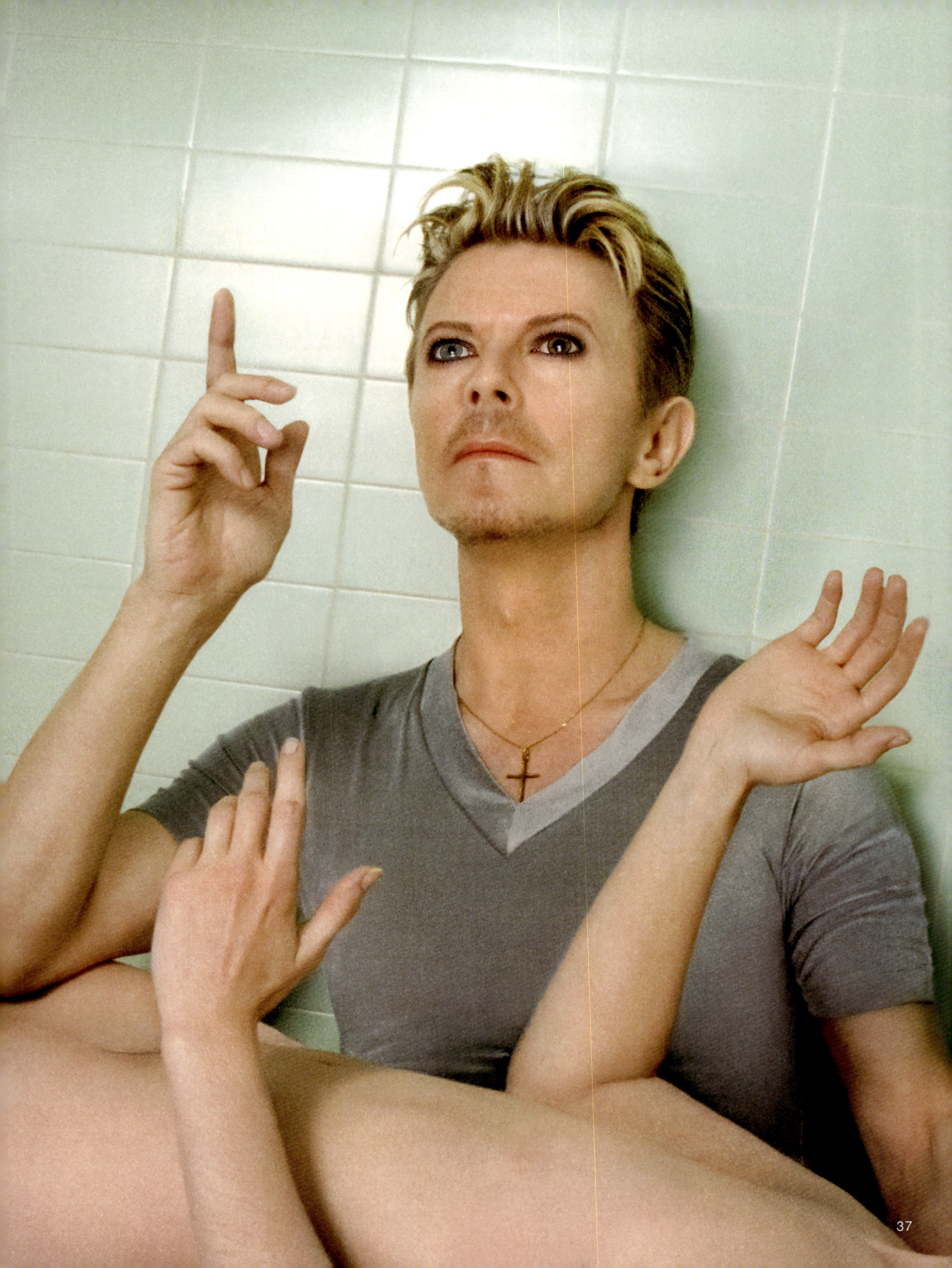

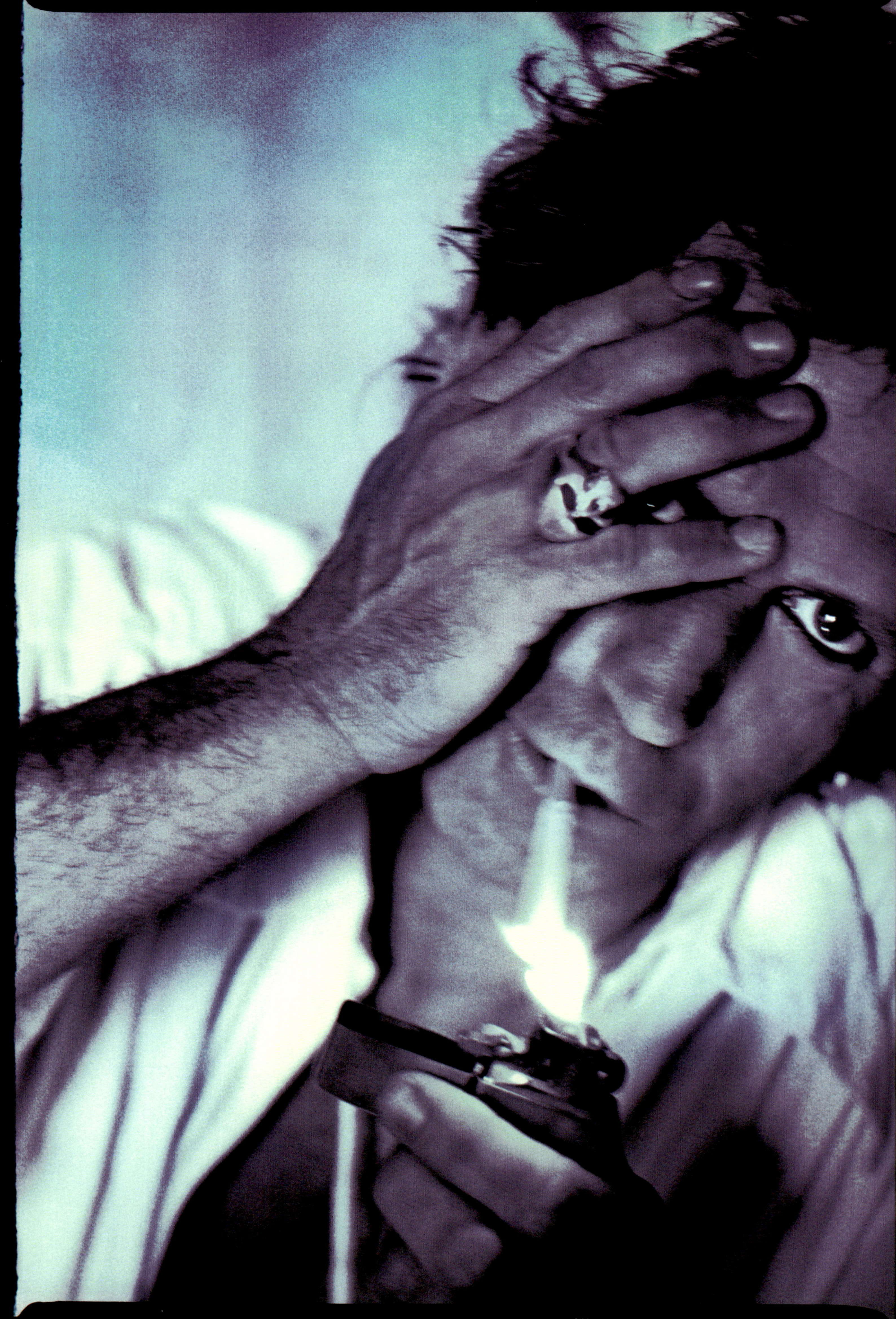

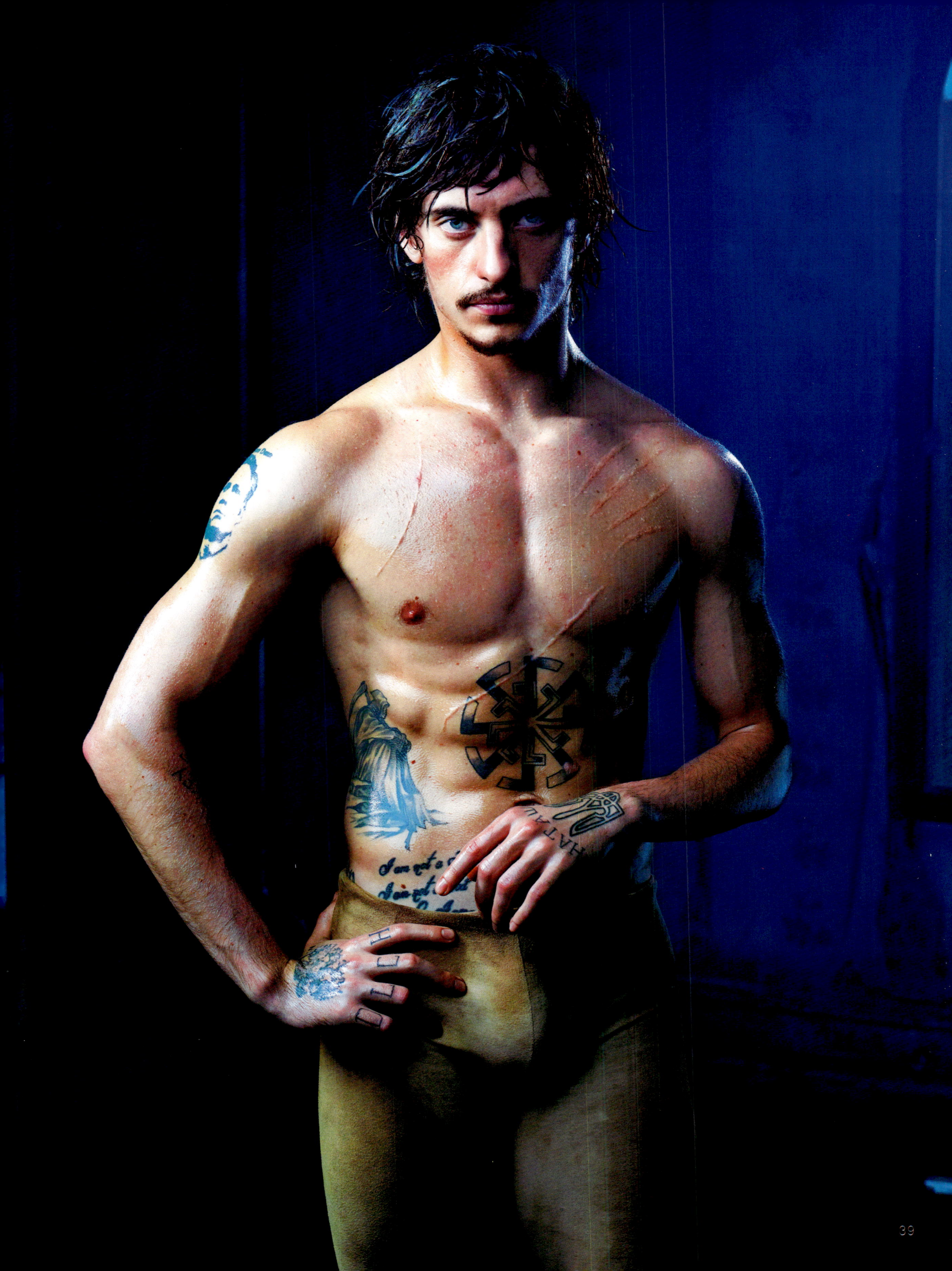

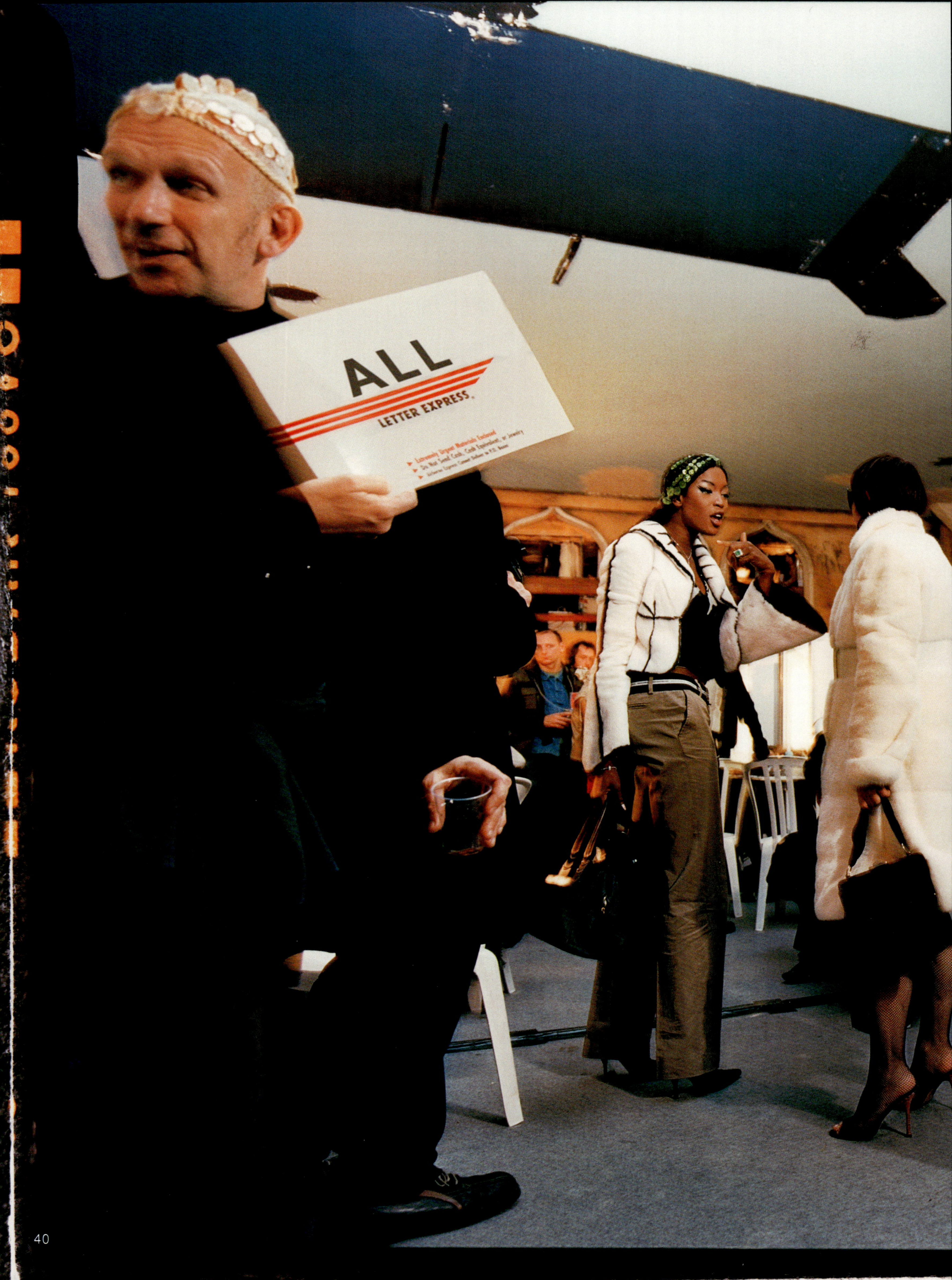
ALL
LETTER EXPRESS

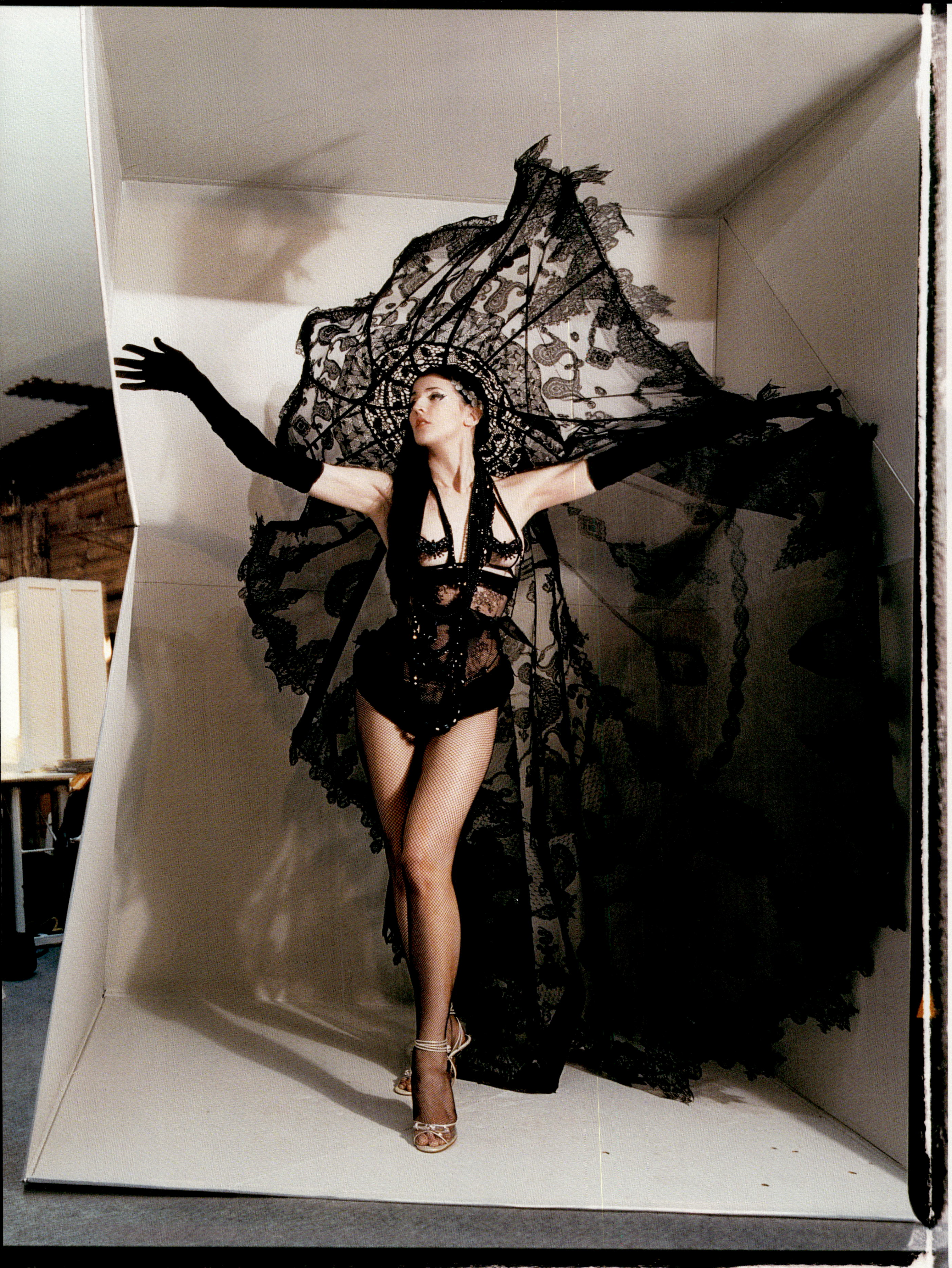

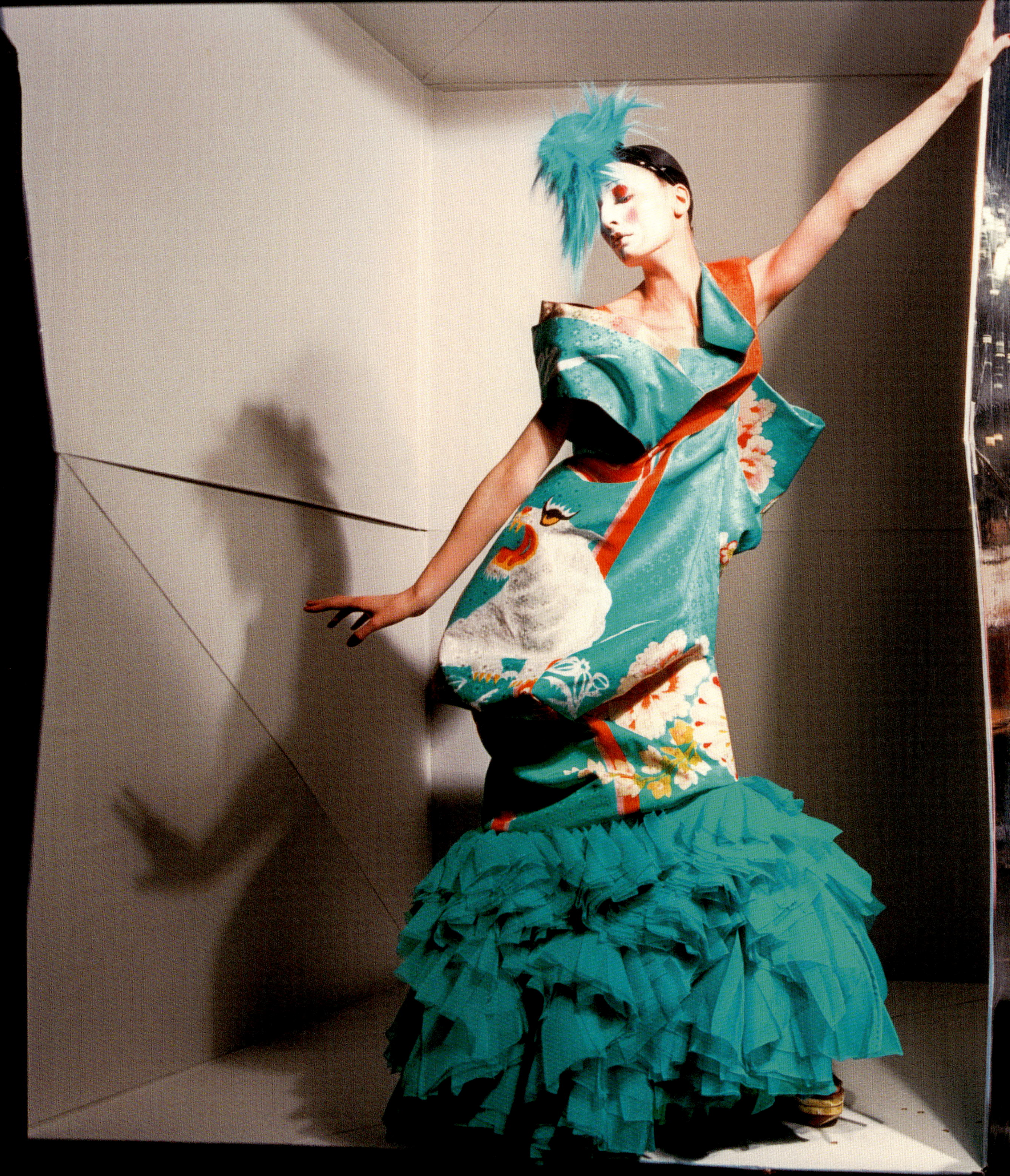

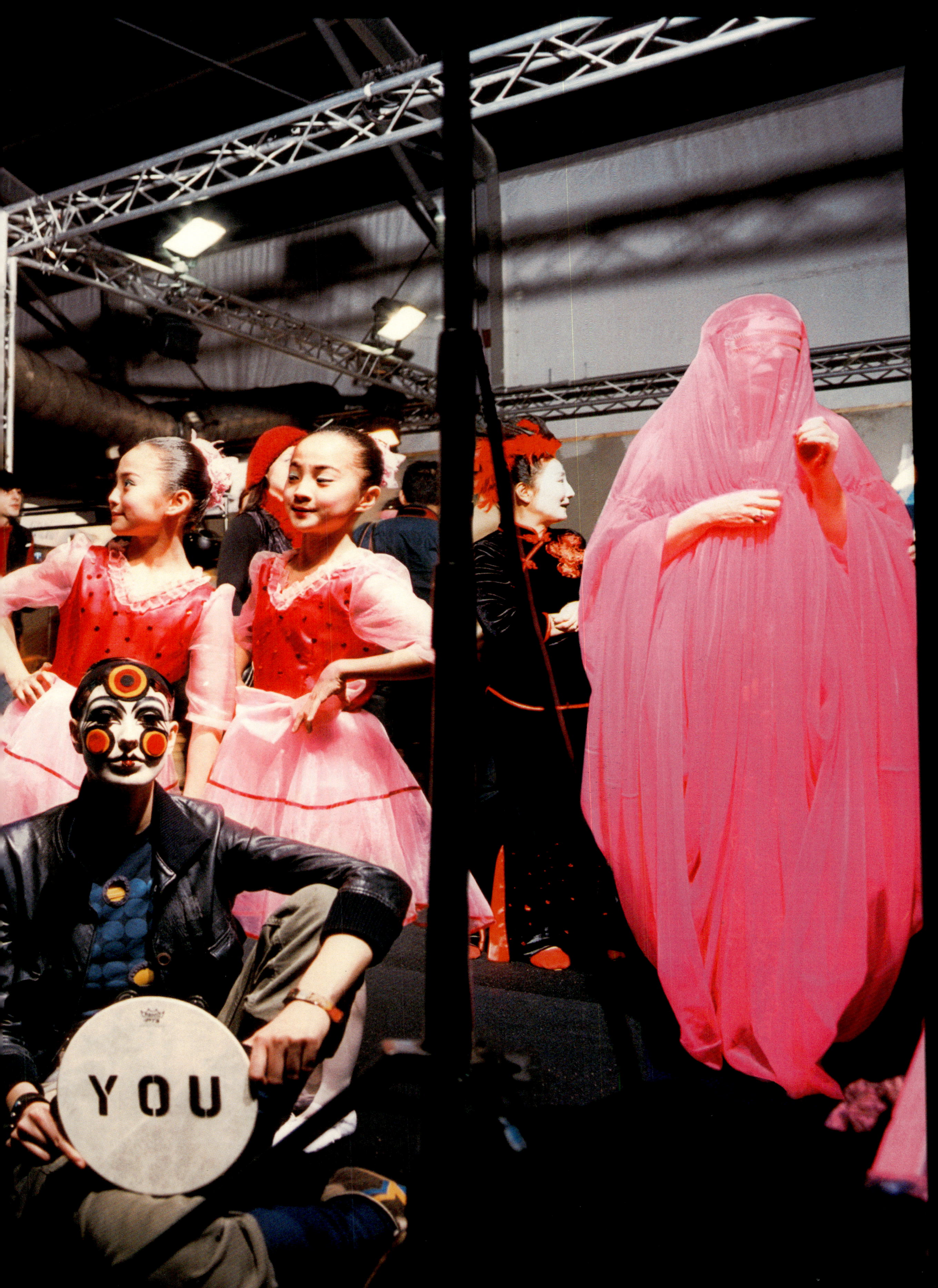
YOU

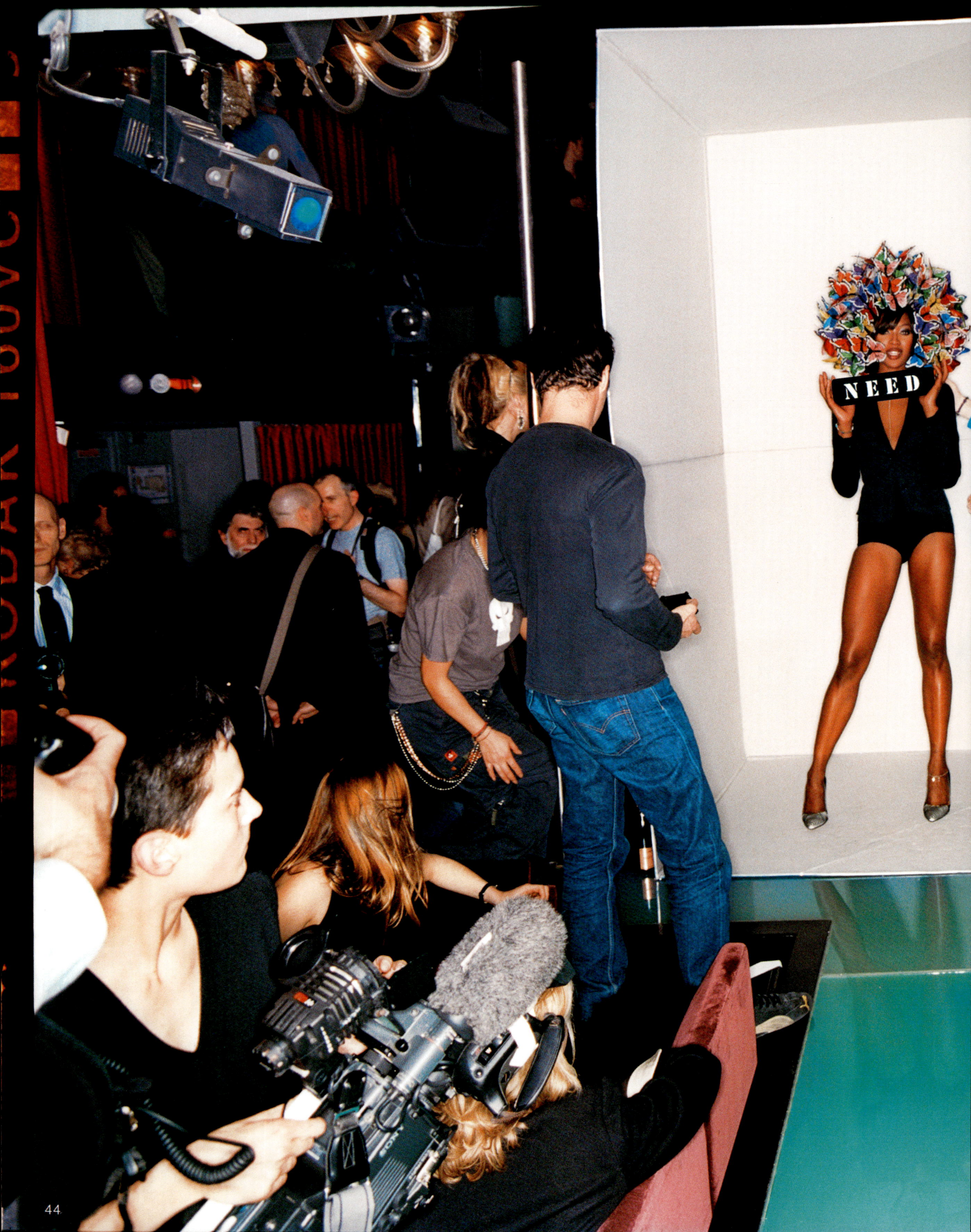
NEED

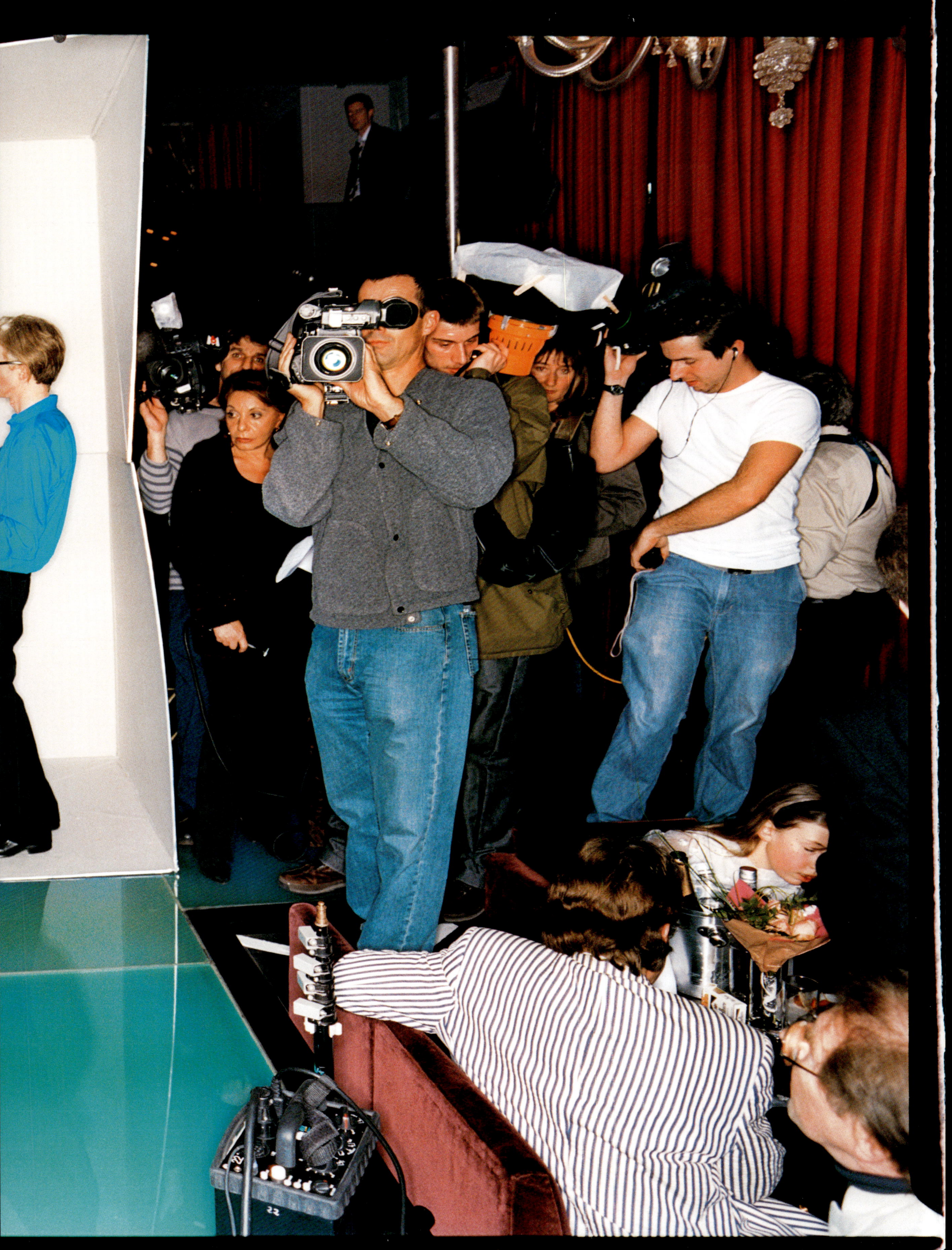

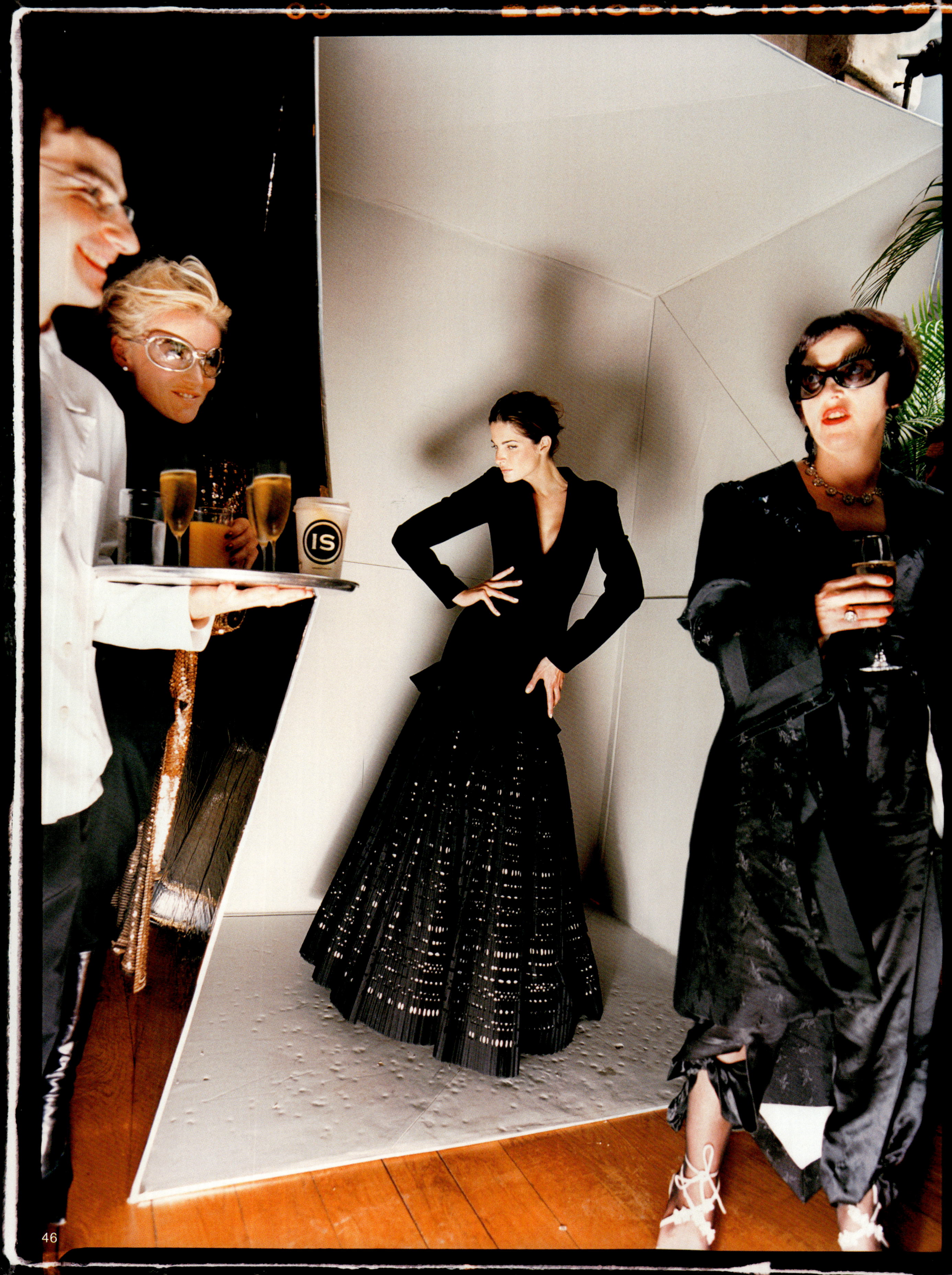
IS

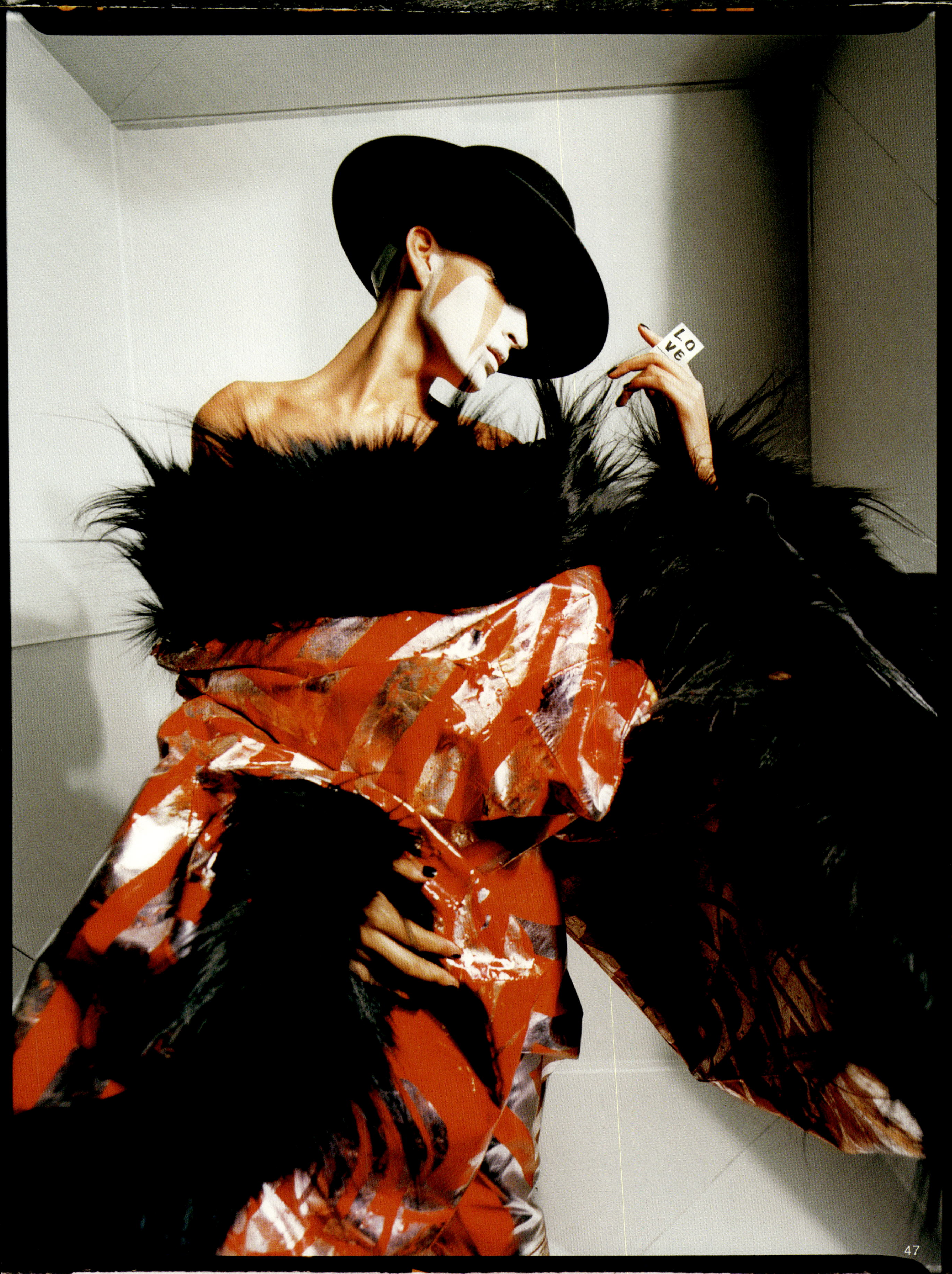
LO
VE

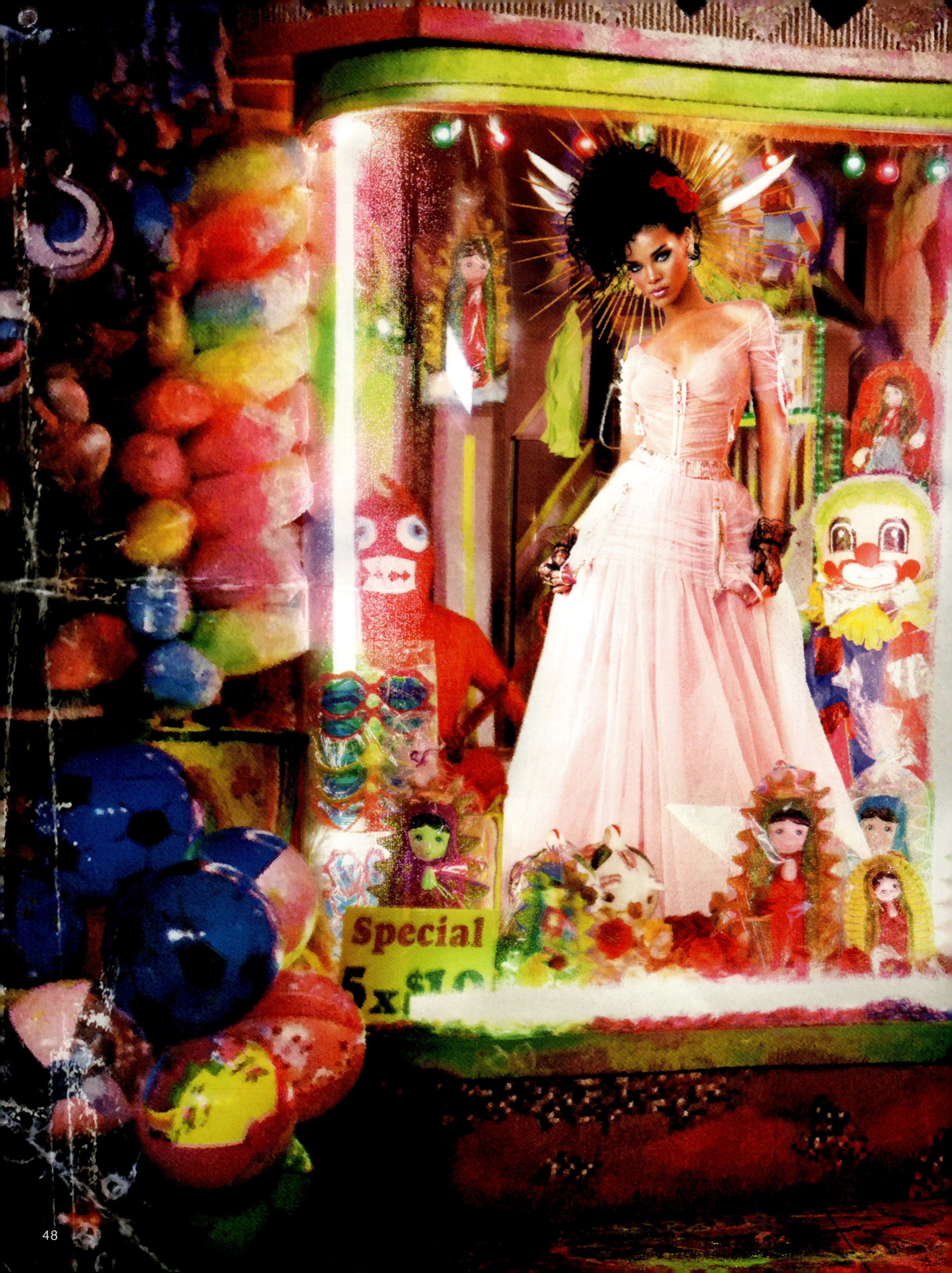
Special
5x

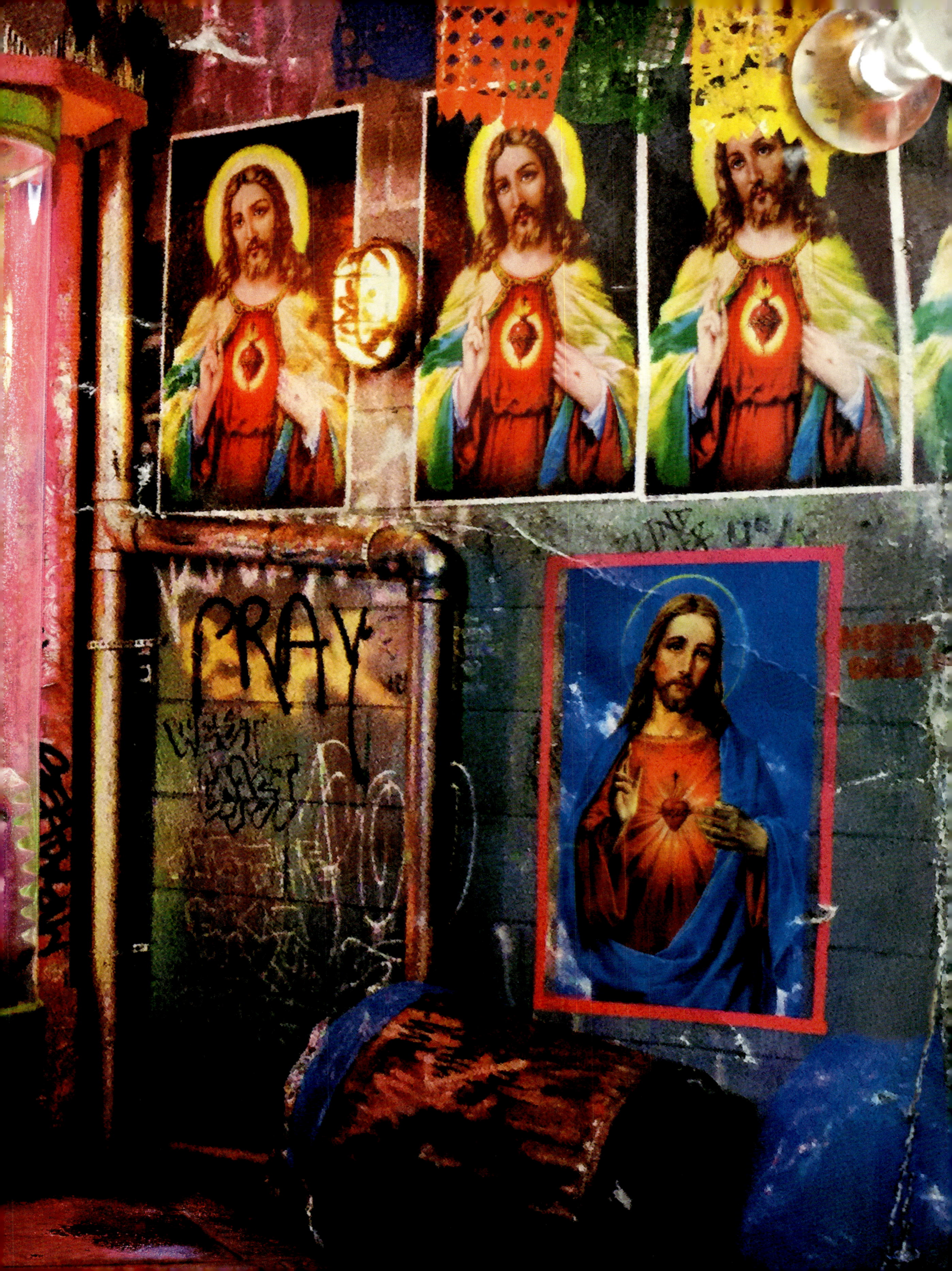
PRAY

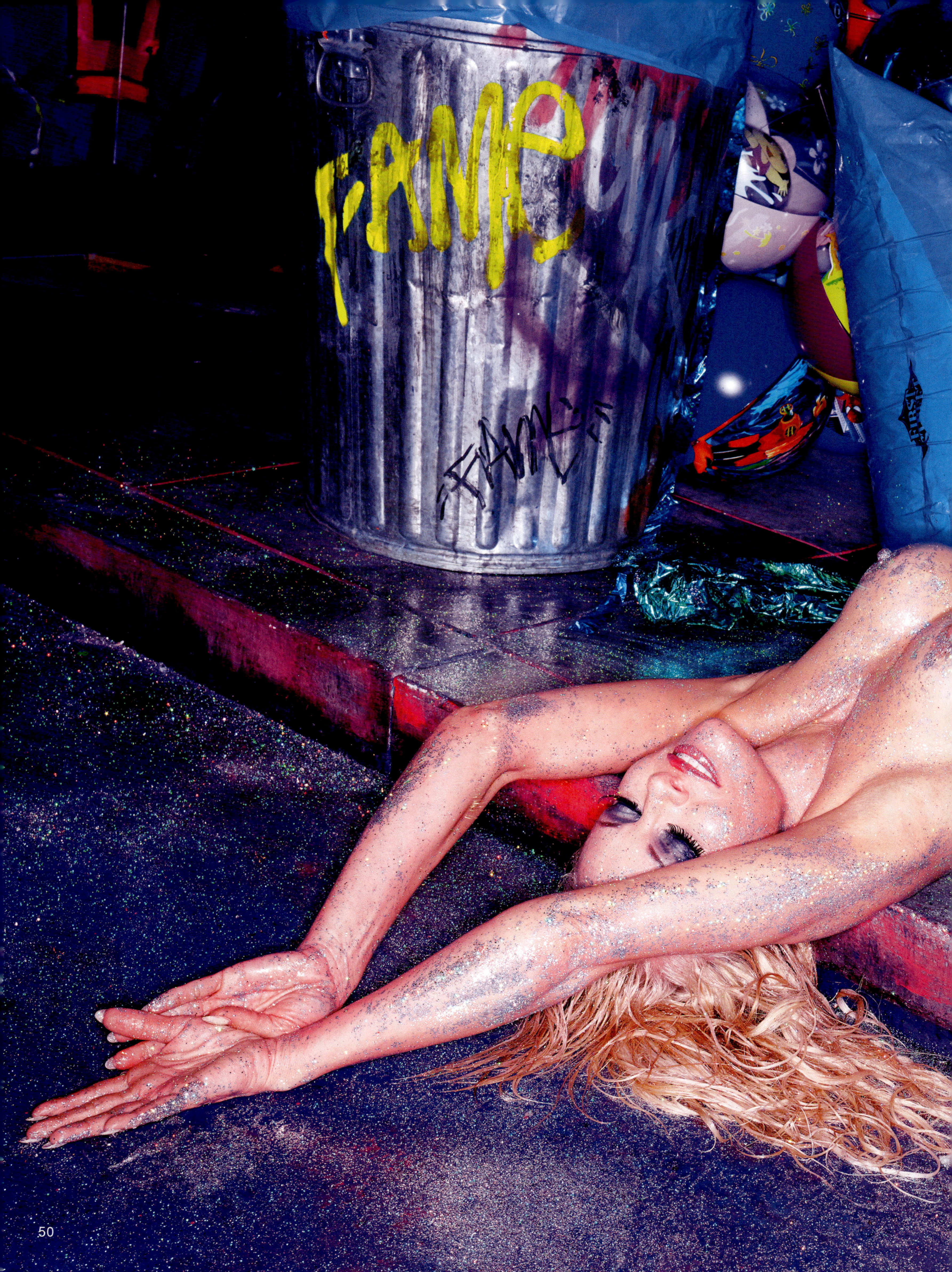
FAME

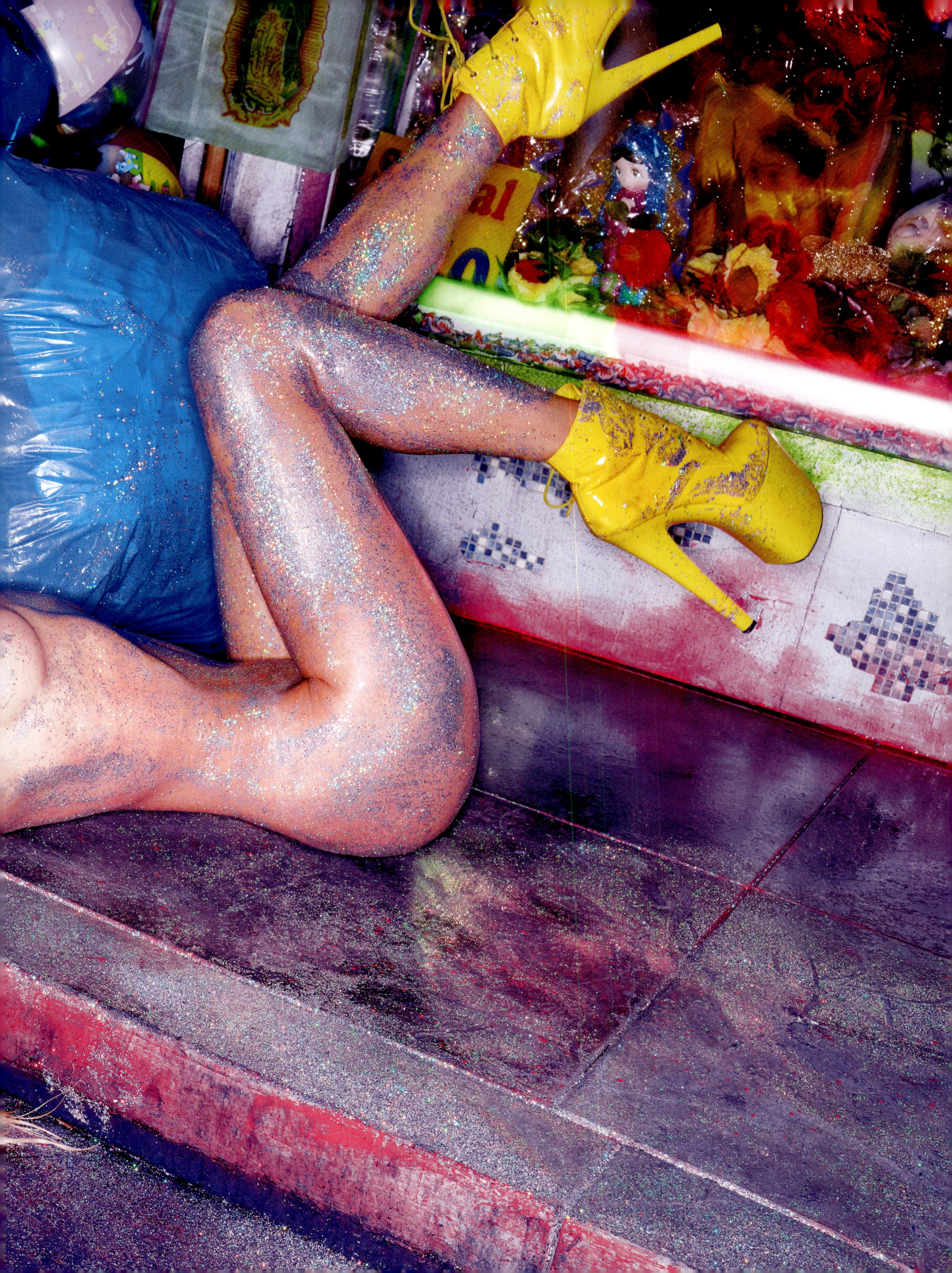

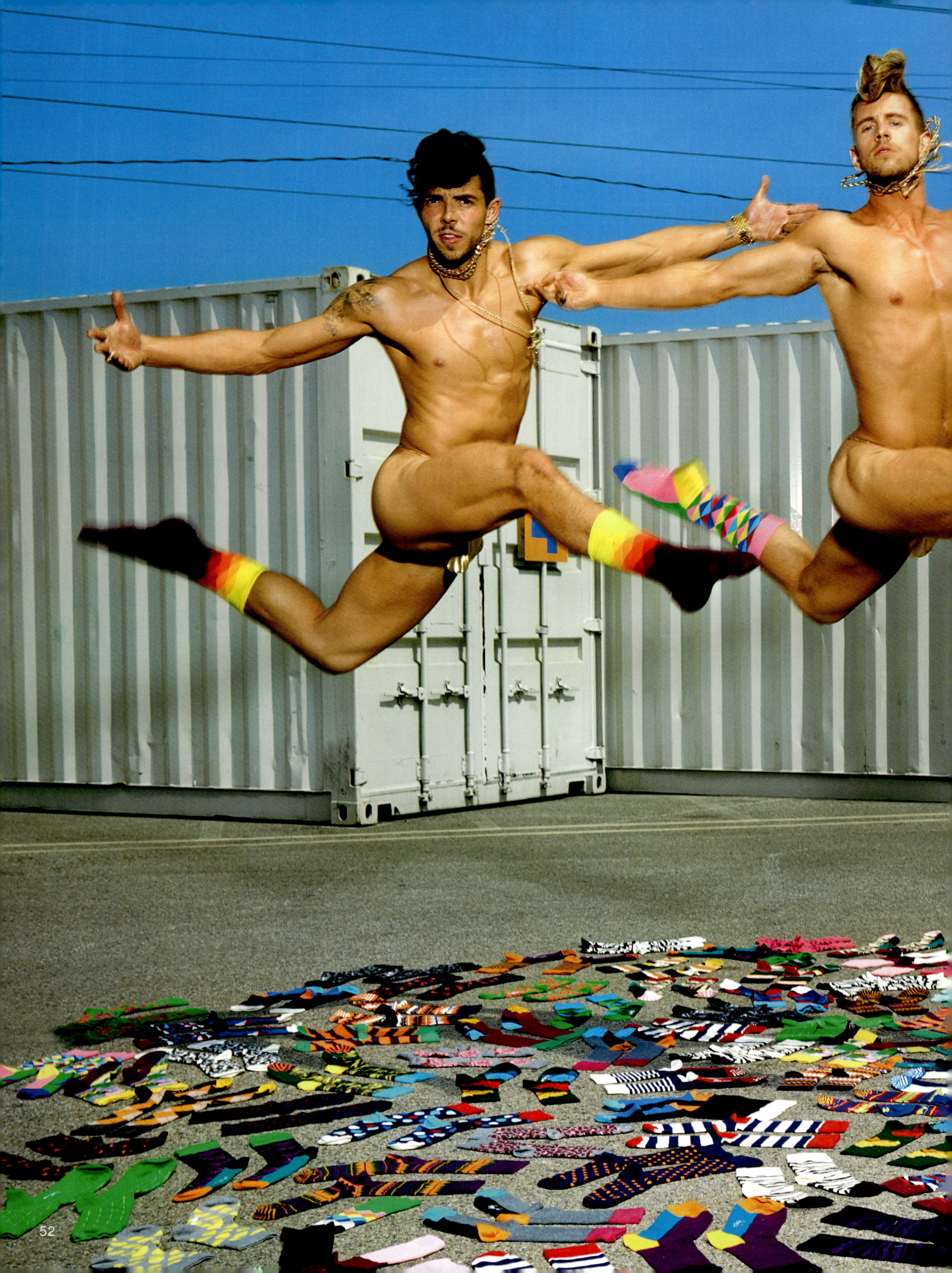

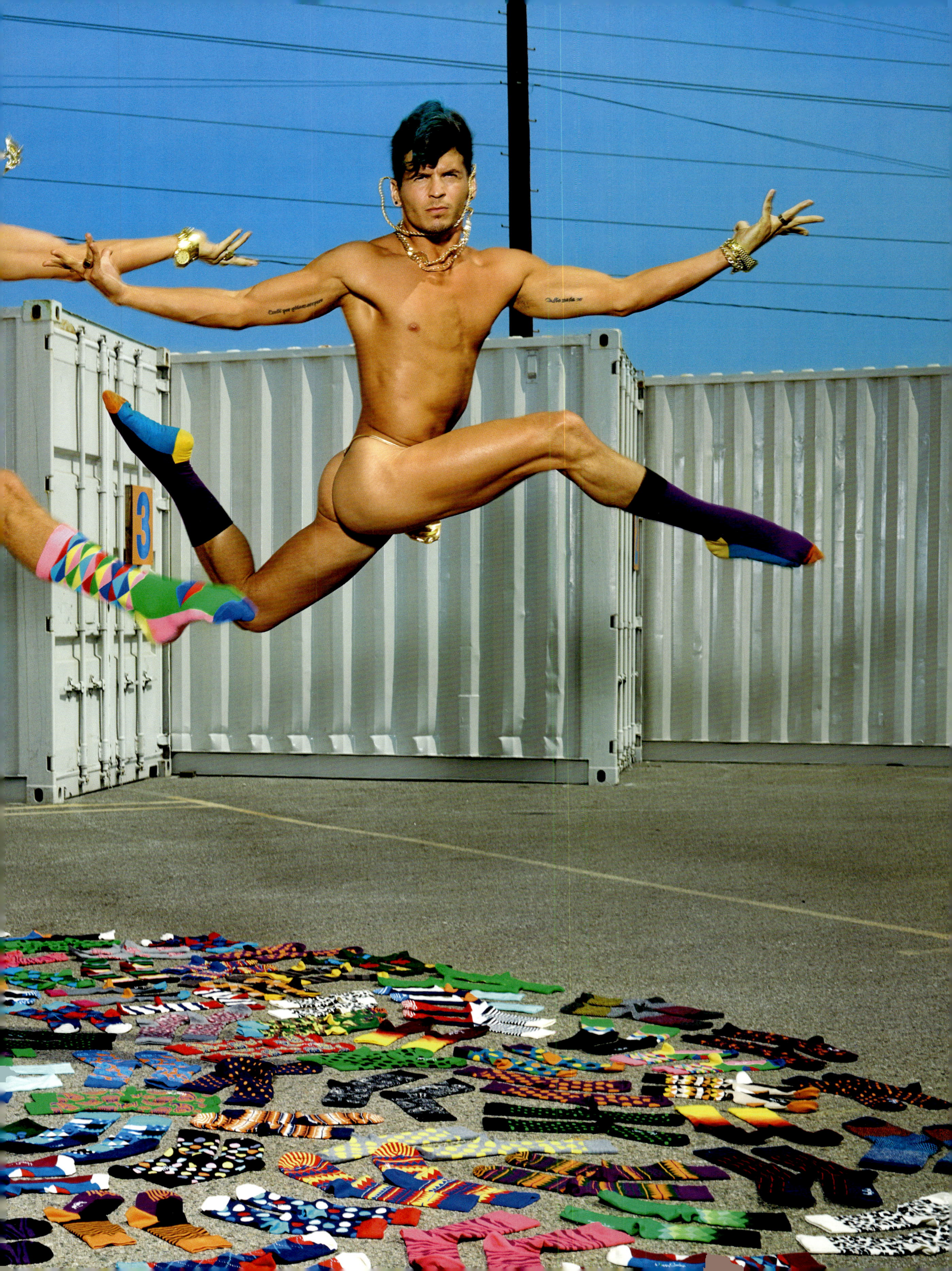

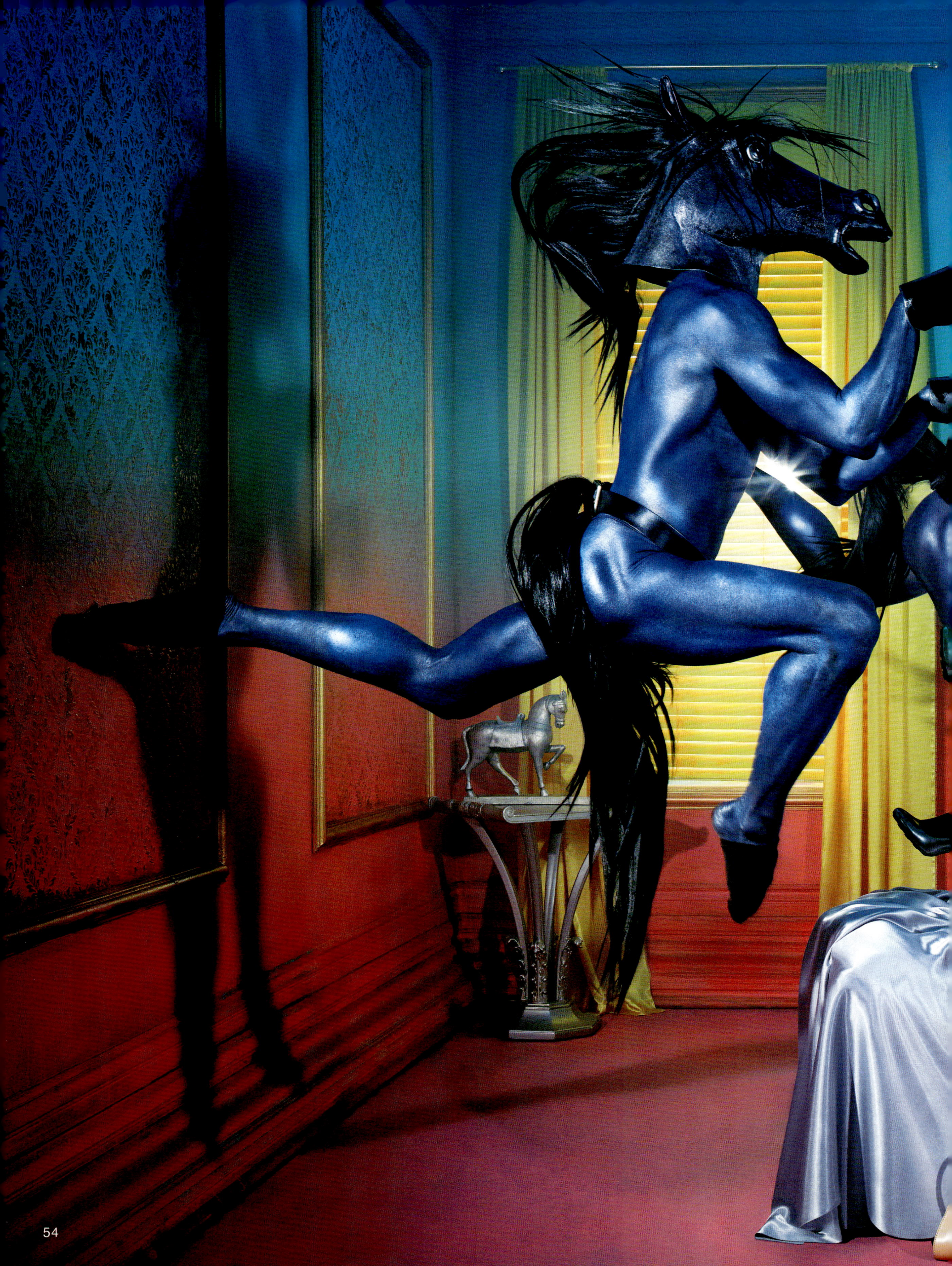

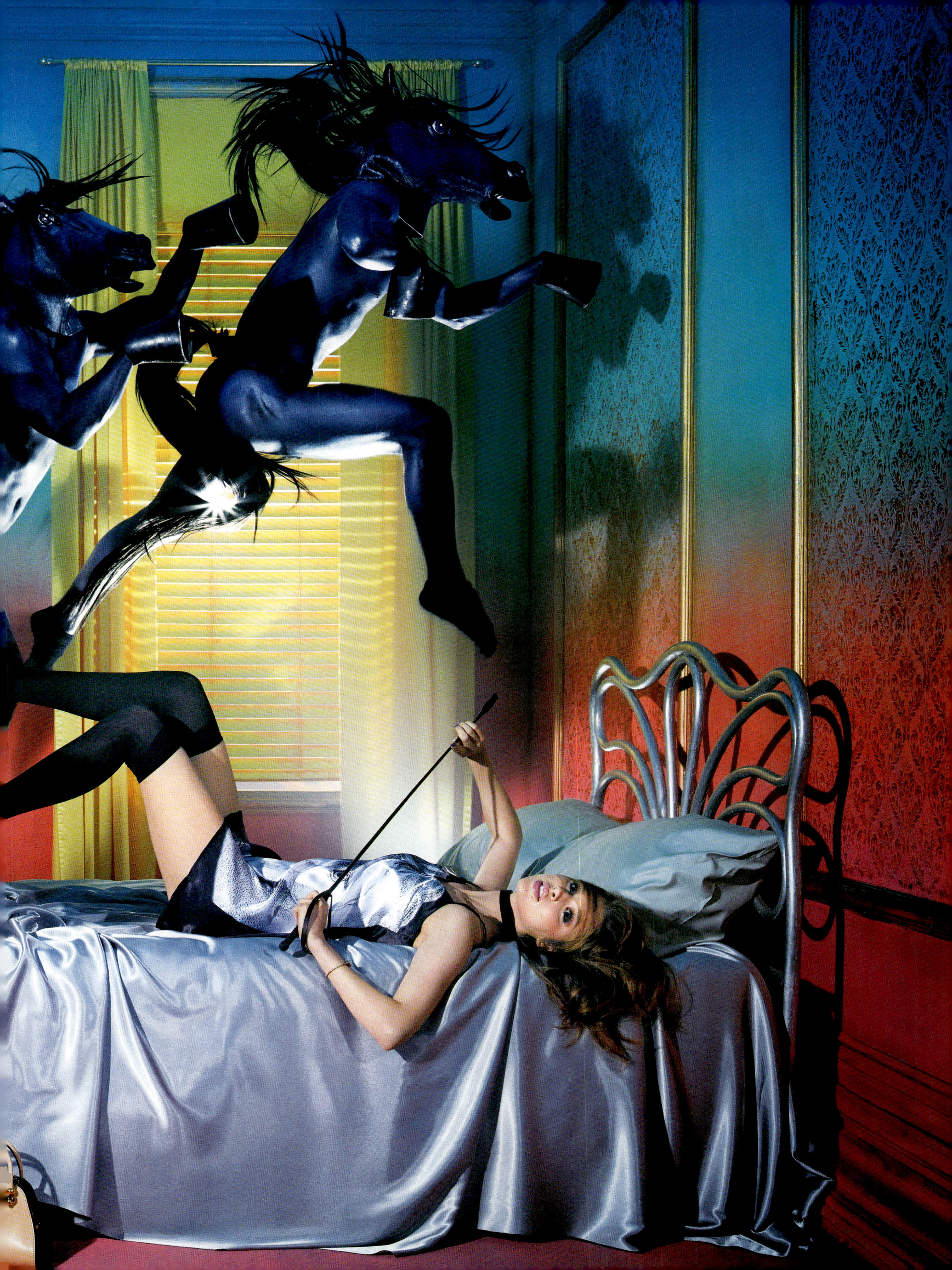

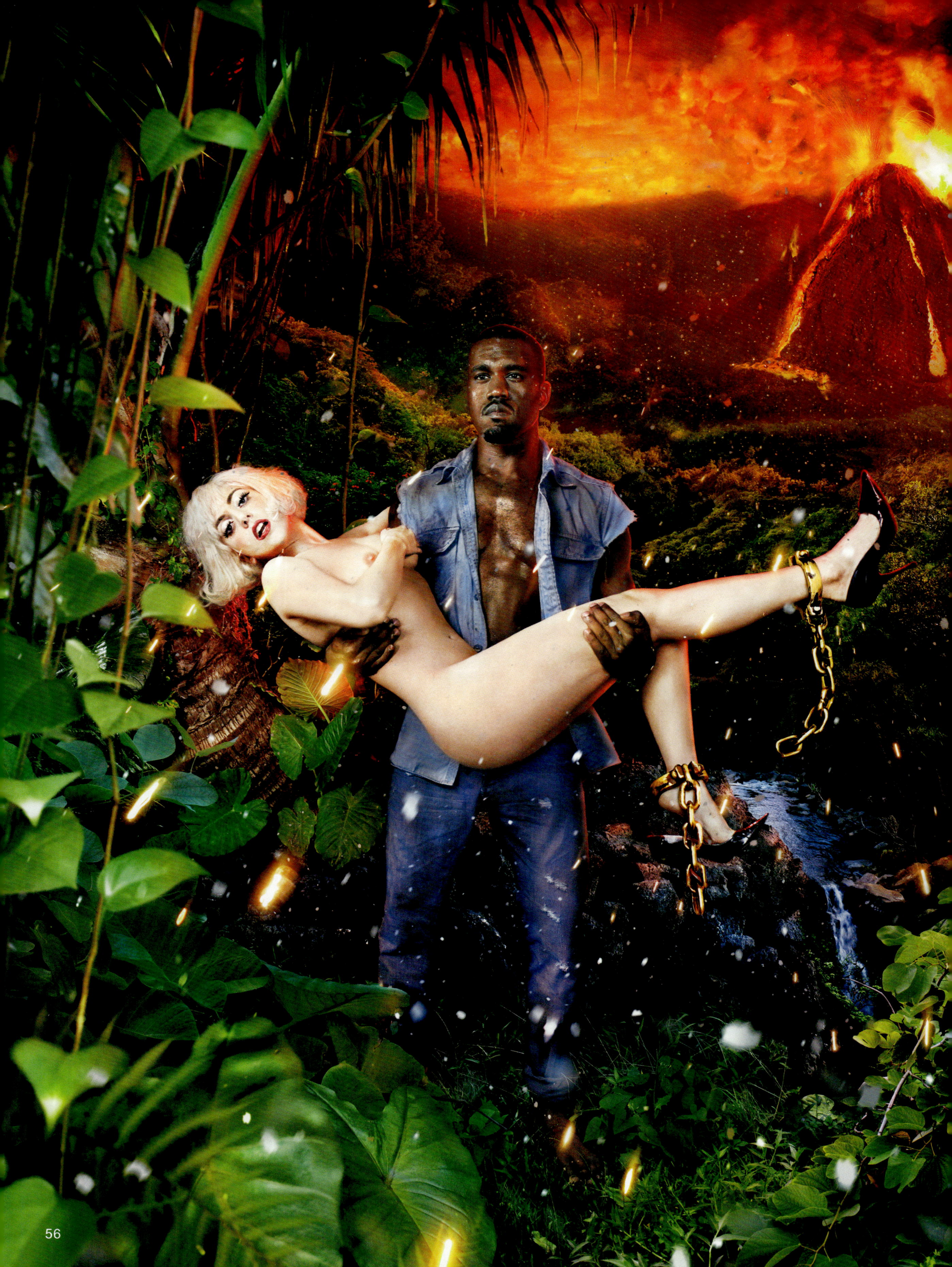

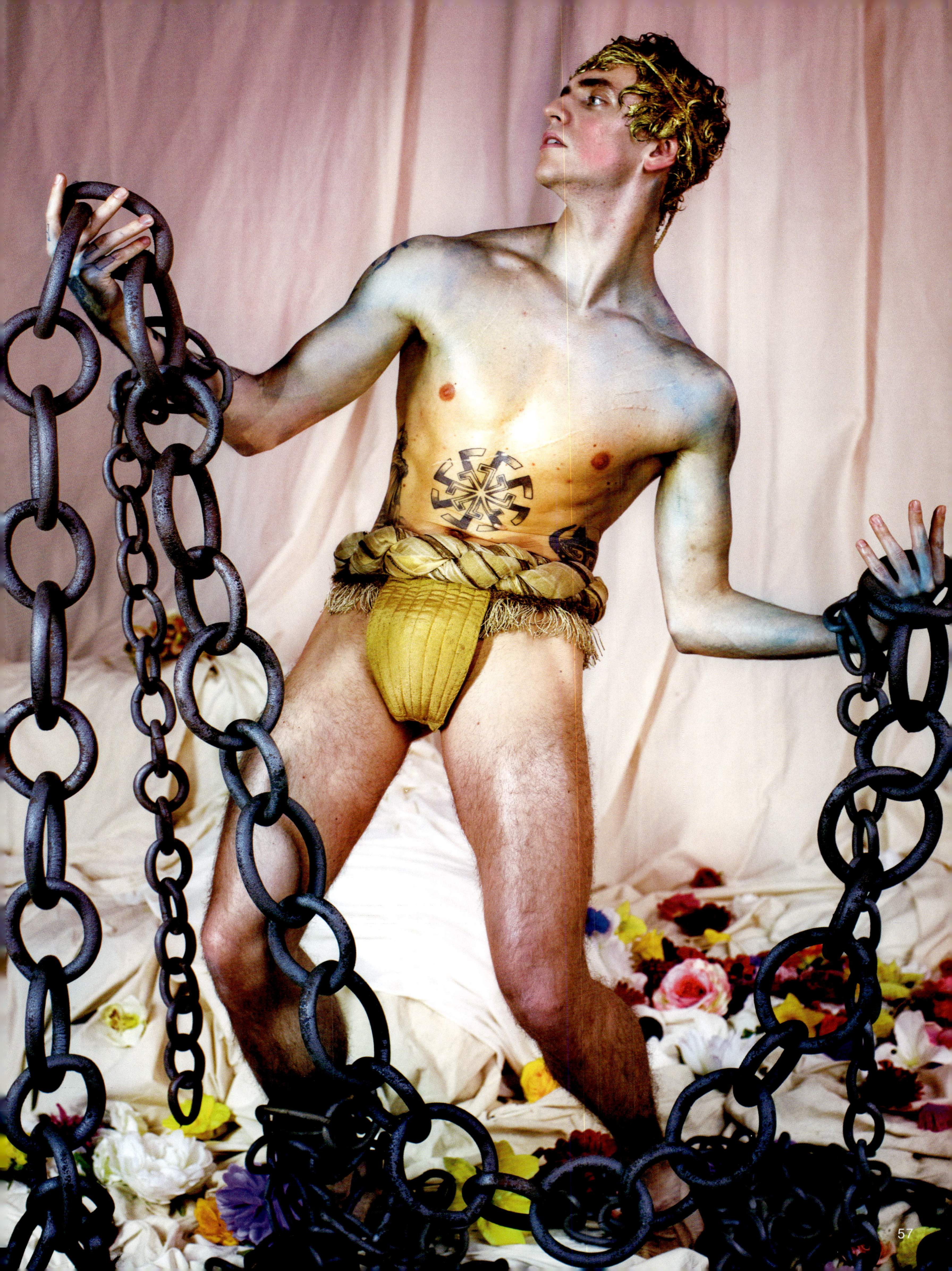

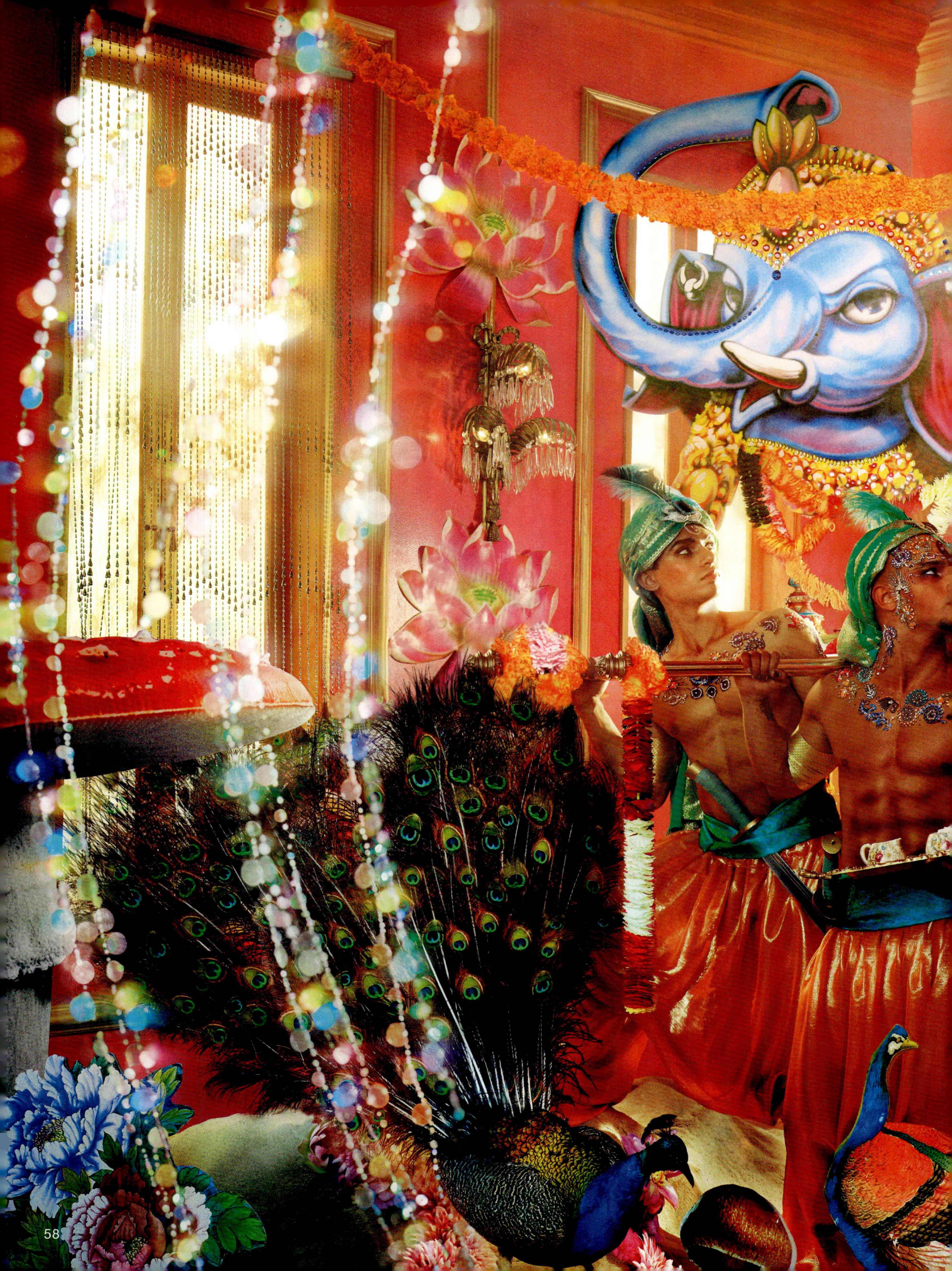

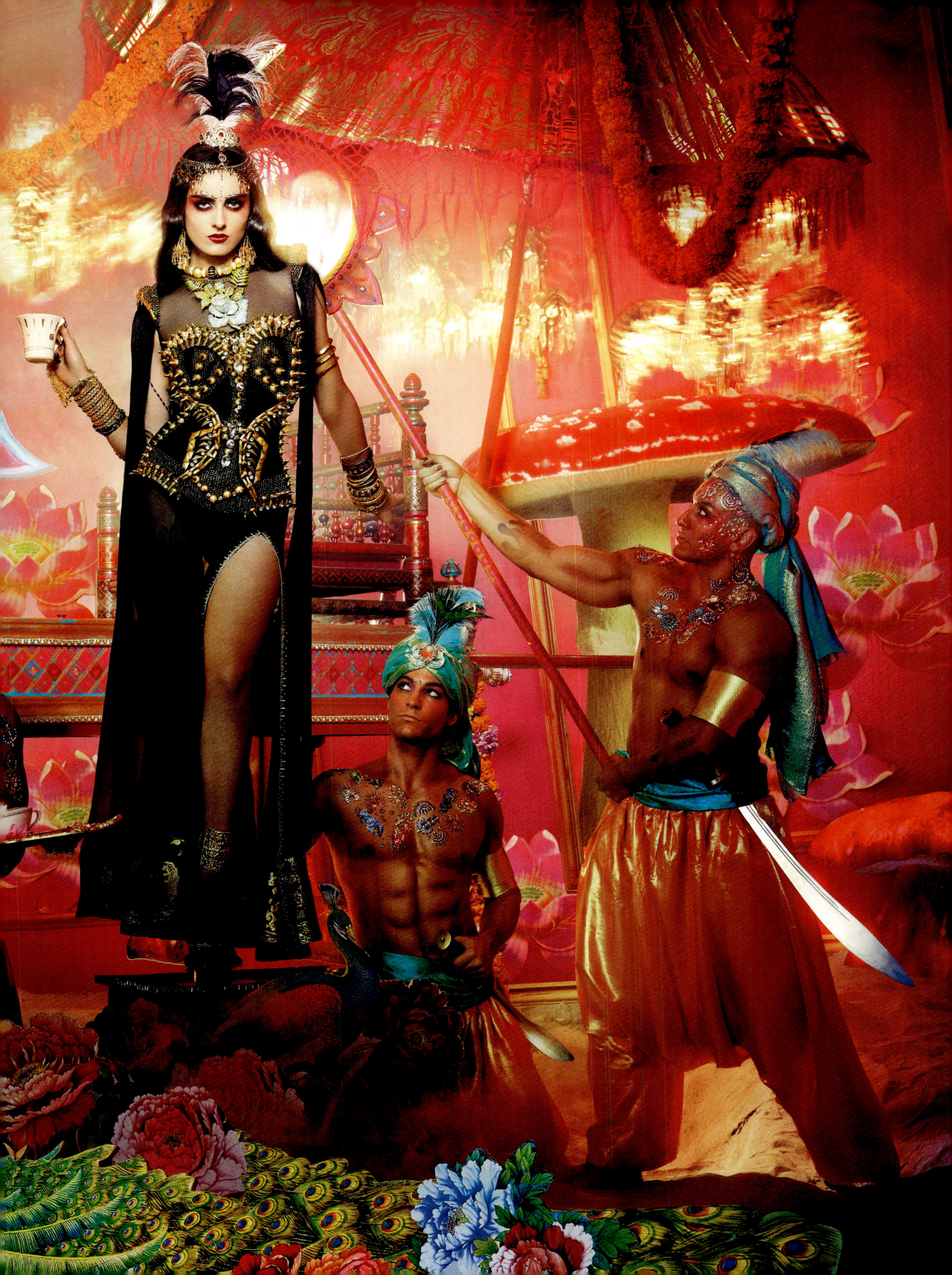

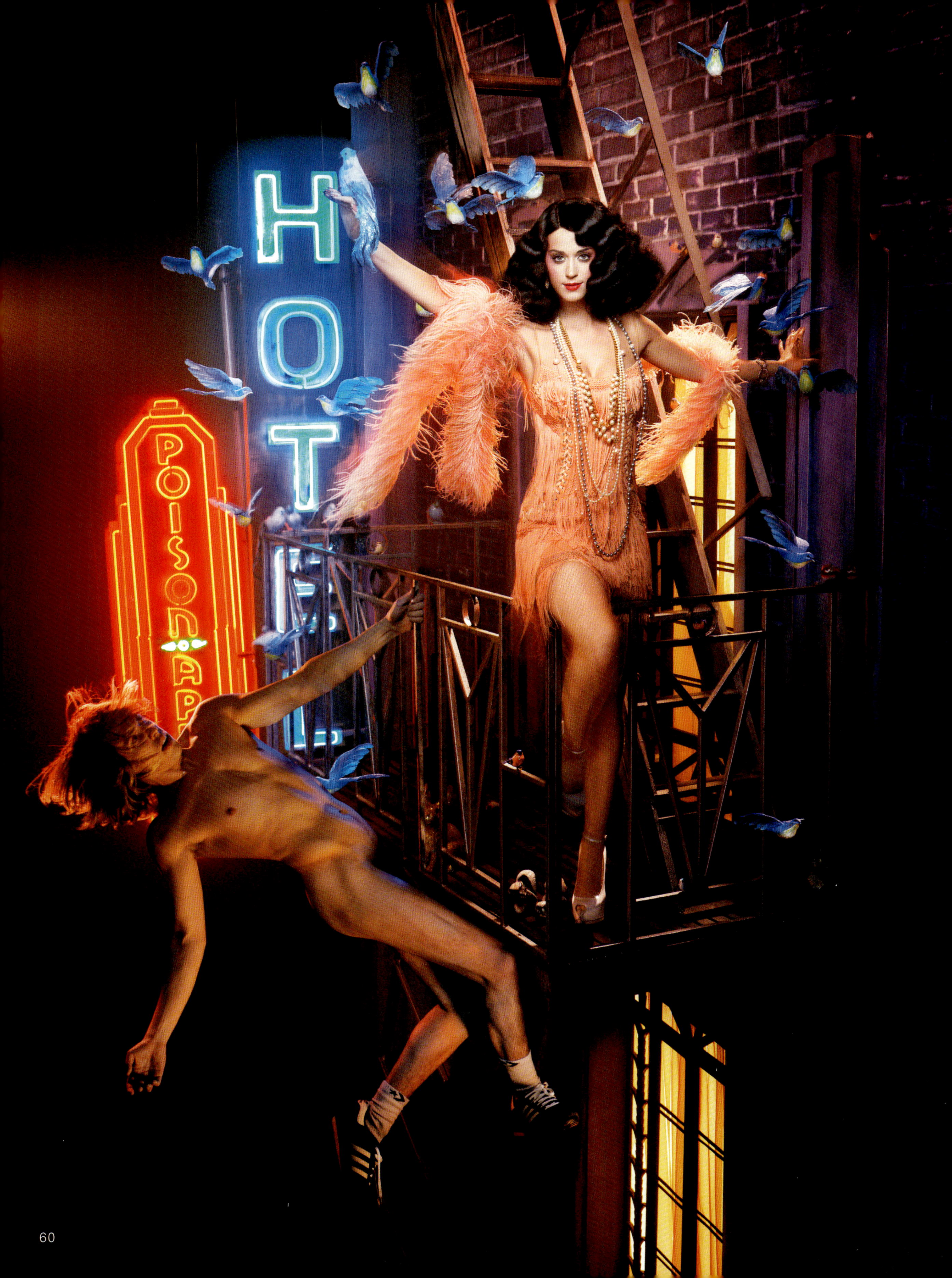
HOT
POISON

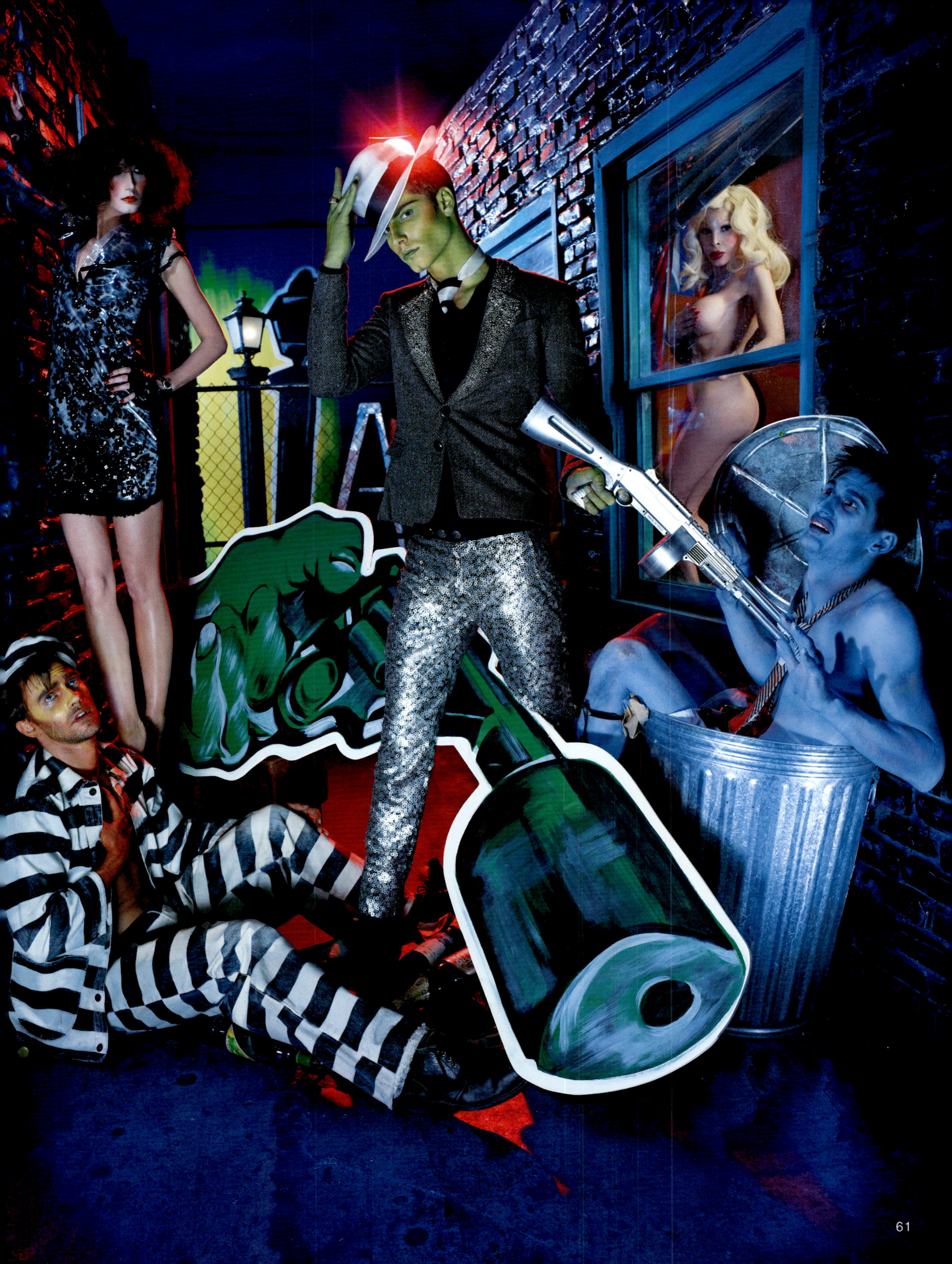

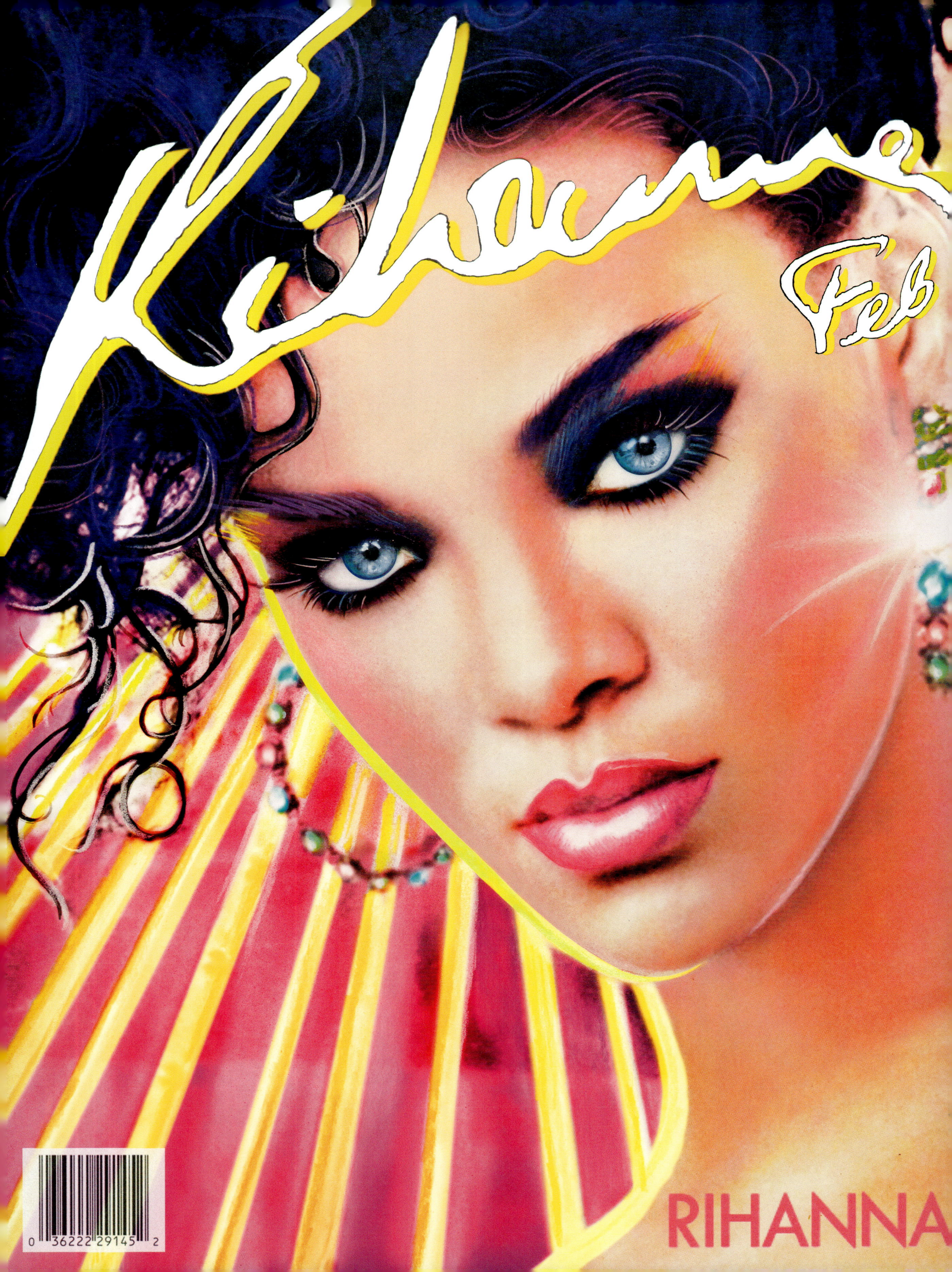

Rihanna
Feb
0 36222 29145 2
RIHANNA

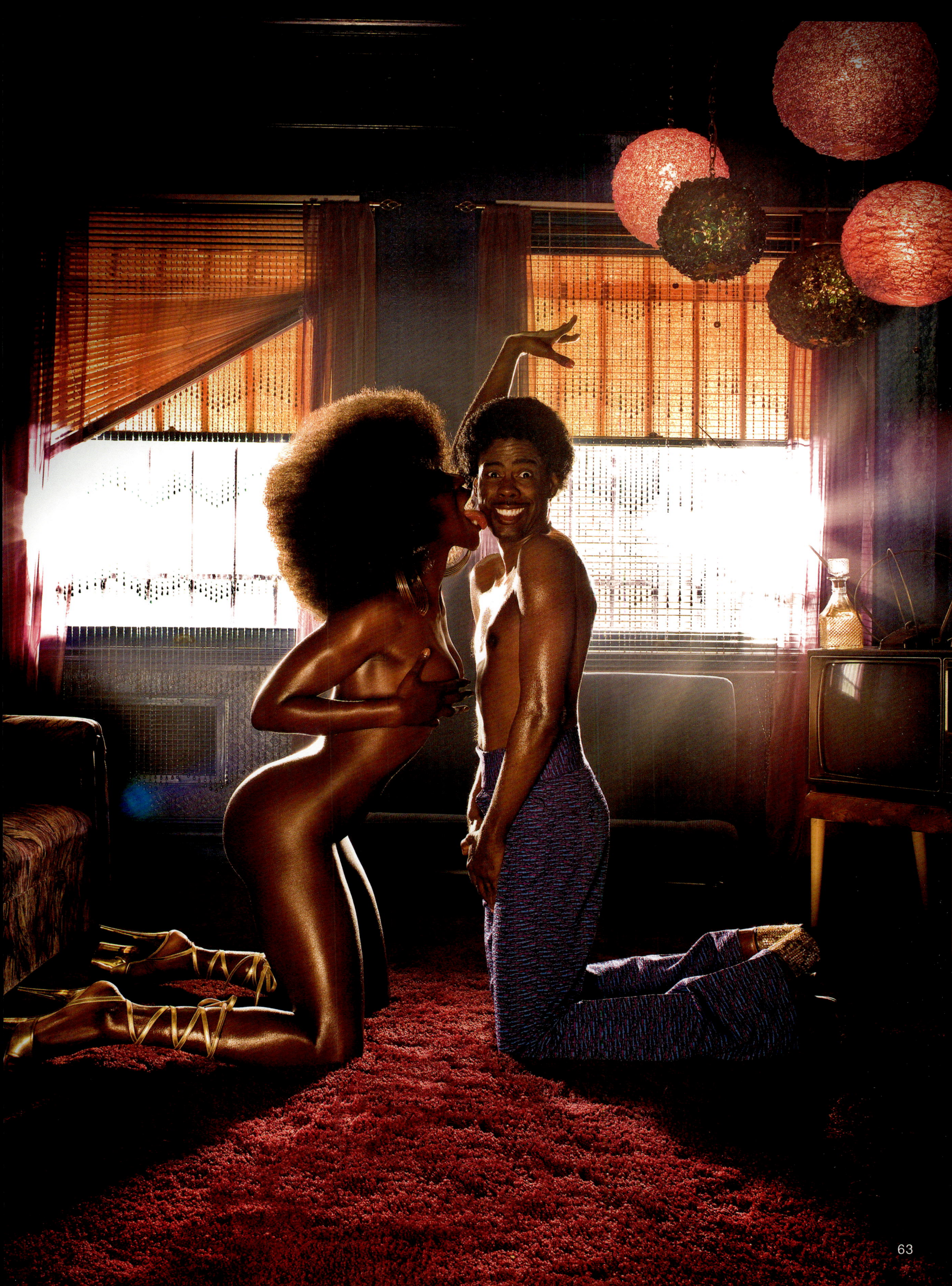

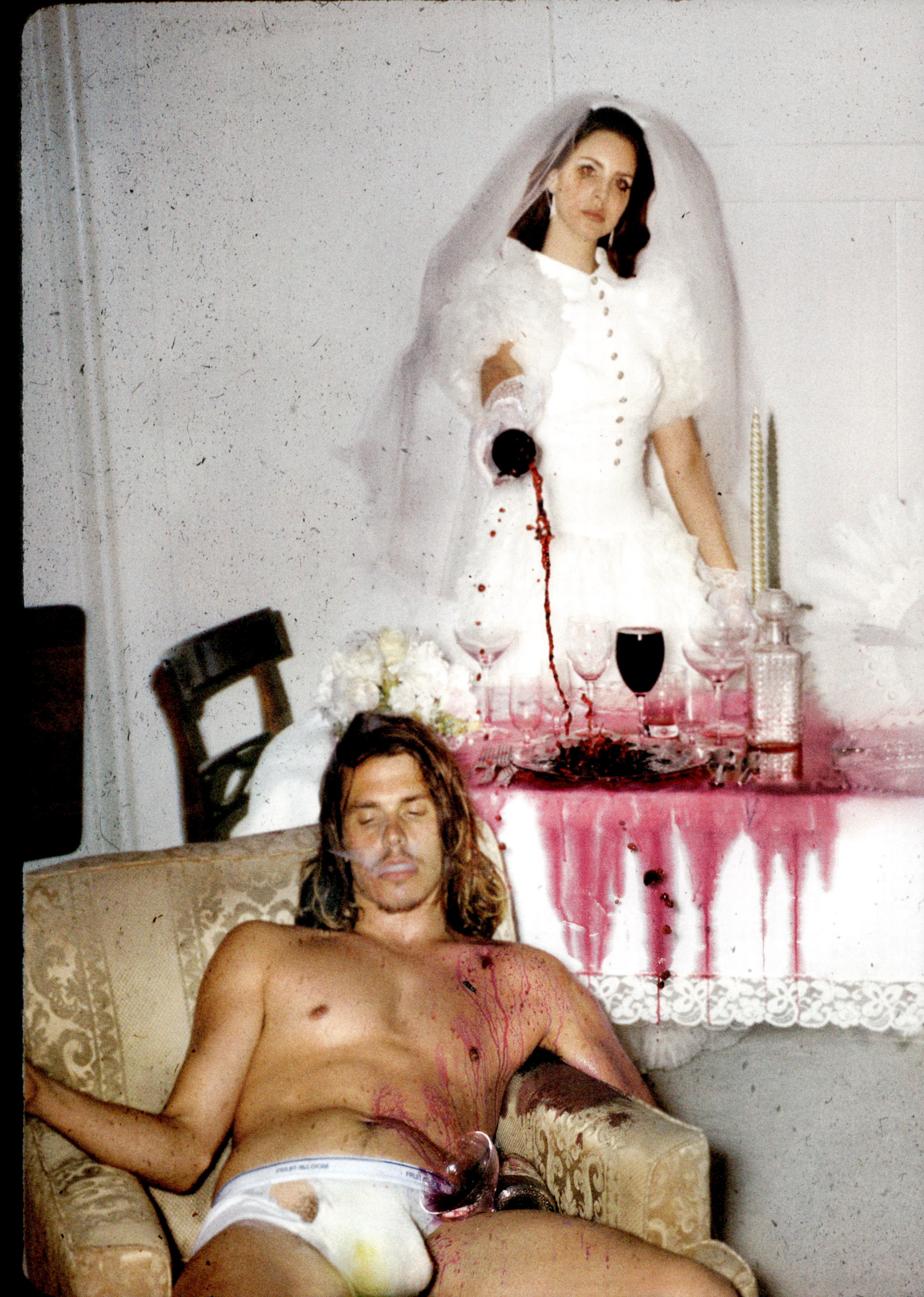

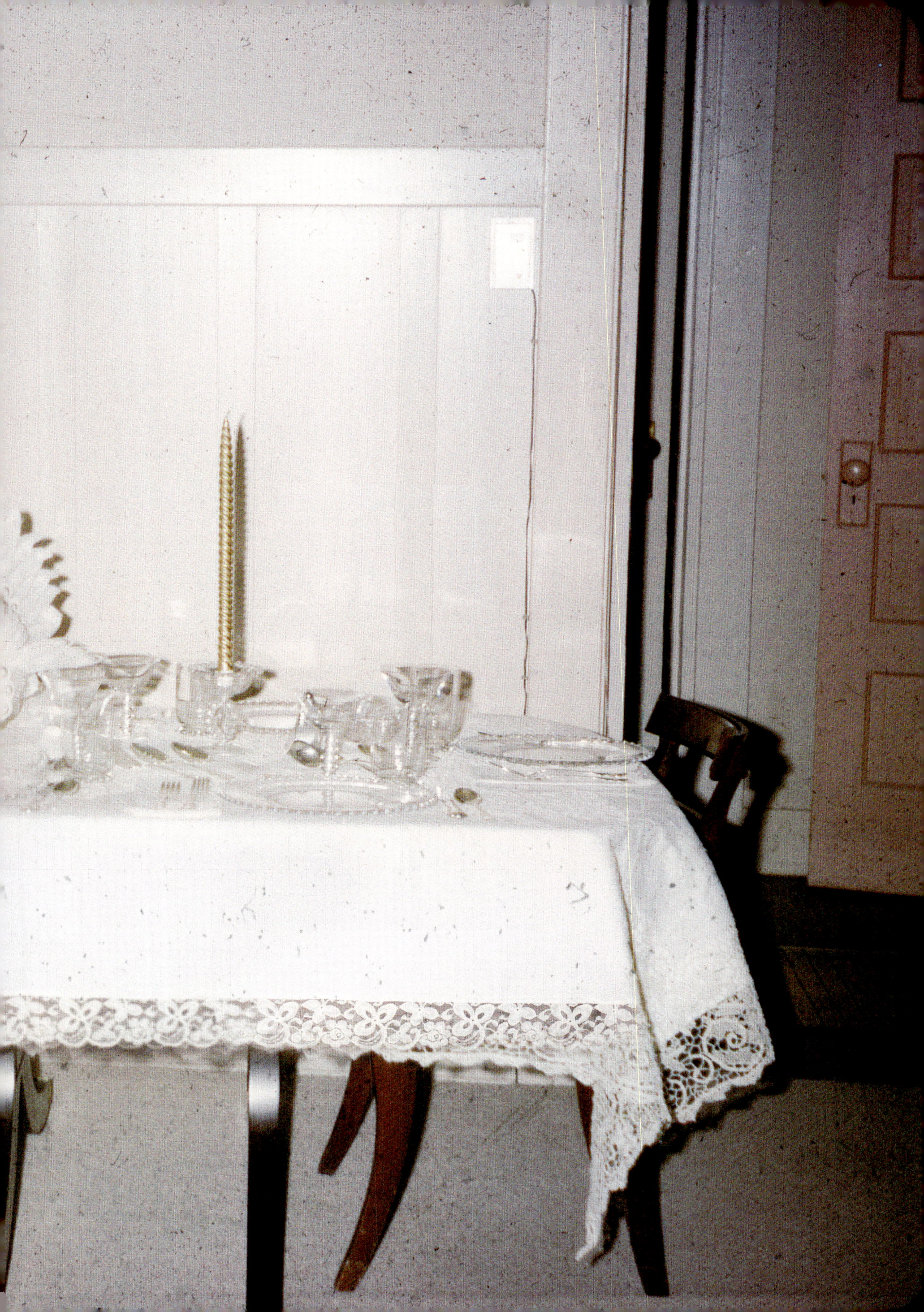

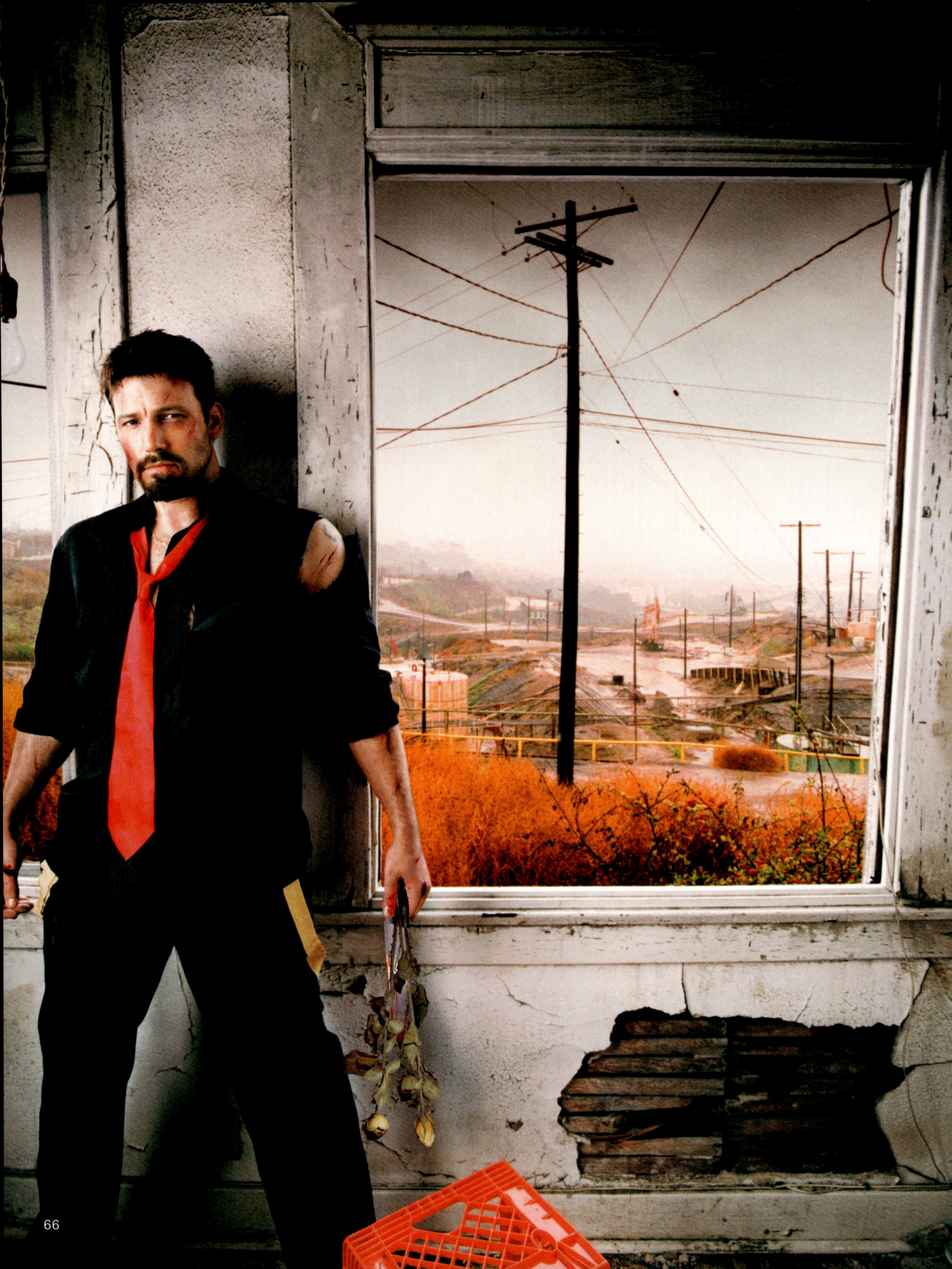

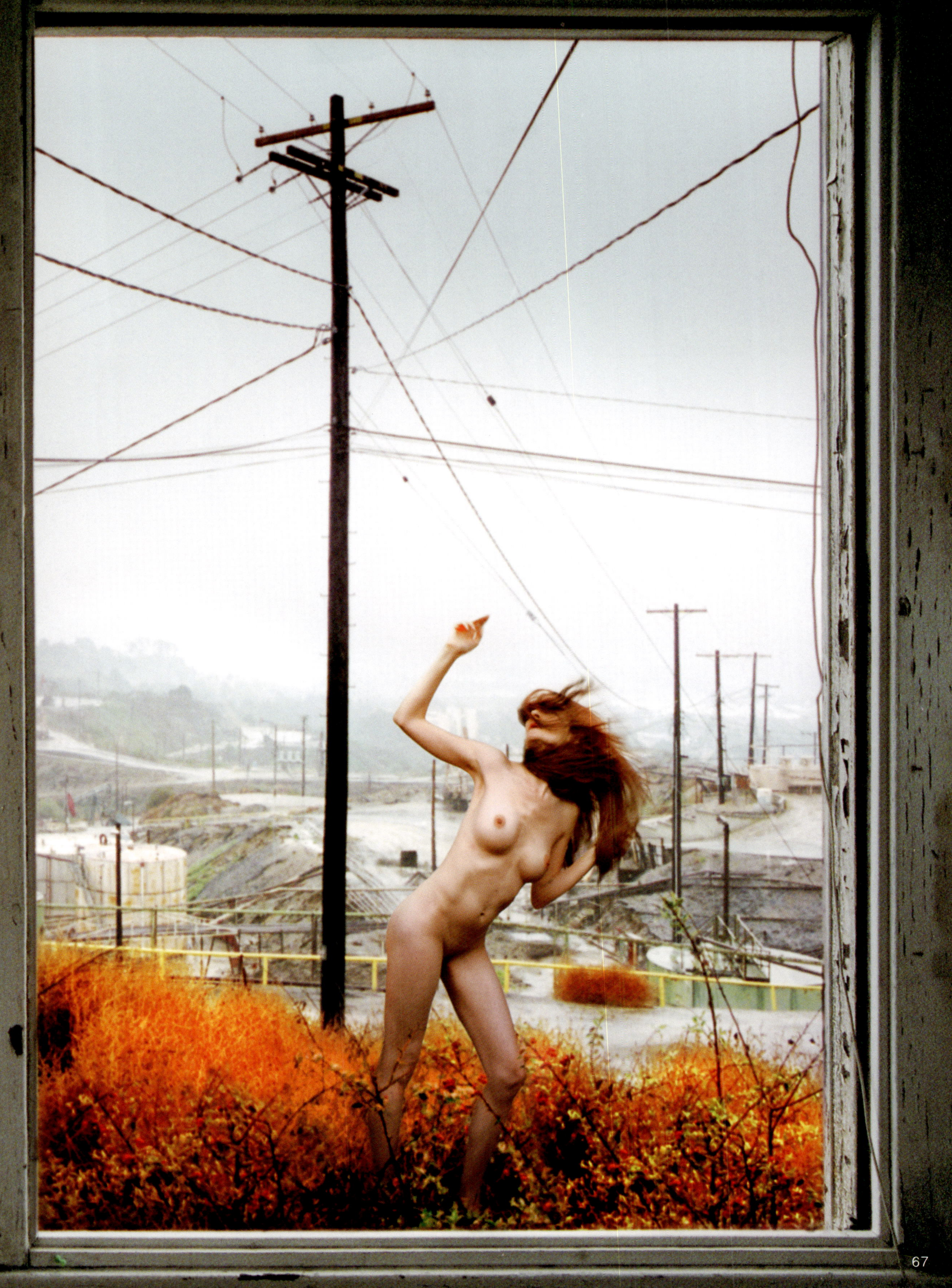

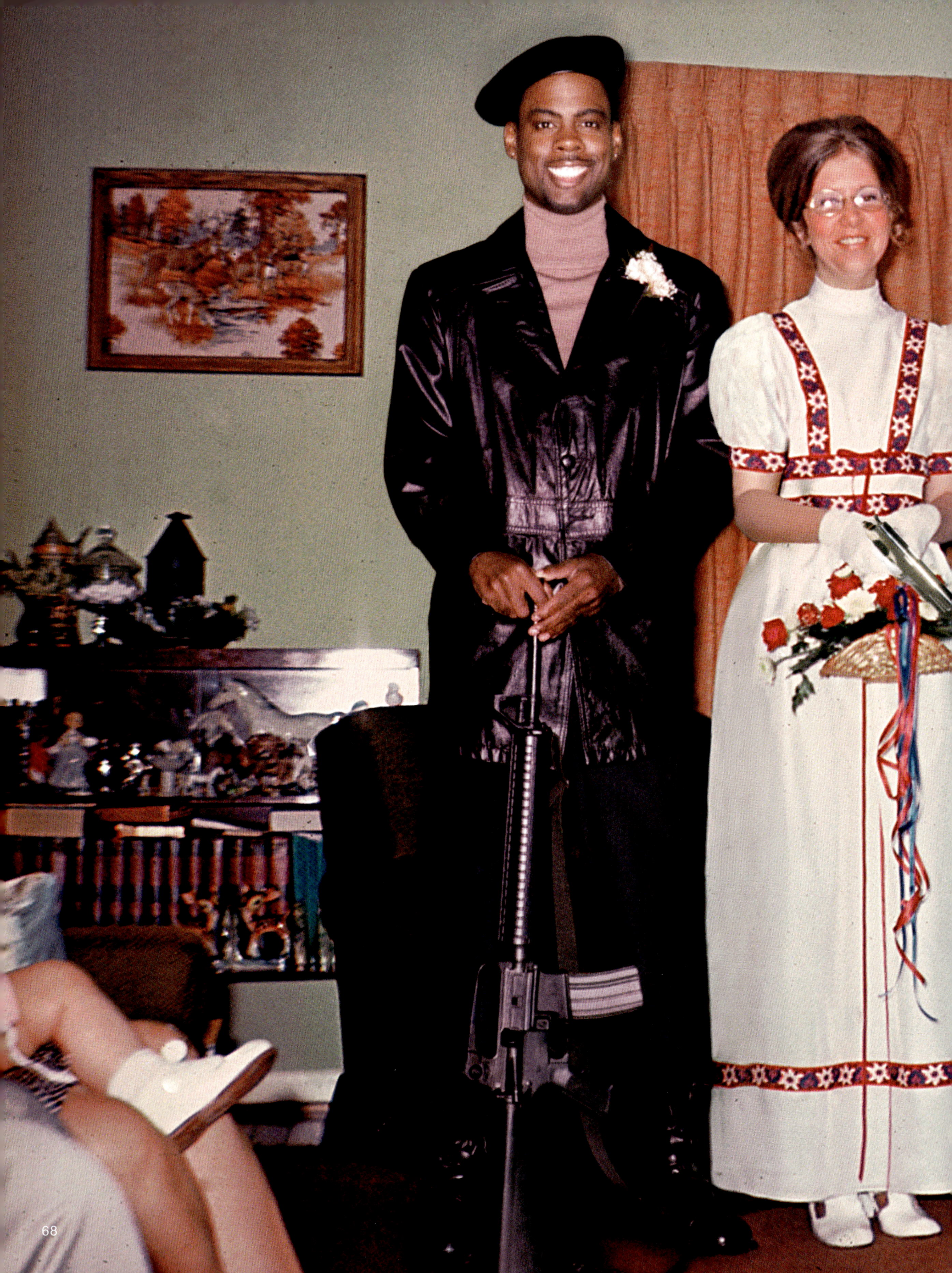

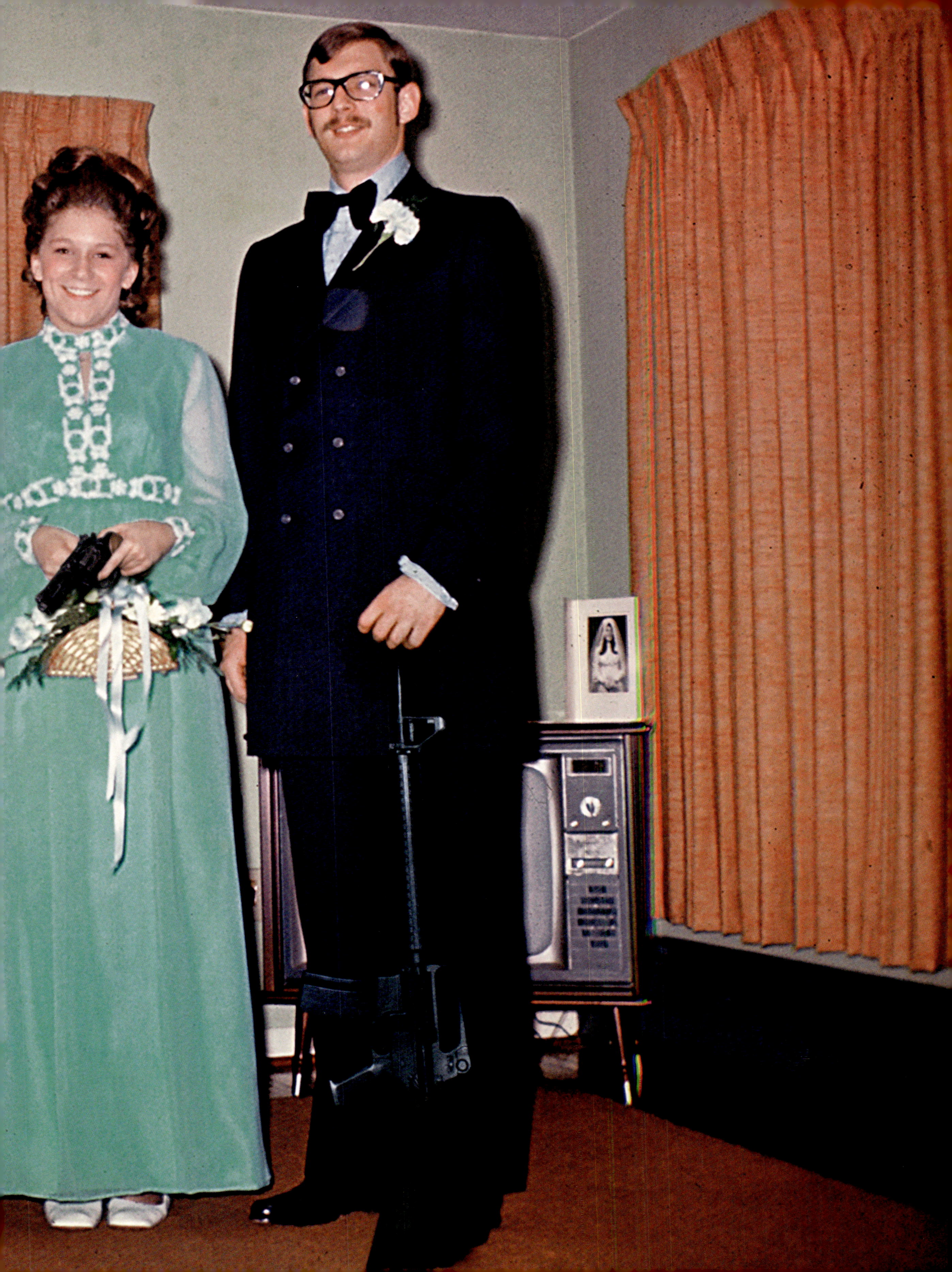

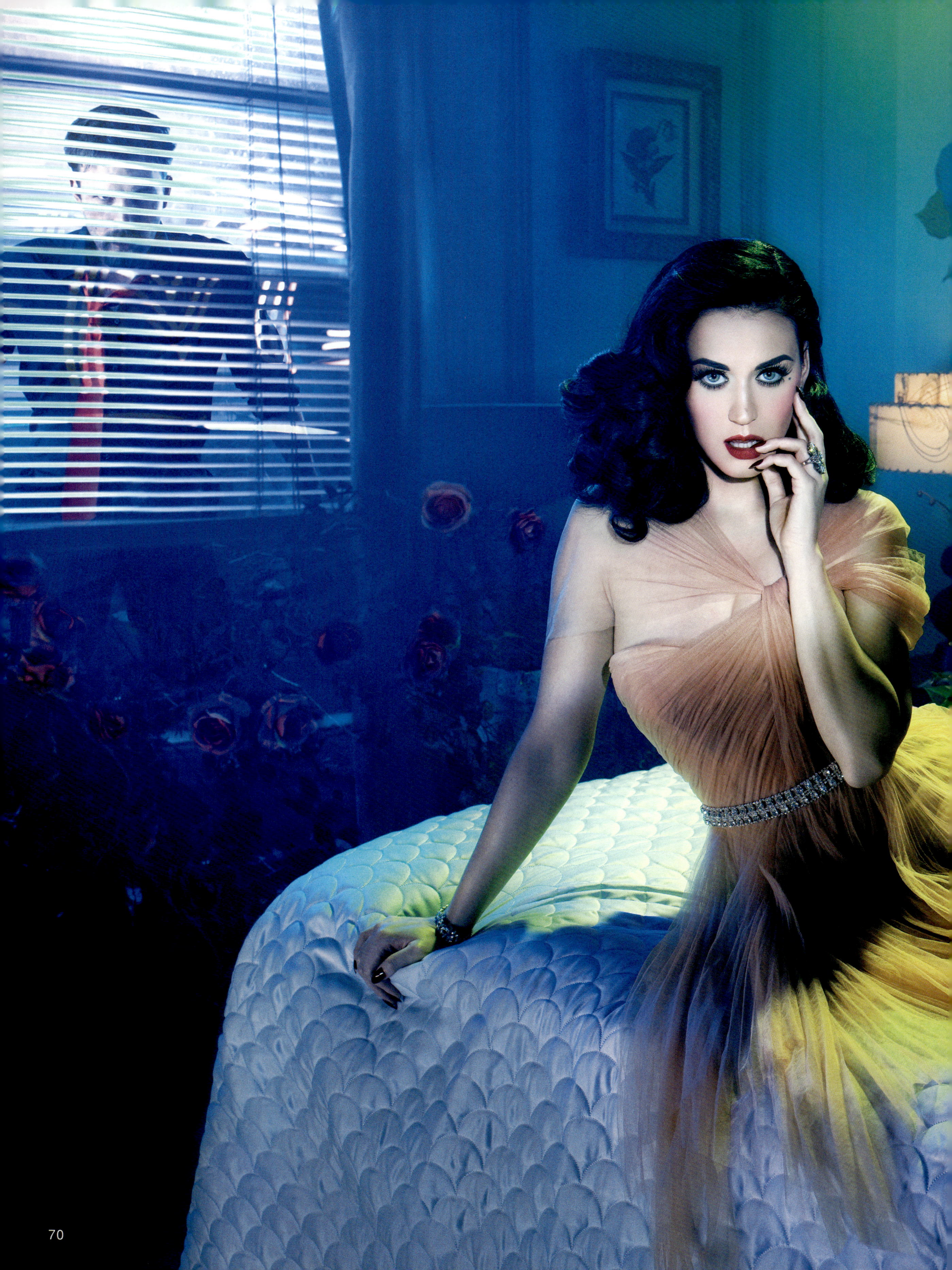

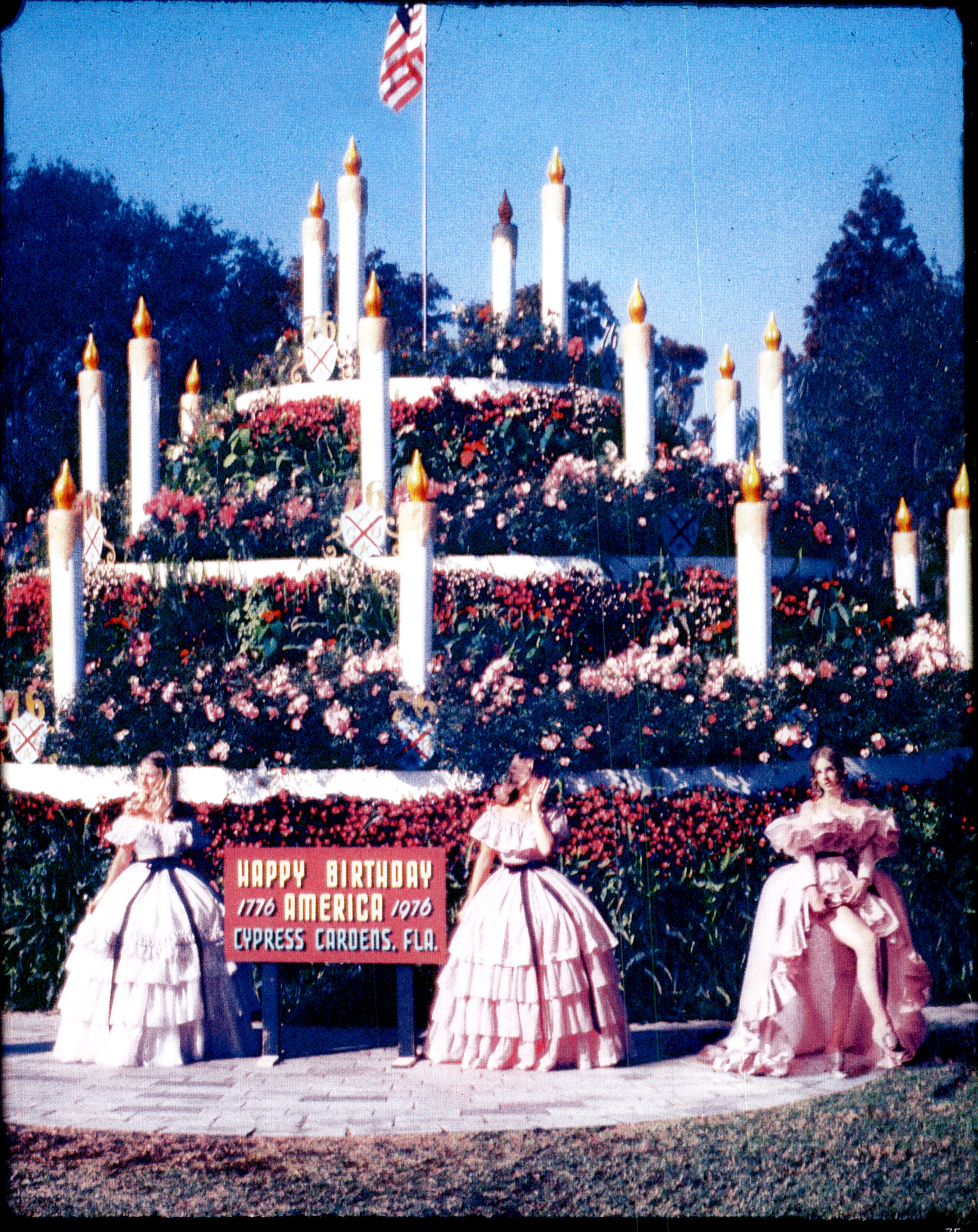
HAPPY BIRTHDAY
1776 AMERICA 1976
CYPRESS GARDENS, FLA.

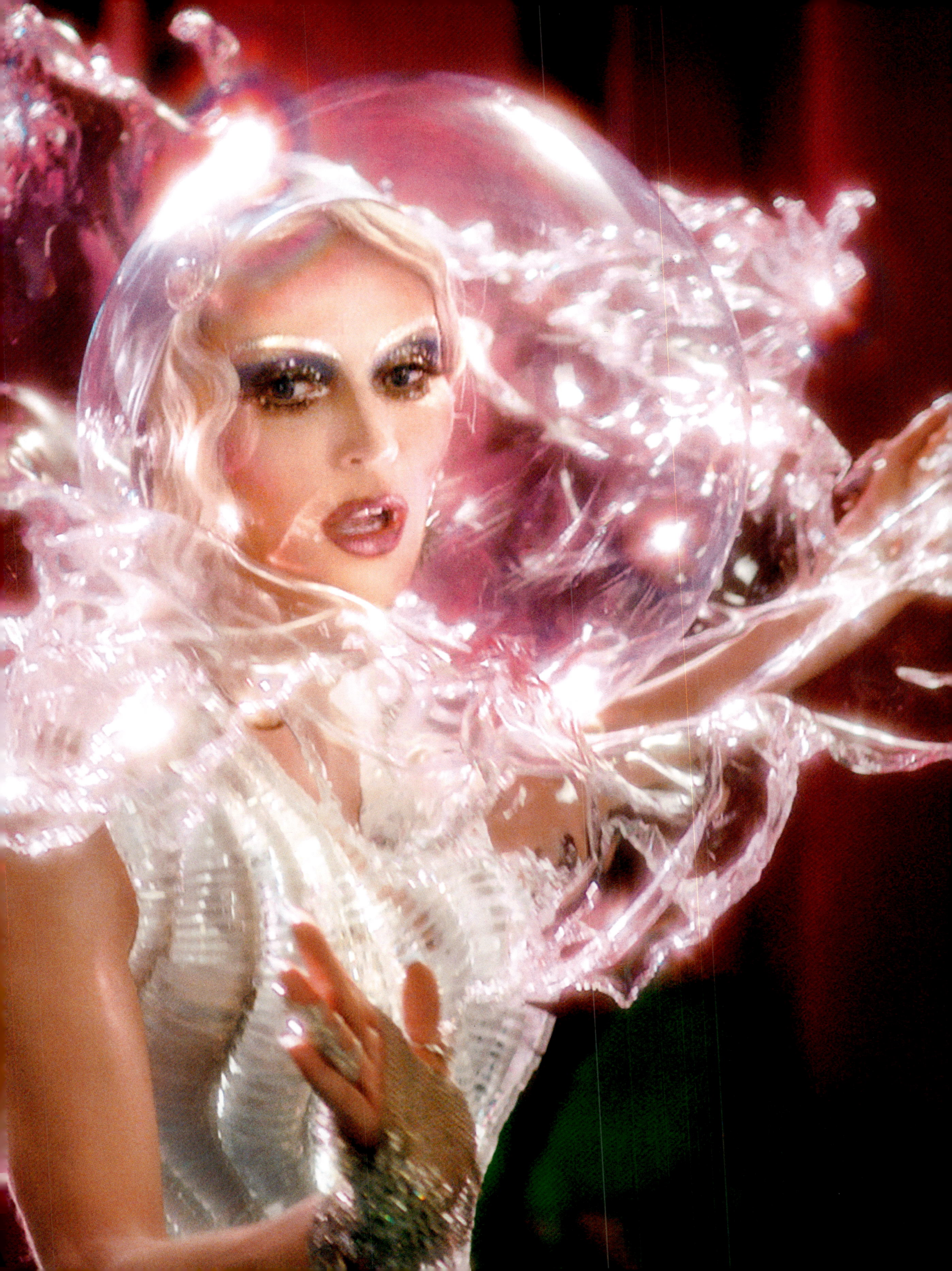

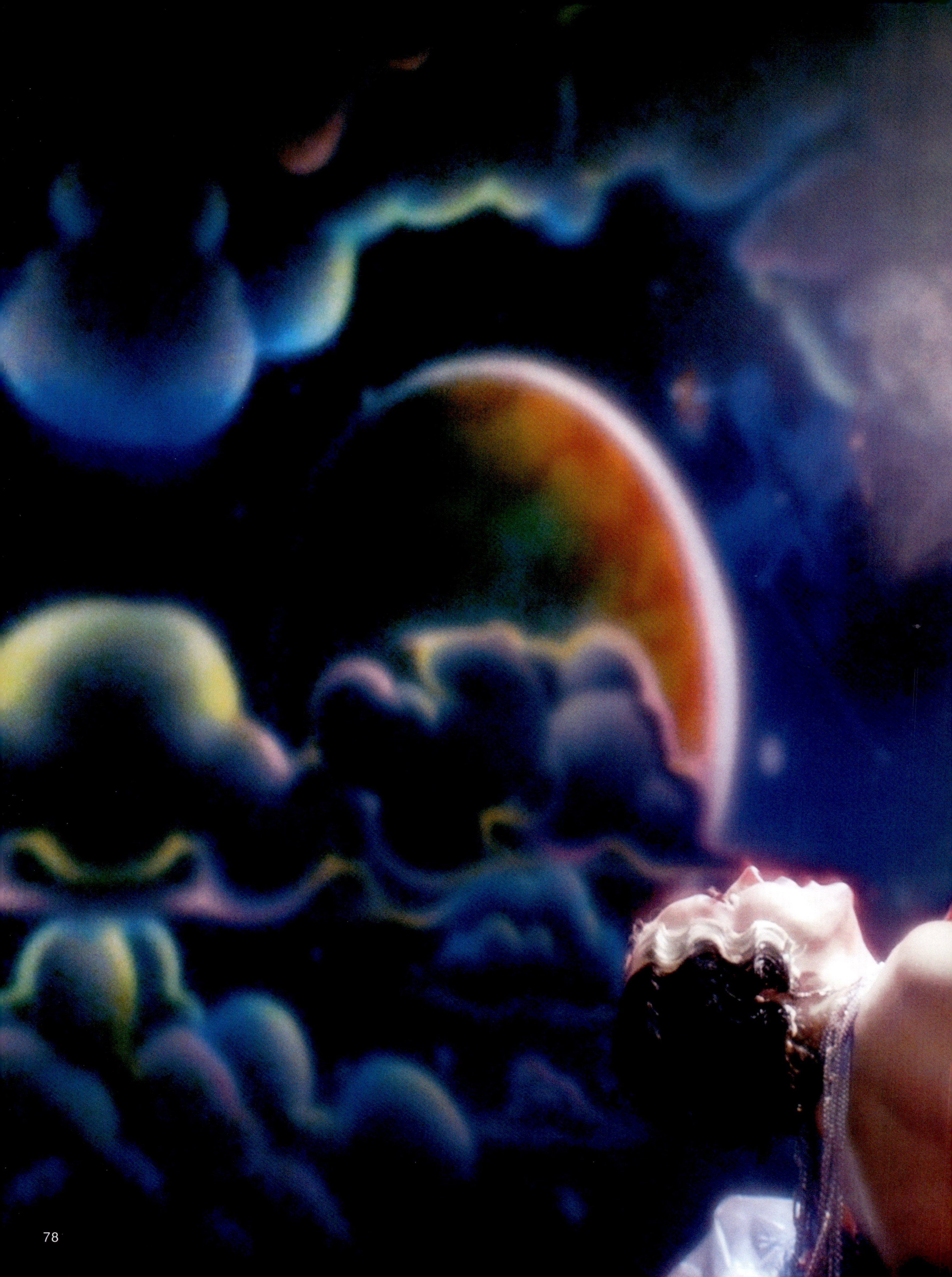

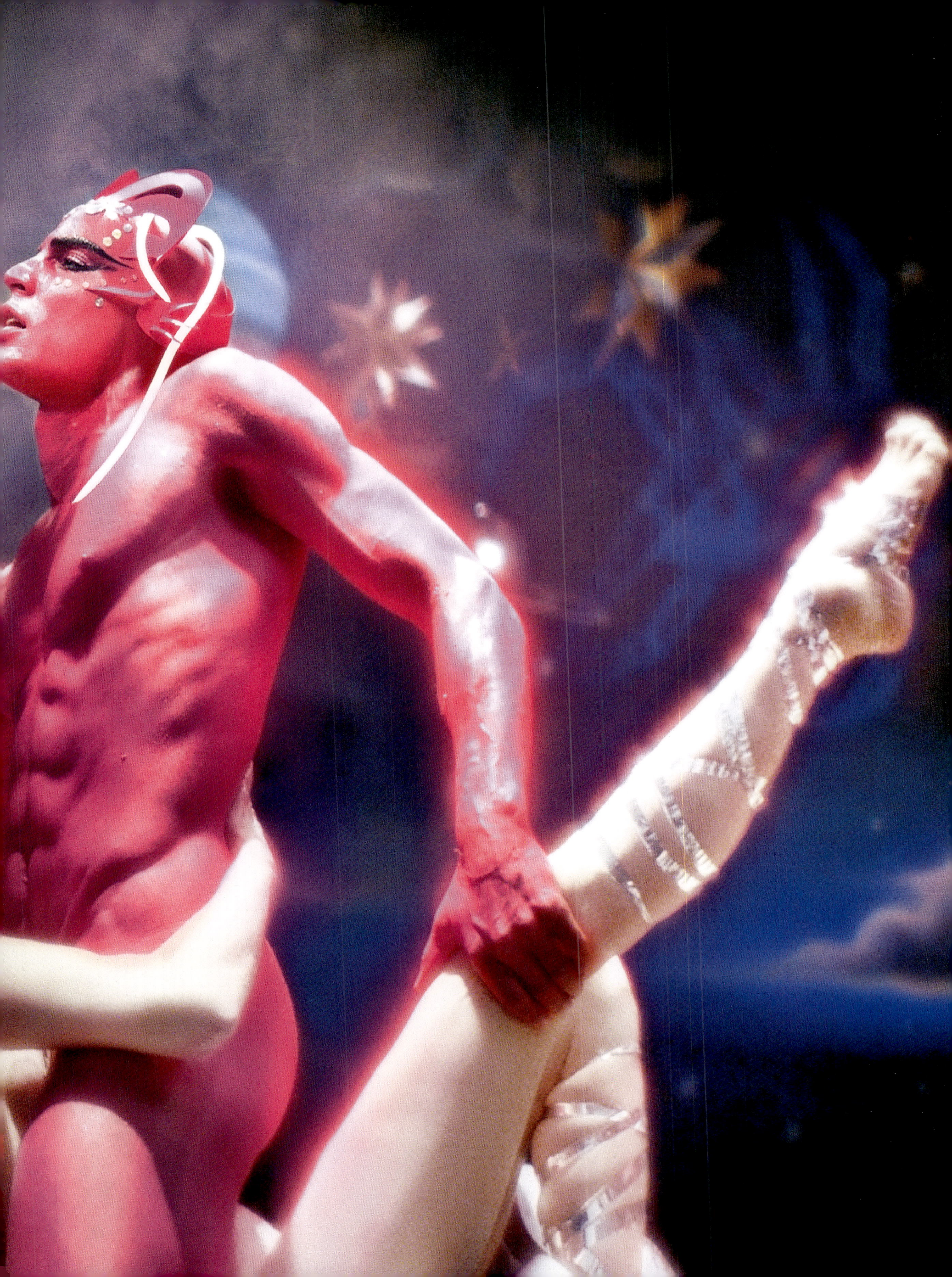

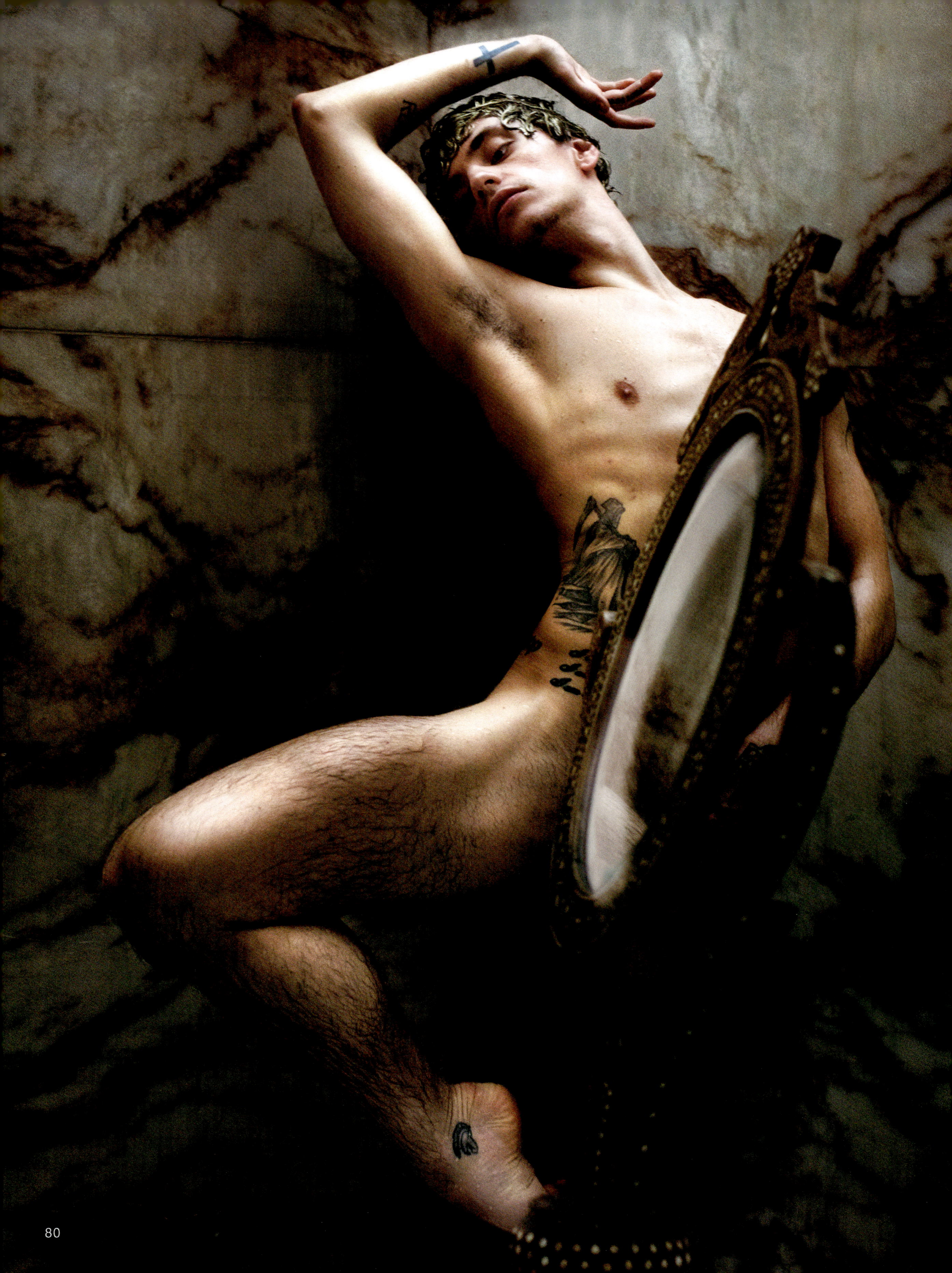

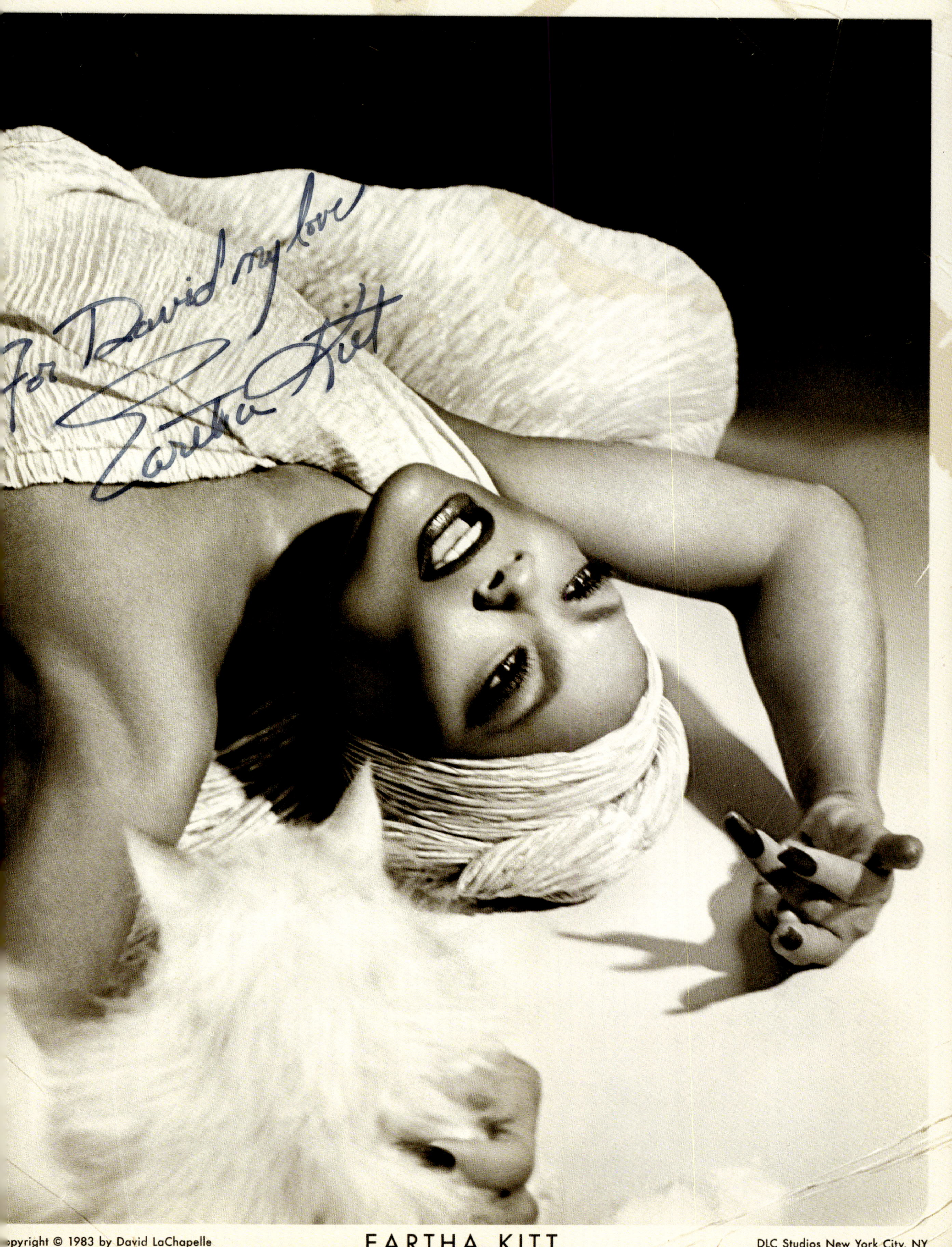

EARTHA KITT

DLC Studios New York City, NY

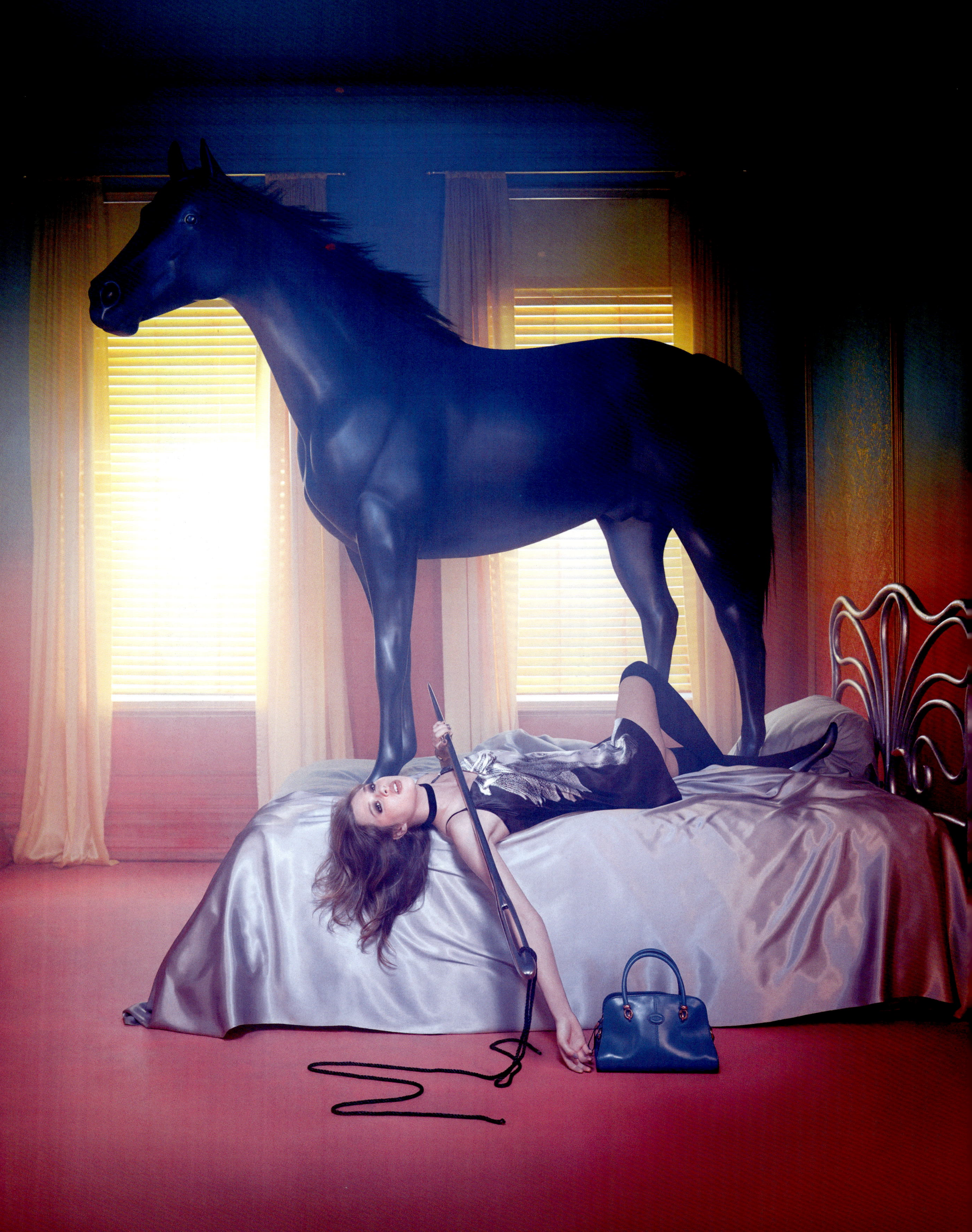

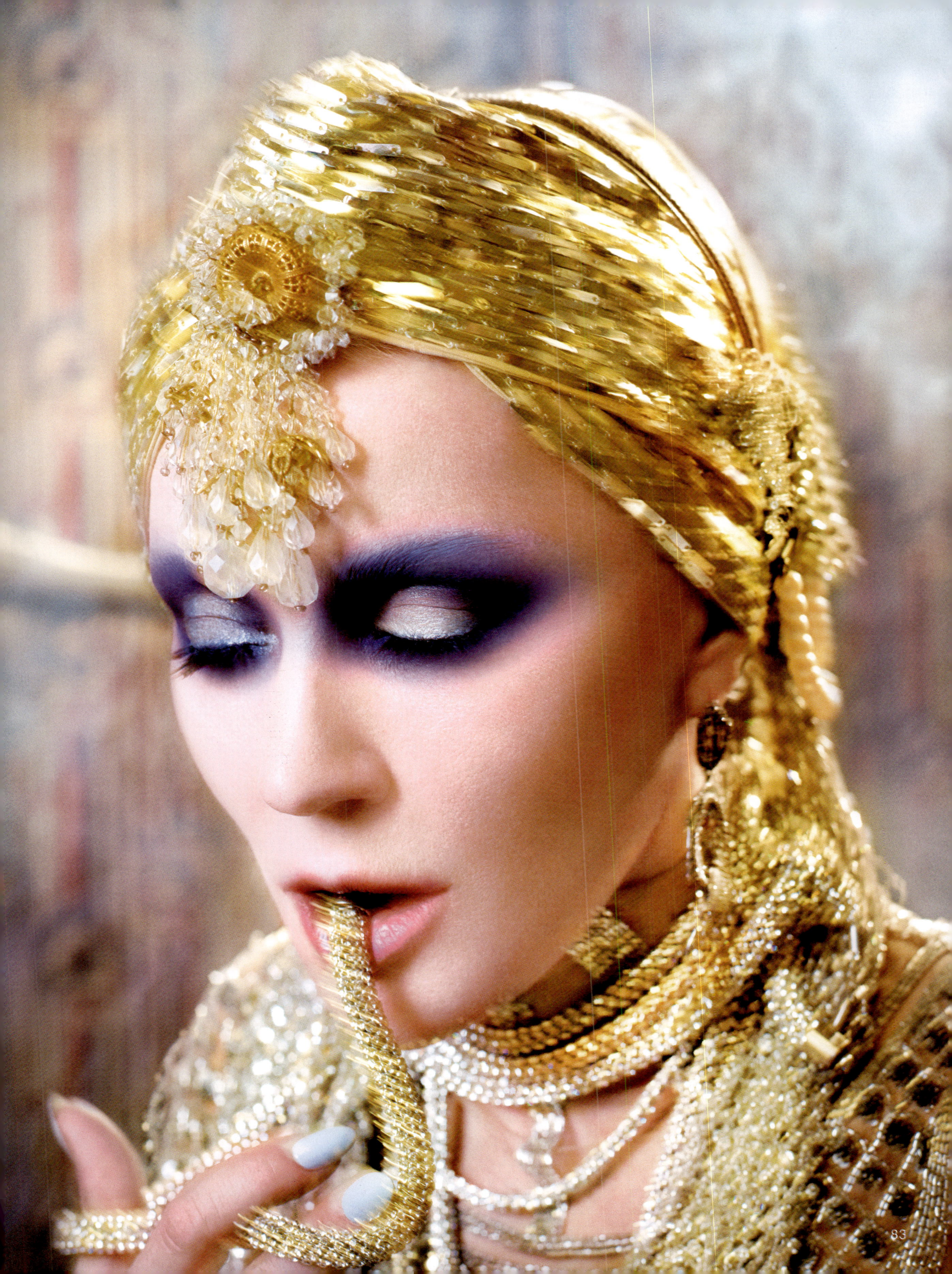

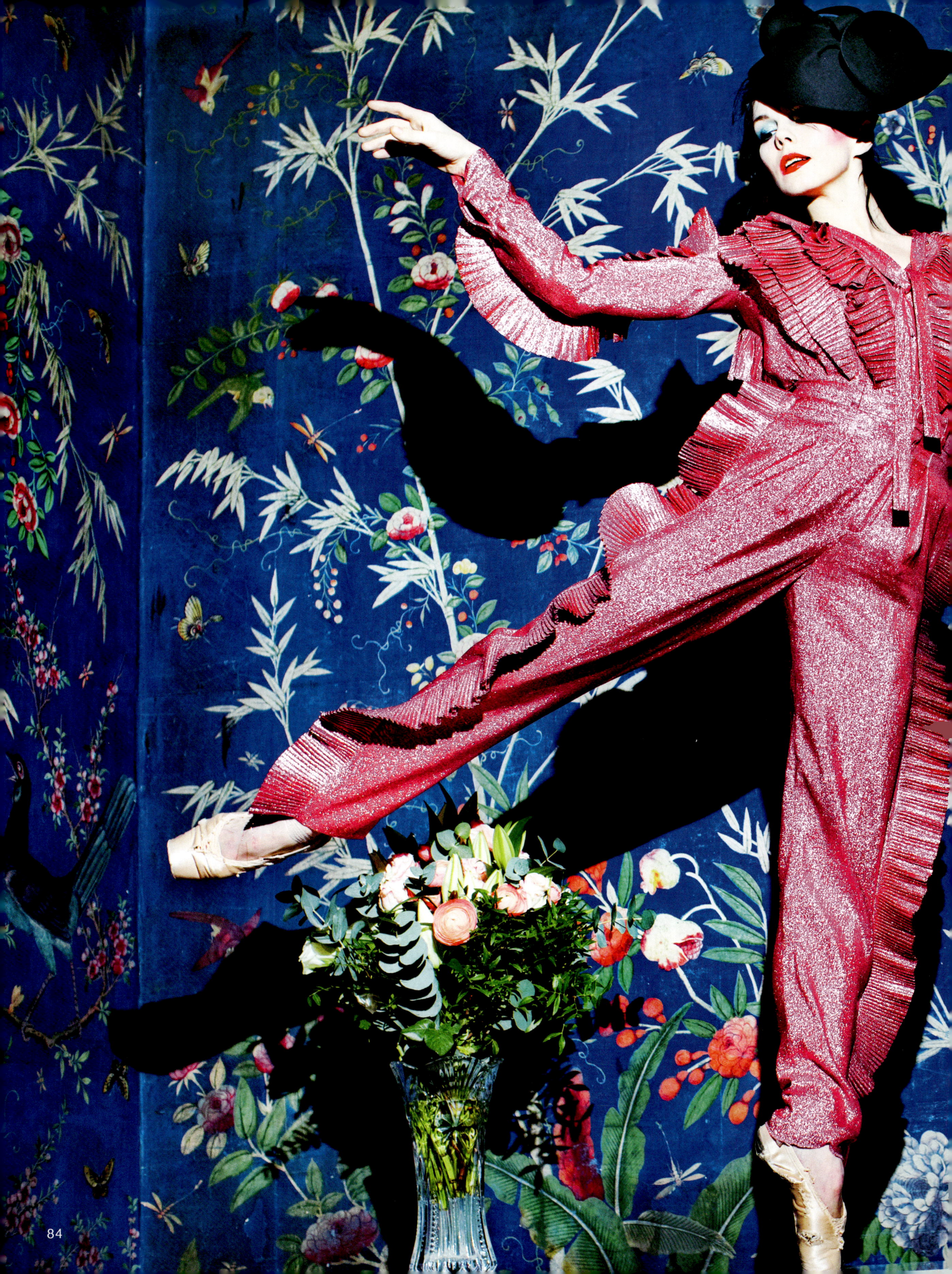

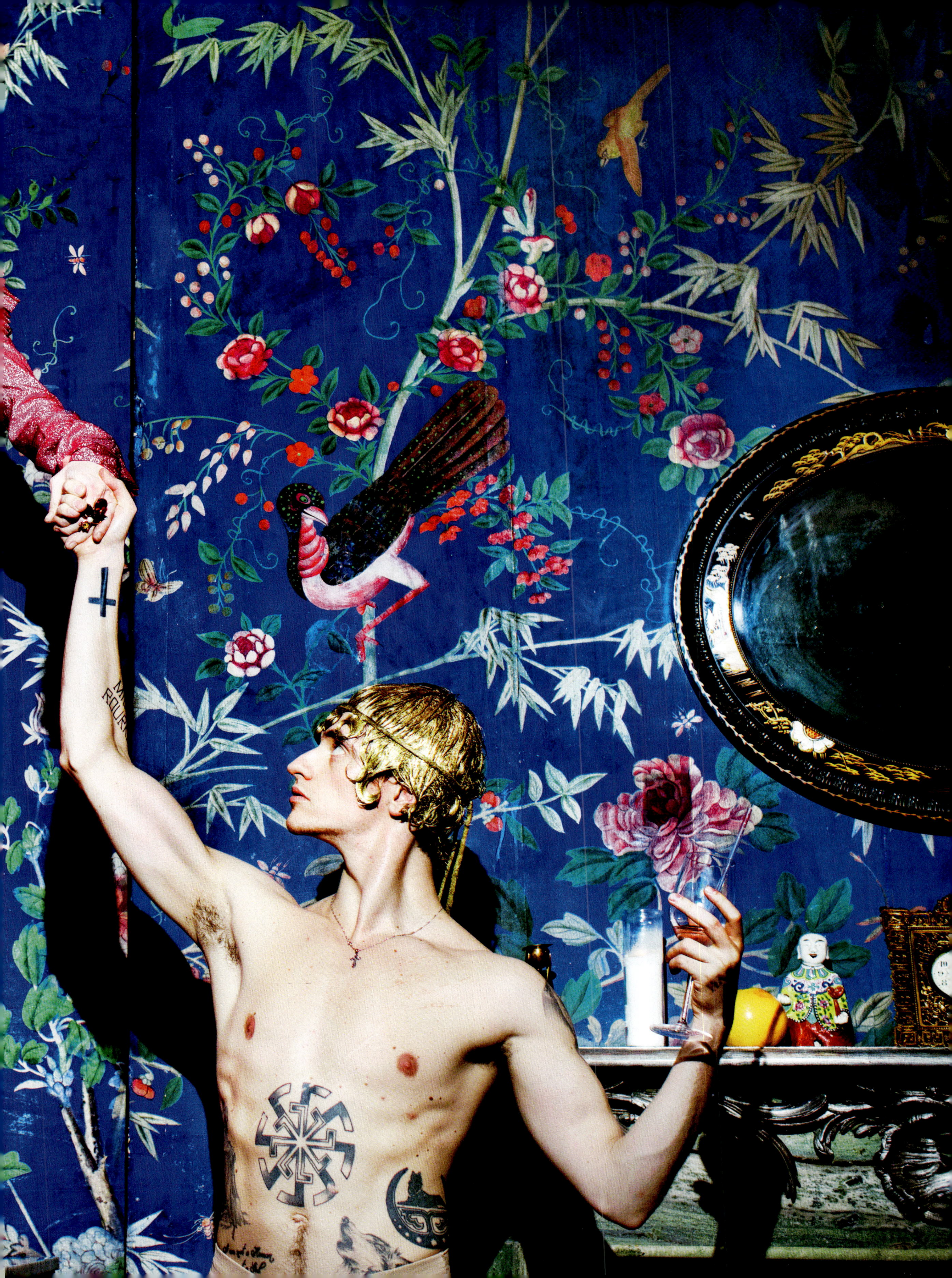

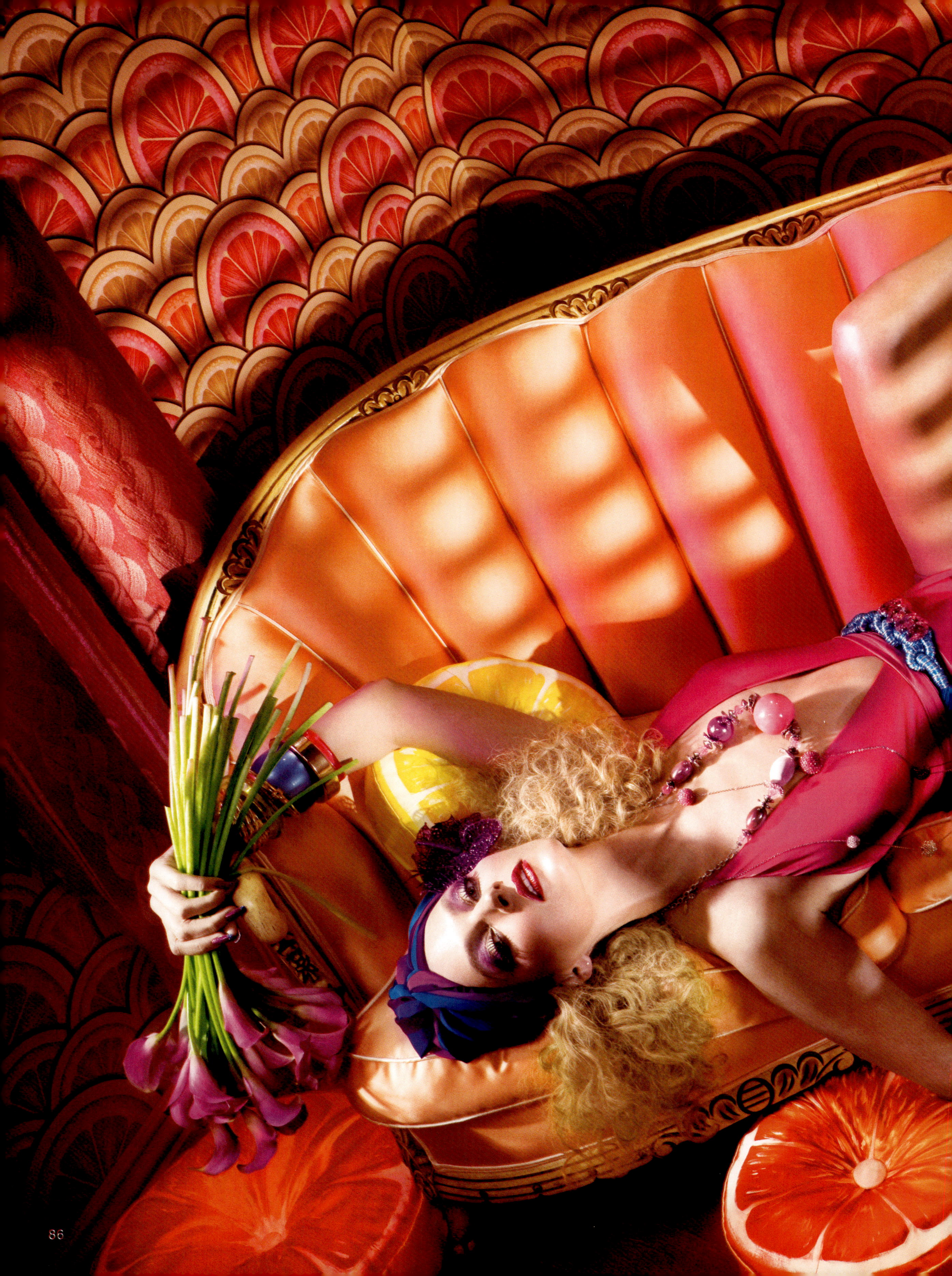

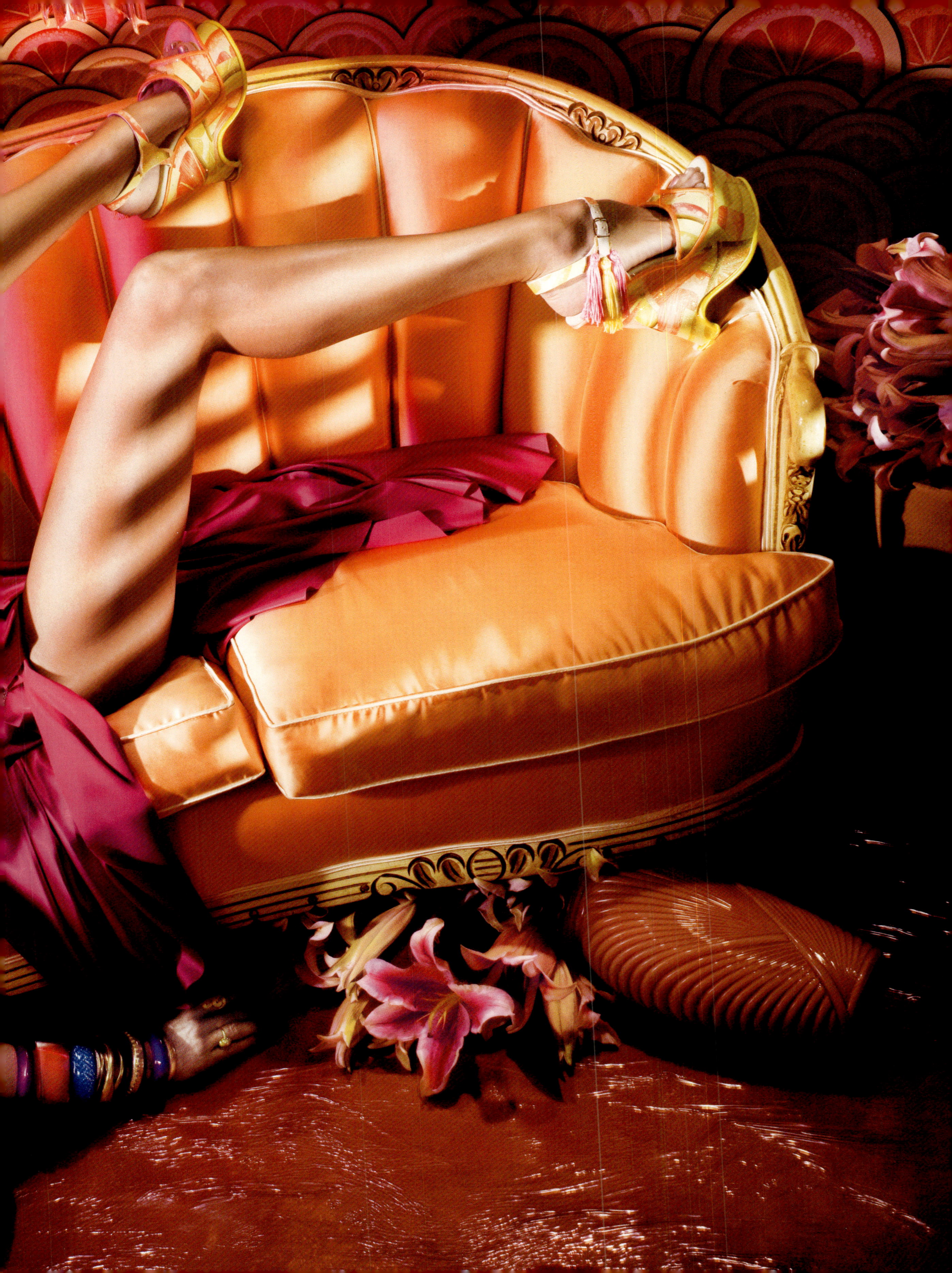

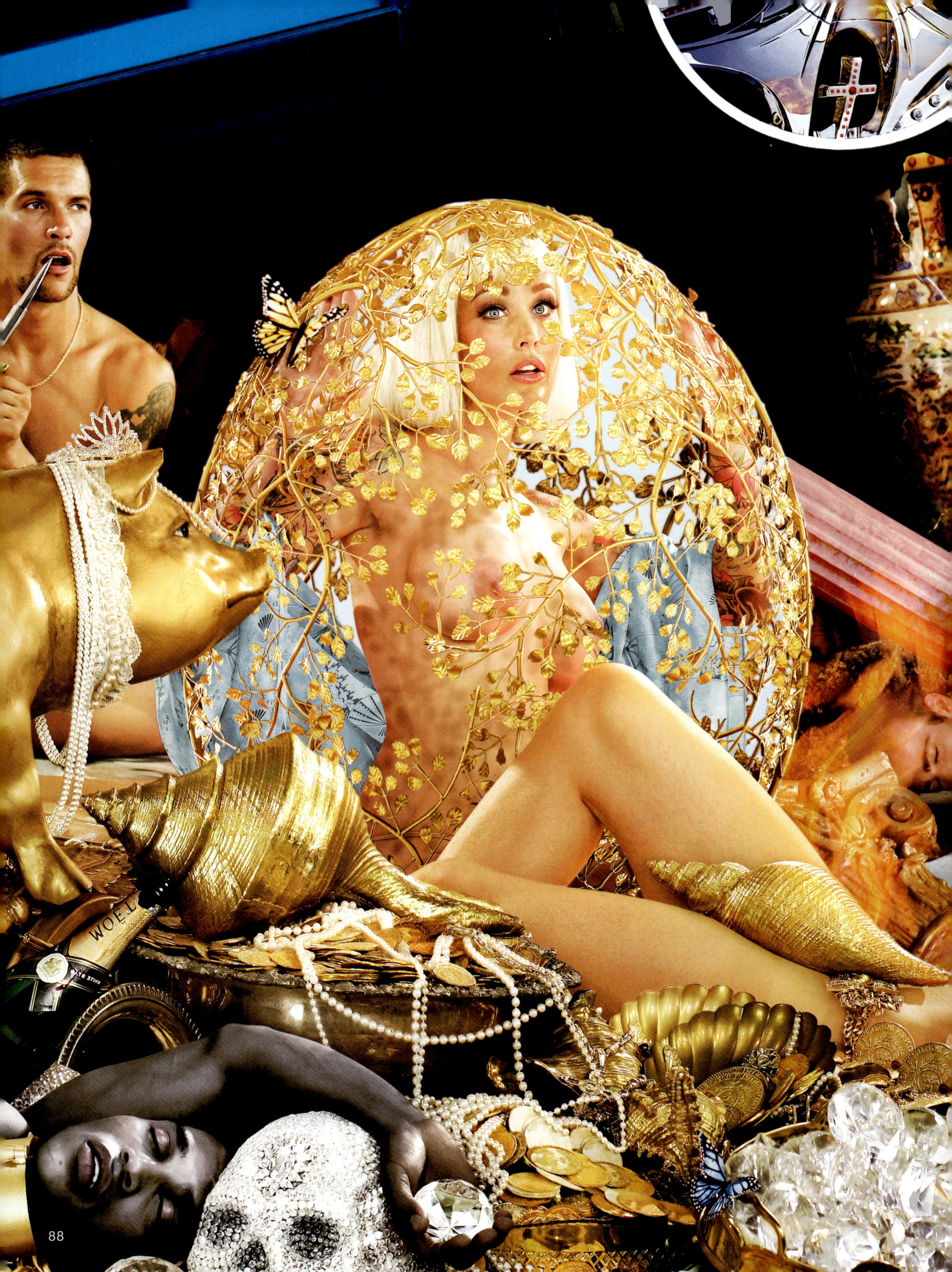

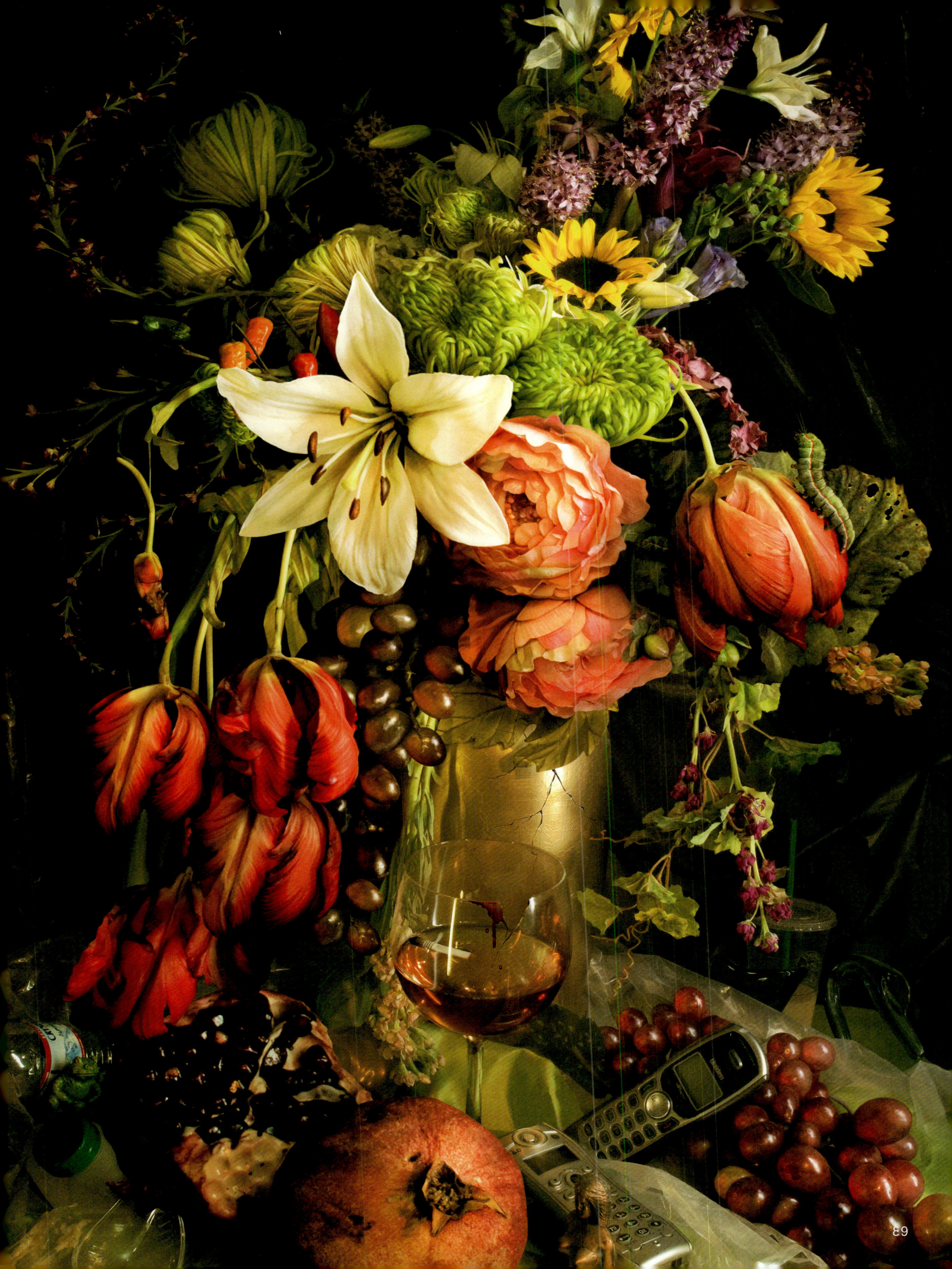

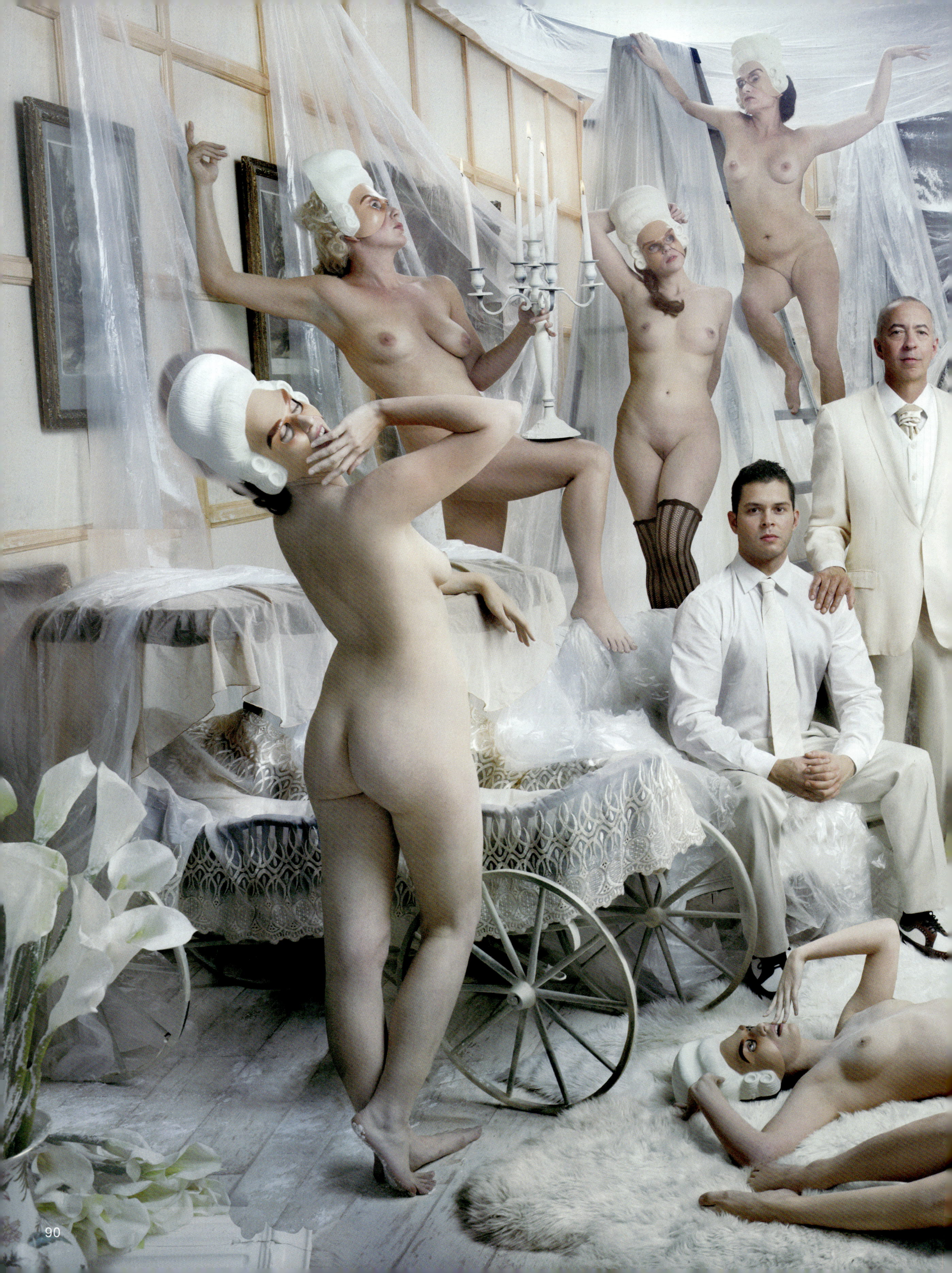

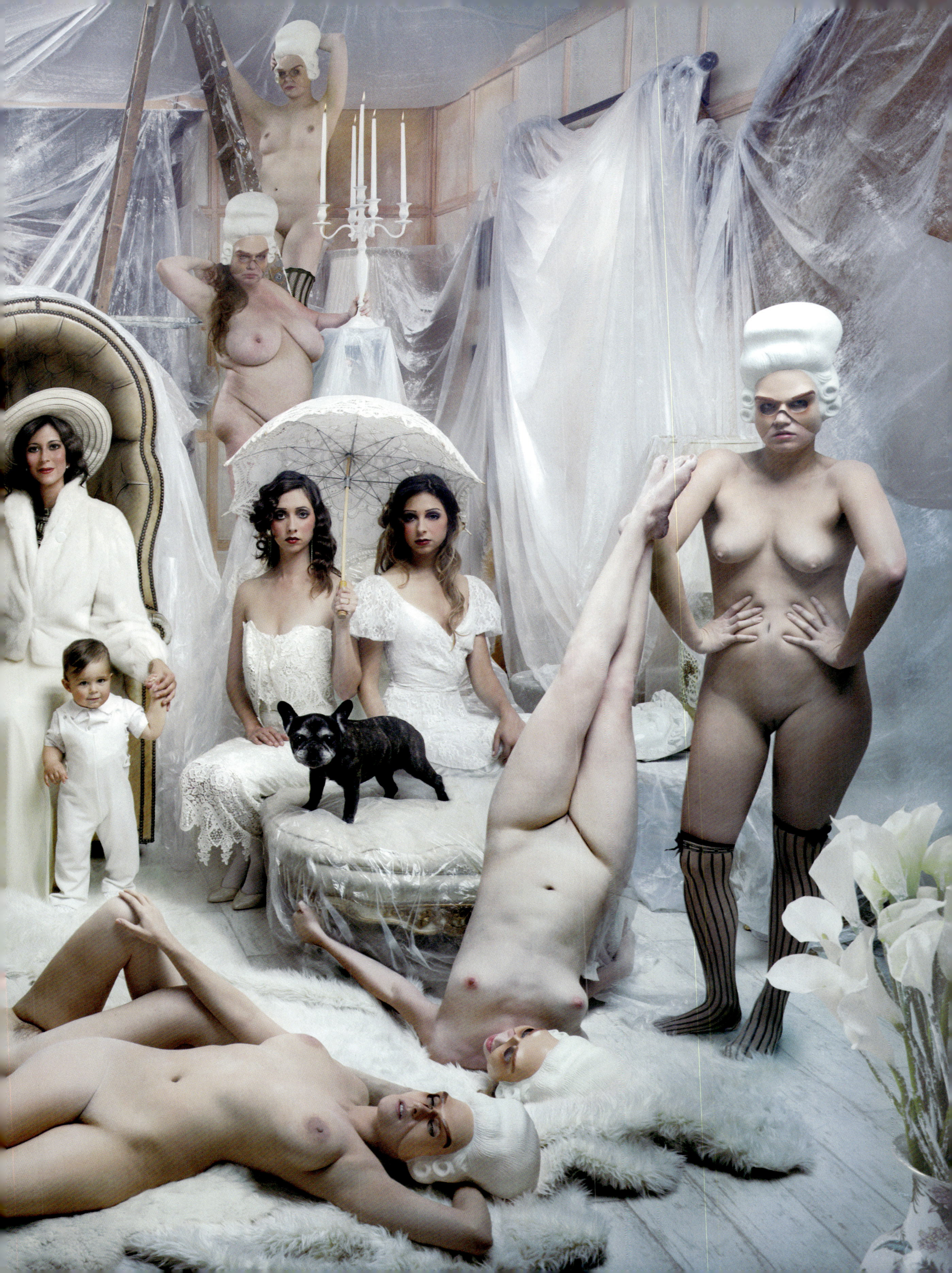

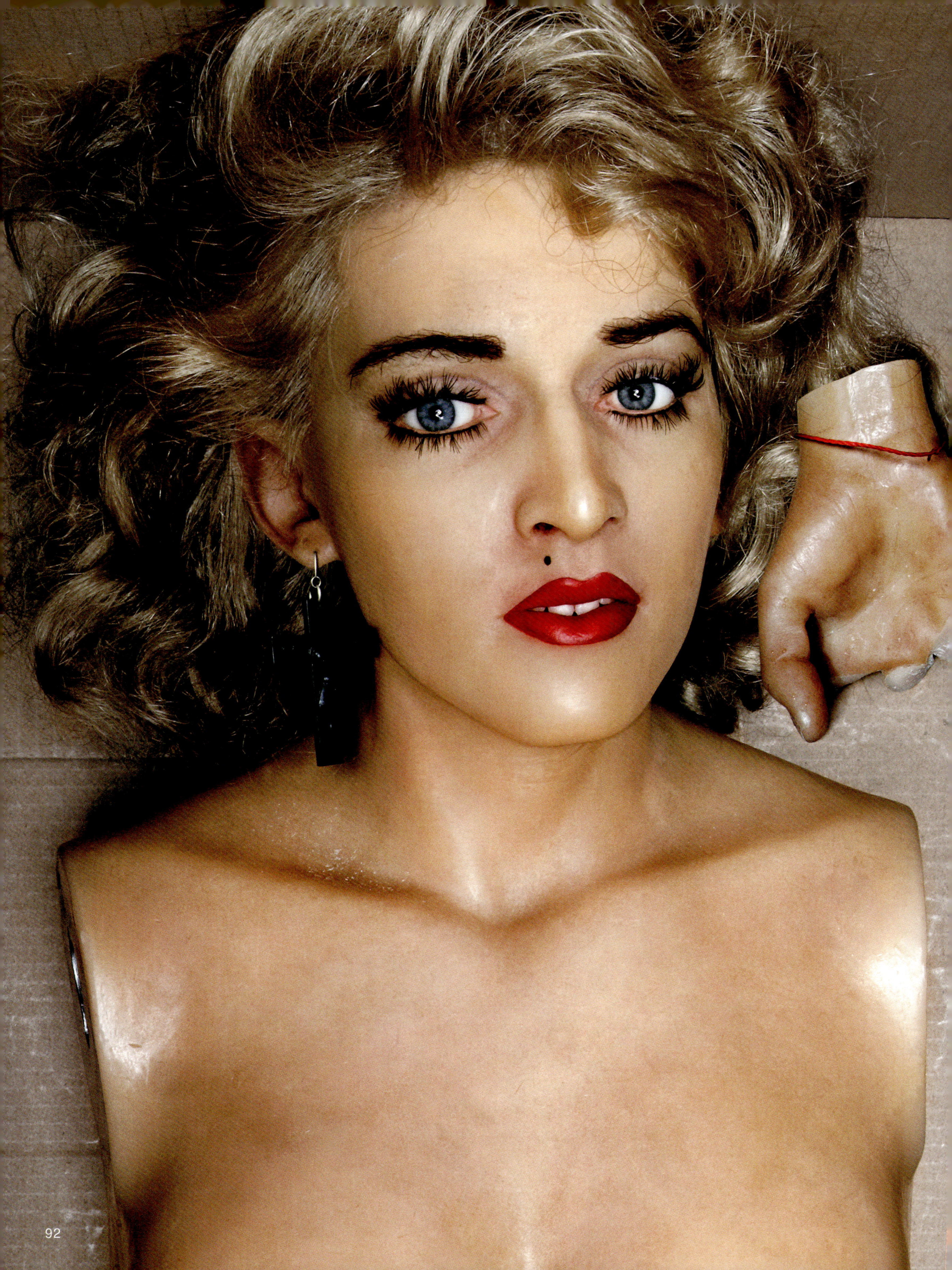

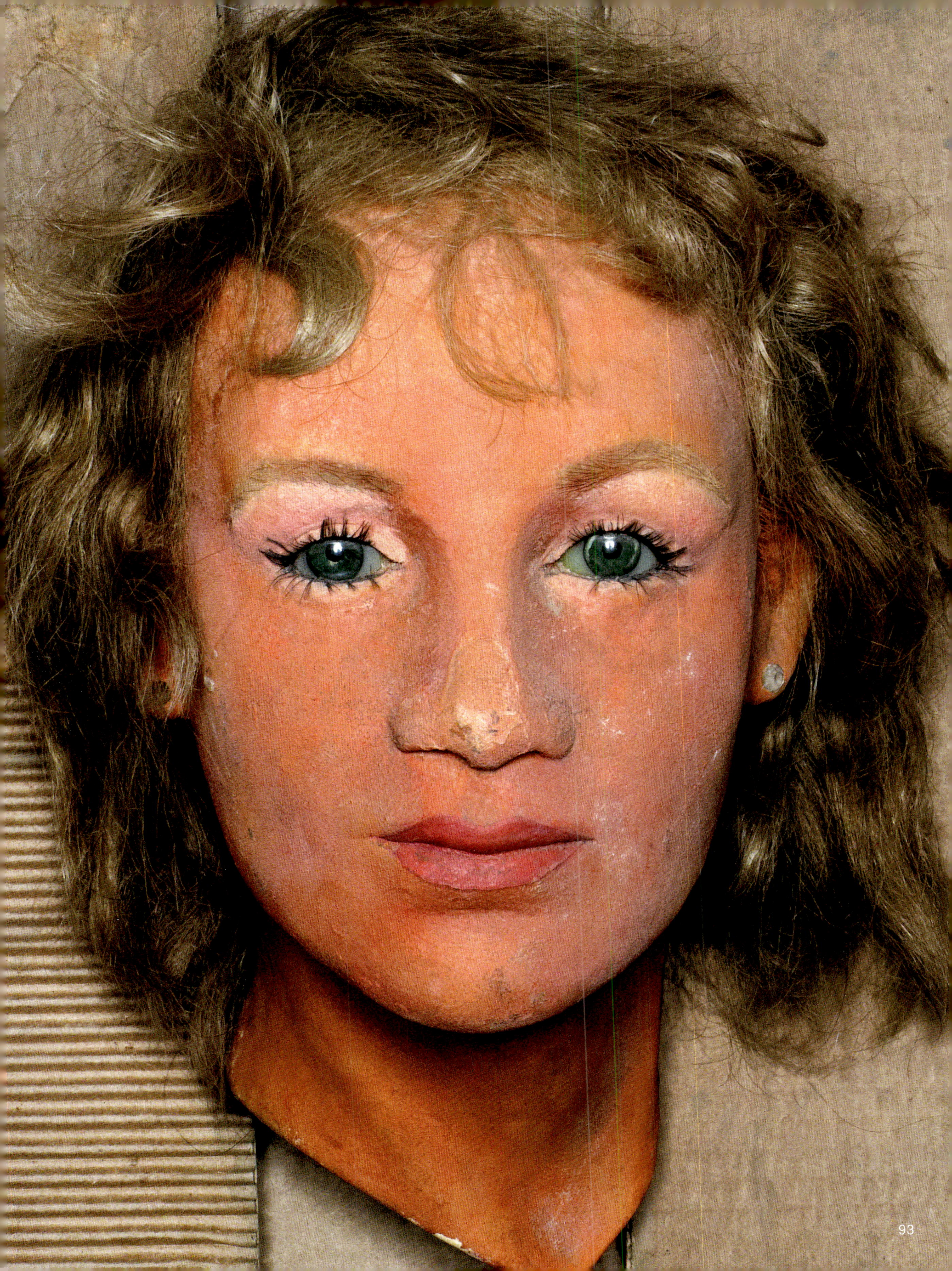

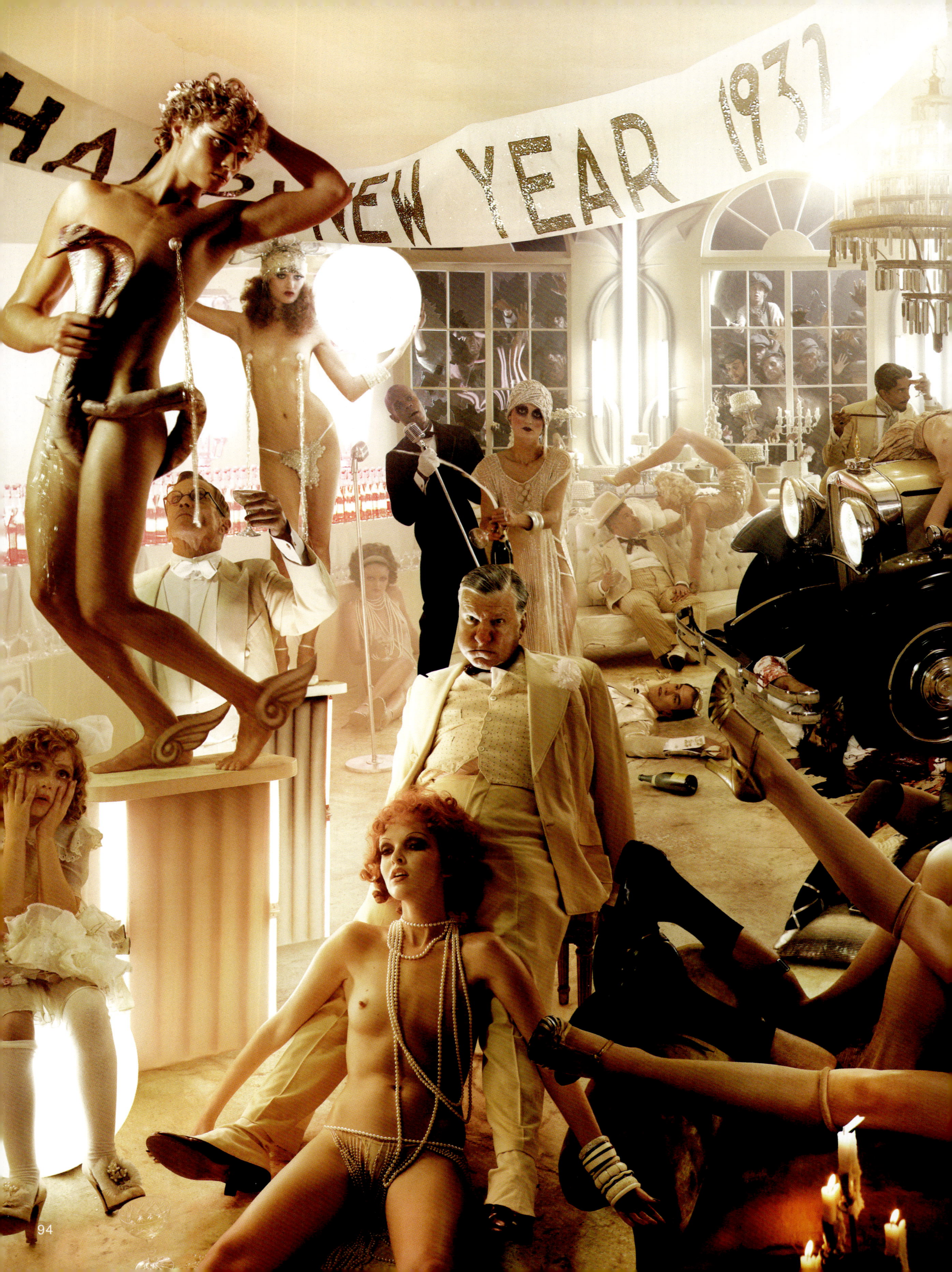
NEW YEAR

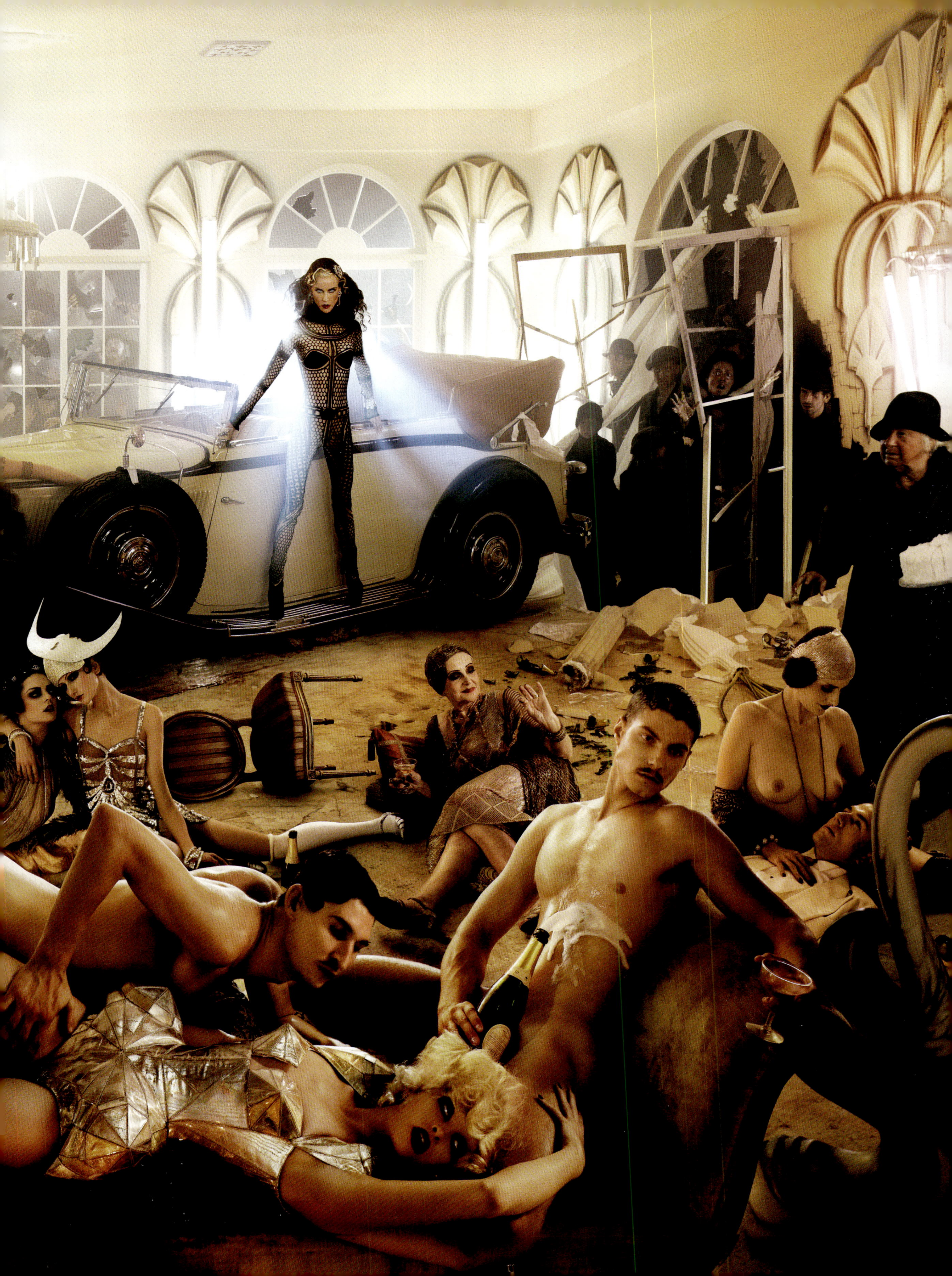

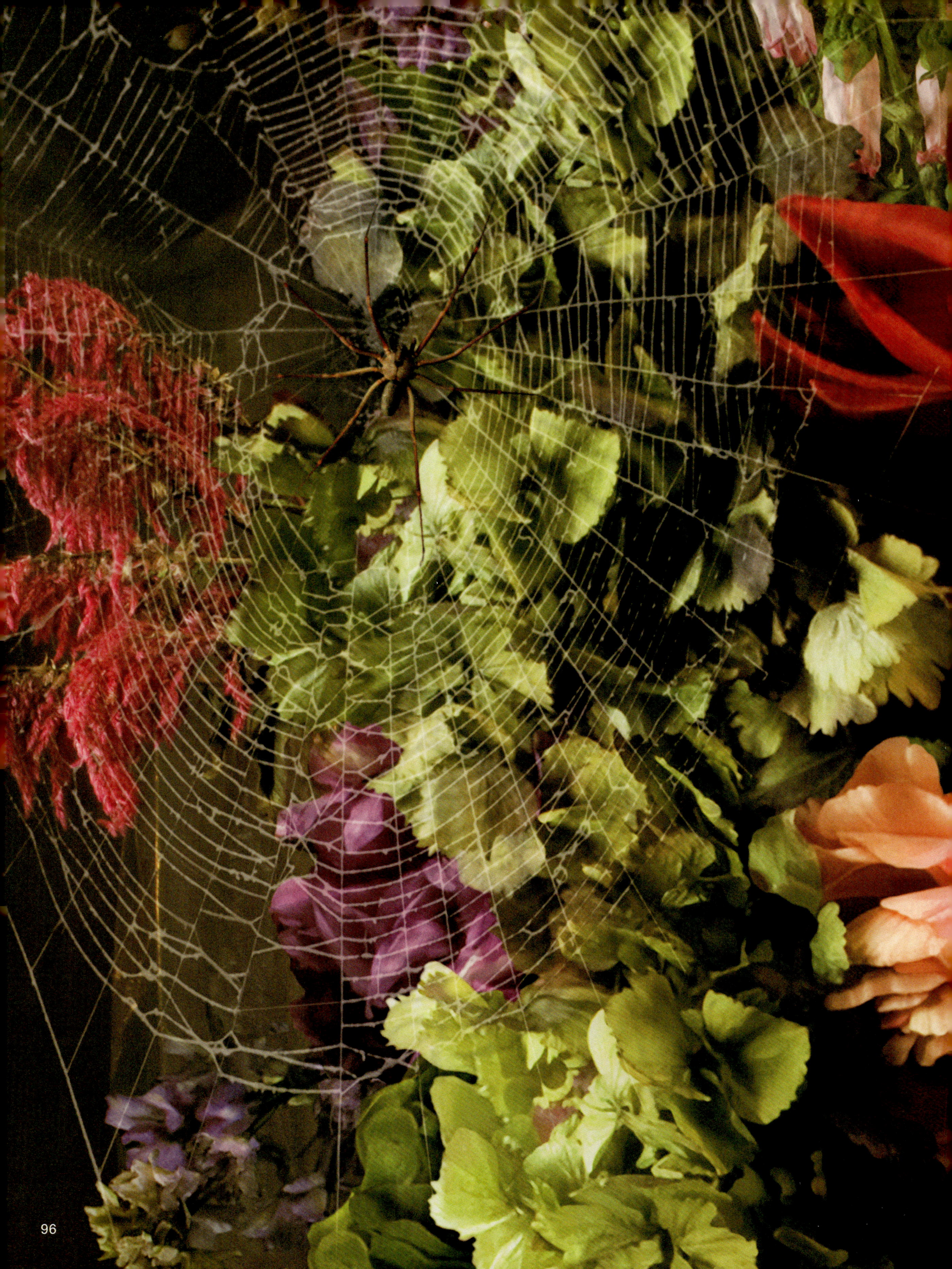

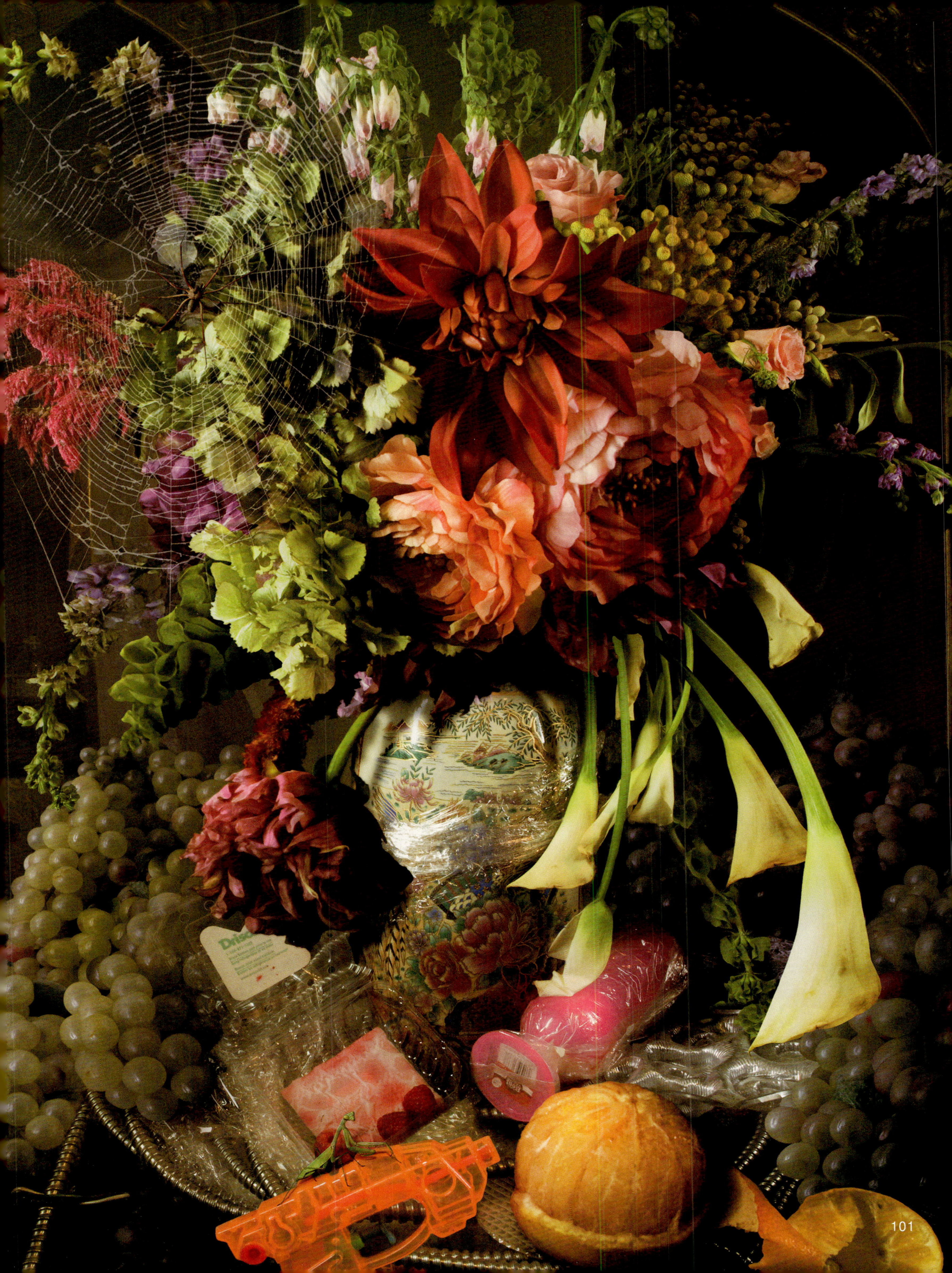

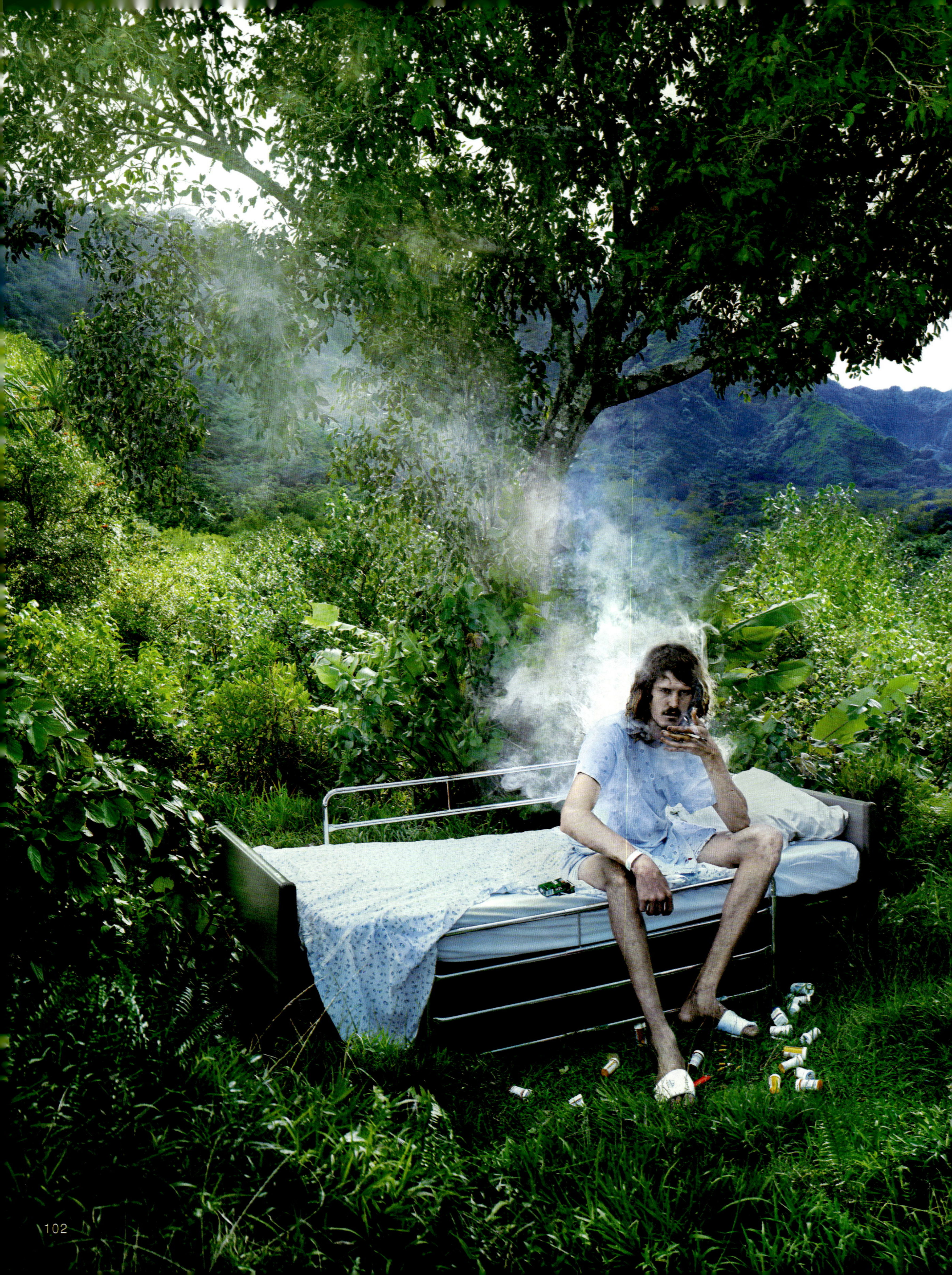

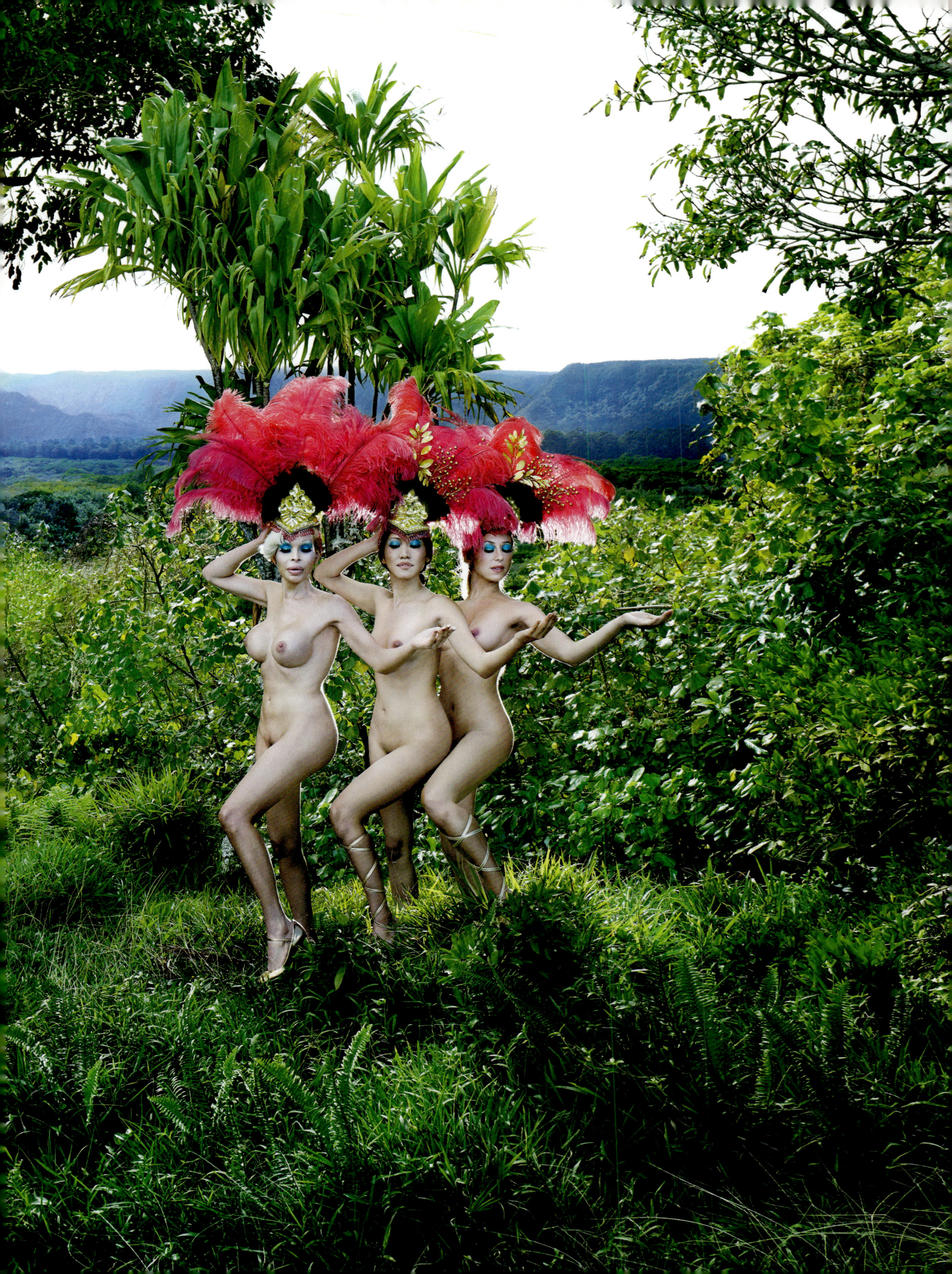

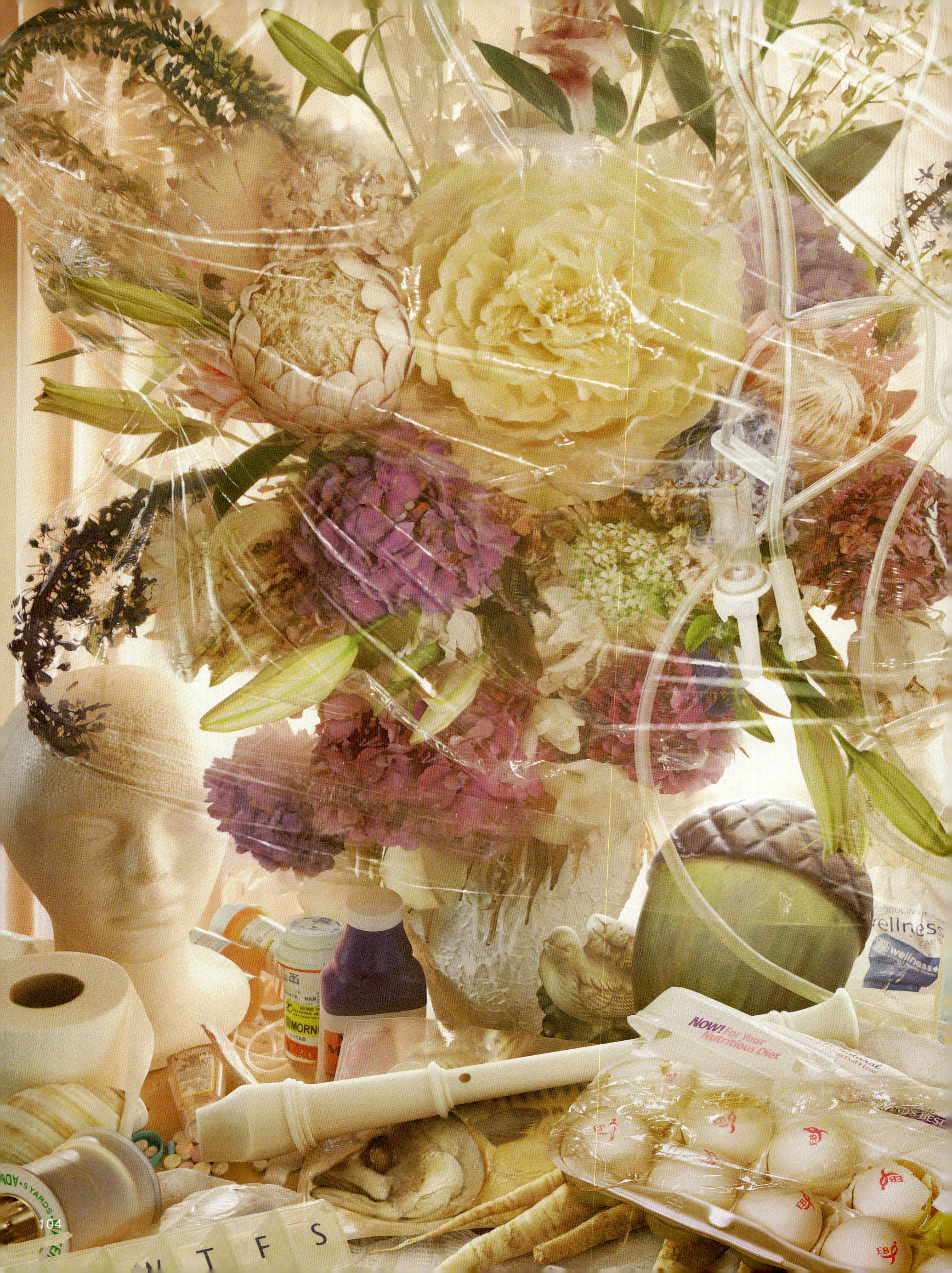
NOW! For Your Nutritious Diet
wellness

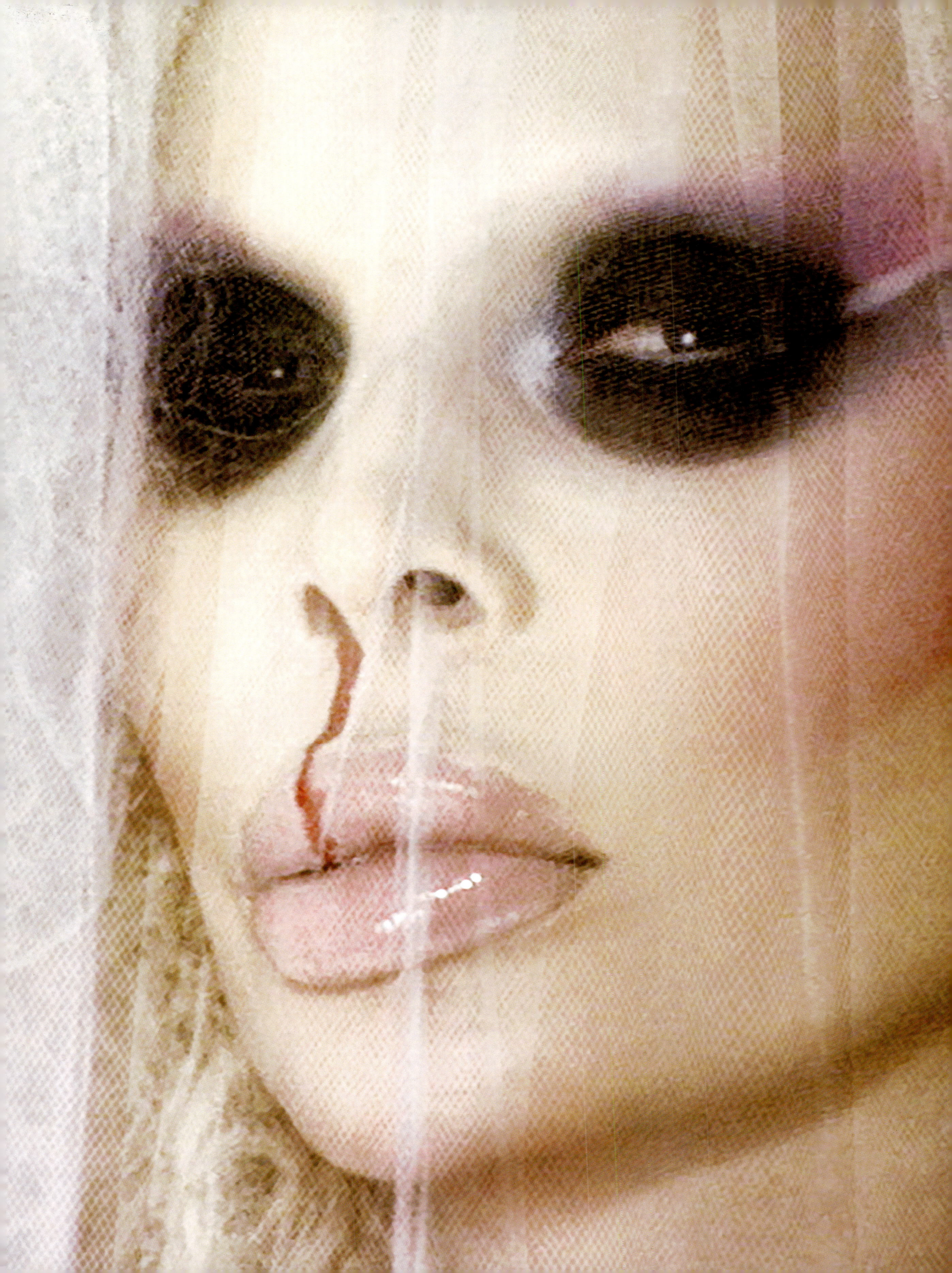

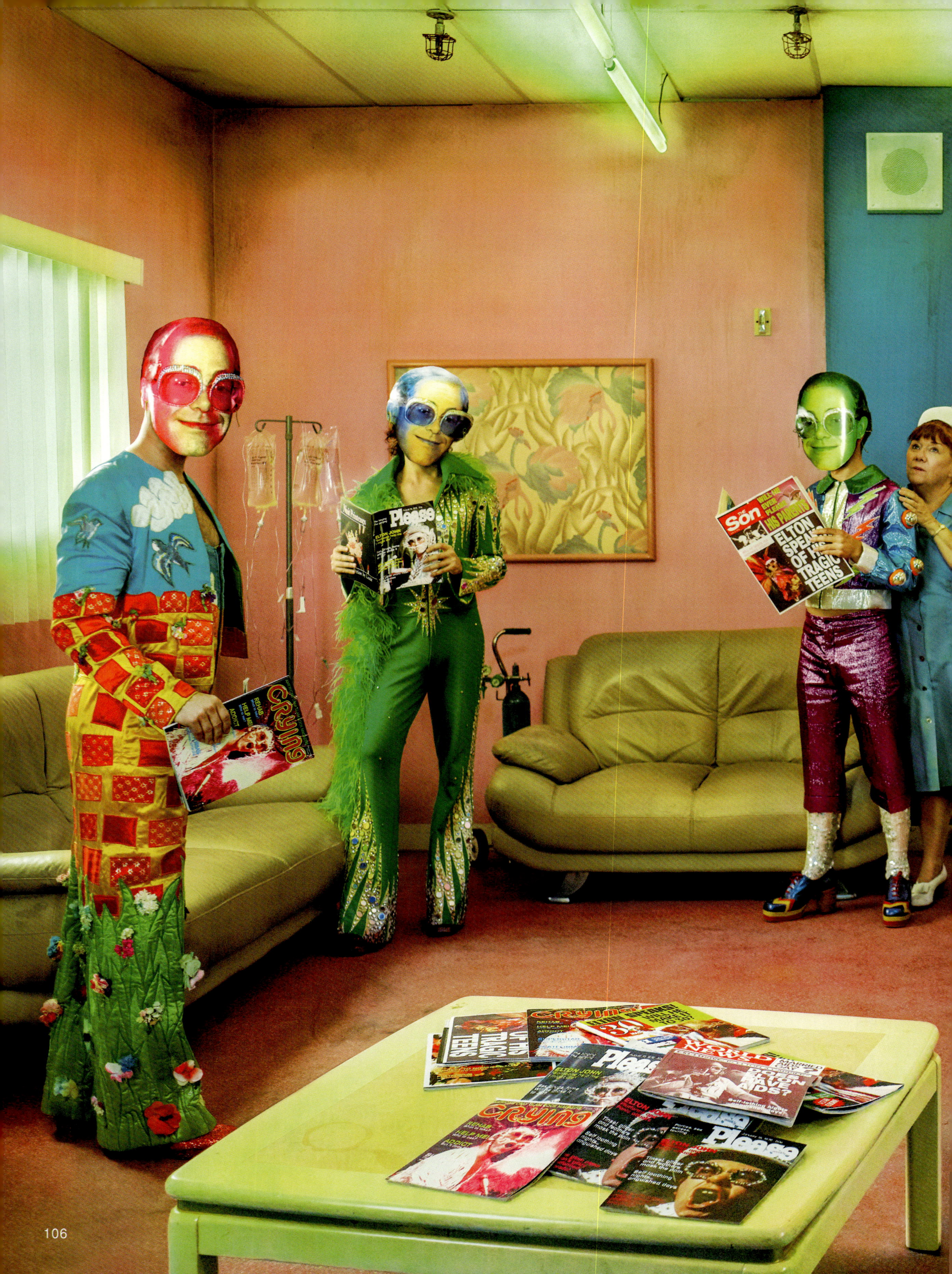
The Son
HIS PARENTS
ELTON
TRAGIC
TEENS
Please
ELTON JOHN
CRYING
REHAB
HELP ME!
ADDICT
TRAGIC
TEENS
ELTON SPEAKS!
WILL HE MAKE IT TO 30?
30
WORLD NEWS
MARRIED
DOES ELTON HAVE AIDS?
Tinsel, glitter and feathers mask the pain
Self loathing nights, anguished days

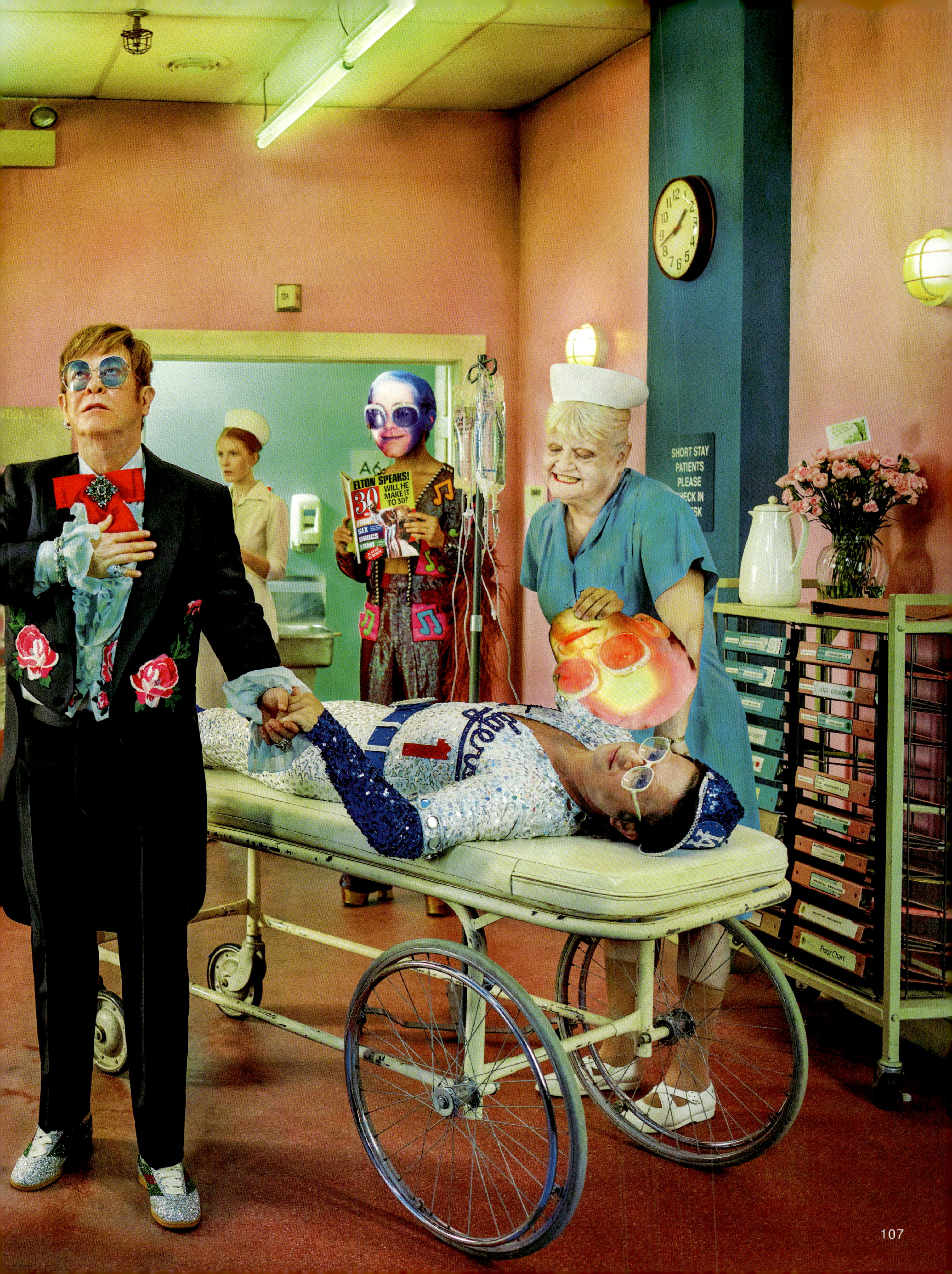
ELTON SPEAKS!
30
WILL HE MAKE IT TO 30?
SEX
DRUGS
FAME
SHORT STAY
PATIENTS
PLEASE
Floor Chart

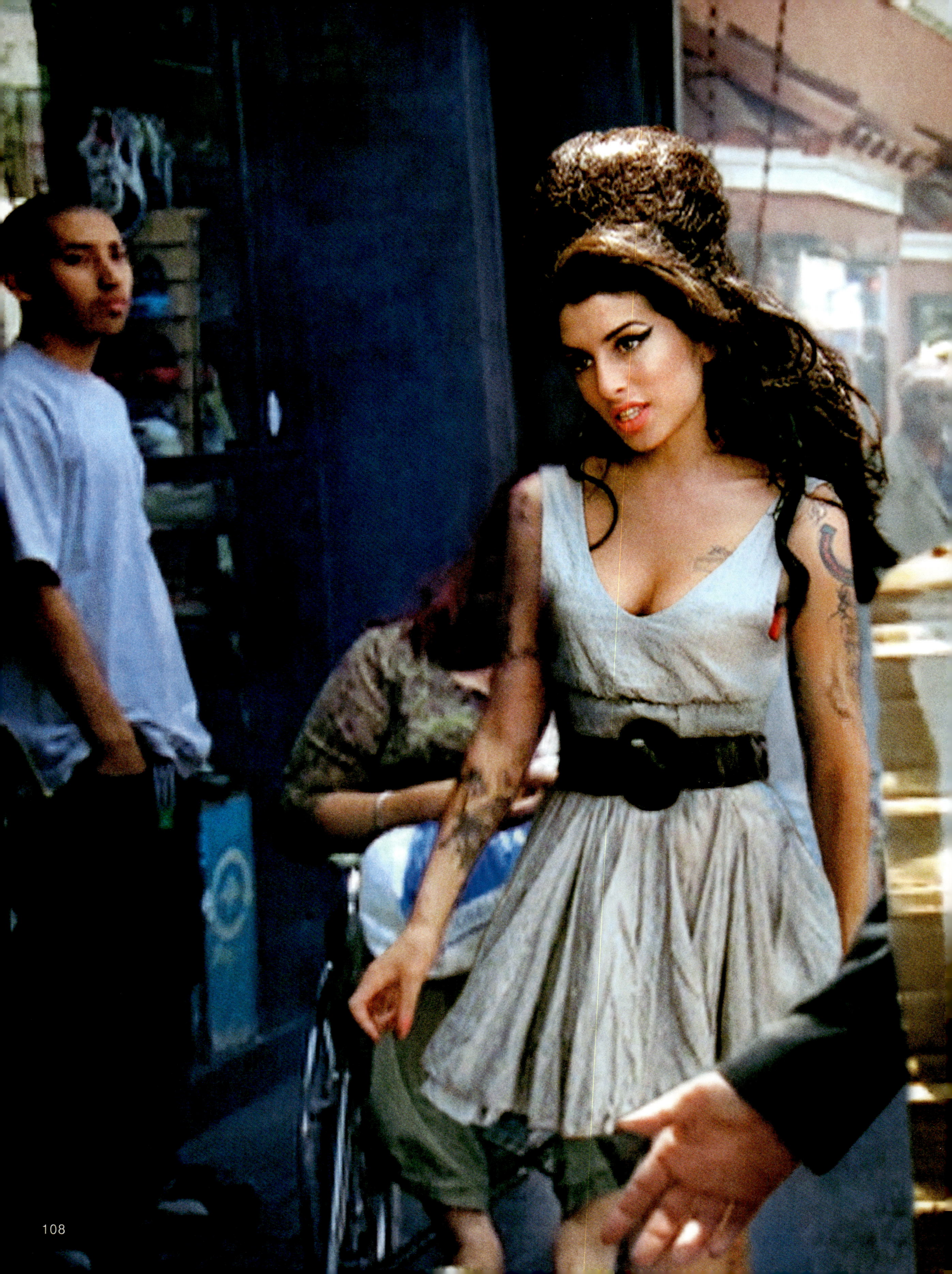

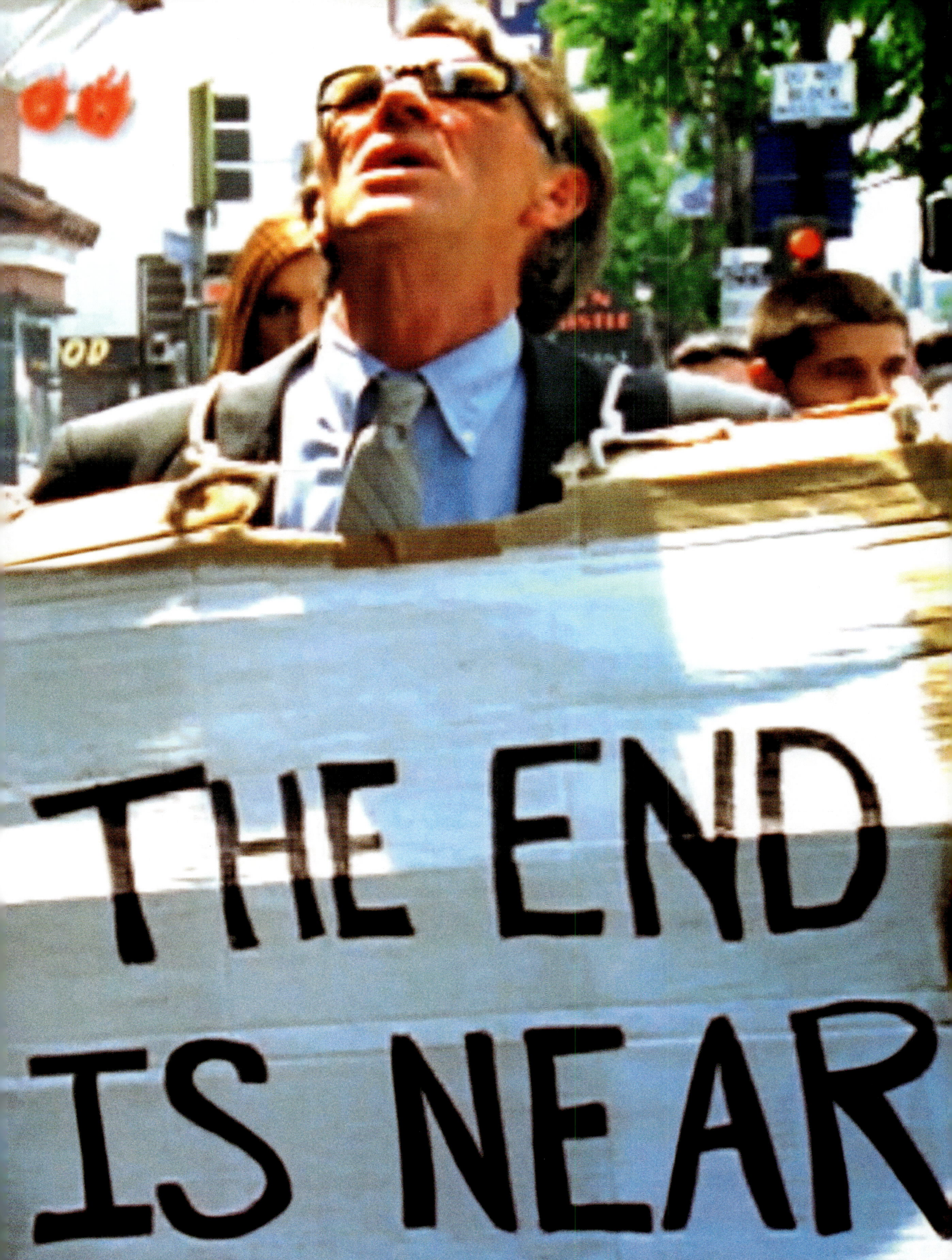
THE END
IS NEAR

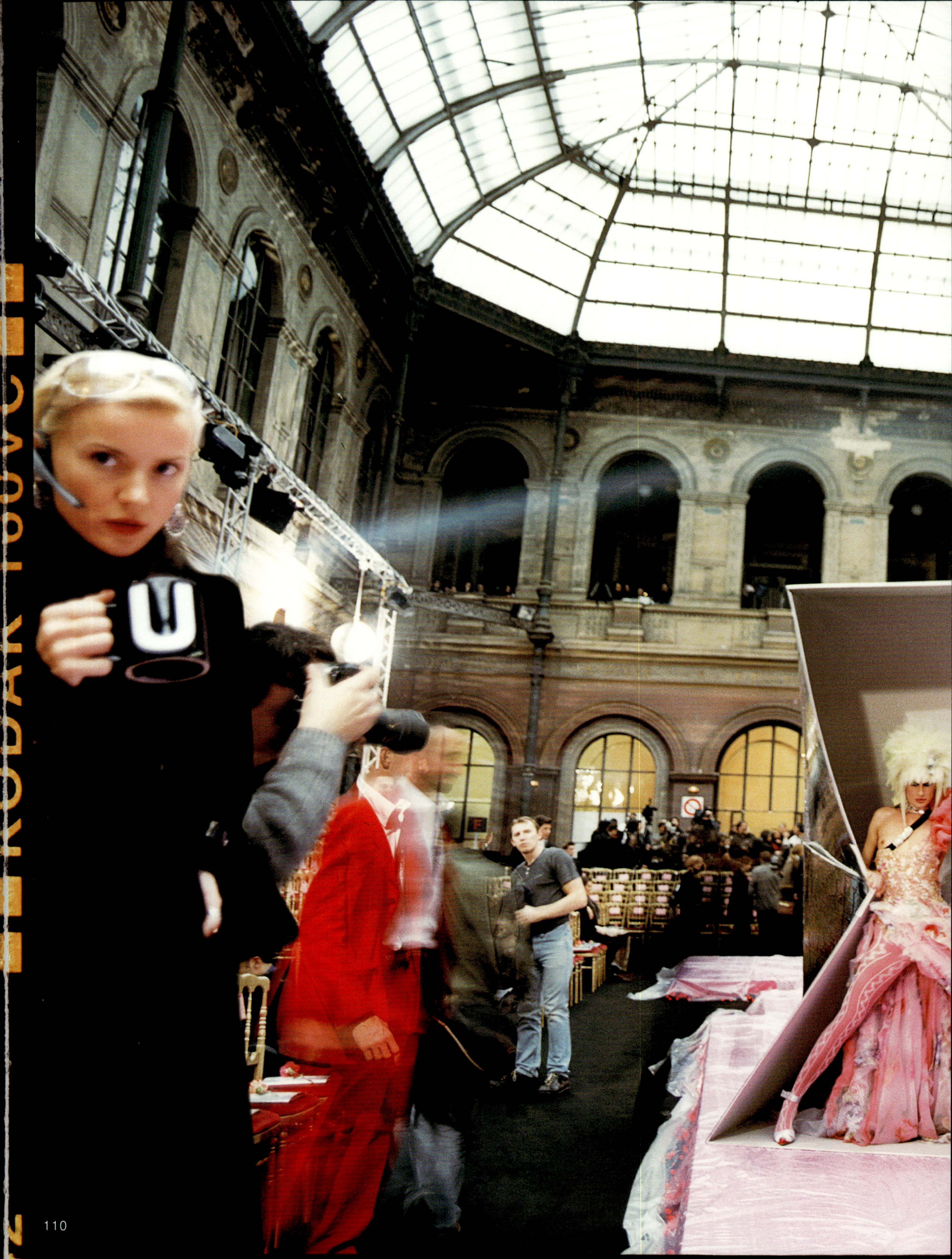

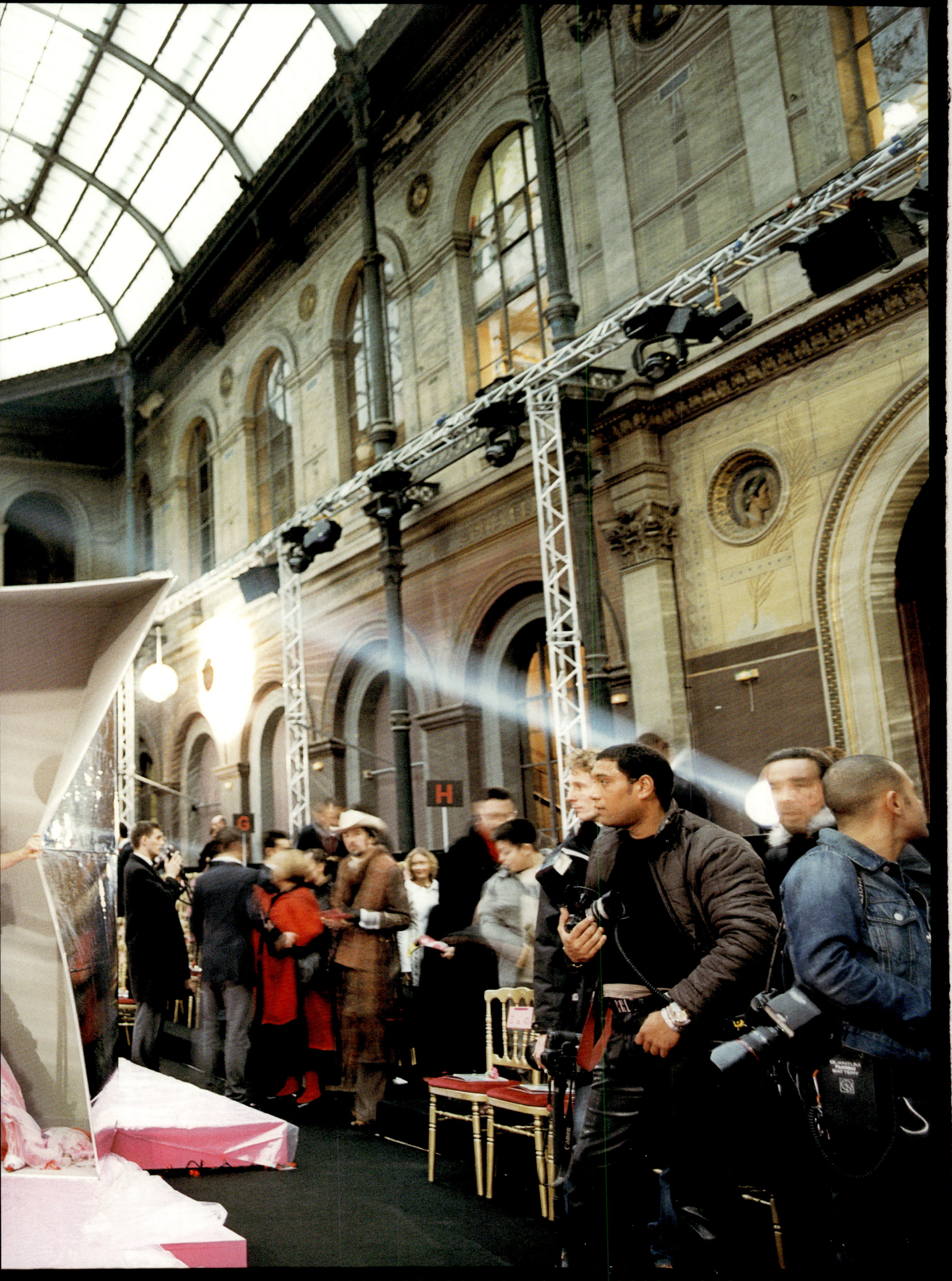
G
H

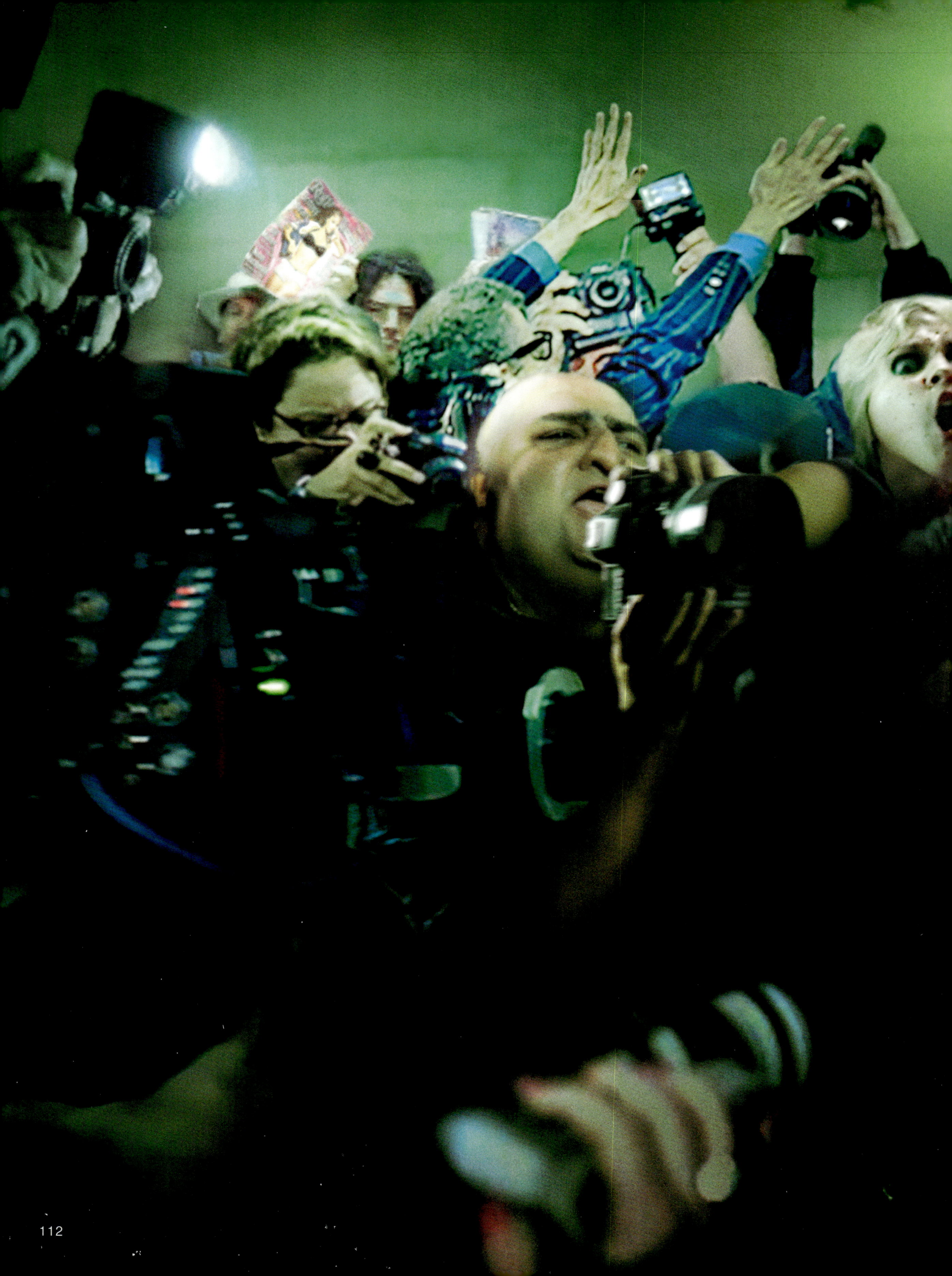

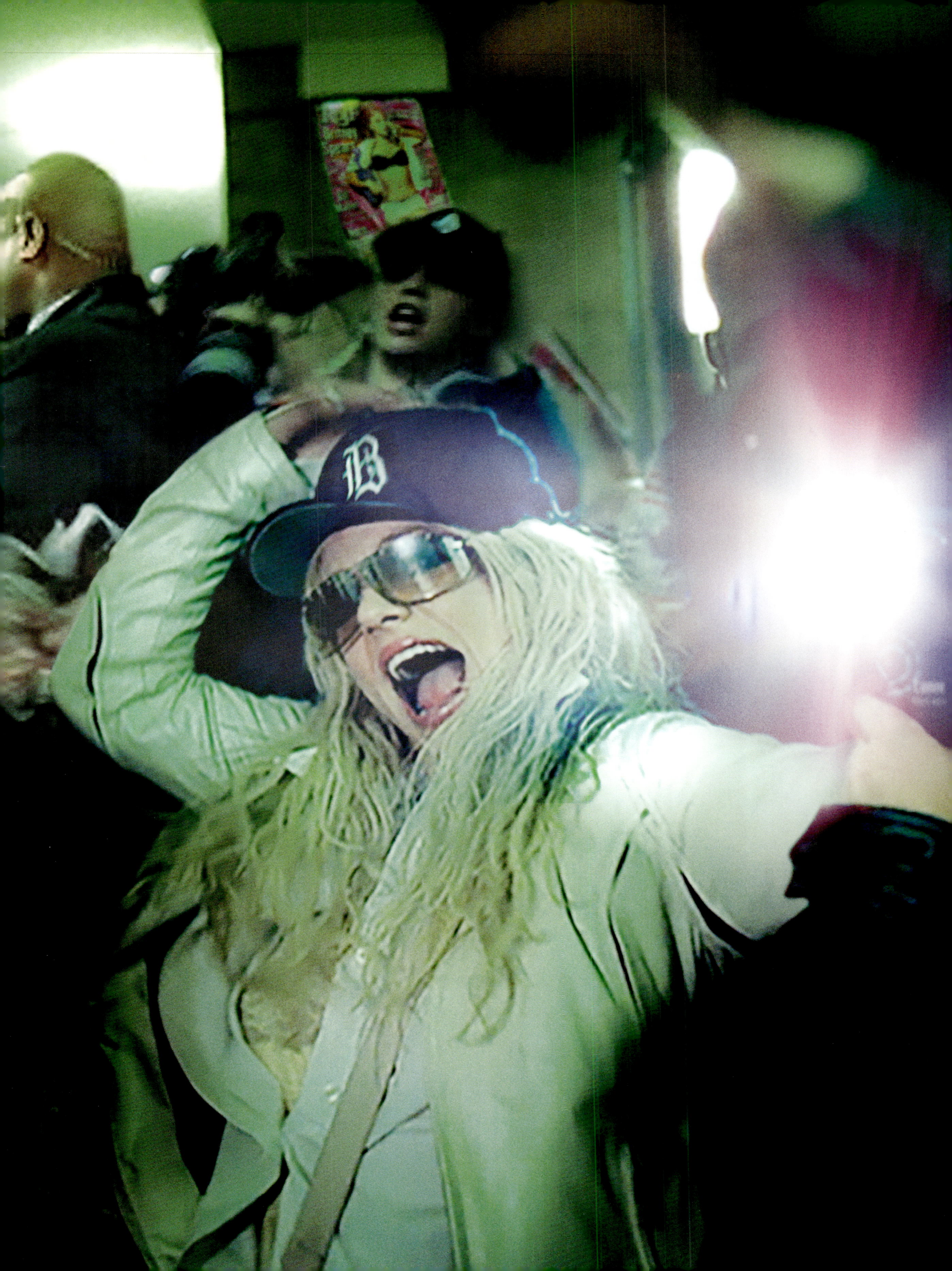

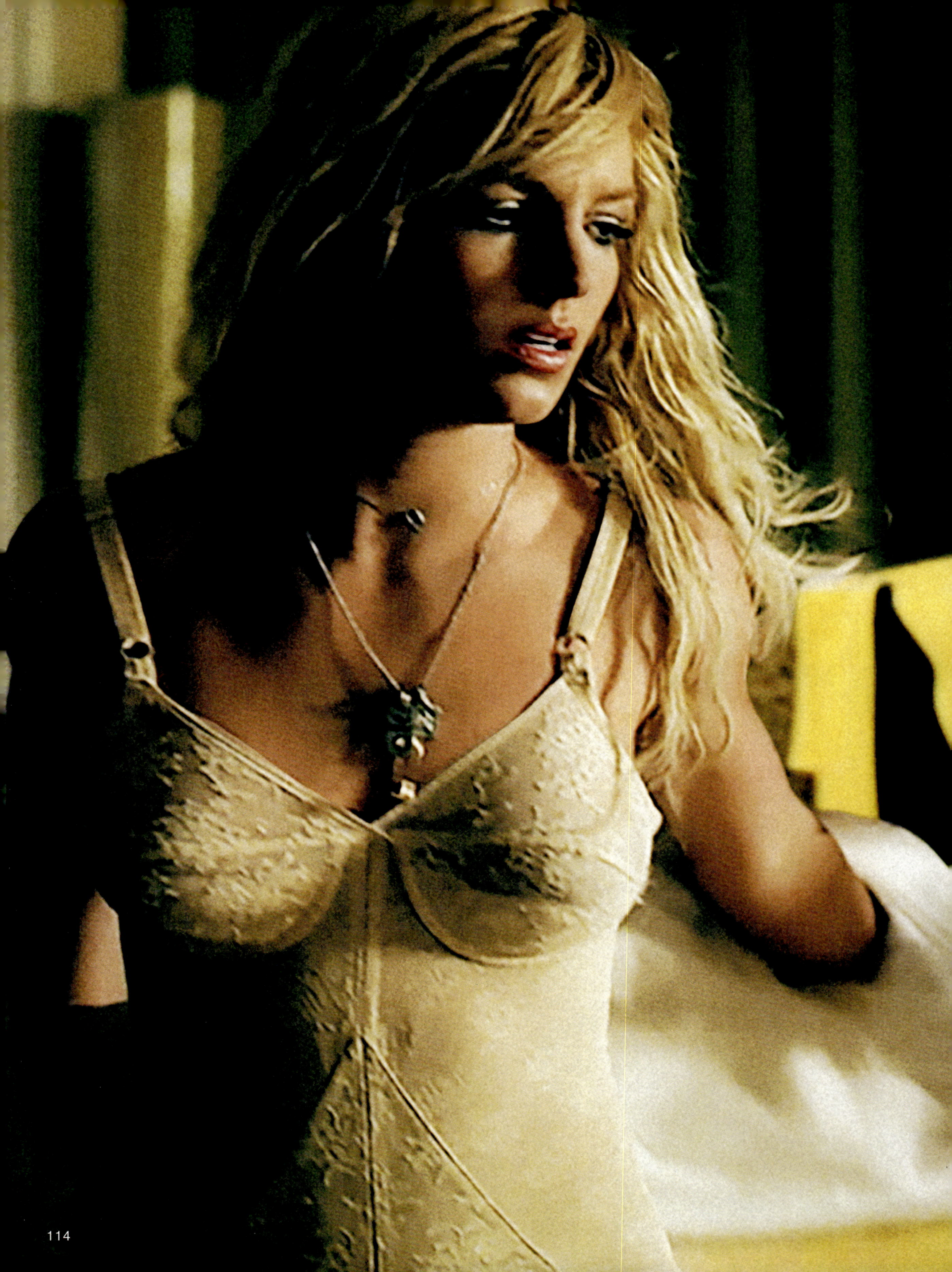

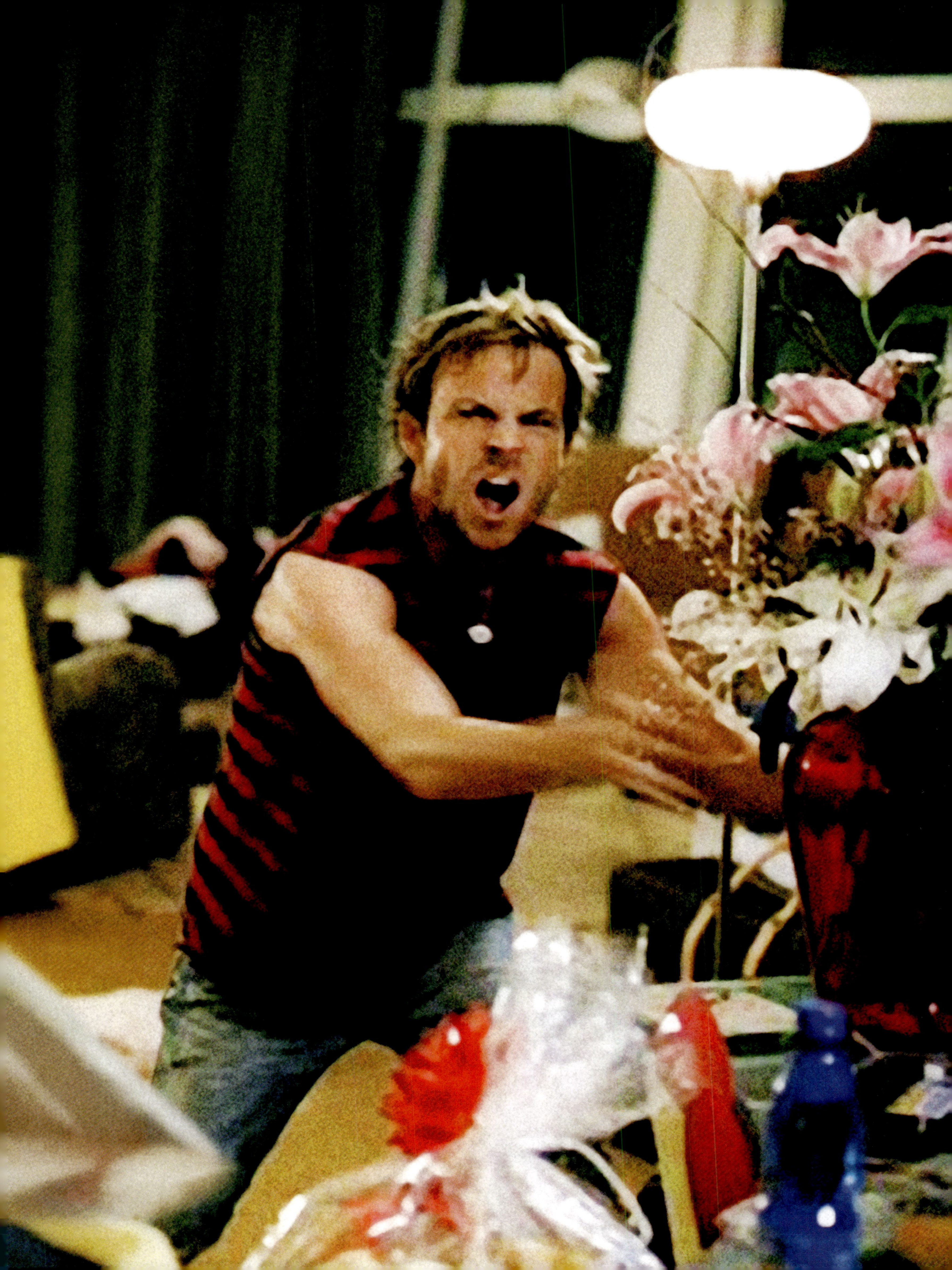

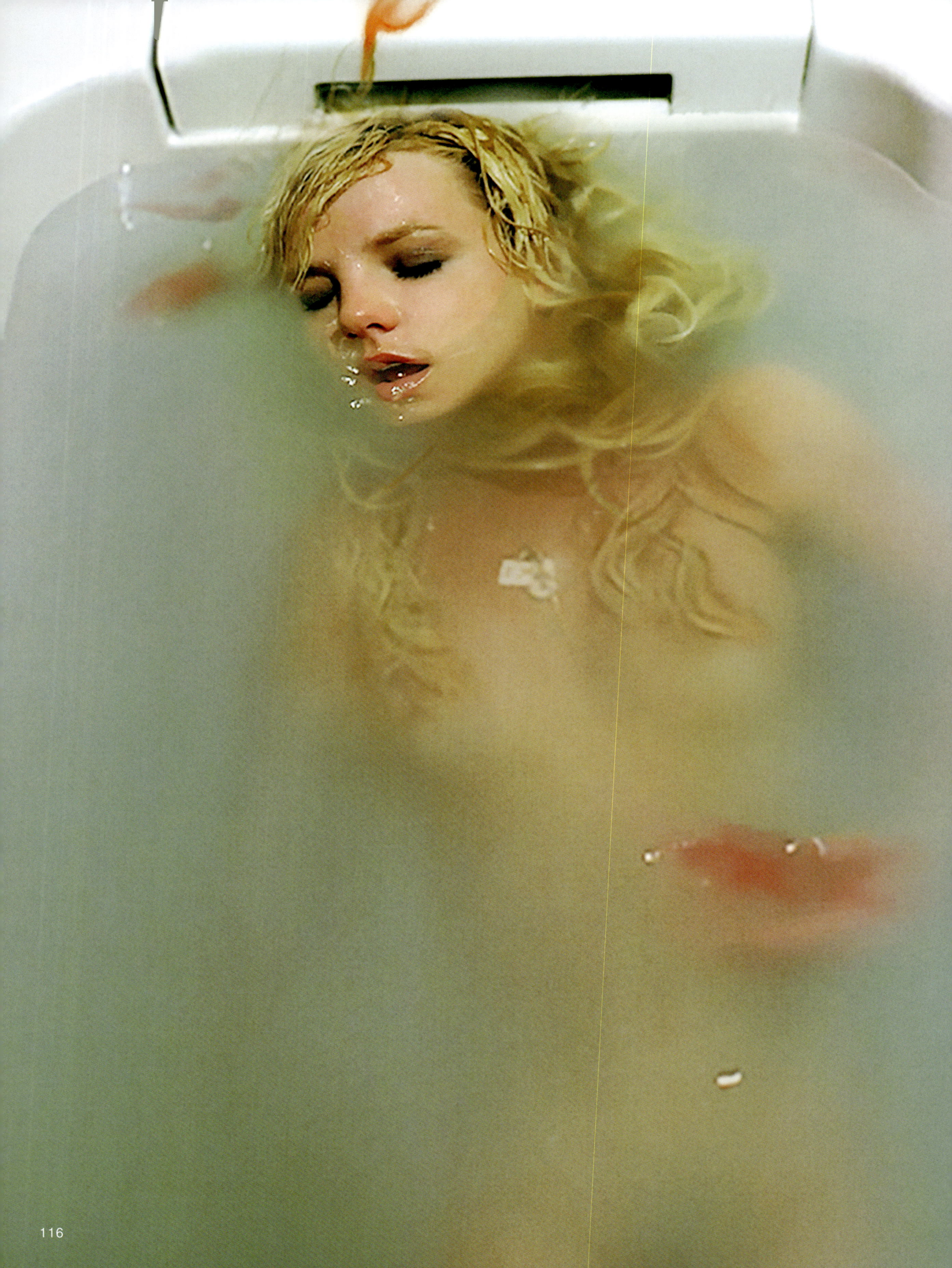

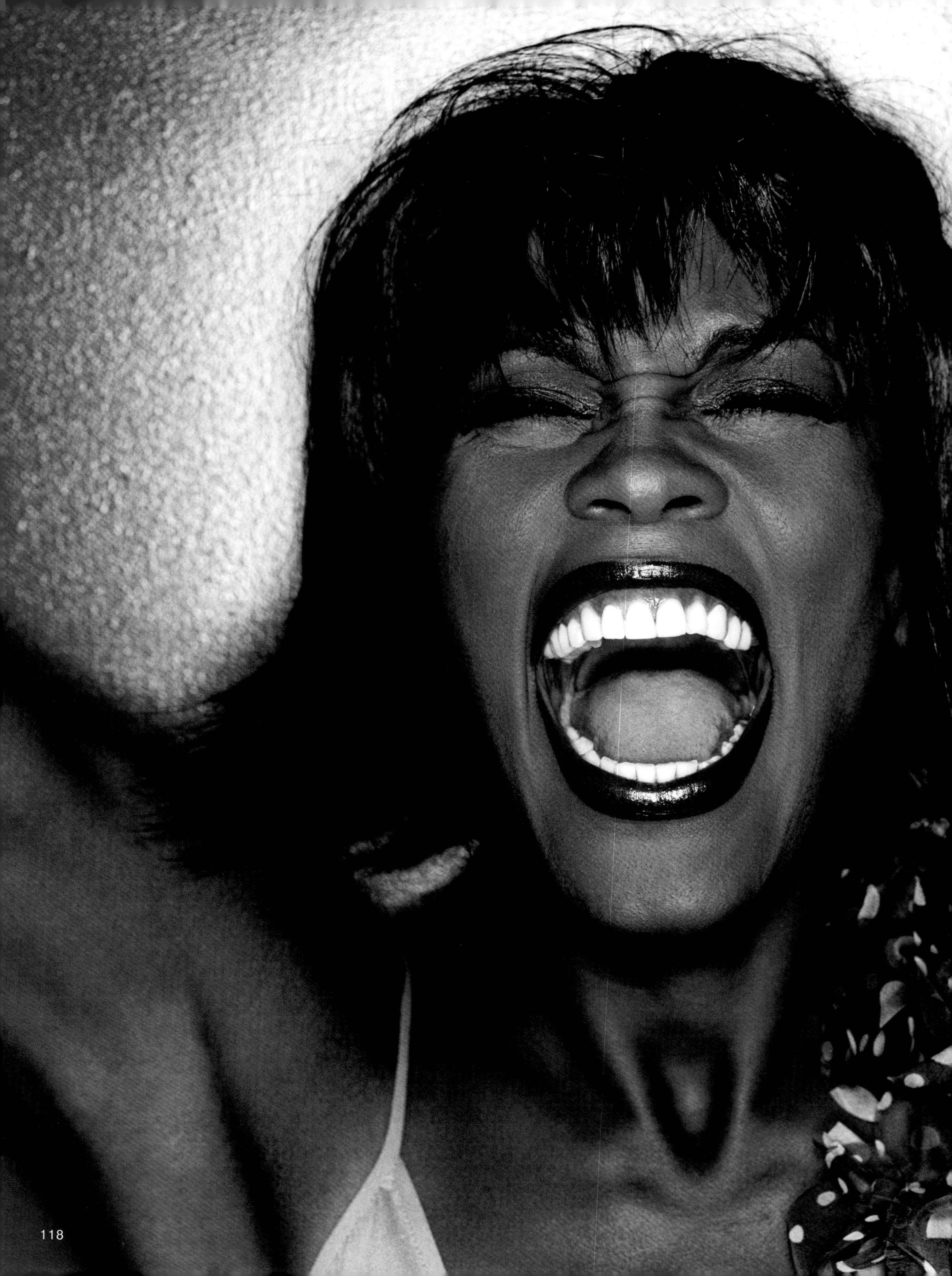

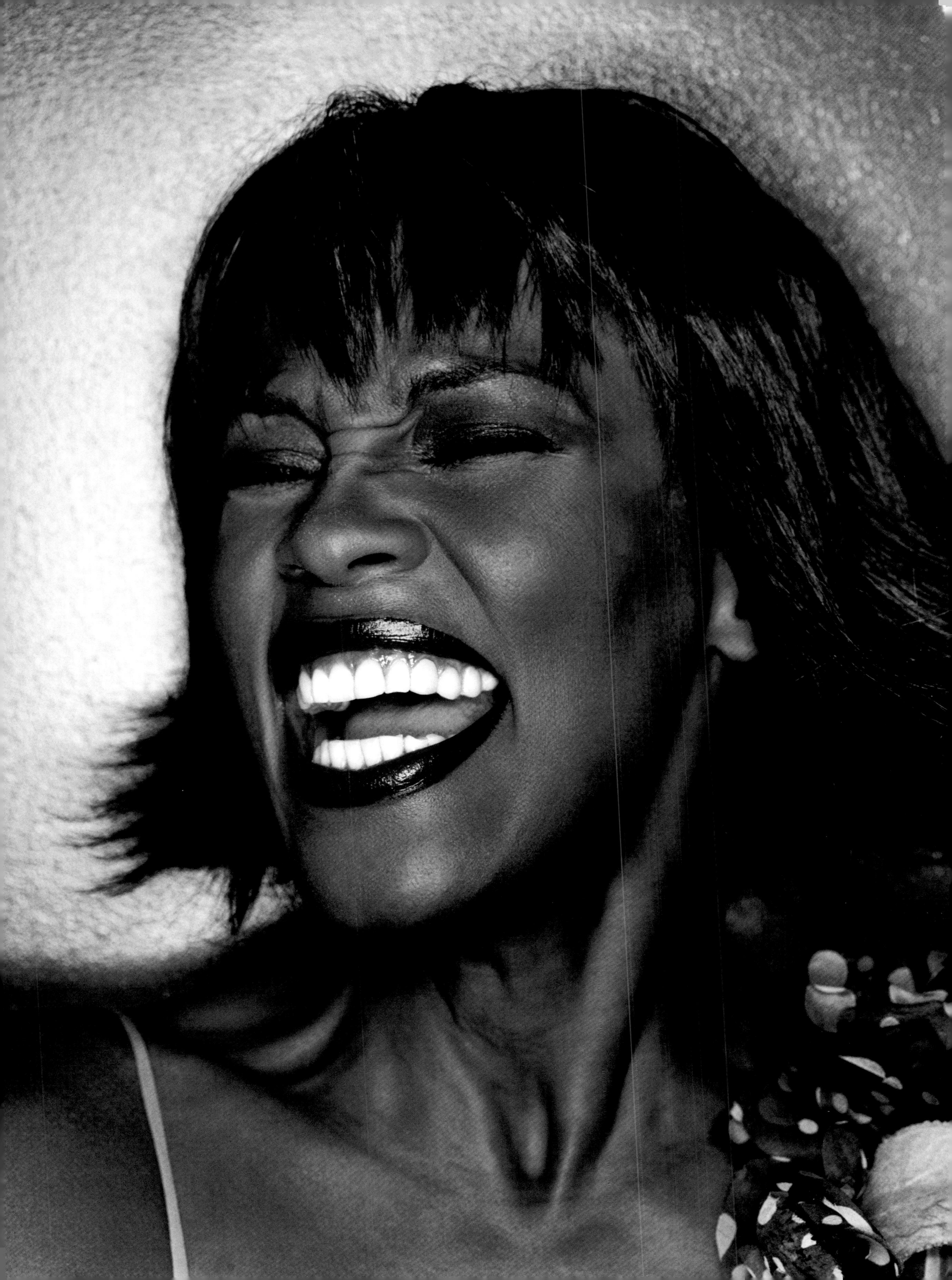

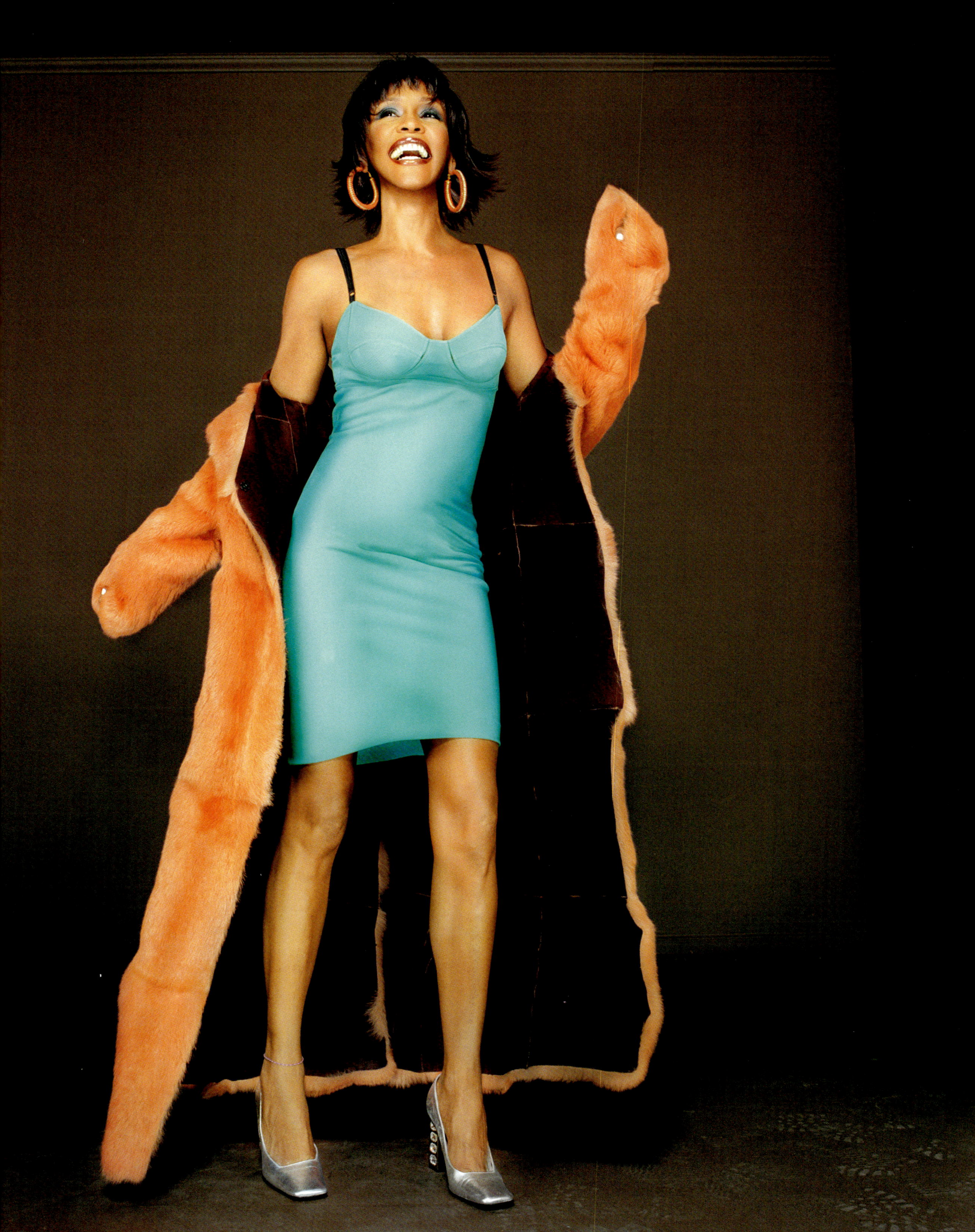

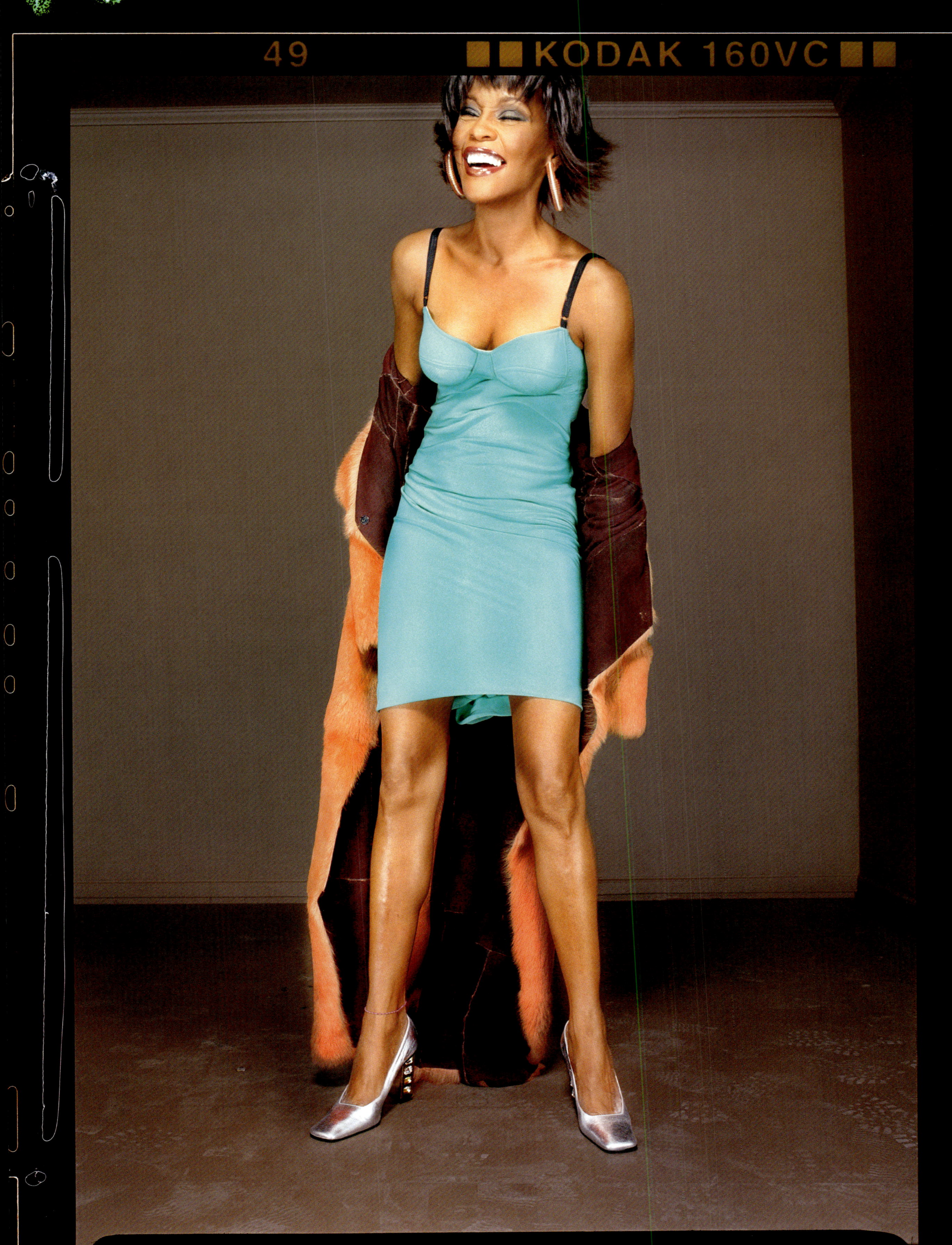
49
KODAK 160VC

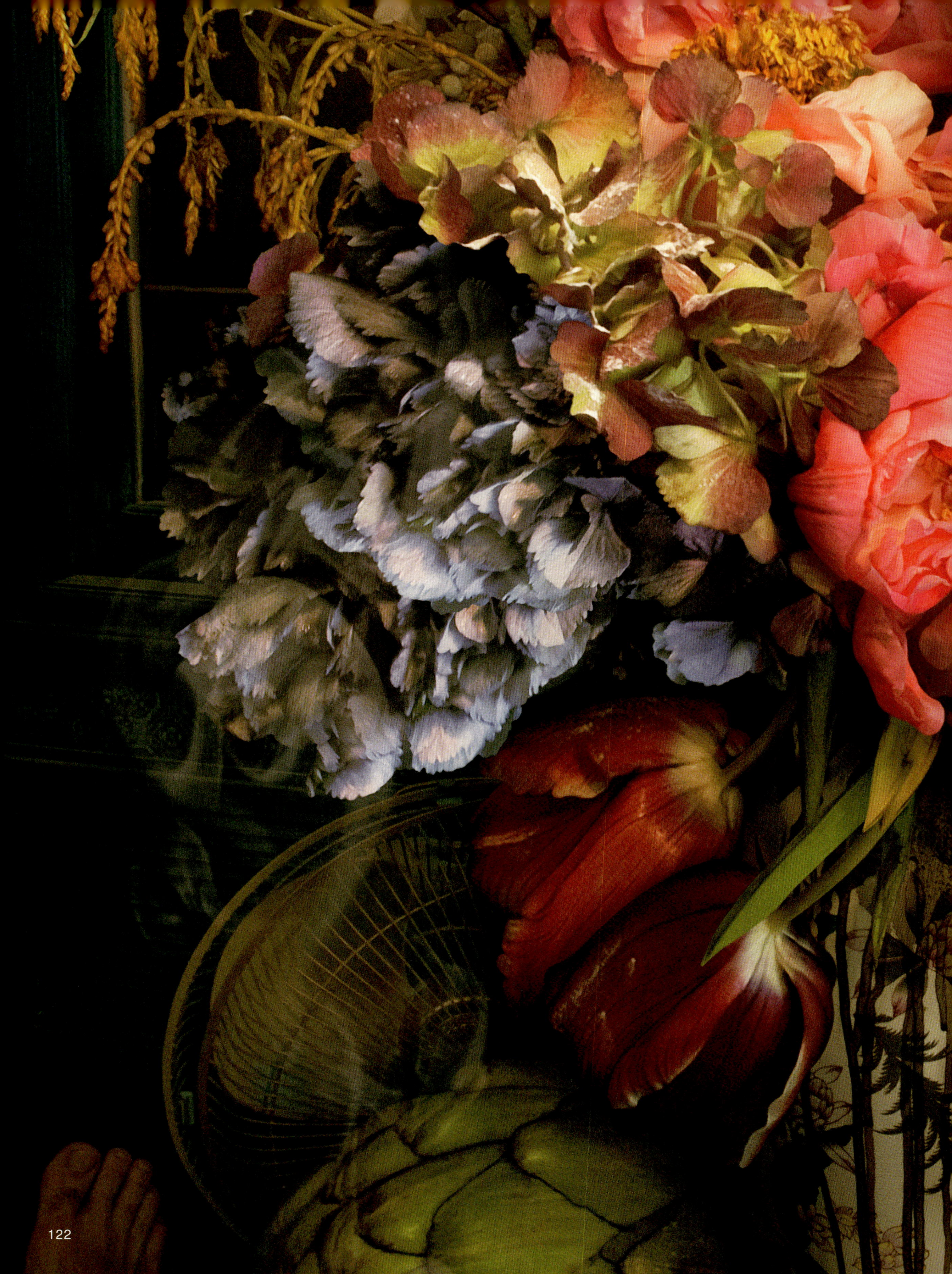

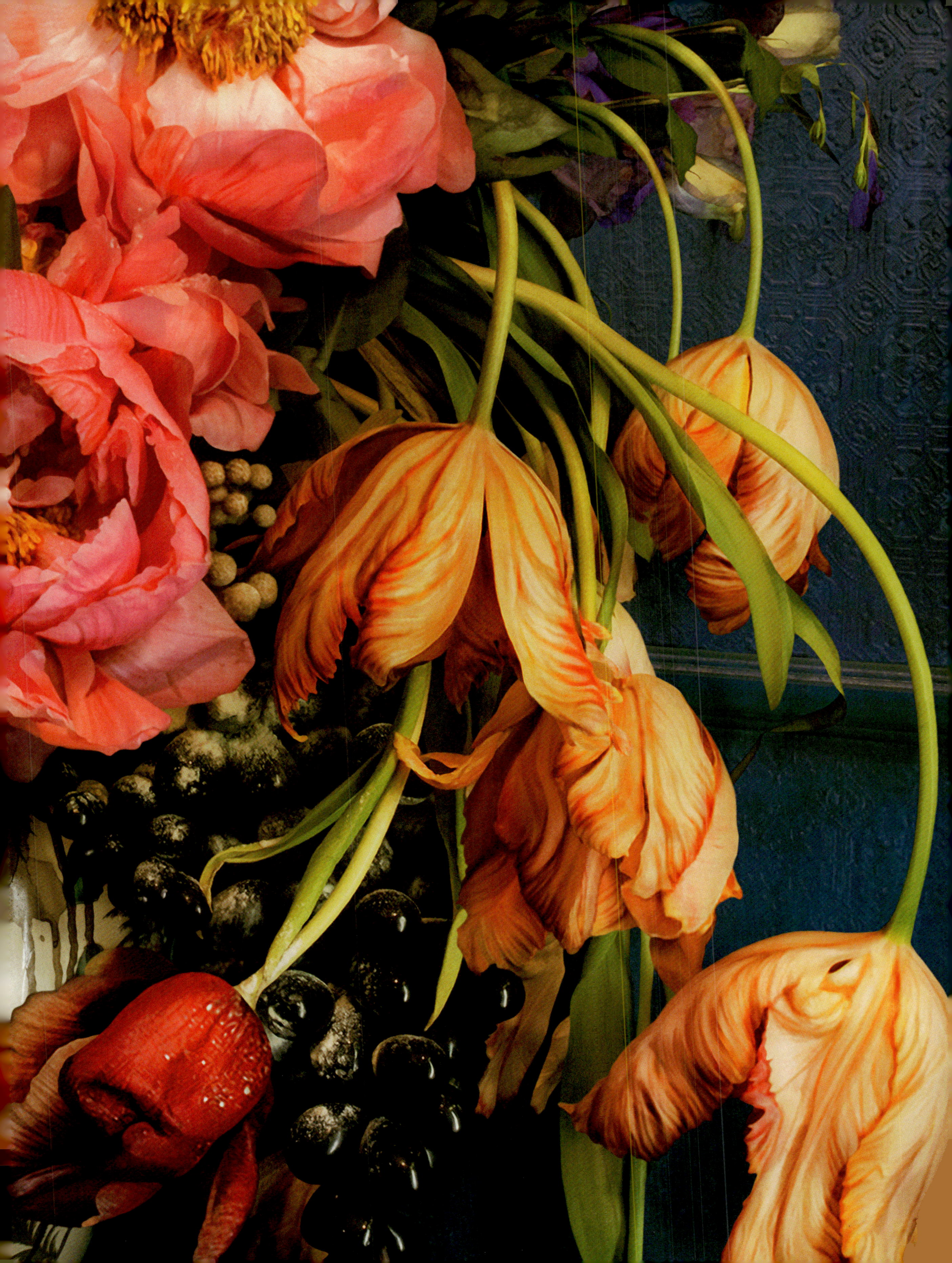

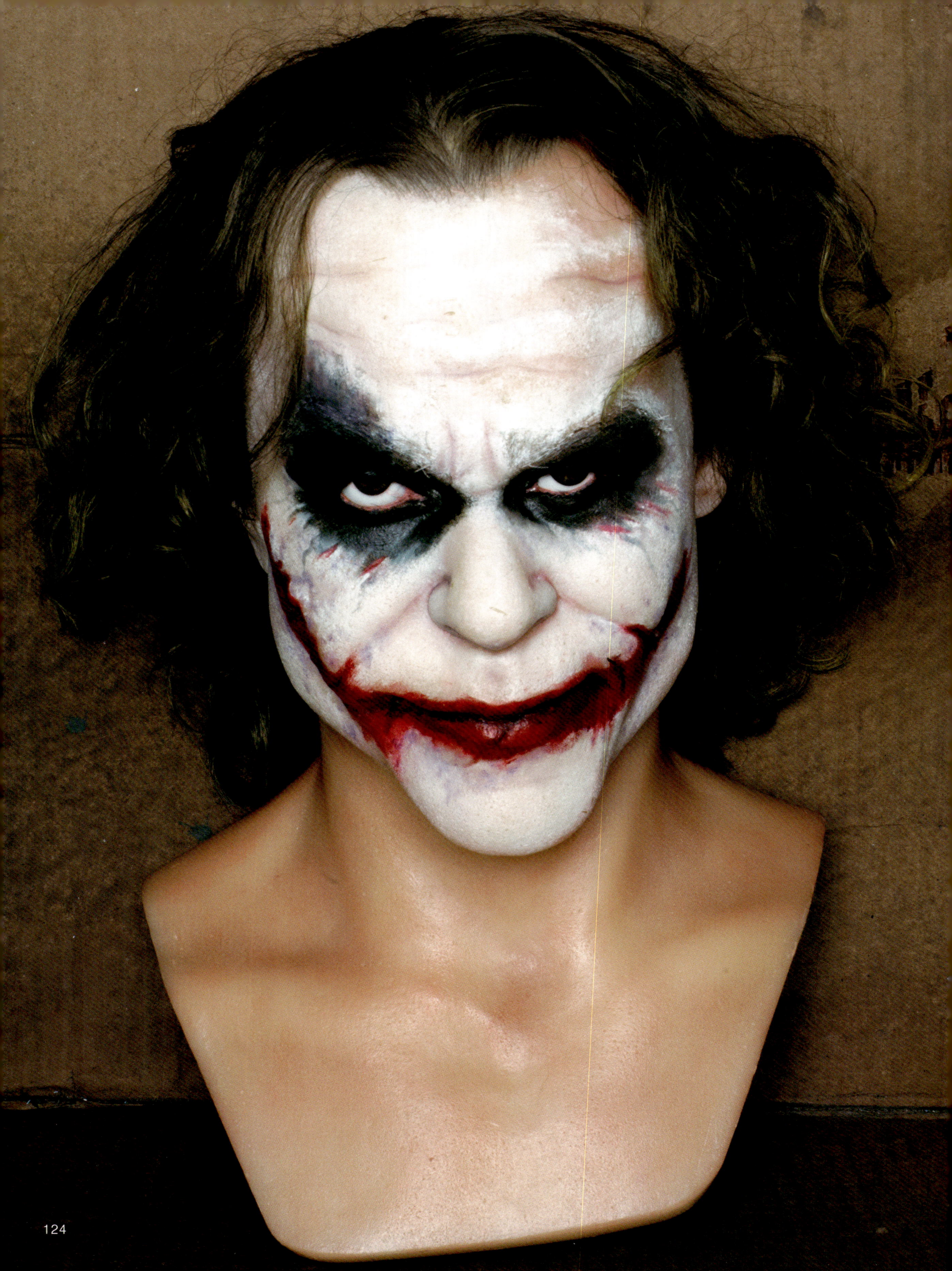

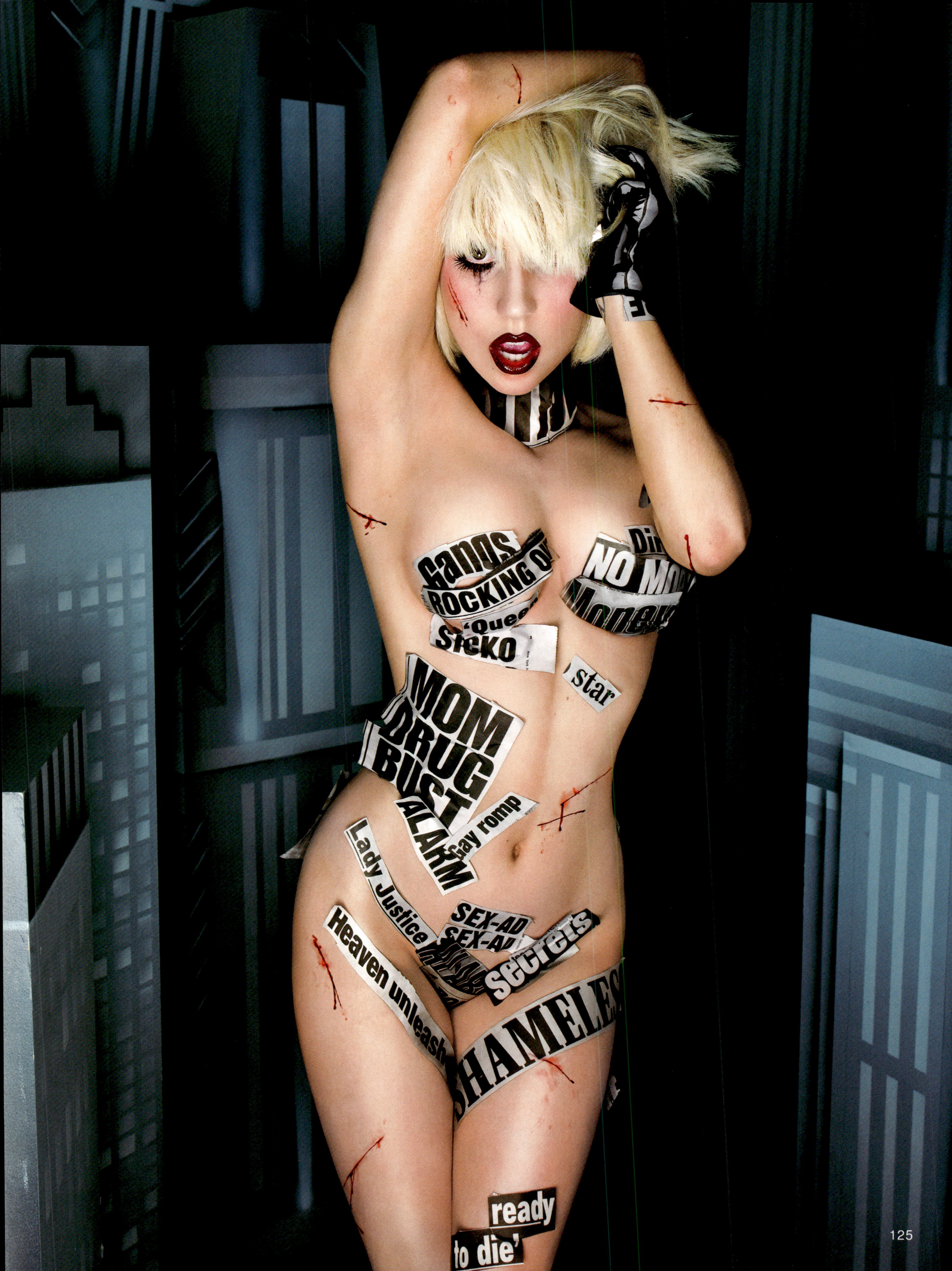
Gangs
ROCKING
NO MO
Money
Sicko
star
MOM
DRUG
BUST
ALARM
Gay romp
Lady Justice
SEX-AD
SEX-AD
secrets
Heaven unleash
SHAMELES
ready
to die'

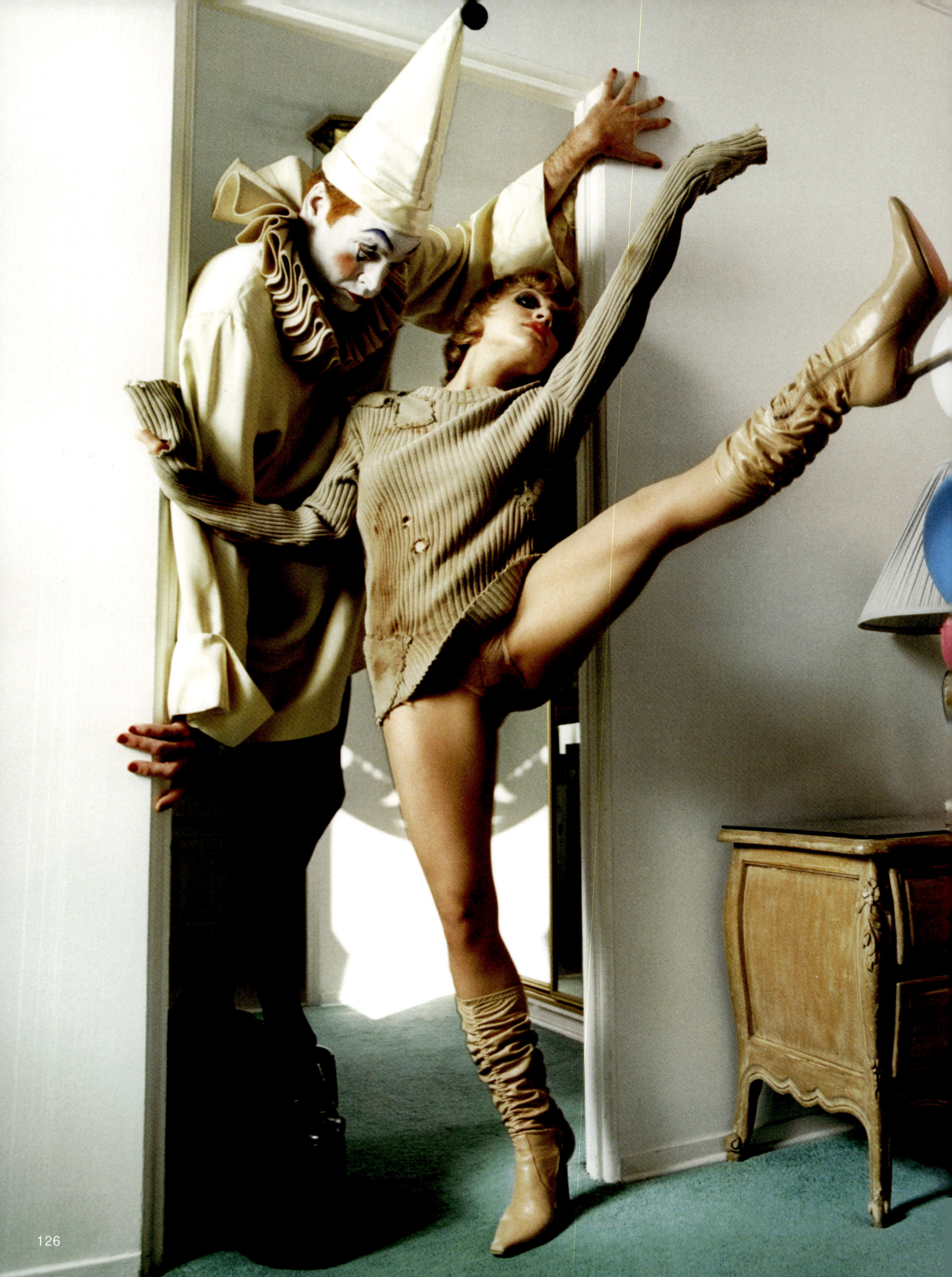

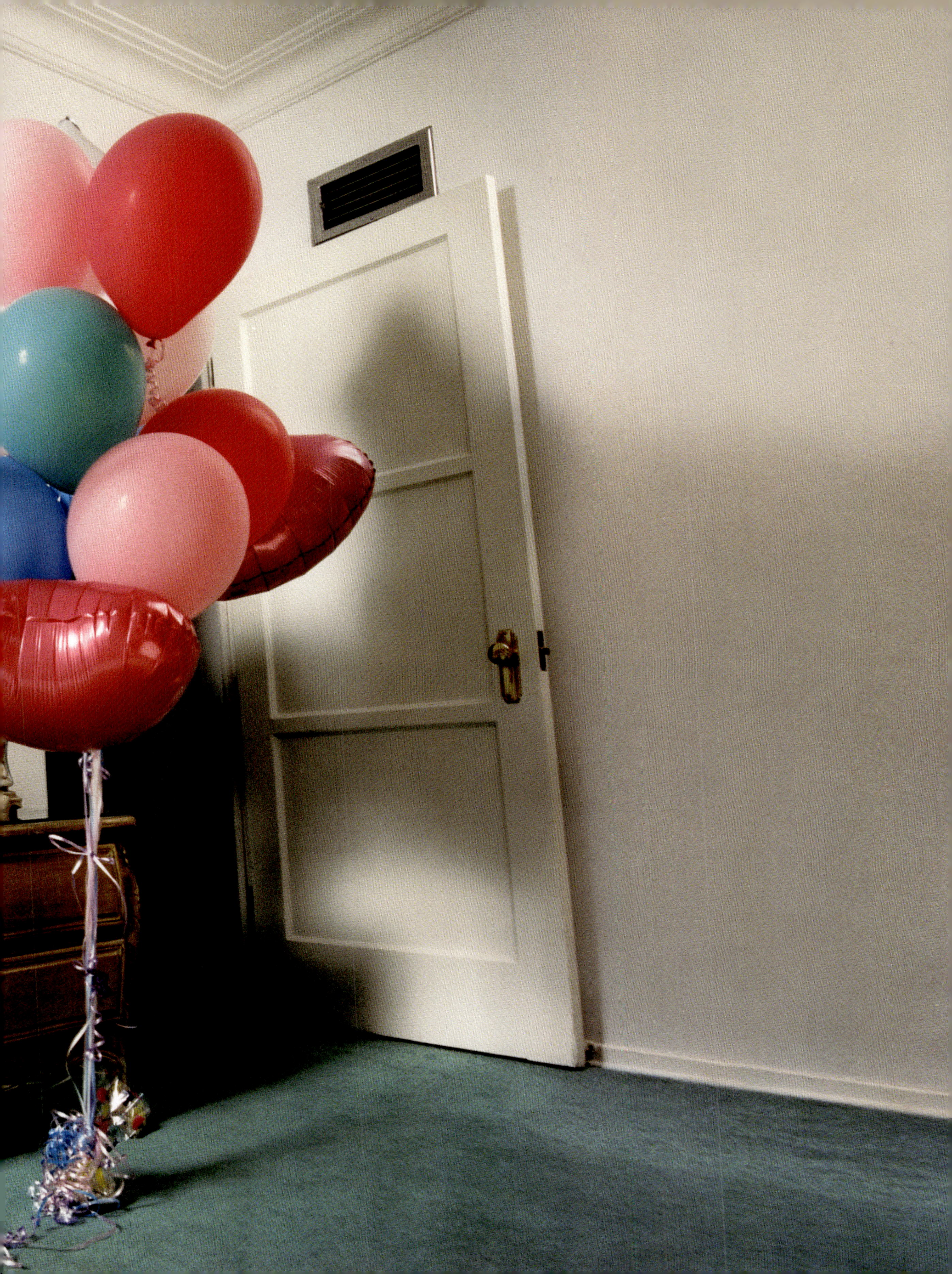

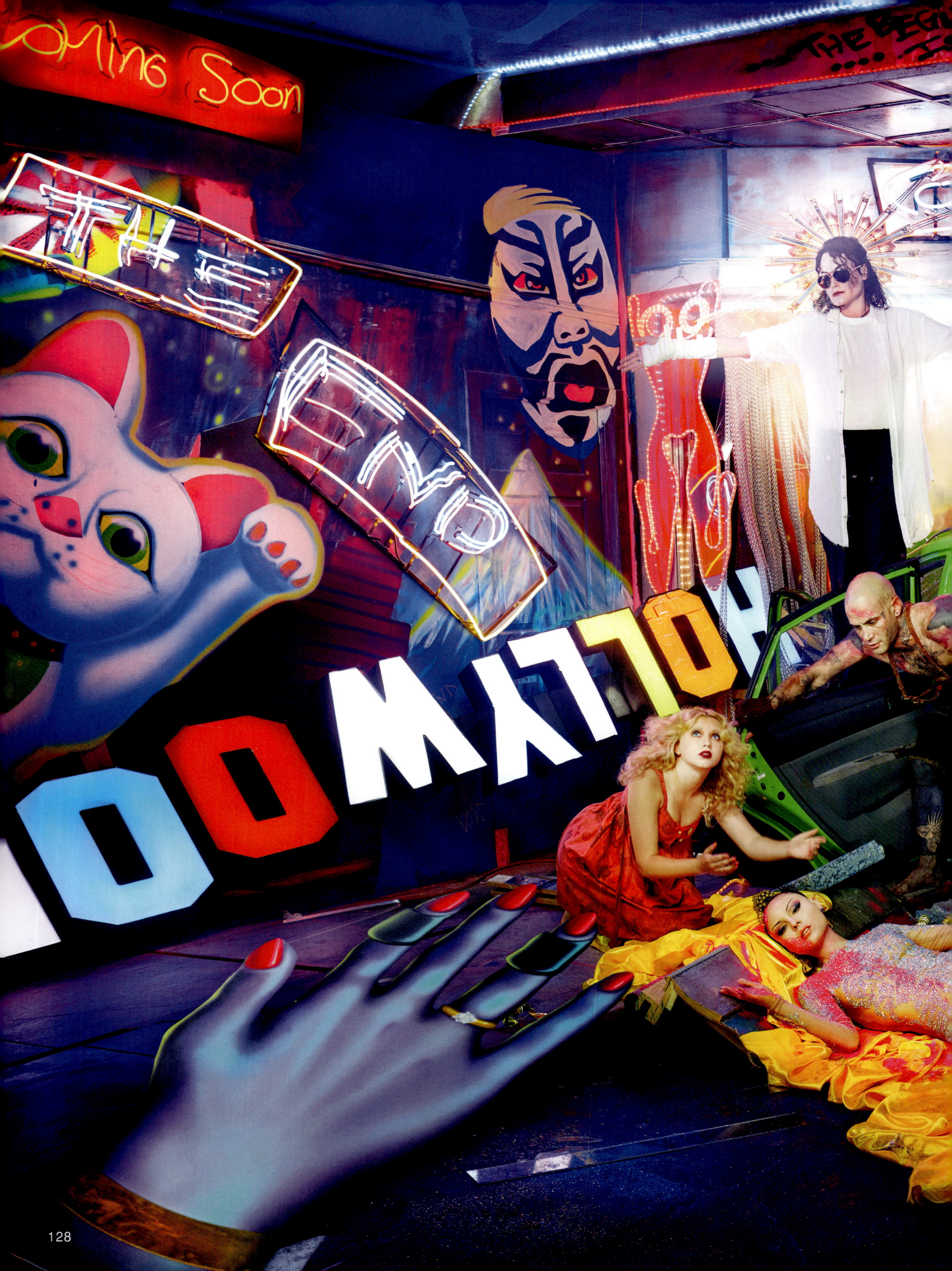
oming Soon
THE
END

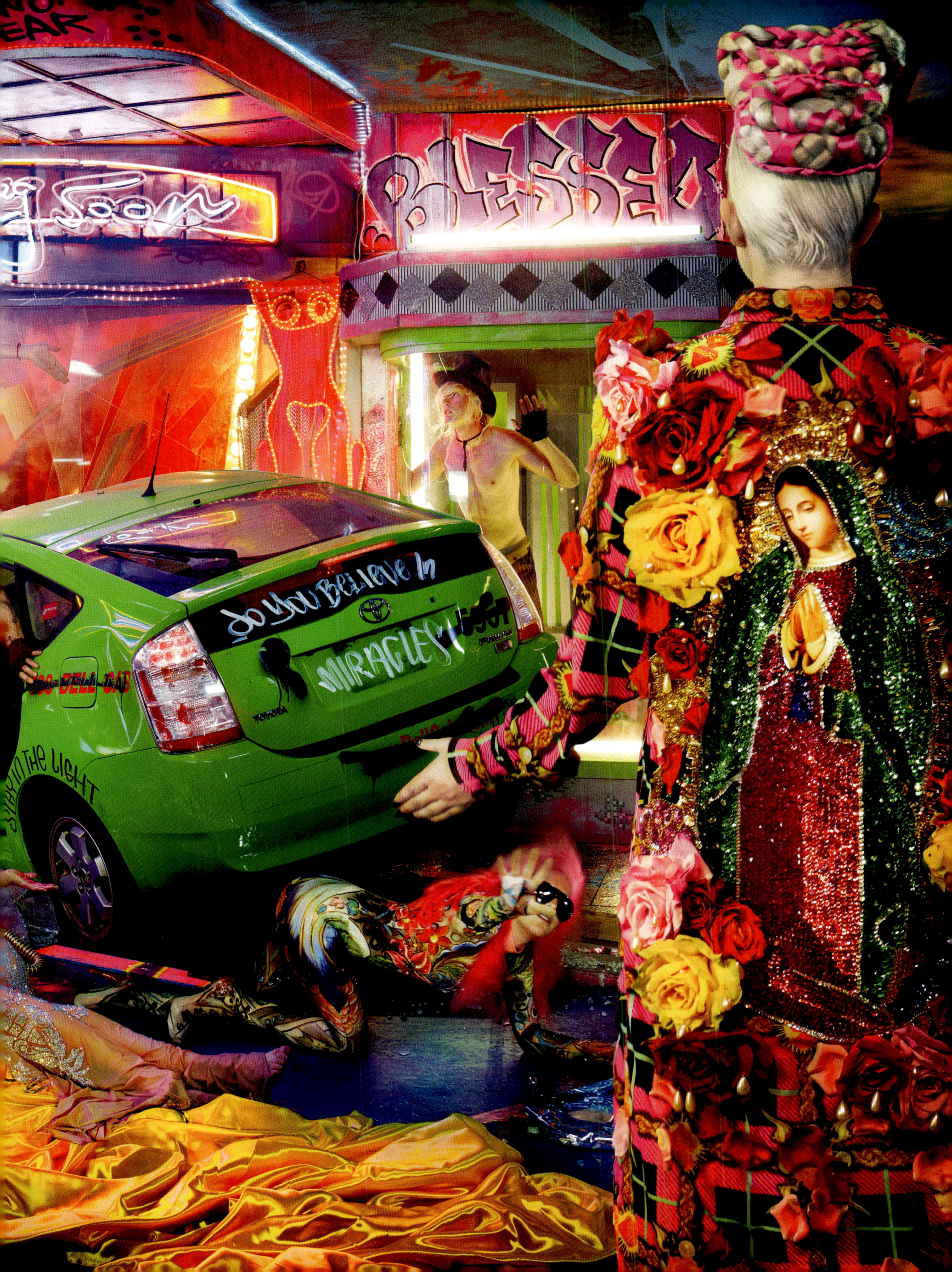

BLESSED
do you Believe In
MIRACLES
STAY IN THE LIGHT

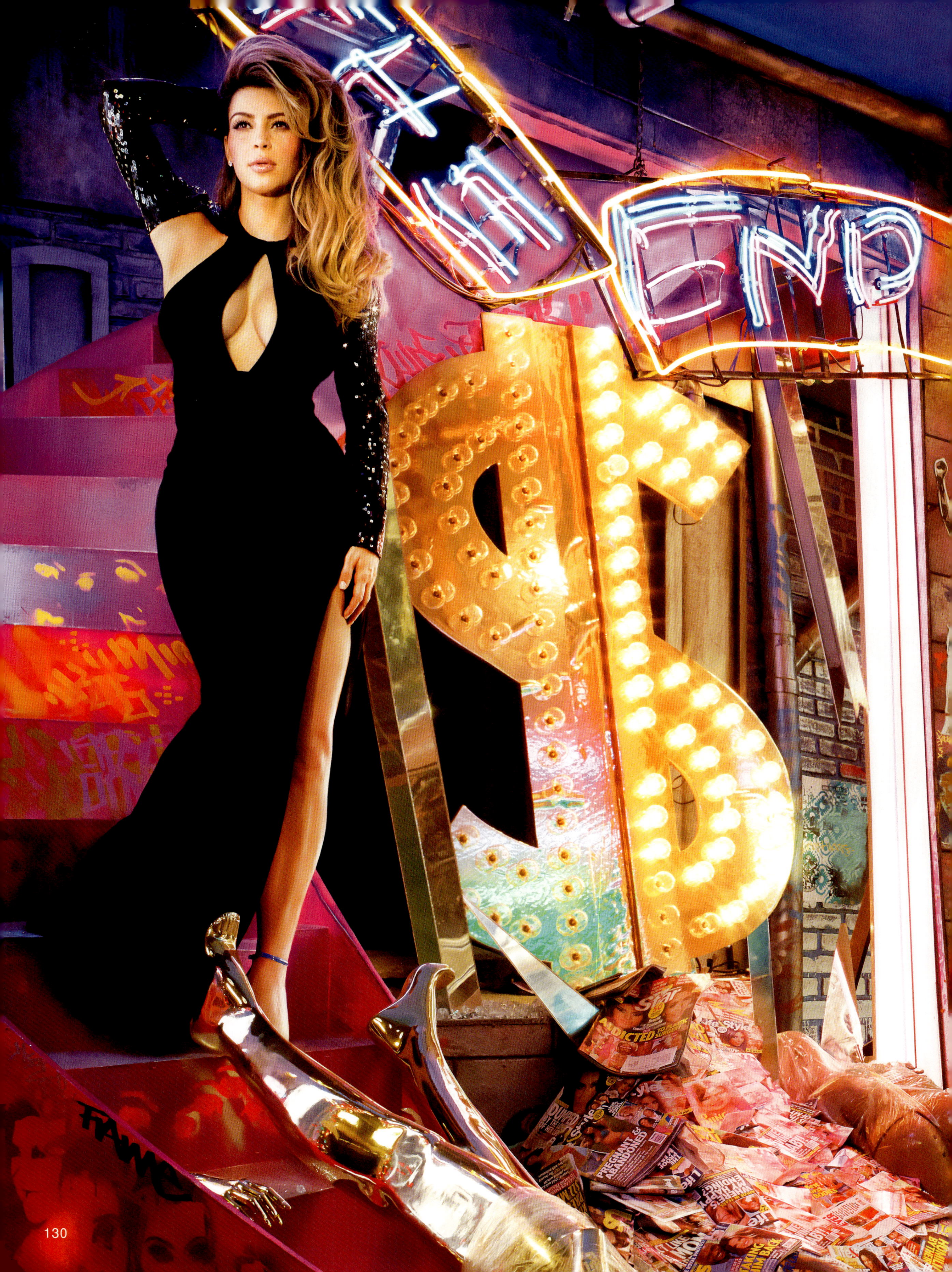
END
ADDICTED
PREGNANT & ABANDONED
FAME

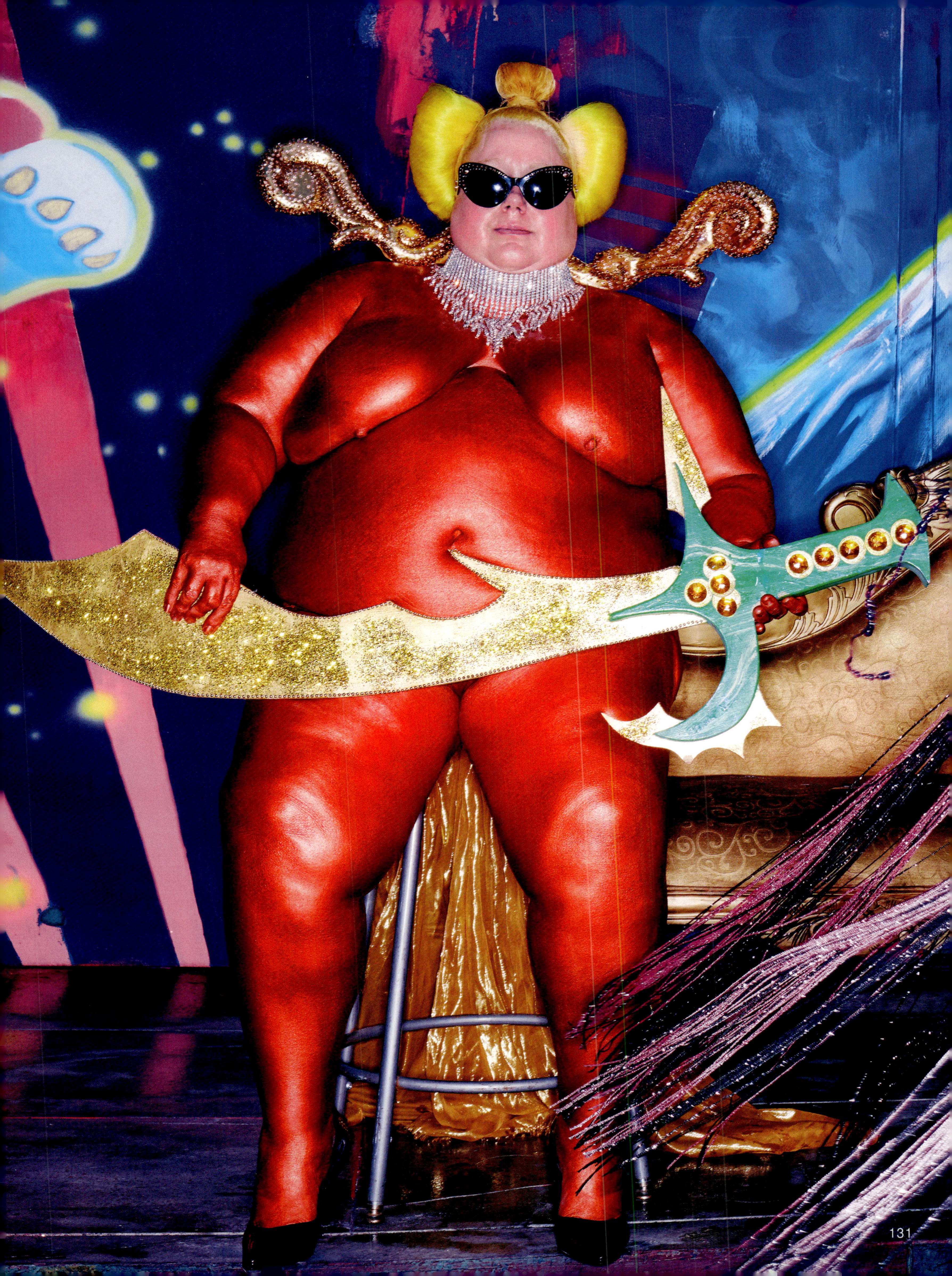

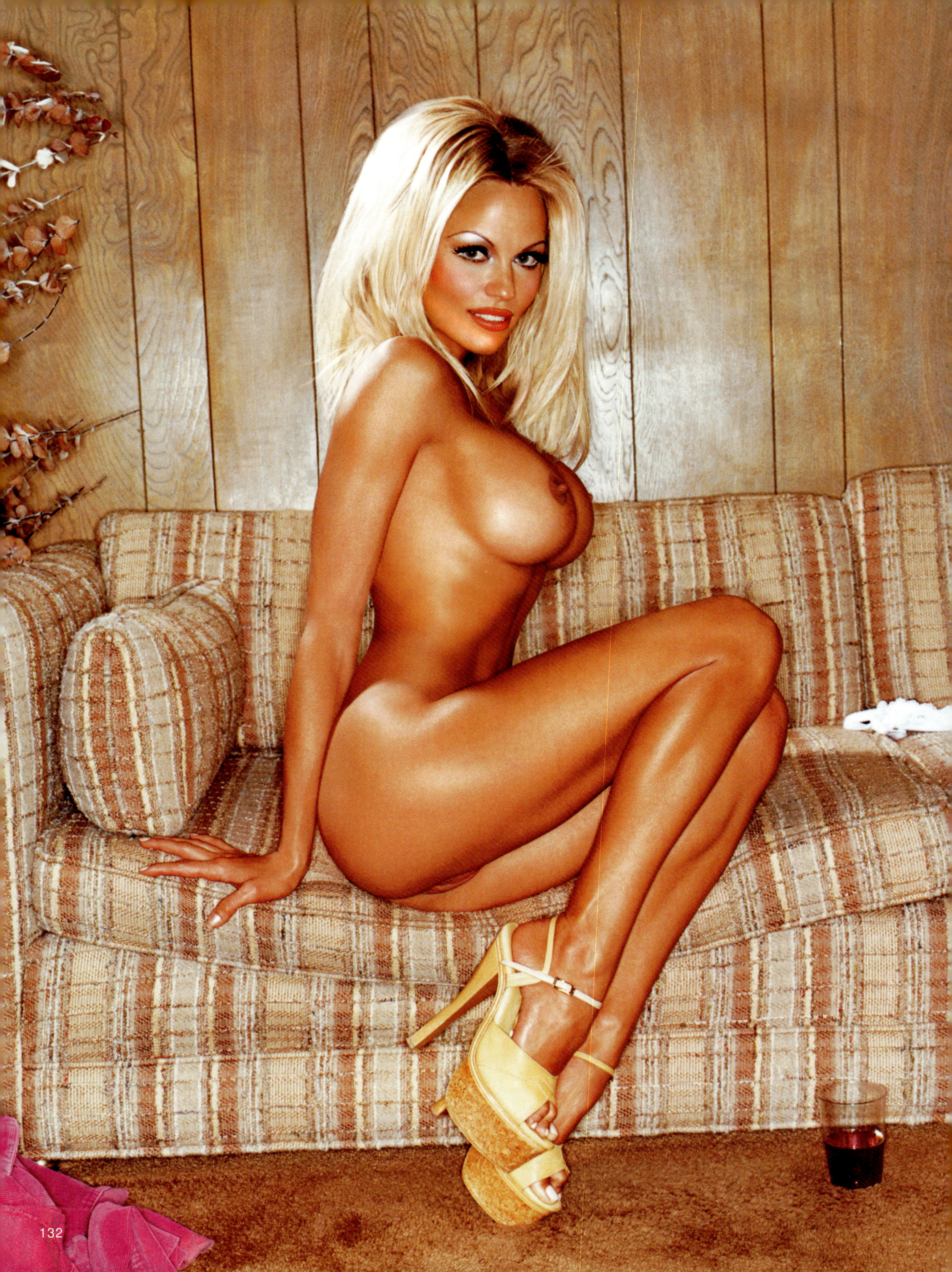

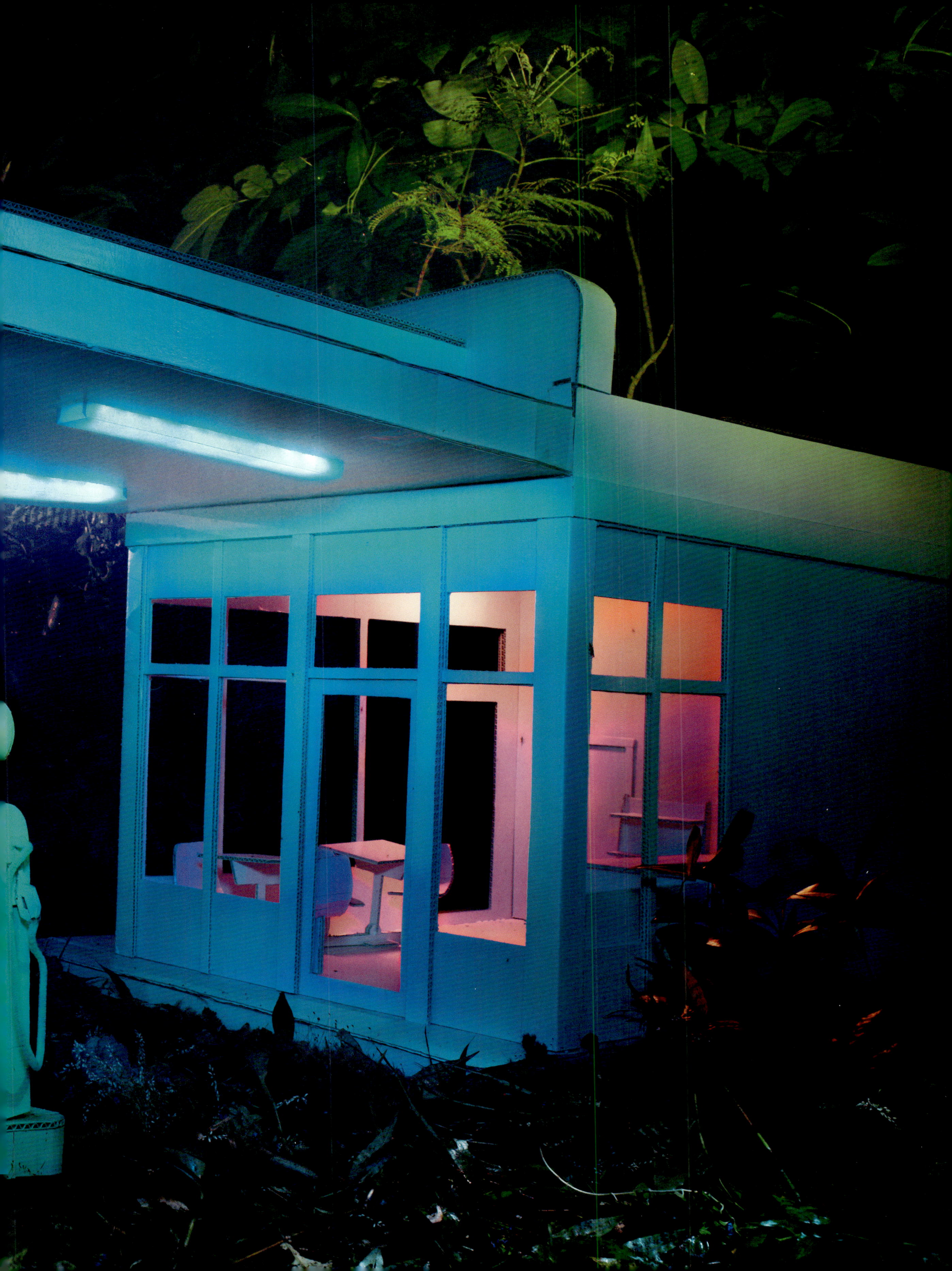

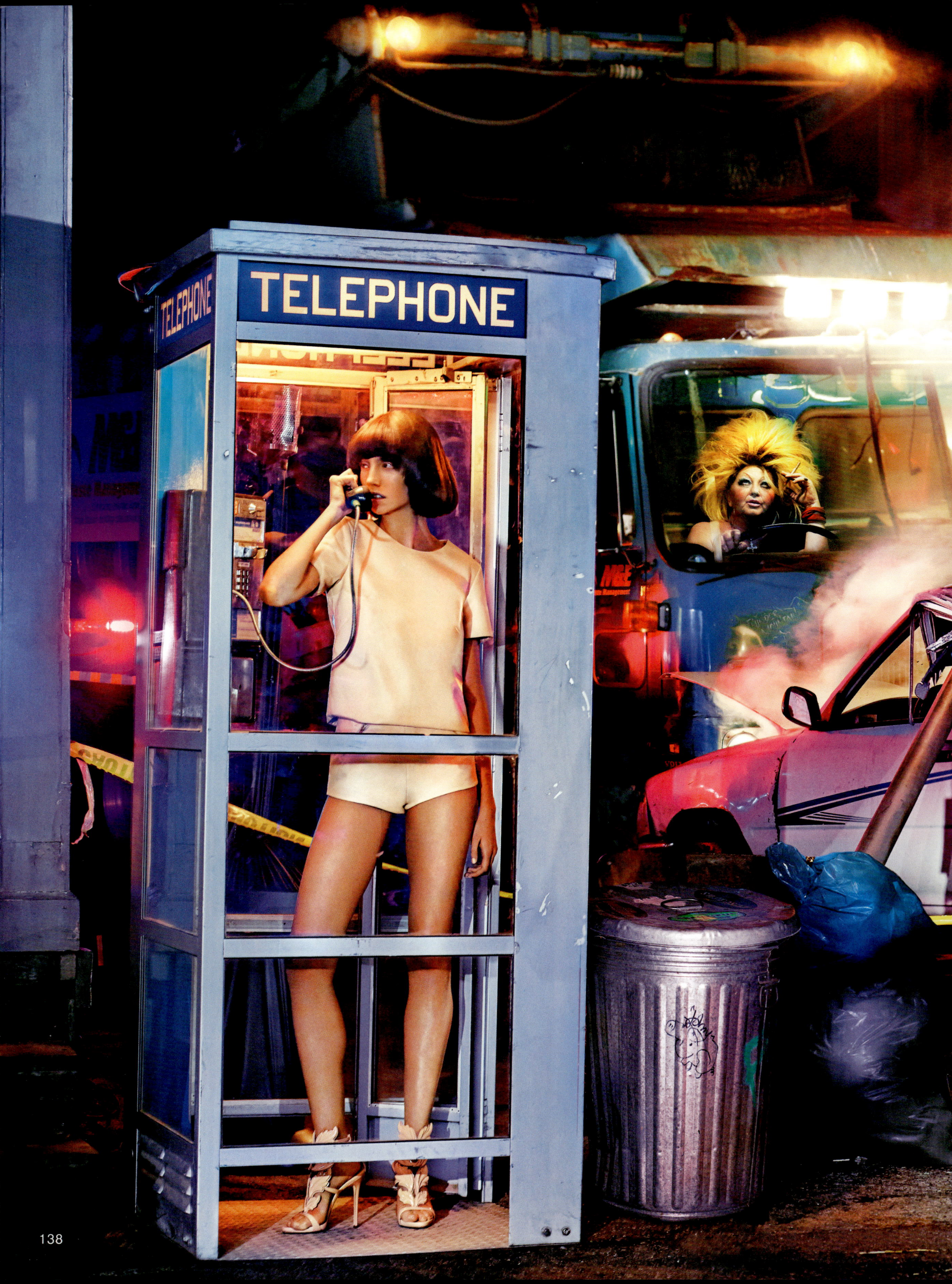
TELEPHONE
TELEPHONE

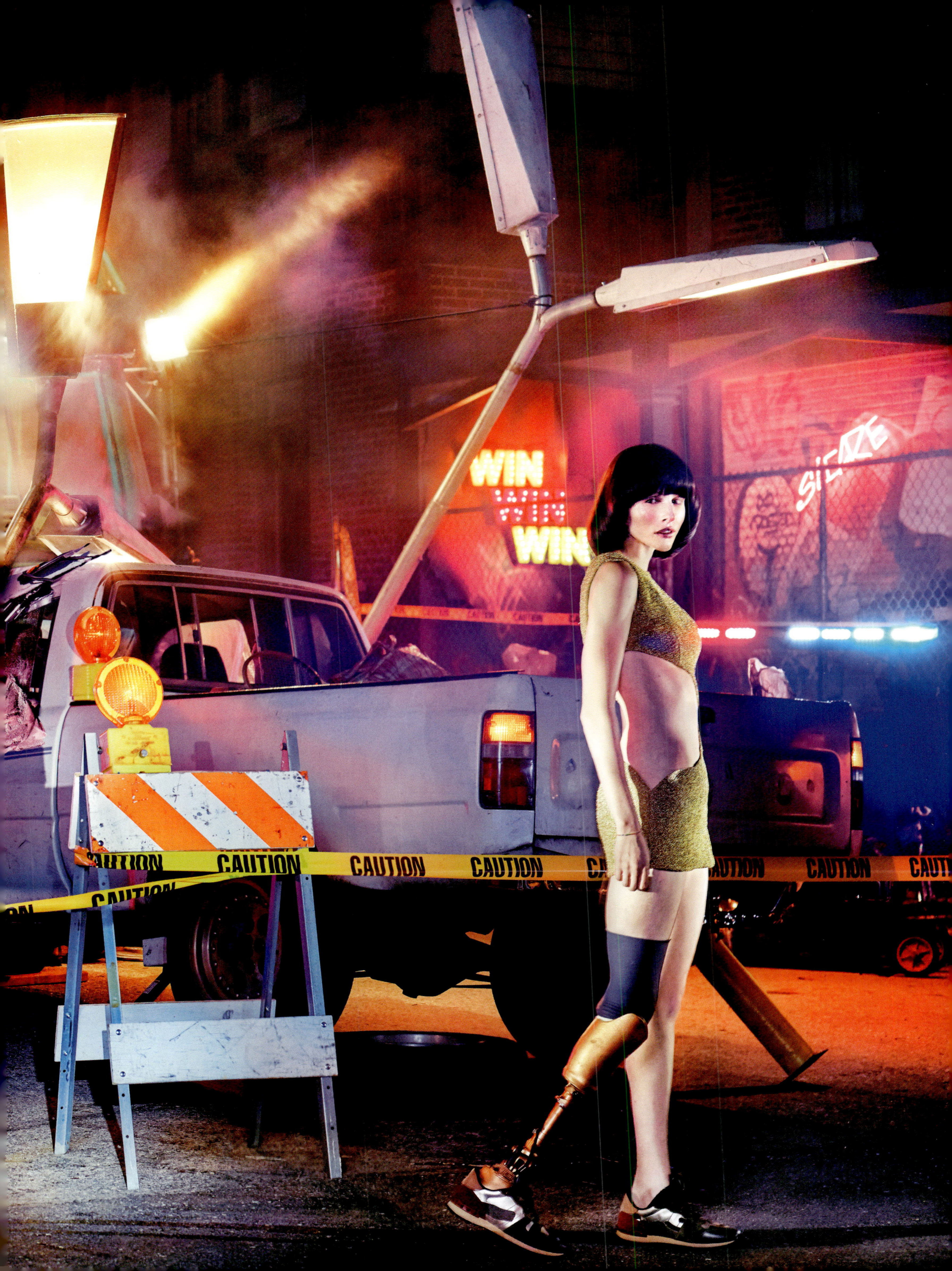
WIN
WIN
WIN
CAUTION

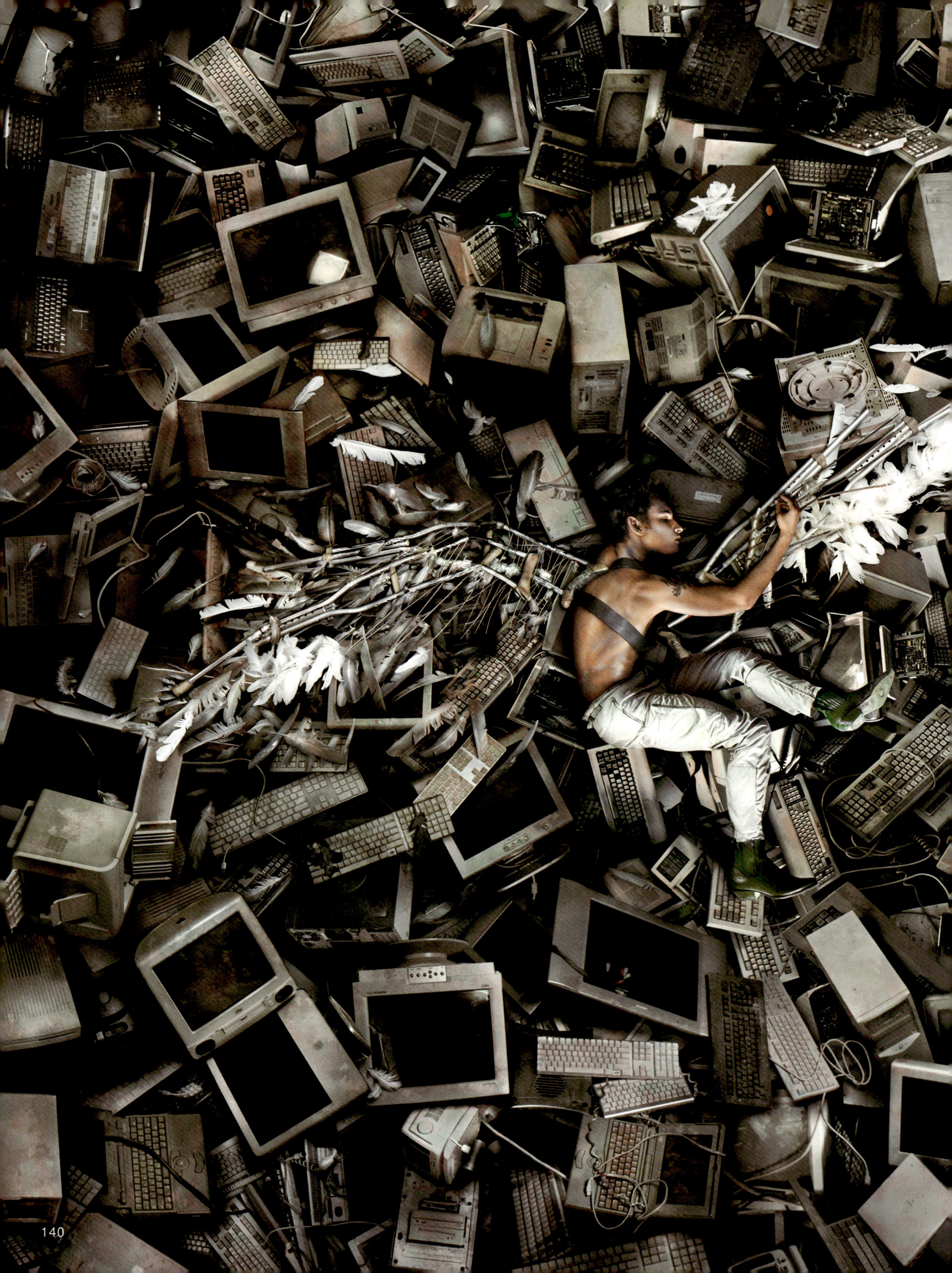

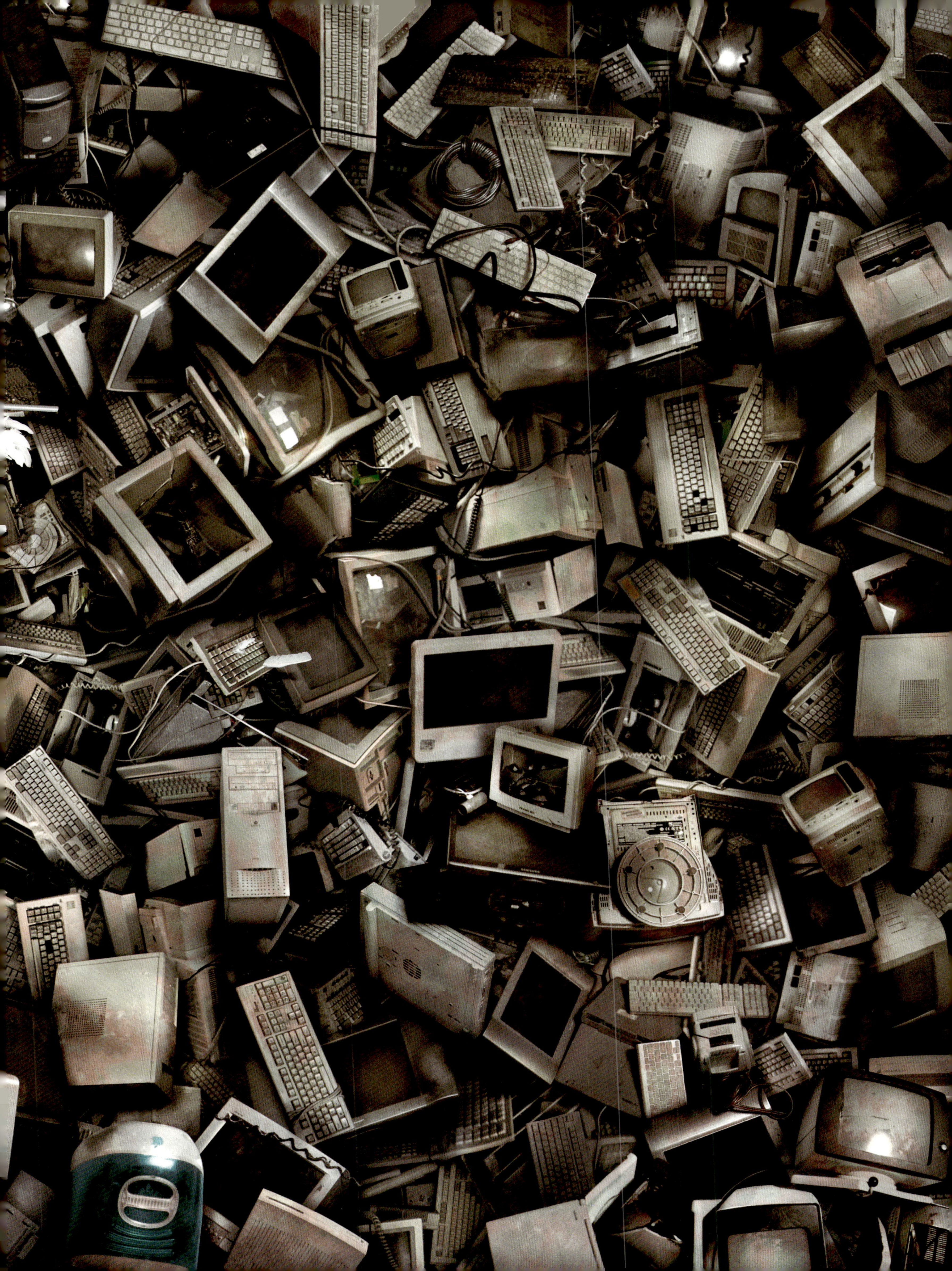

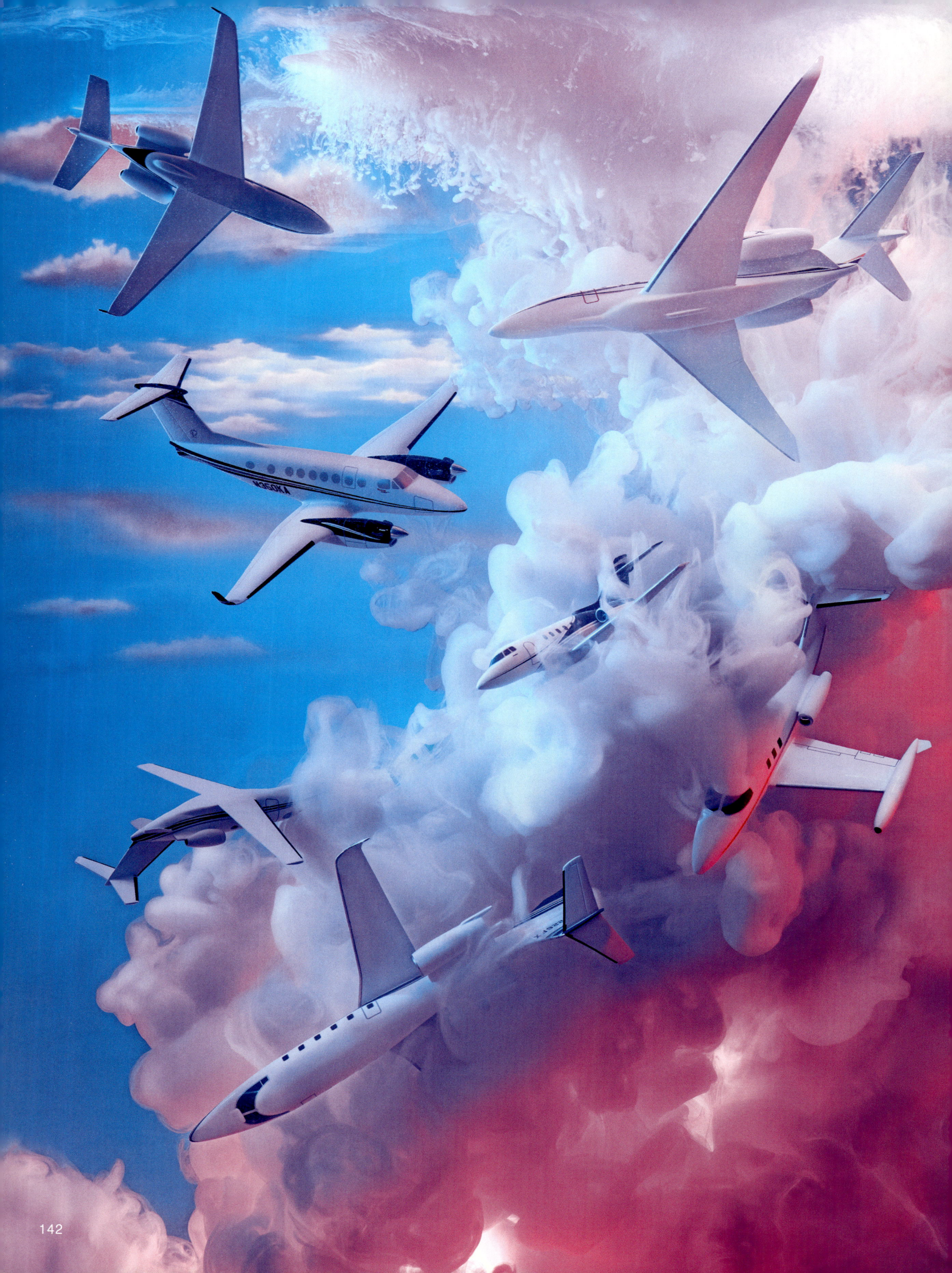
N350KA

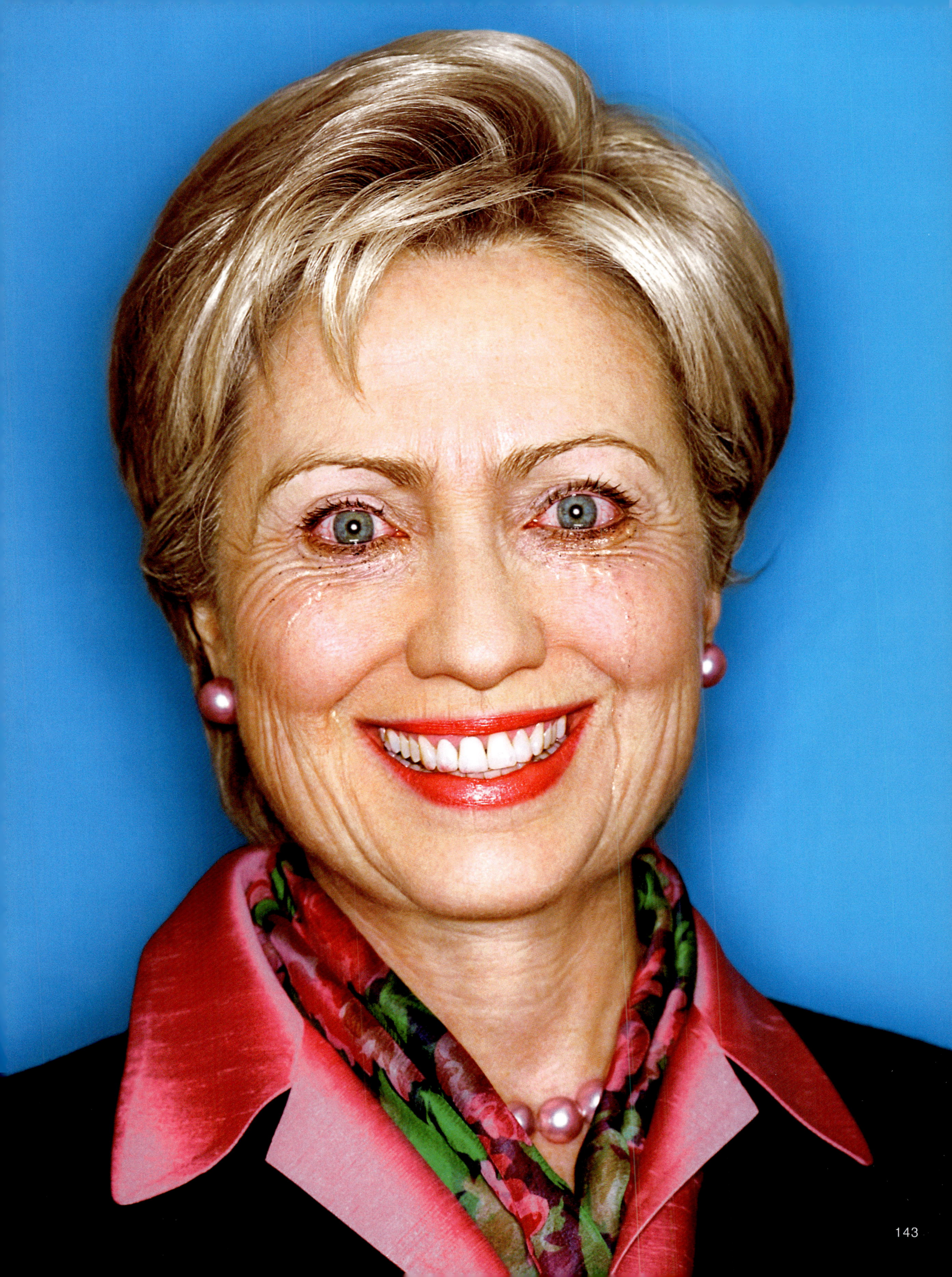

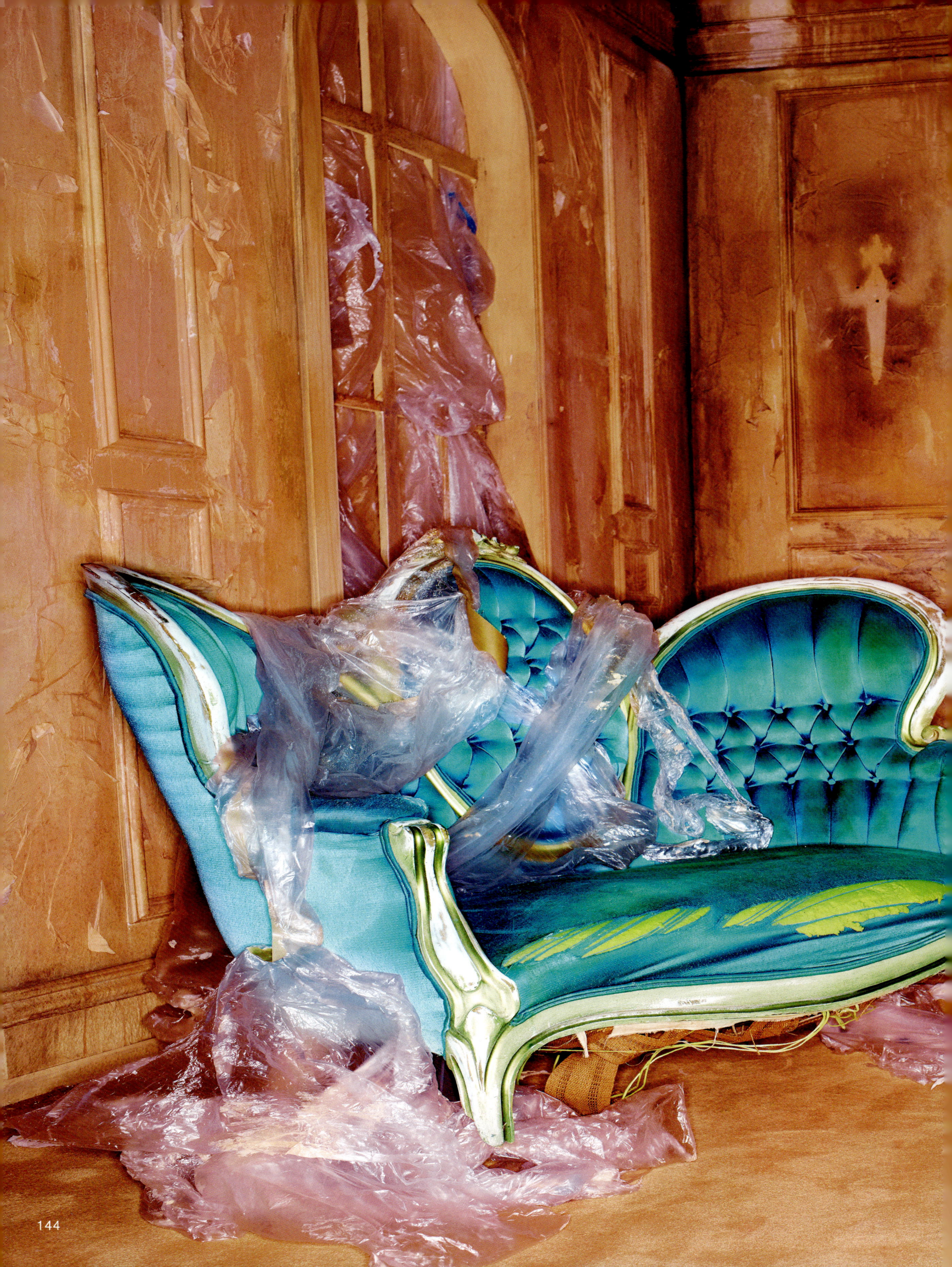

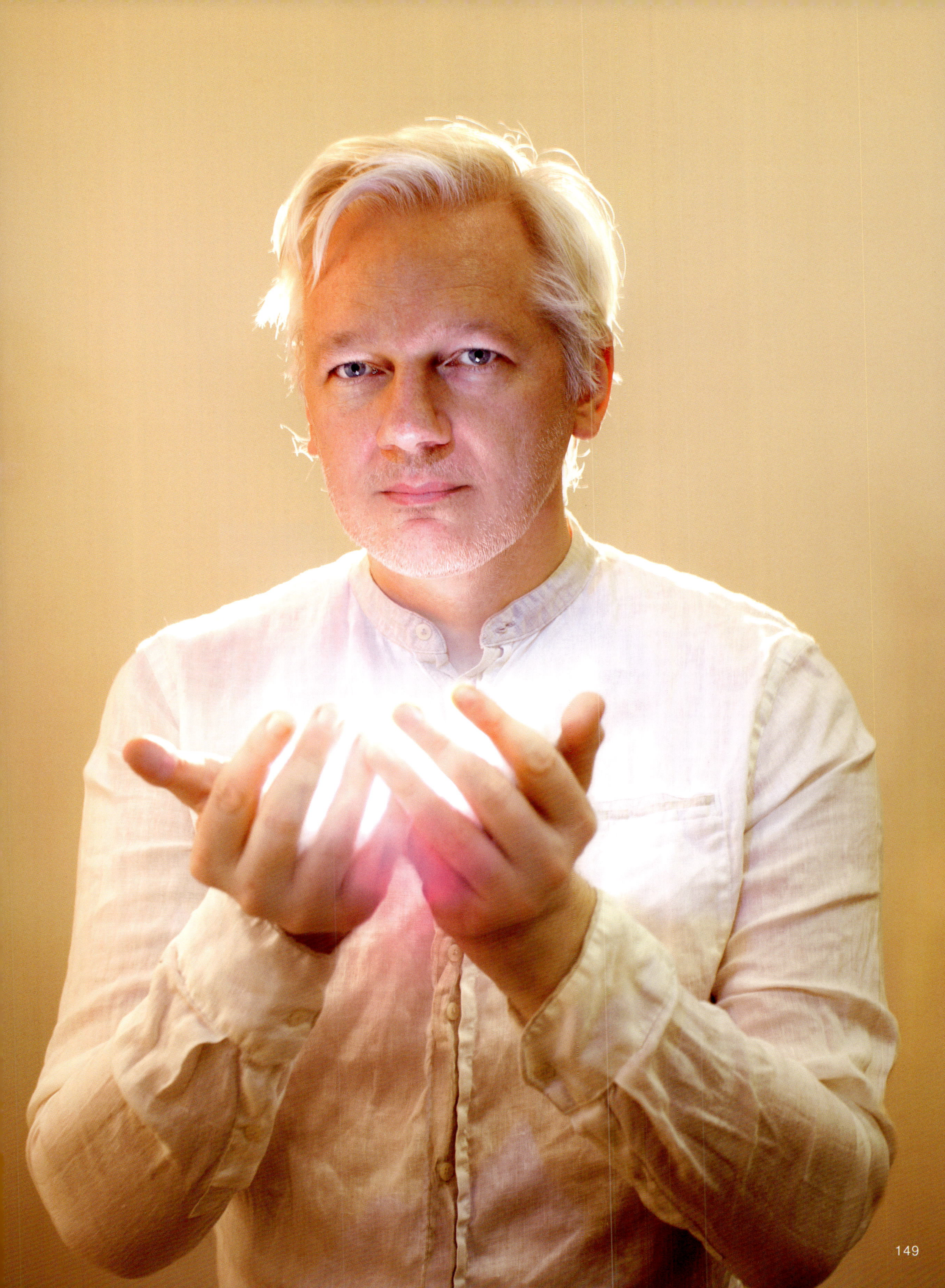

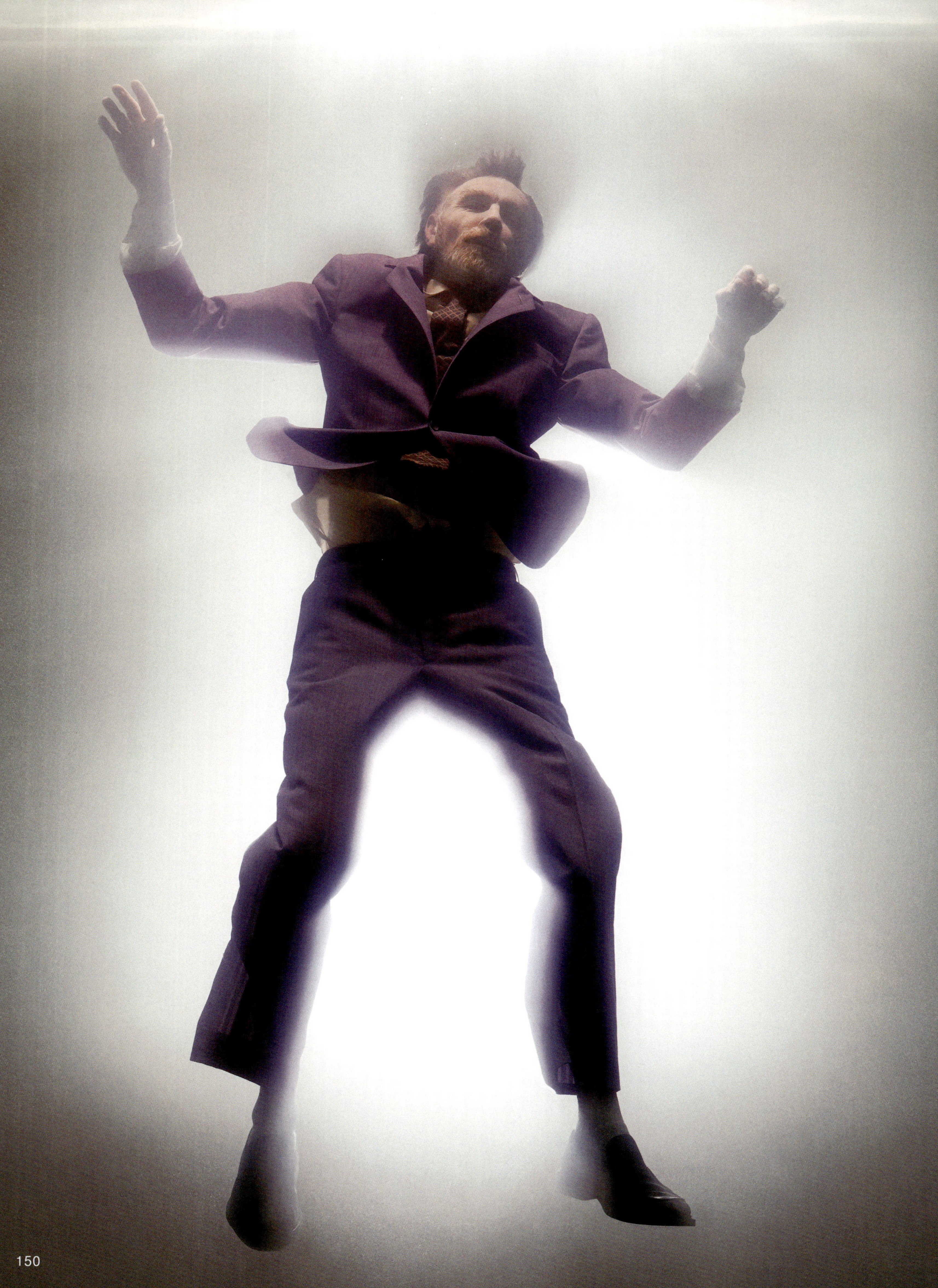

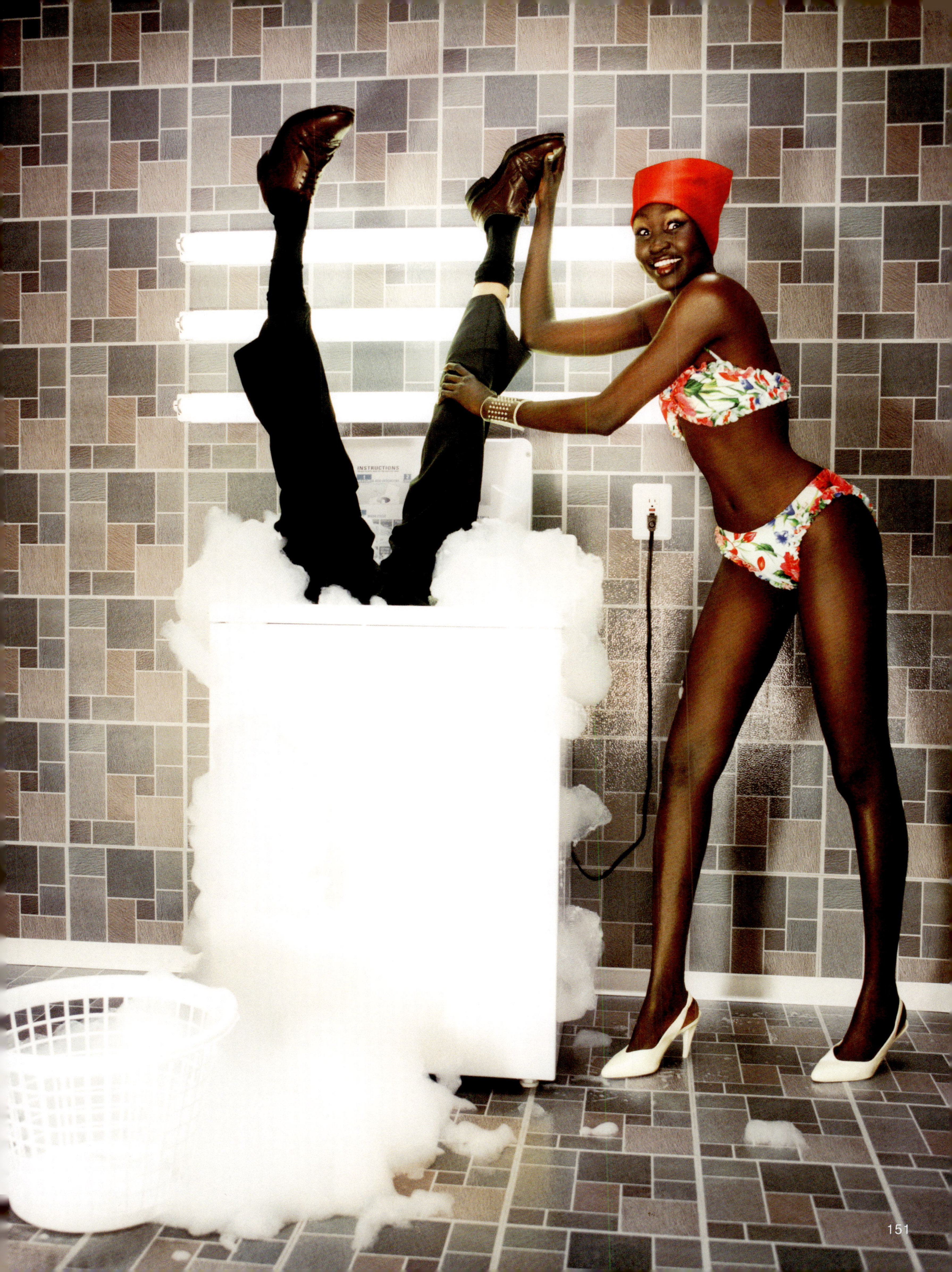
INSTRUCTIONS

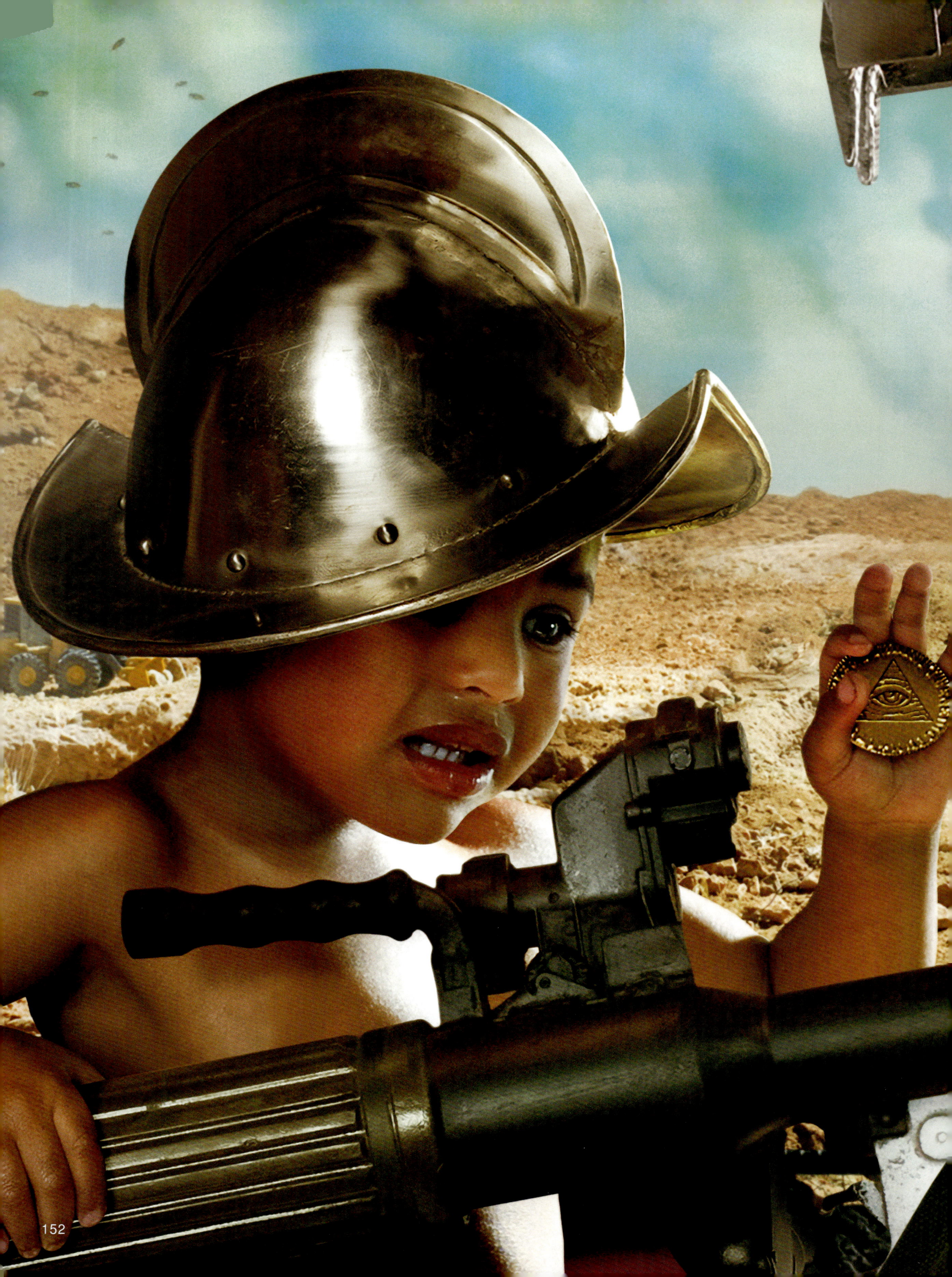

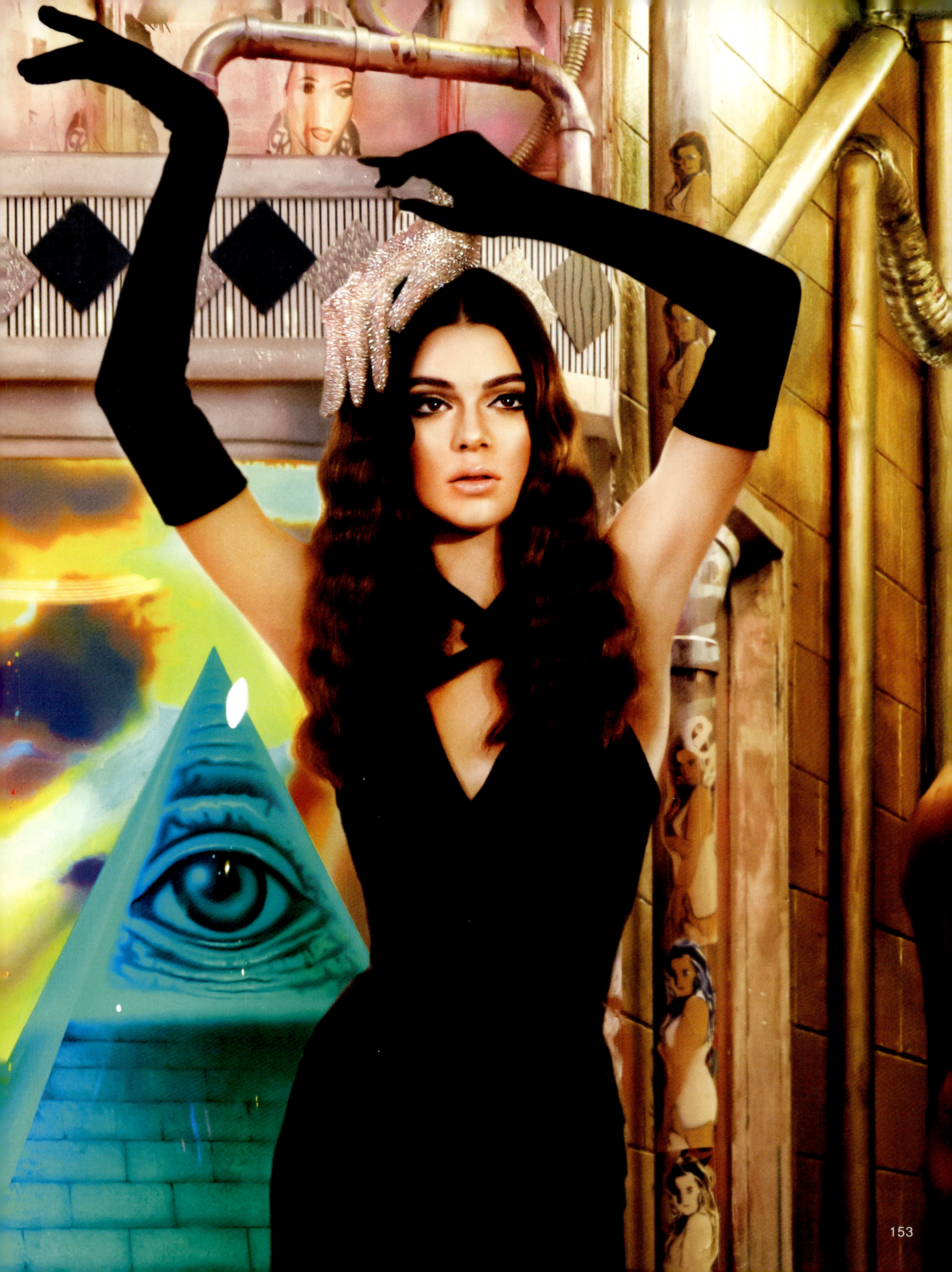

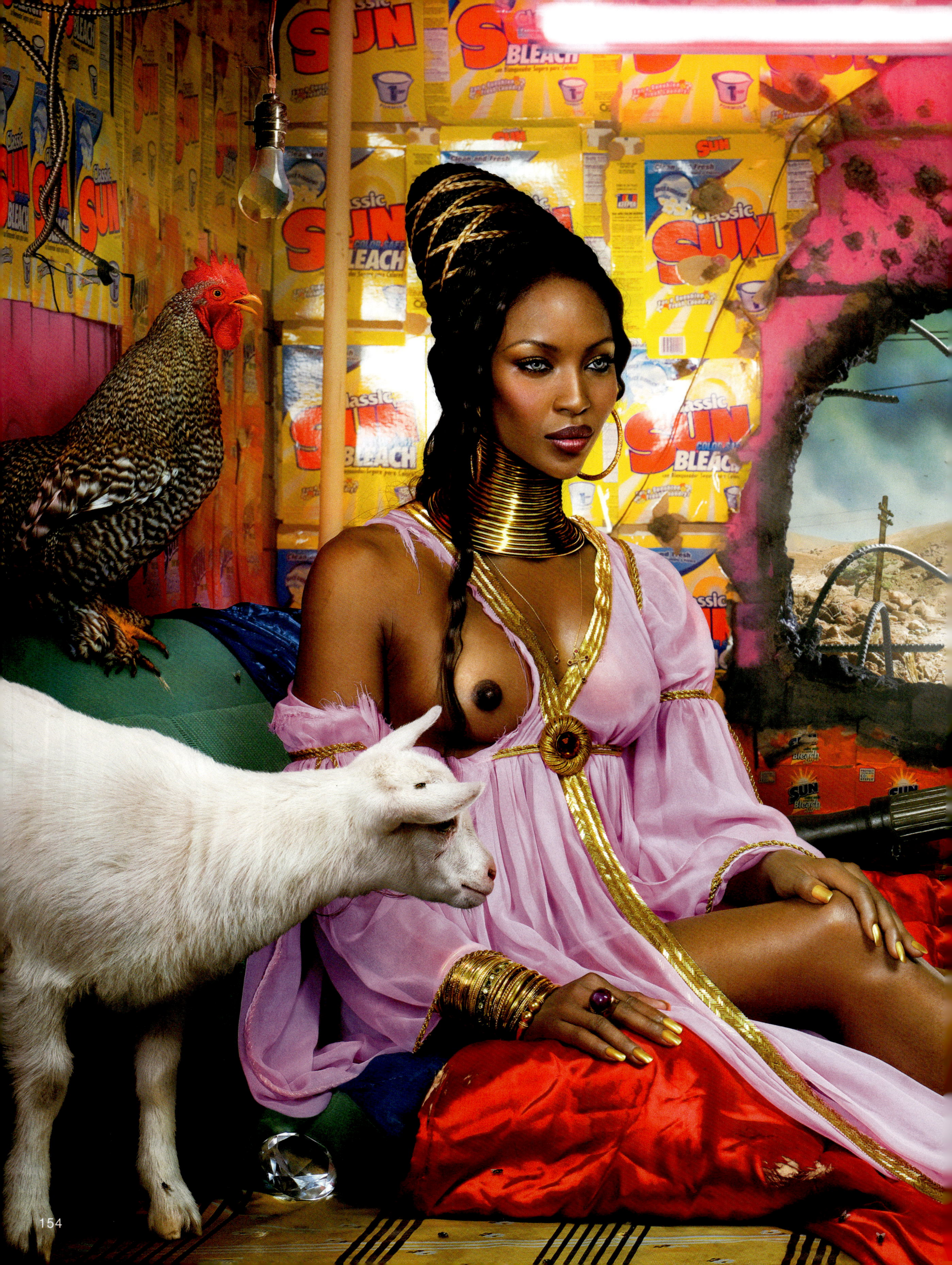
SUN
BLEACH
Classic
SUN
COLOR SAFE
BLEACH
Clean and Fresh

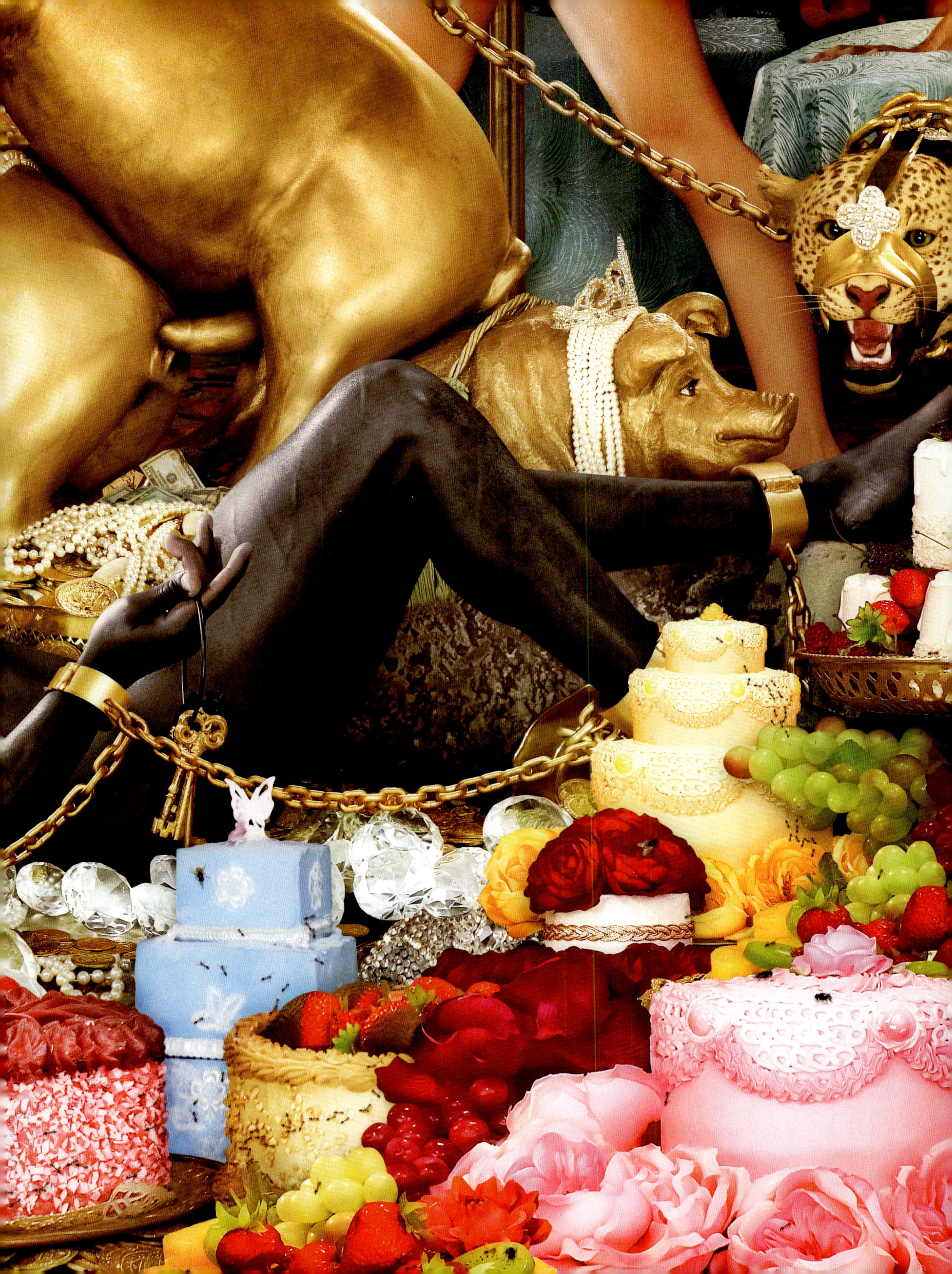

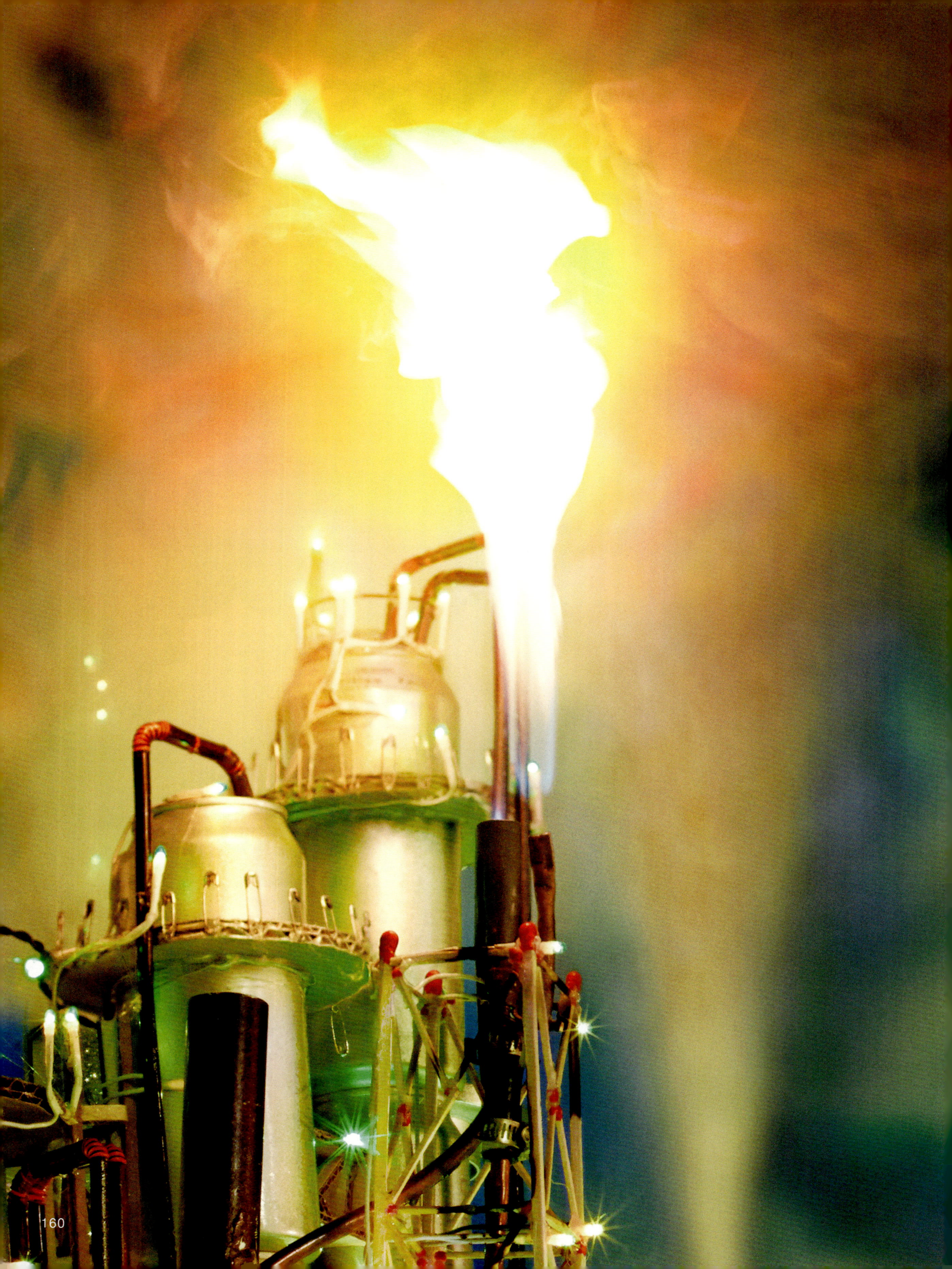

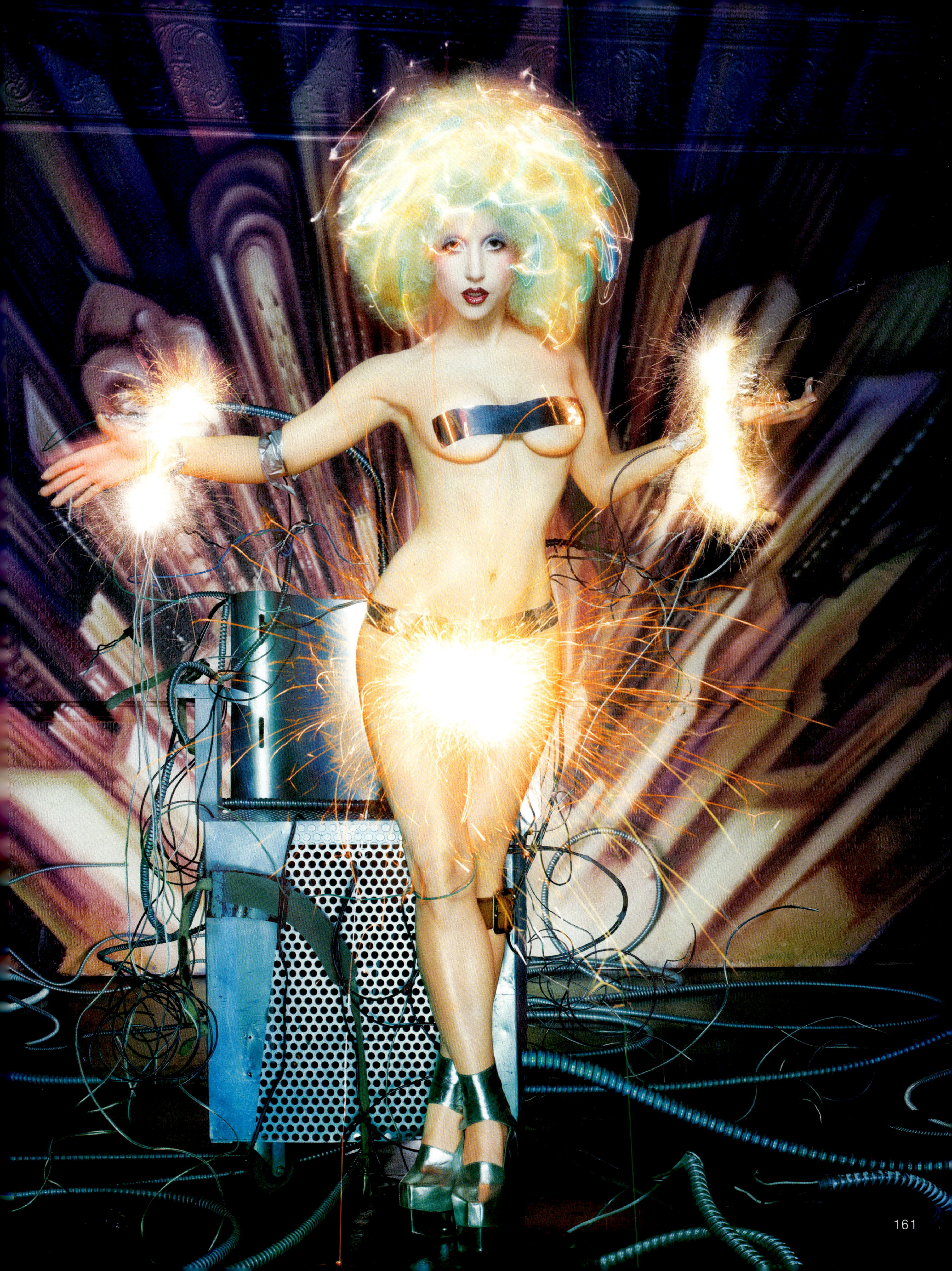

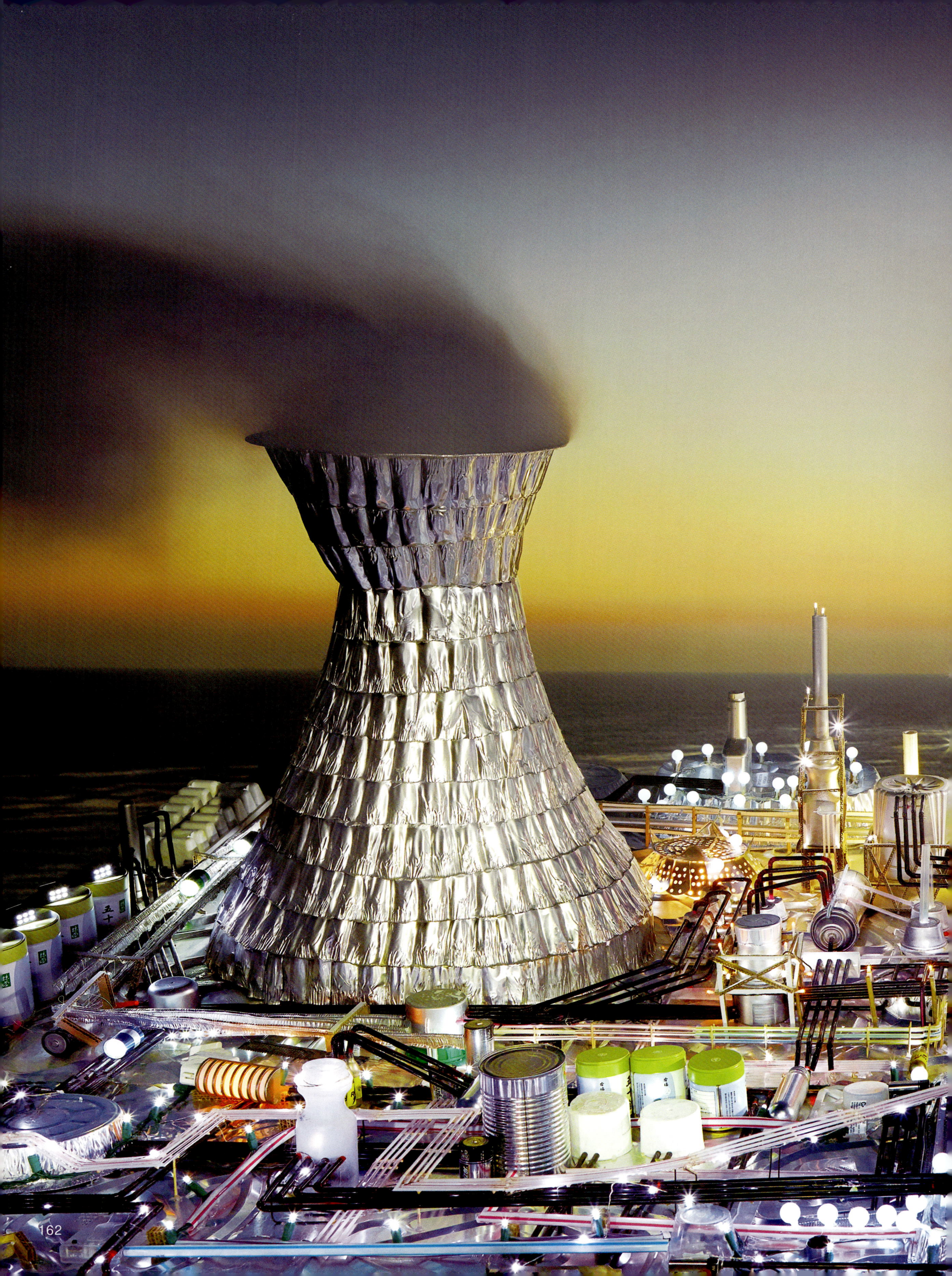

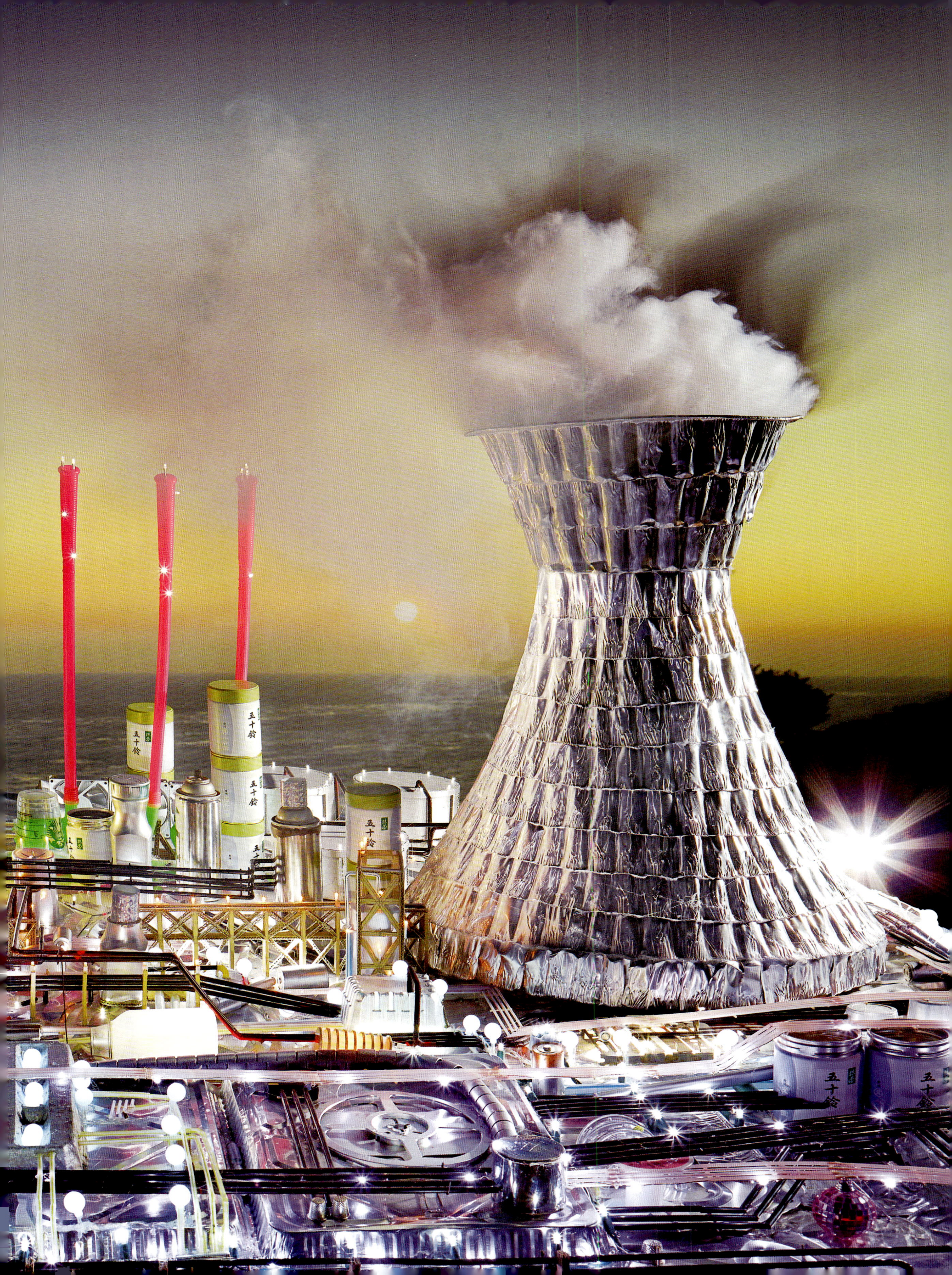
五十鈴

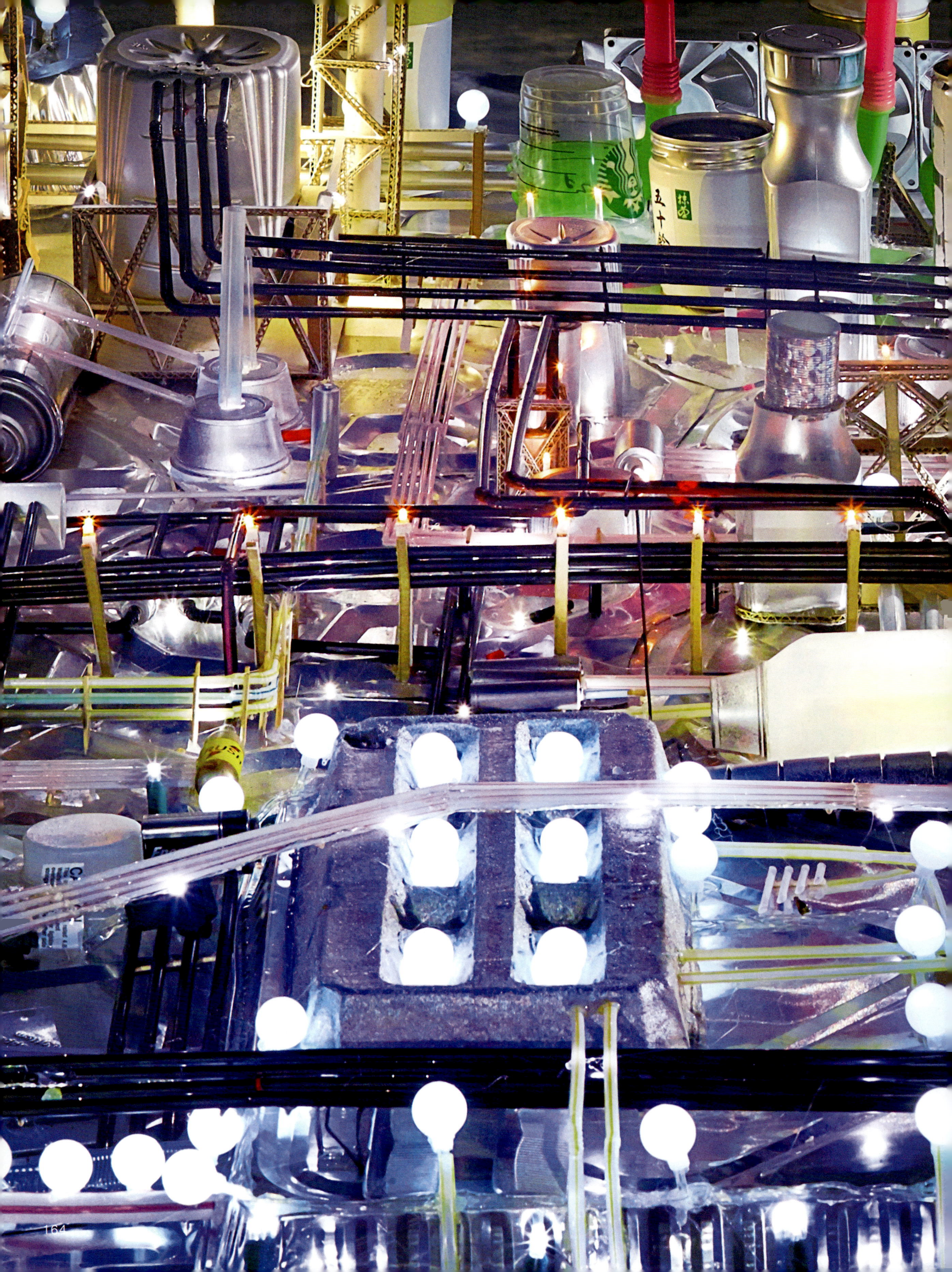

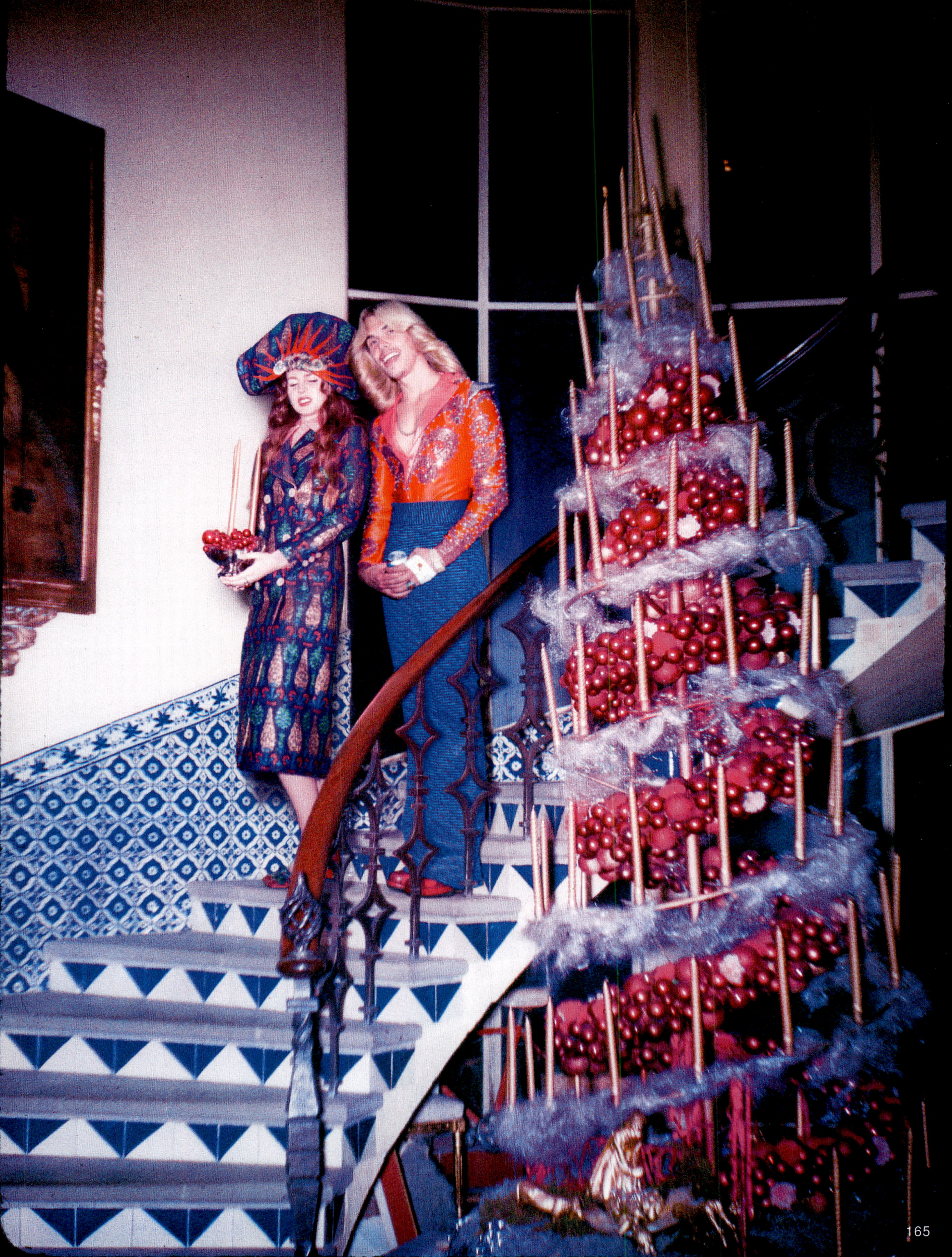

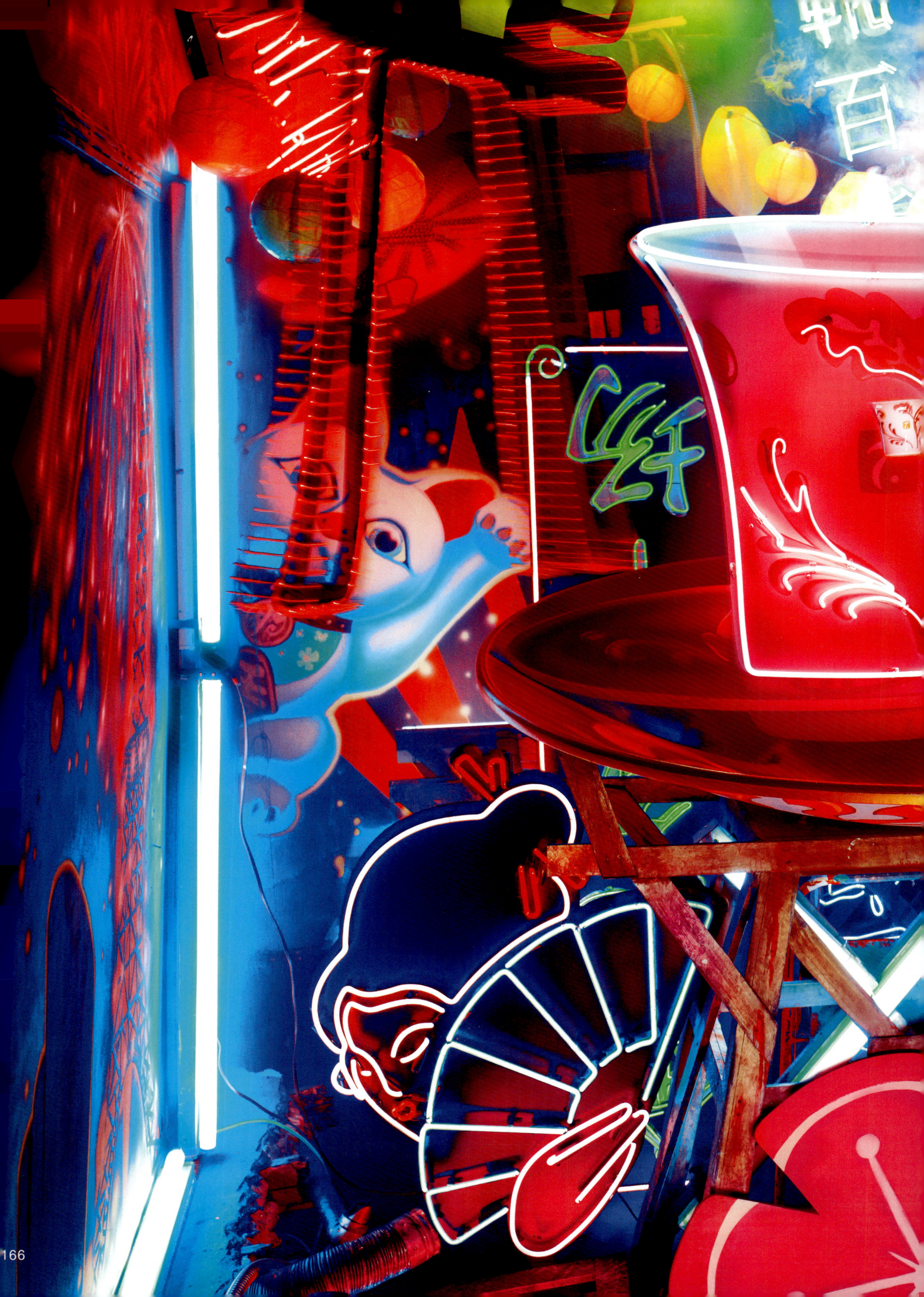

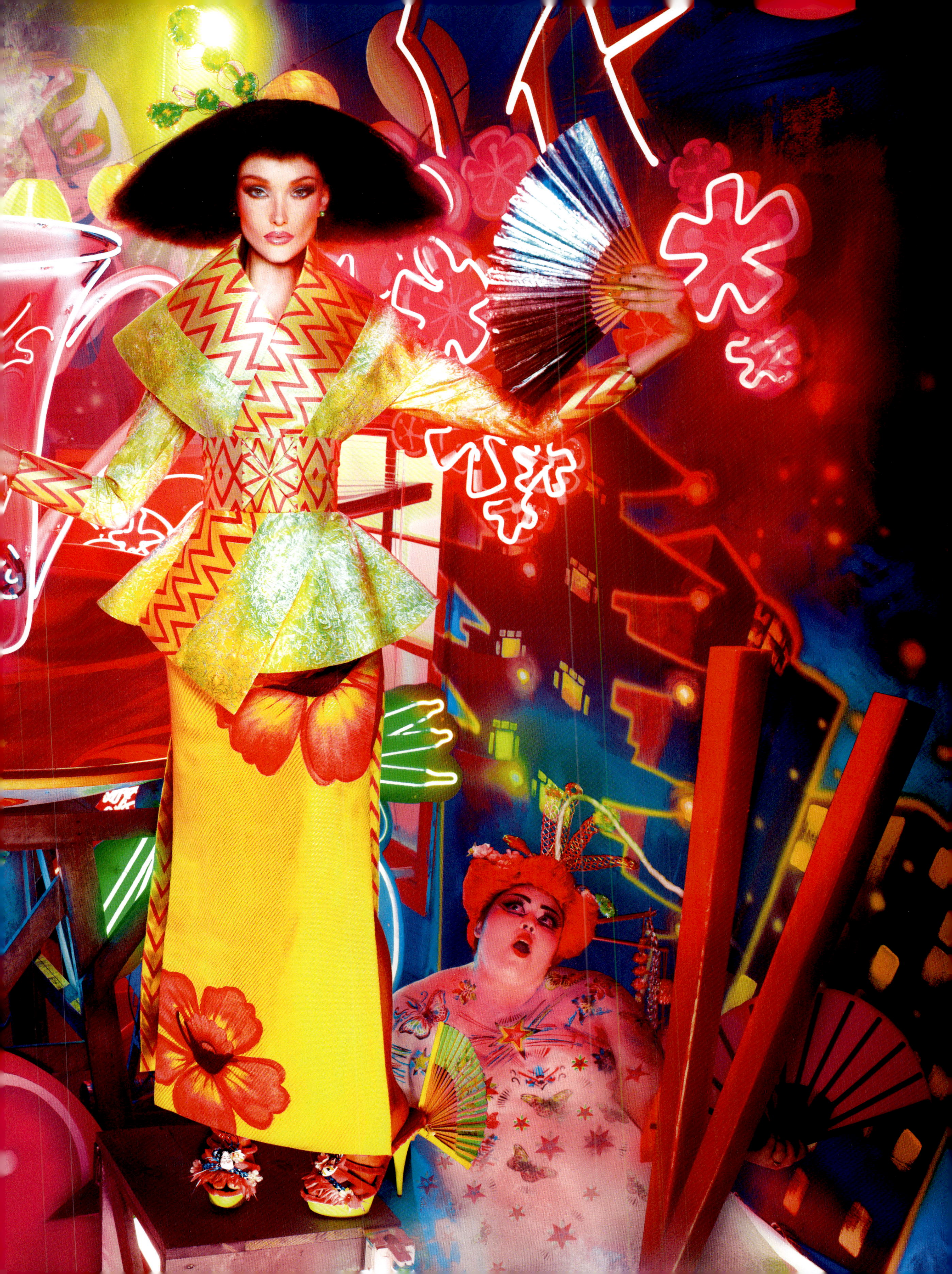

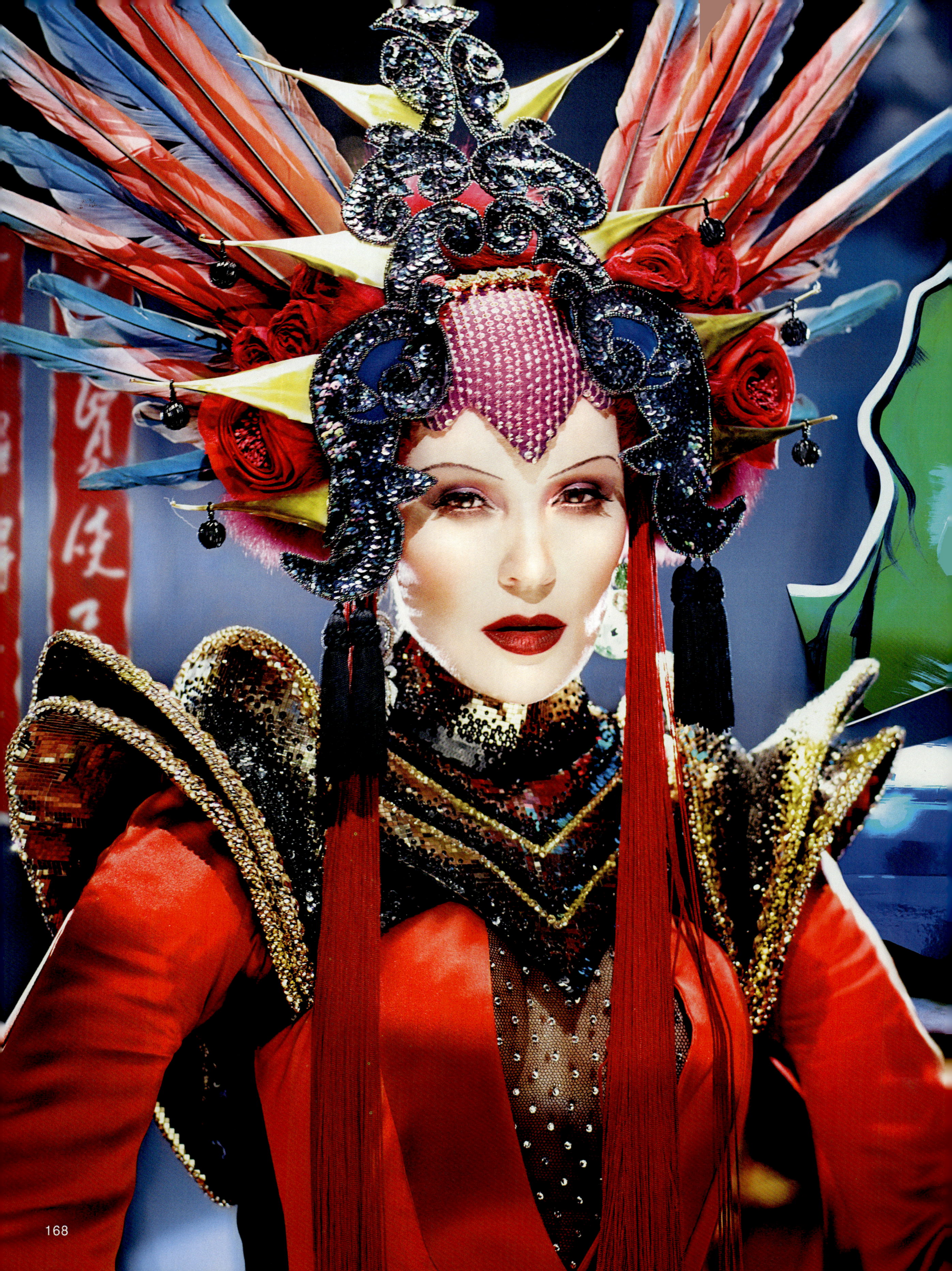

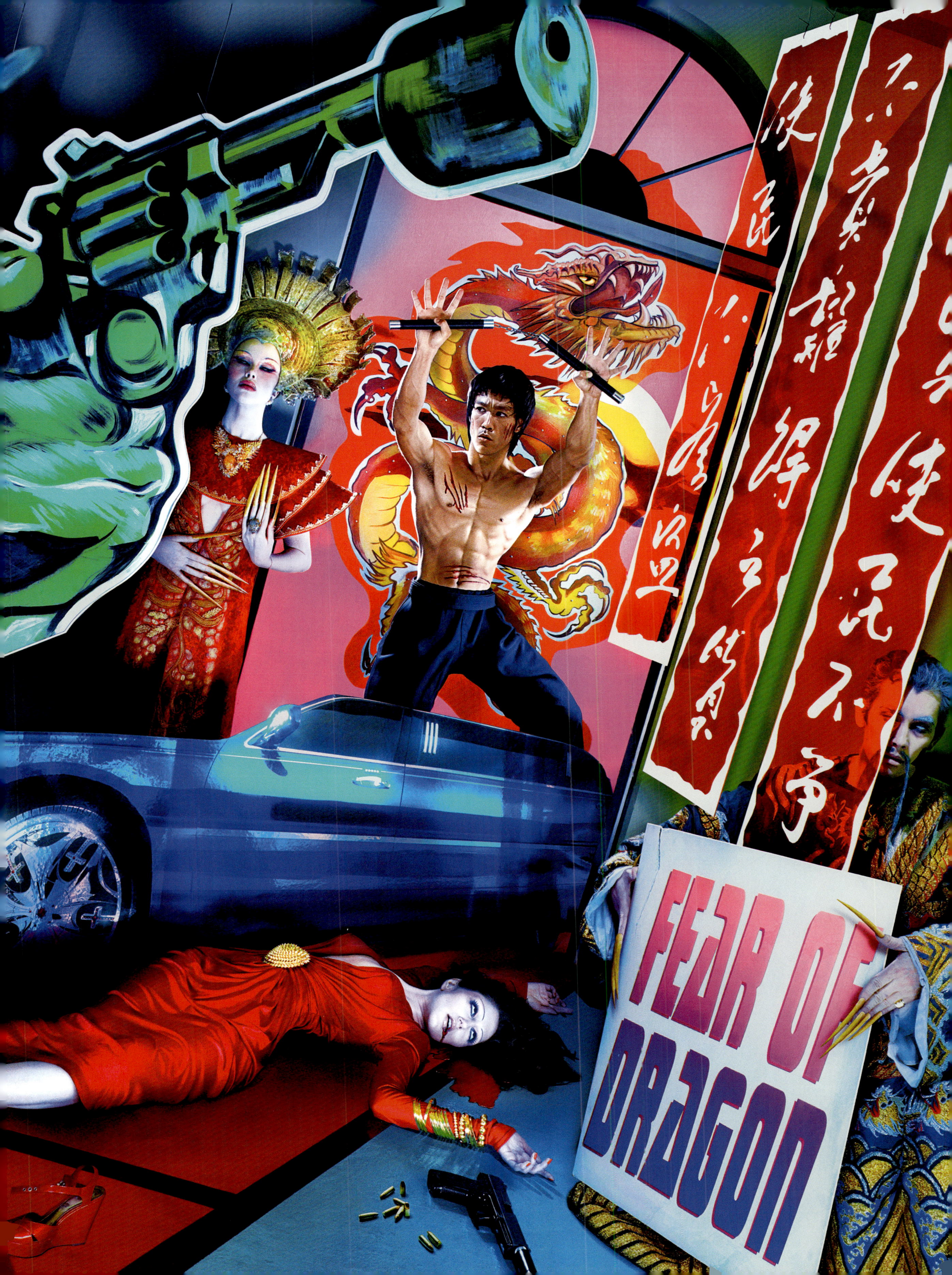
FEAR OF
DRAGON

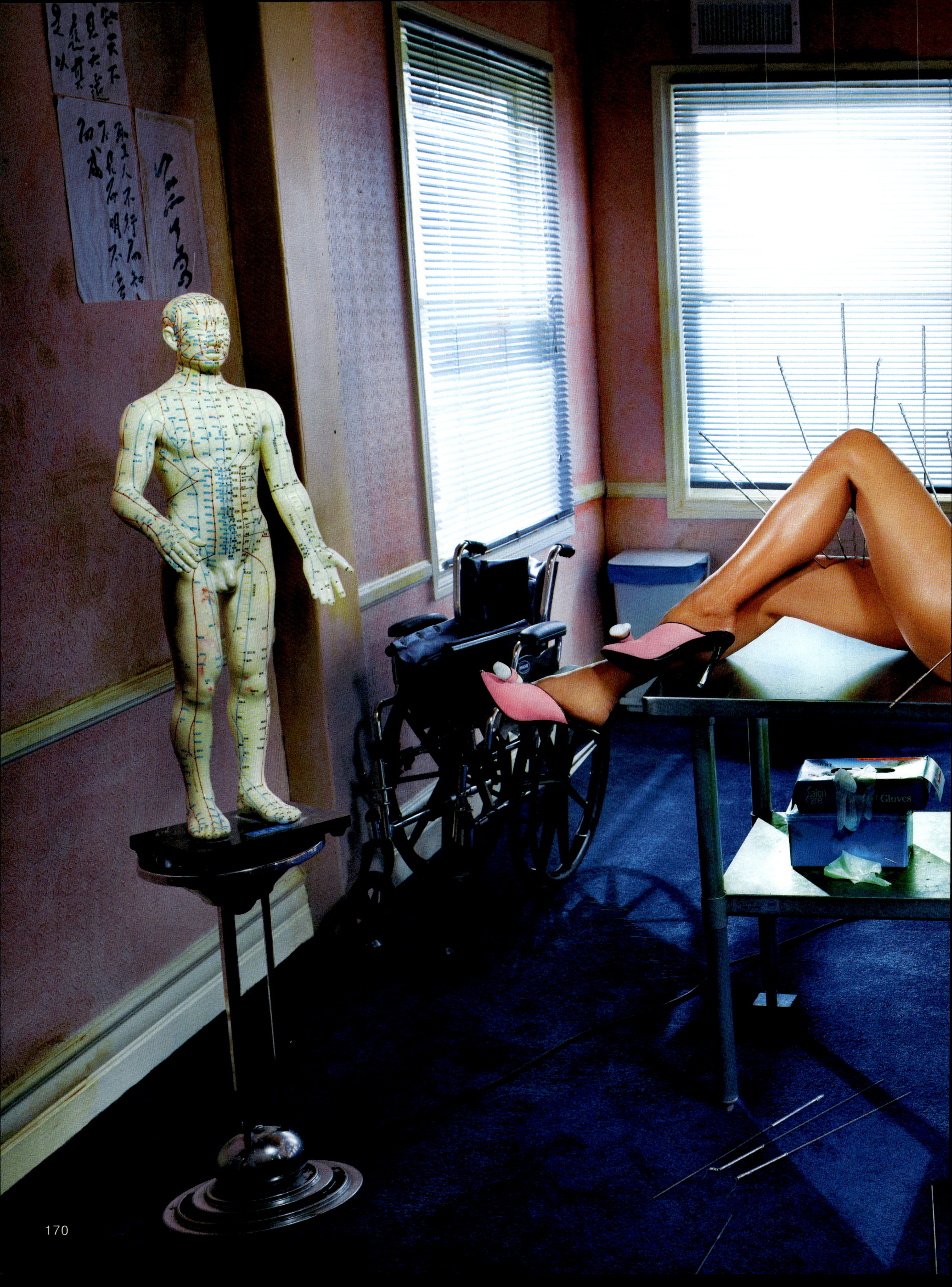
Gloves

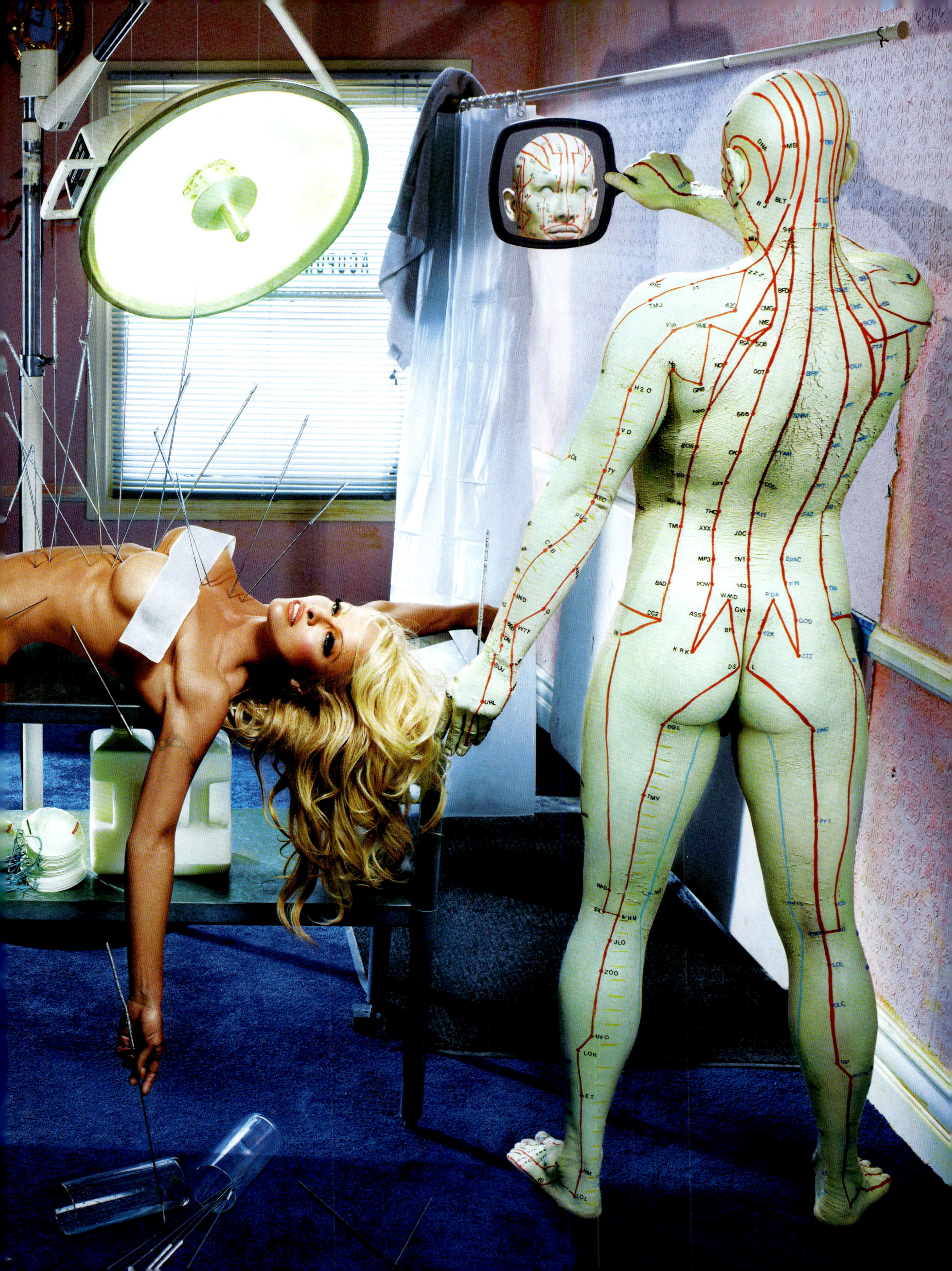

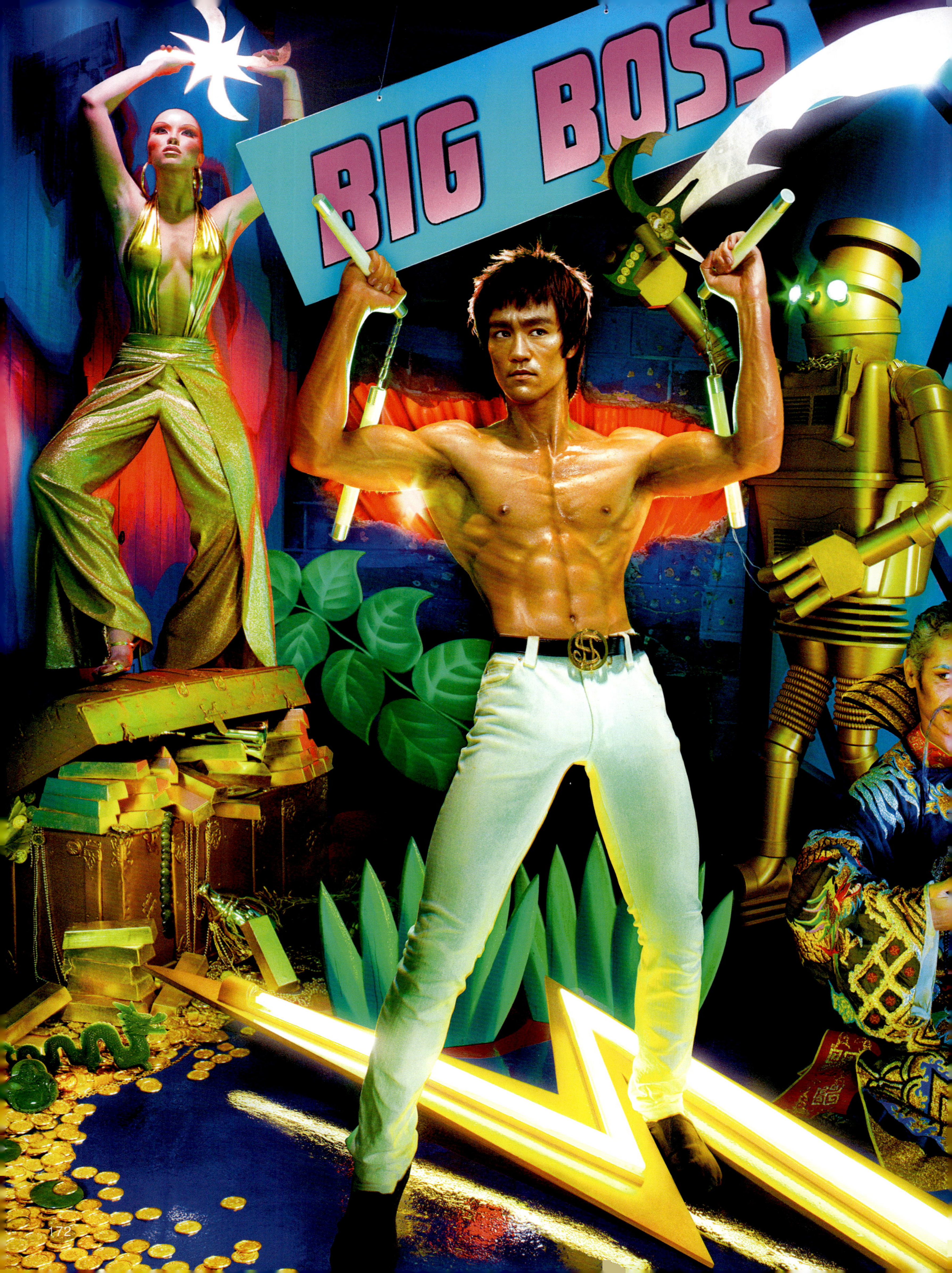
BIG BOSS

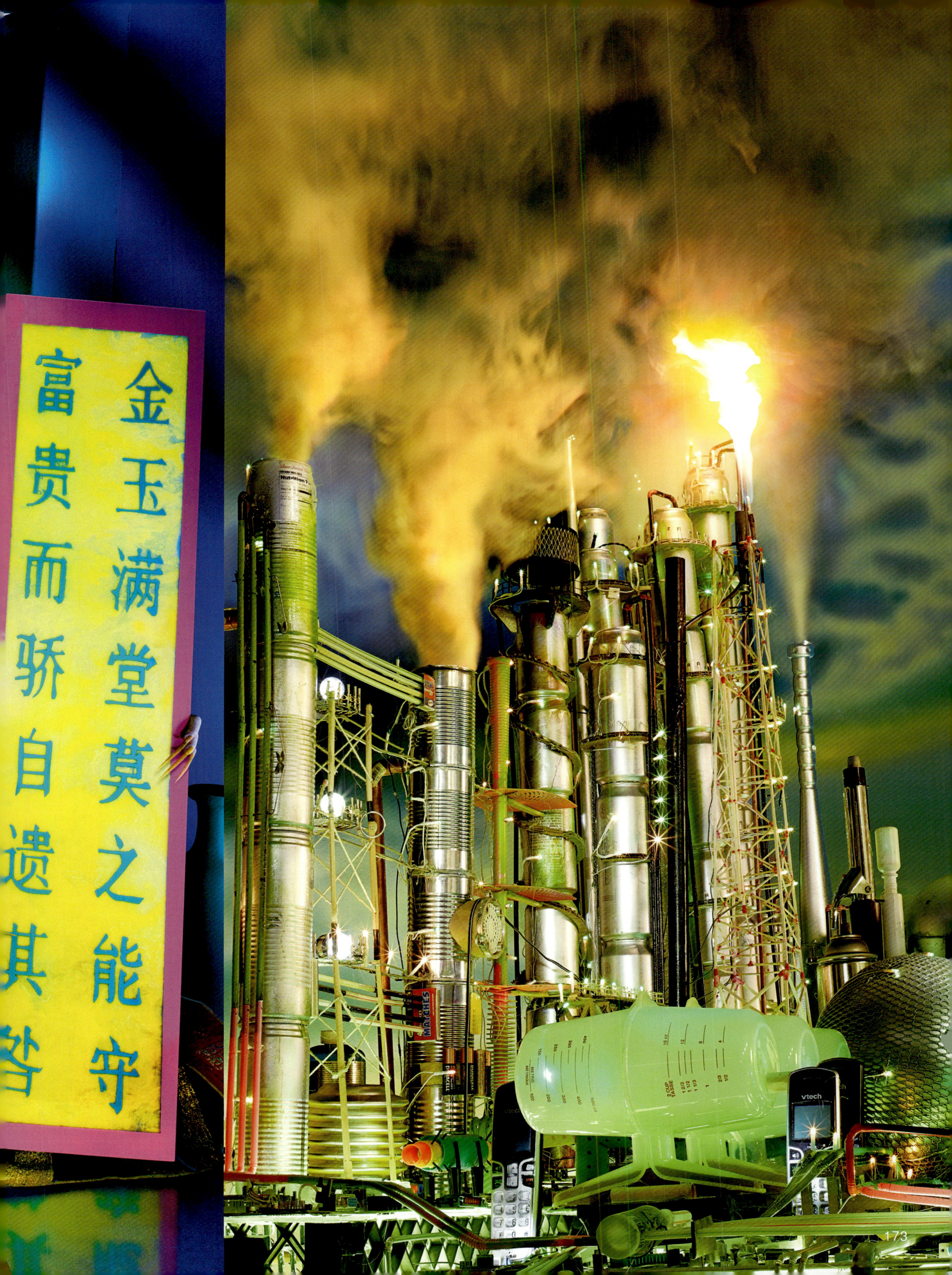
金玉满堂莫之能守
富贵而骄自遗其
MATCHES
vtech

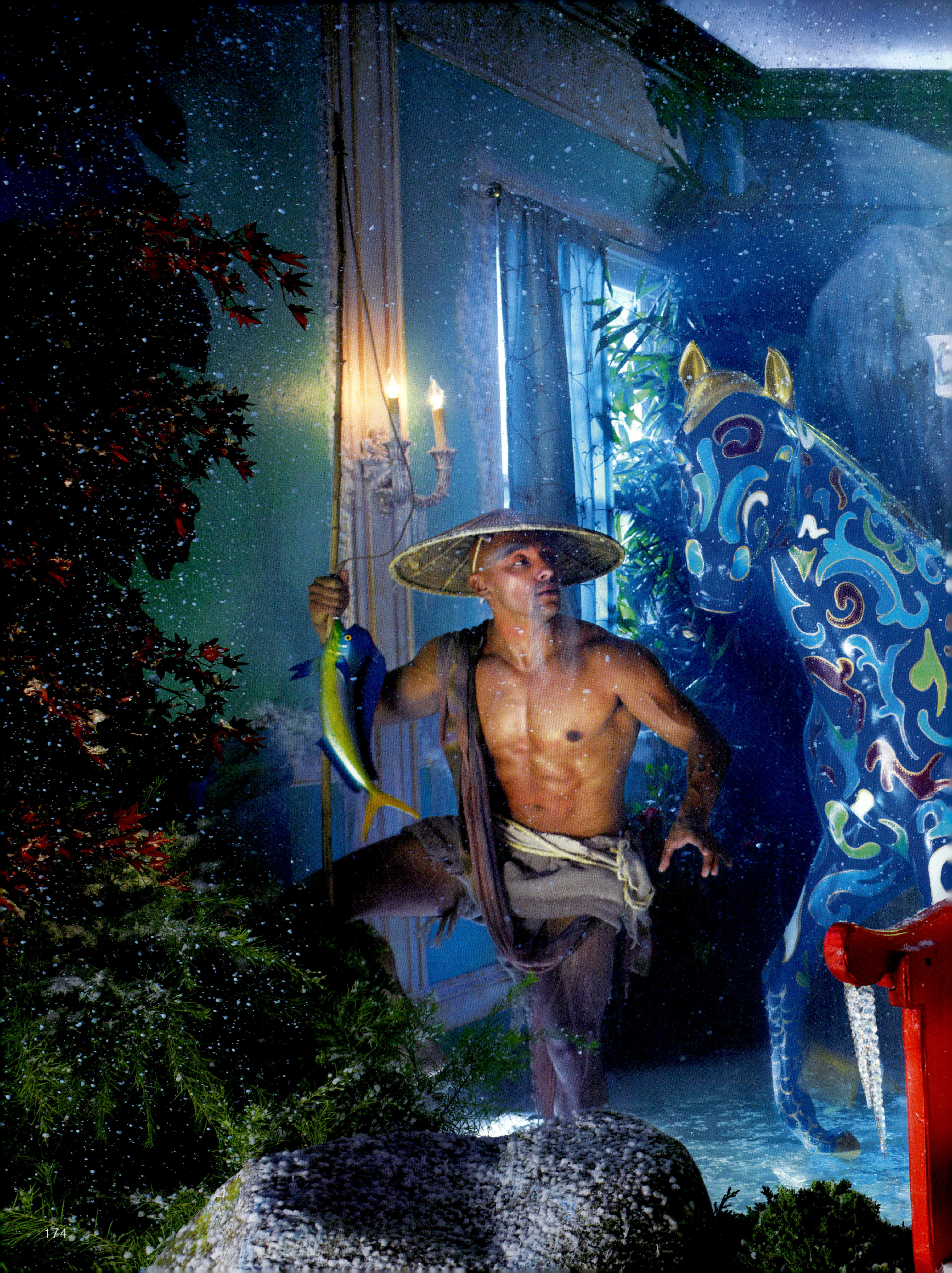

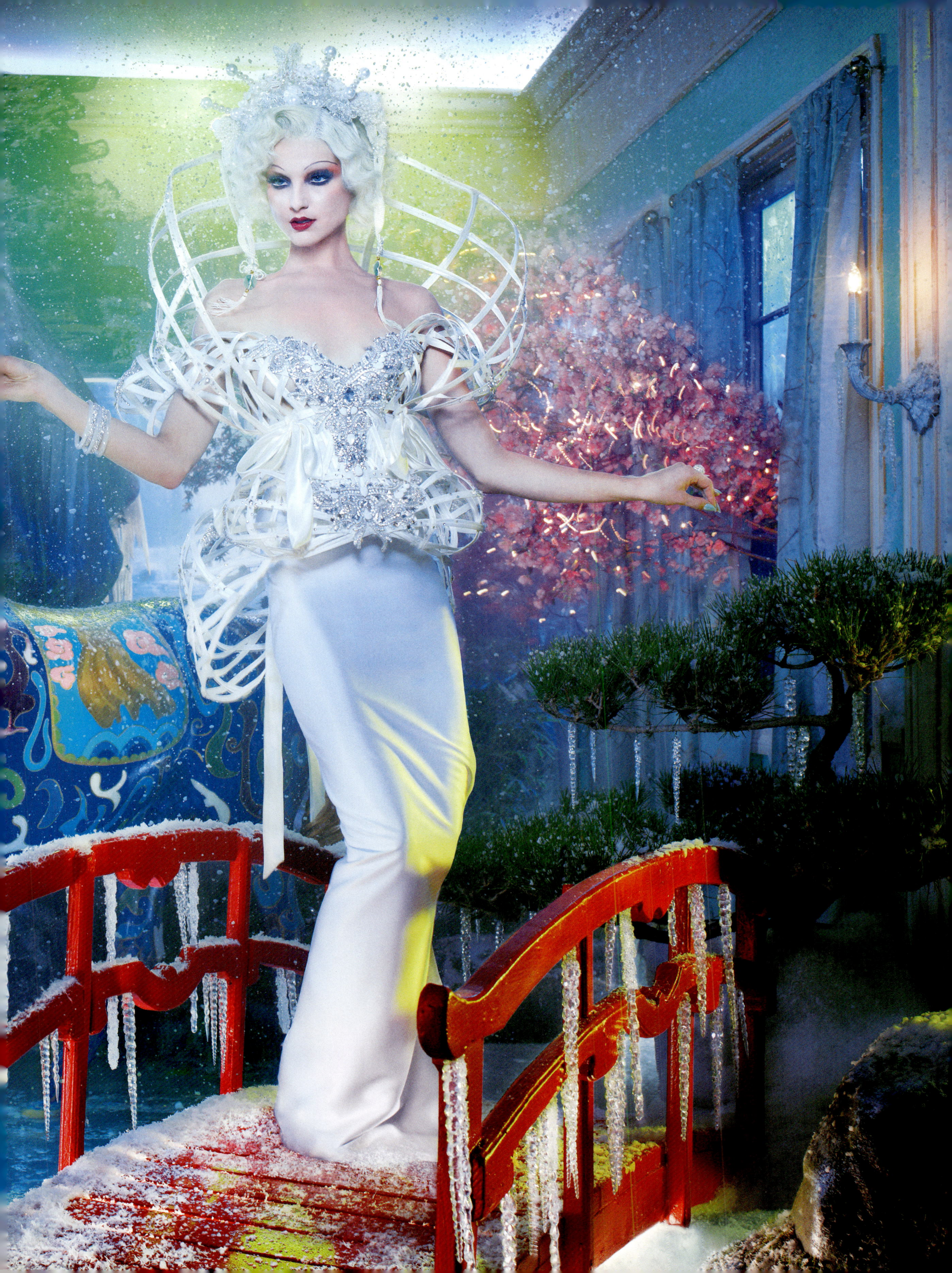

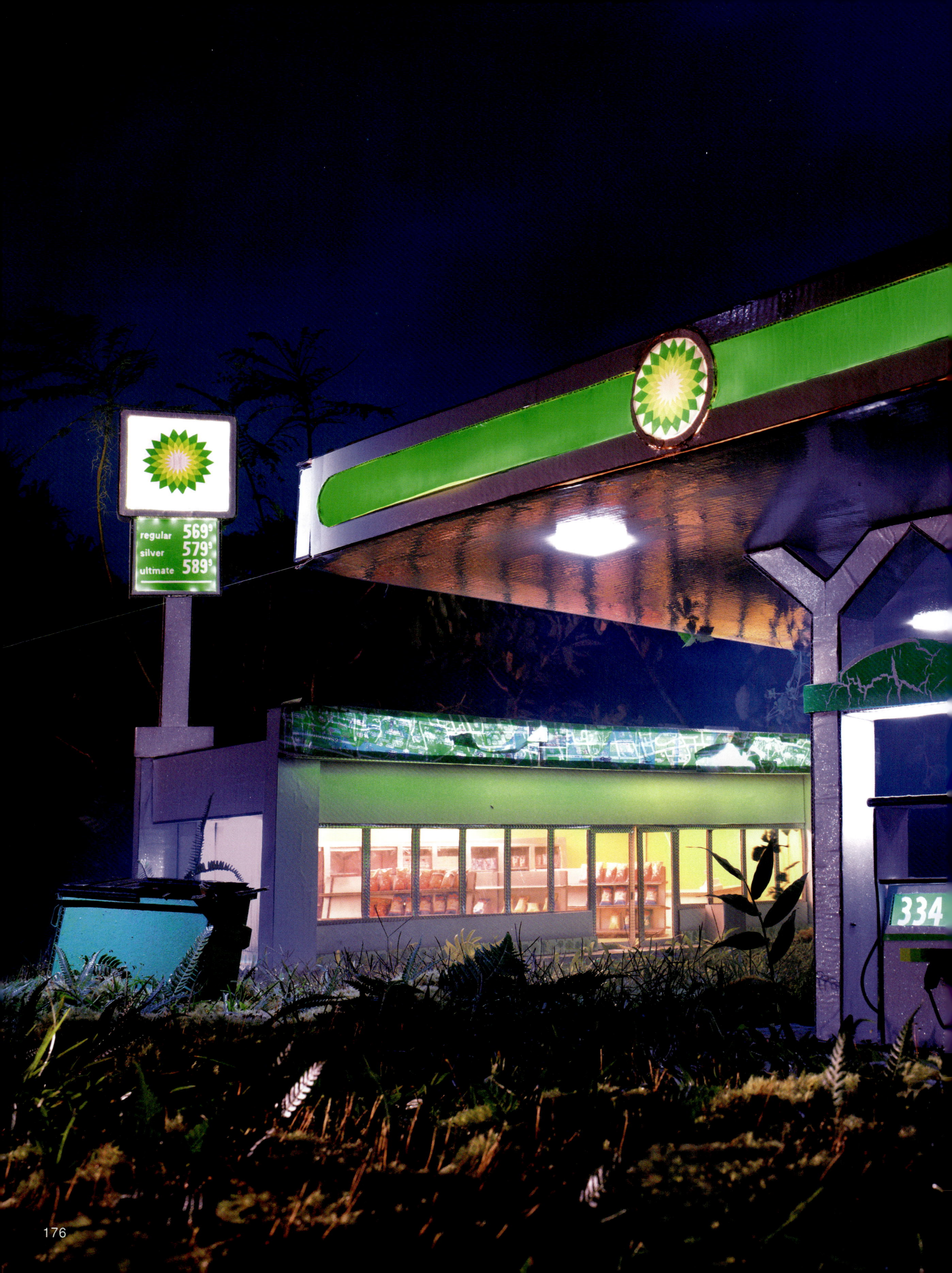
regular 569⁹
silver 579⁹
ultmate 589⁹
334

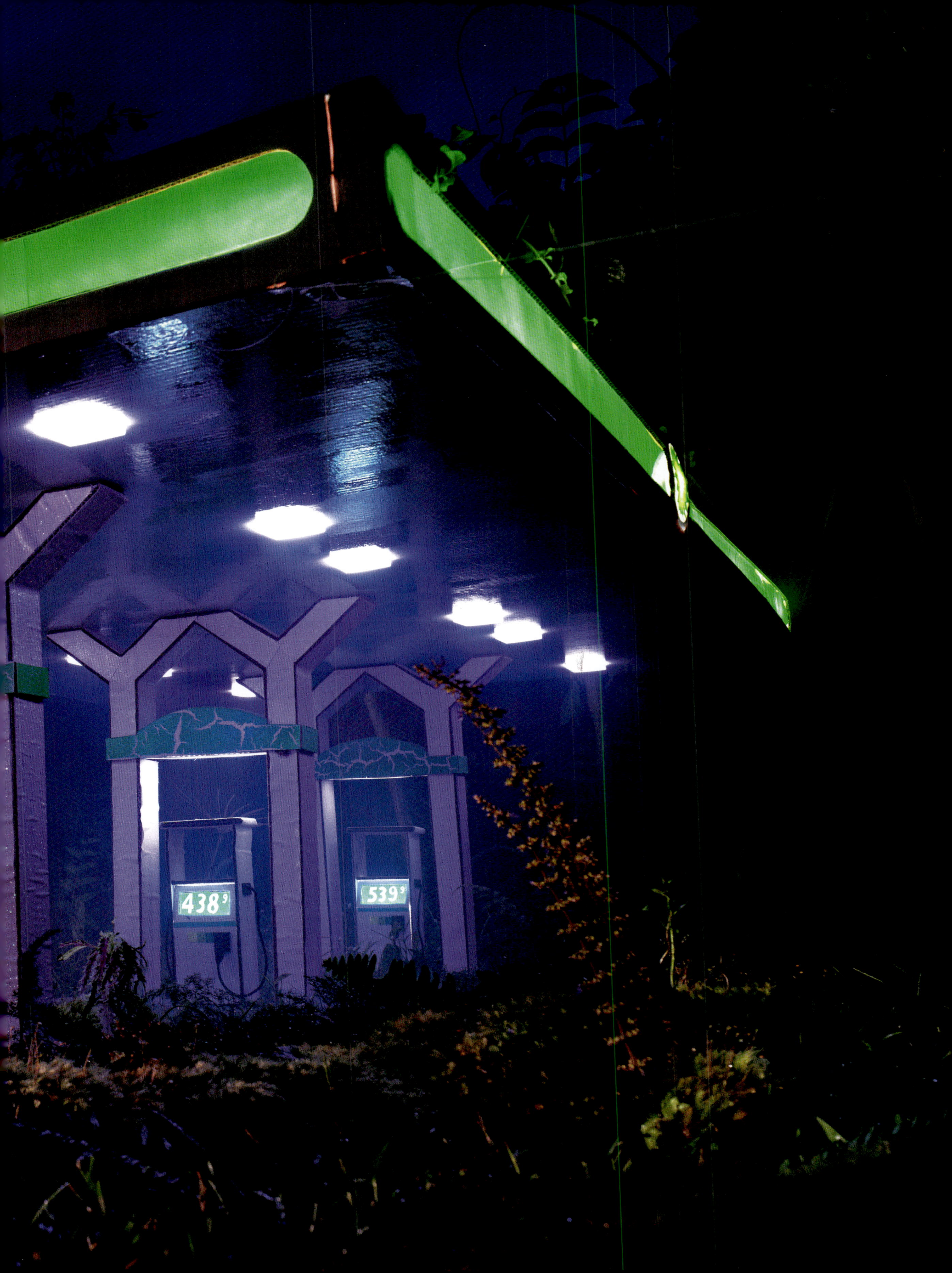
438 9
539 9

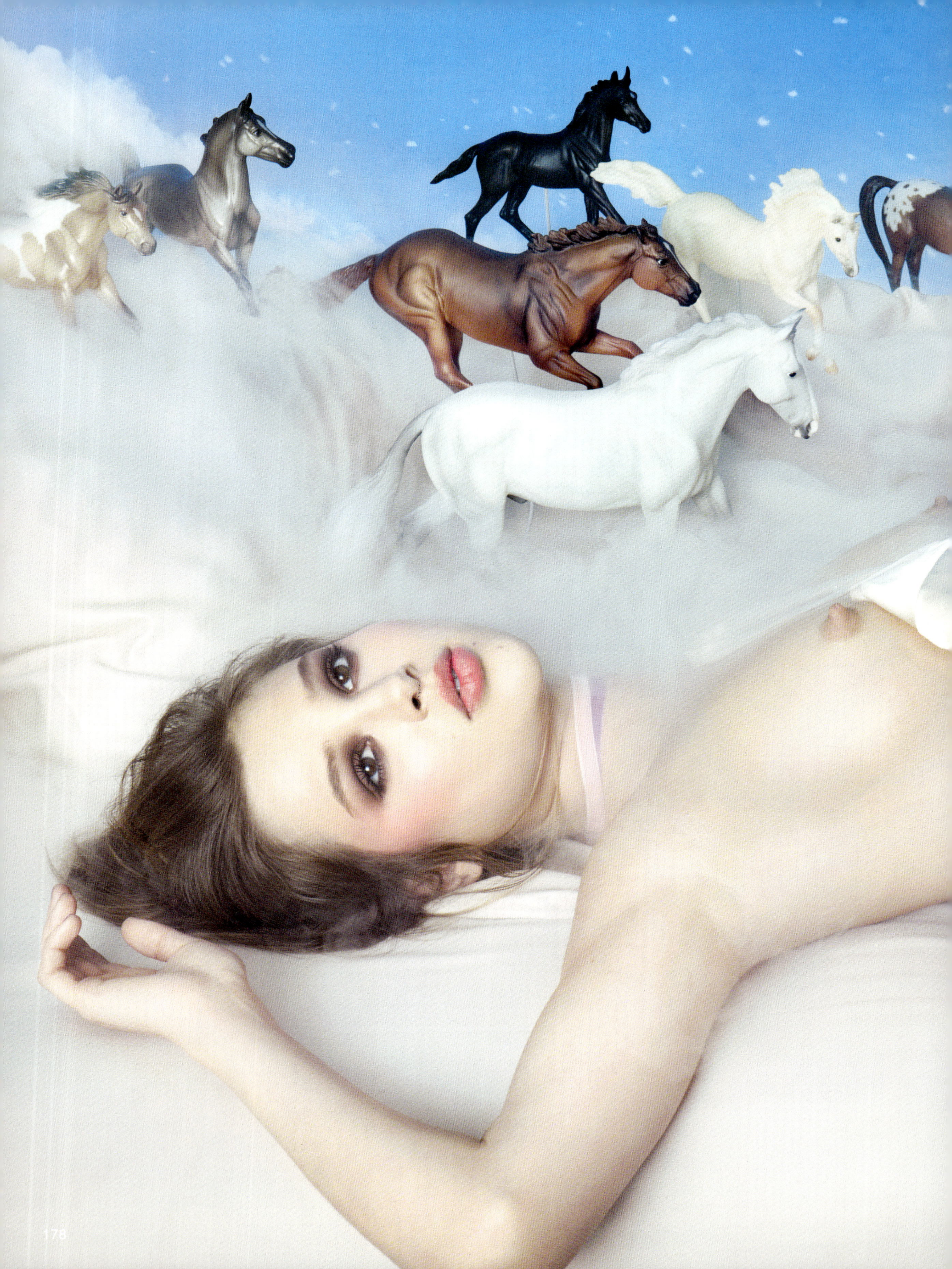

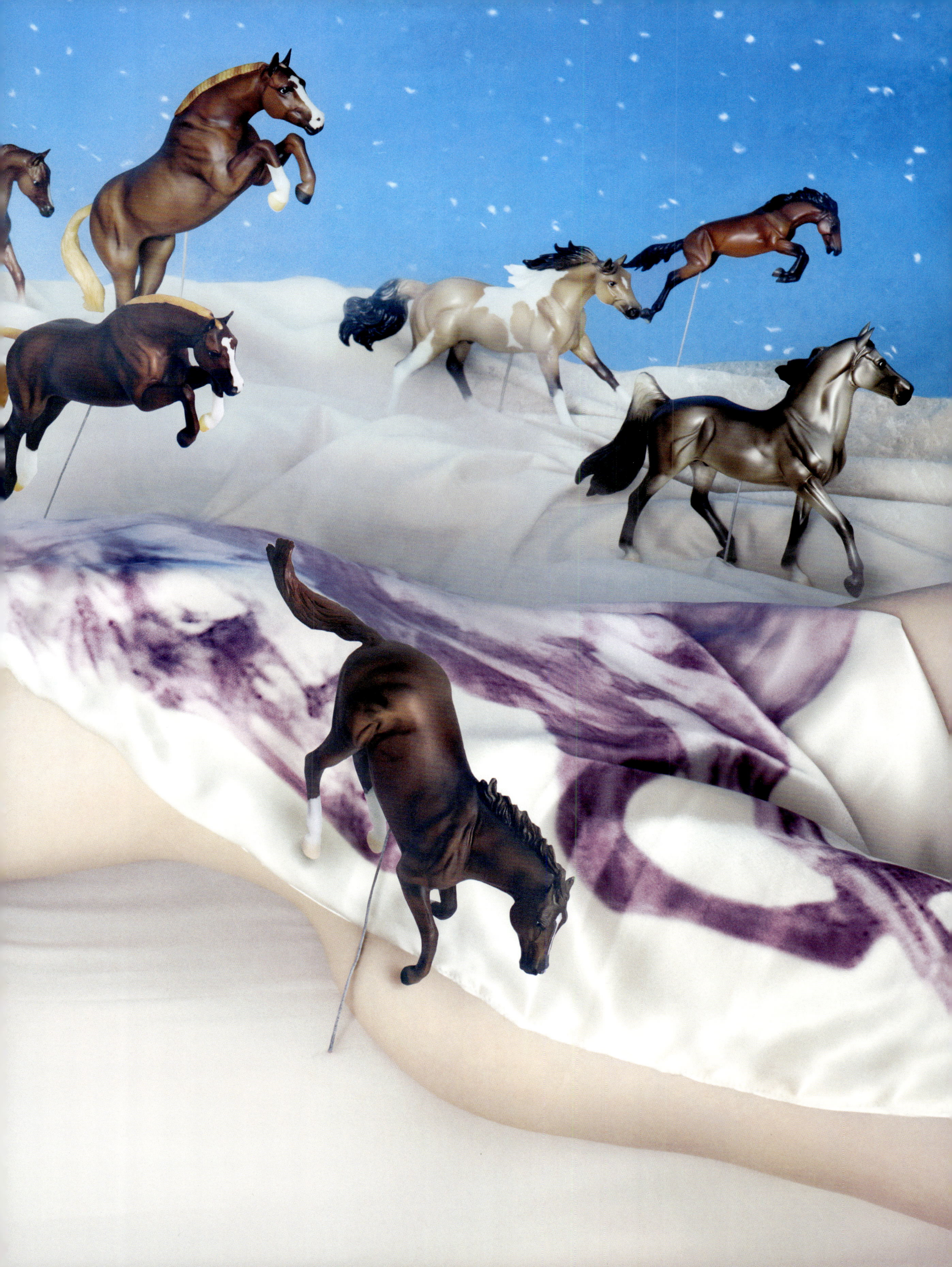

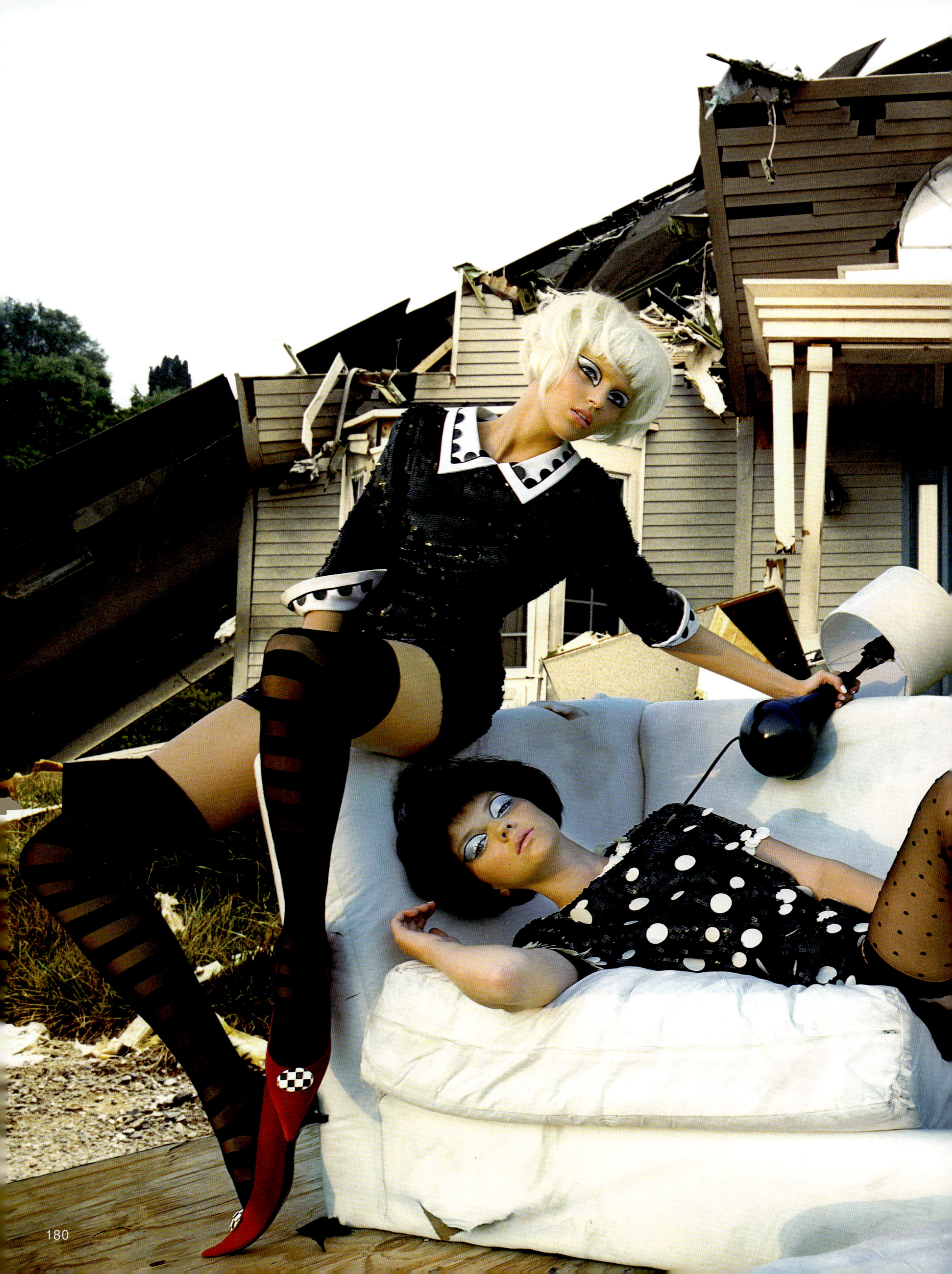

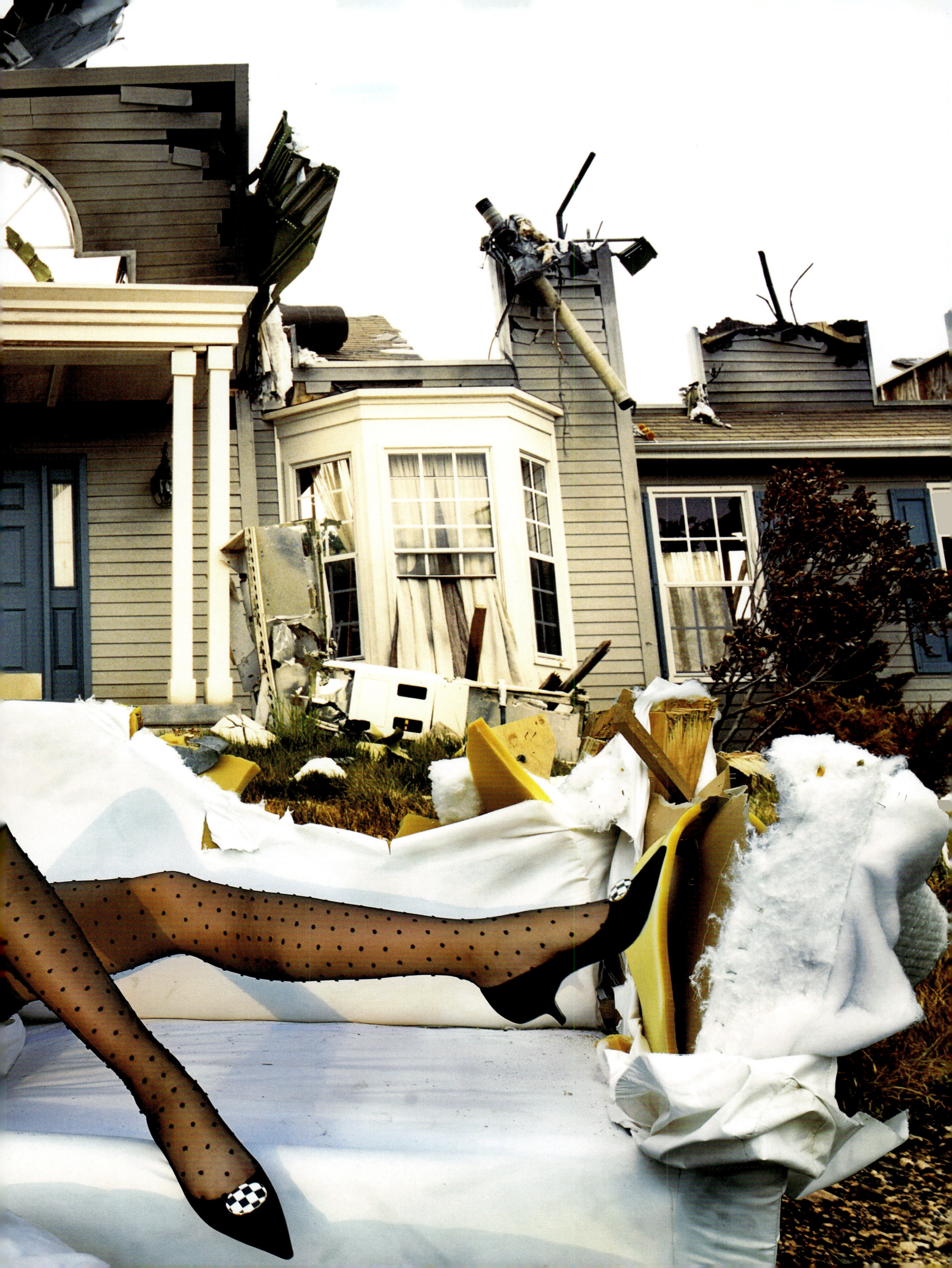

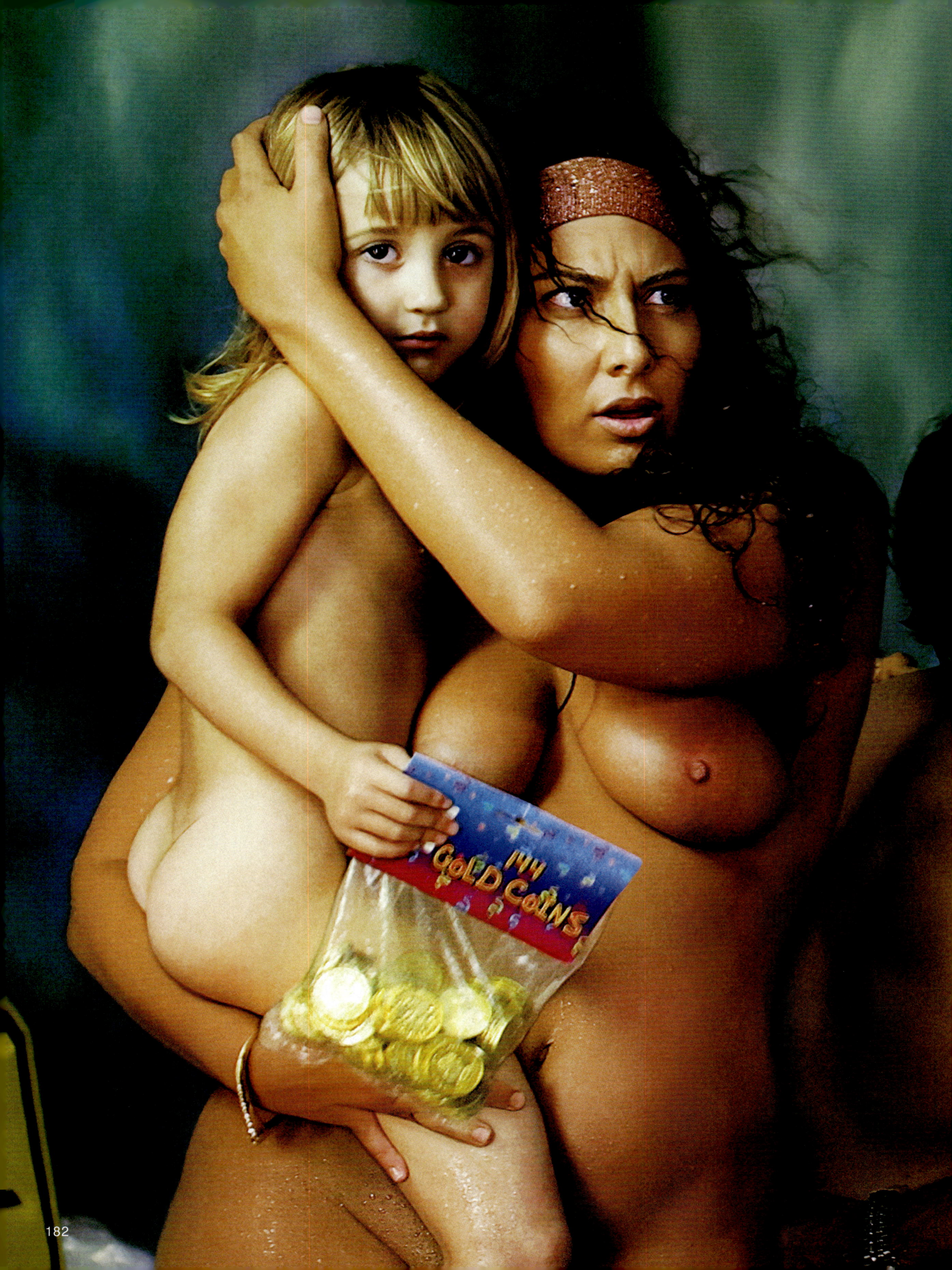
144
GOLD COINS

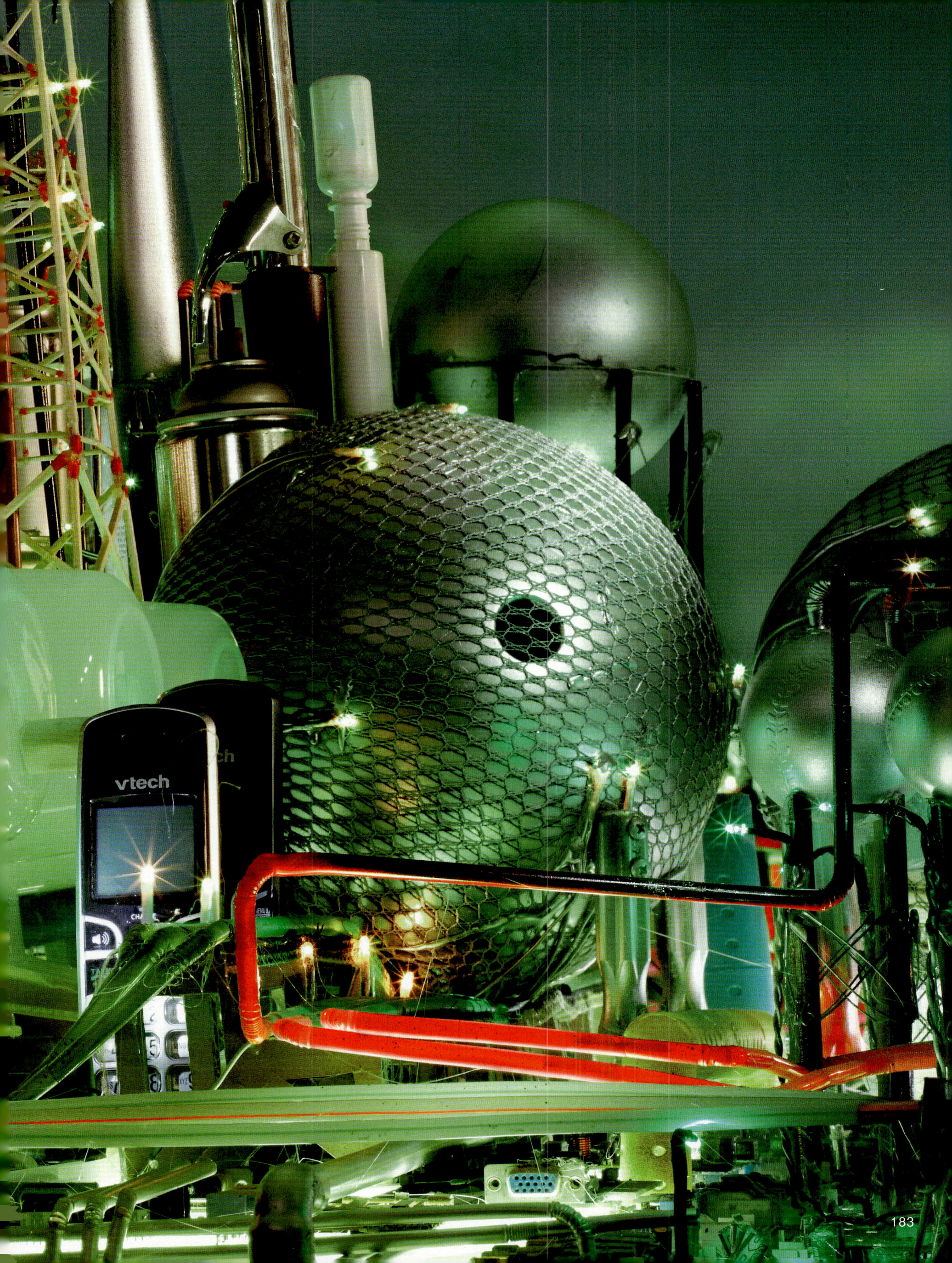
vtech

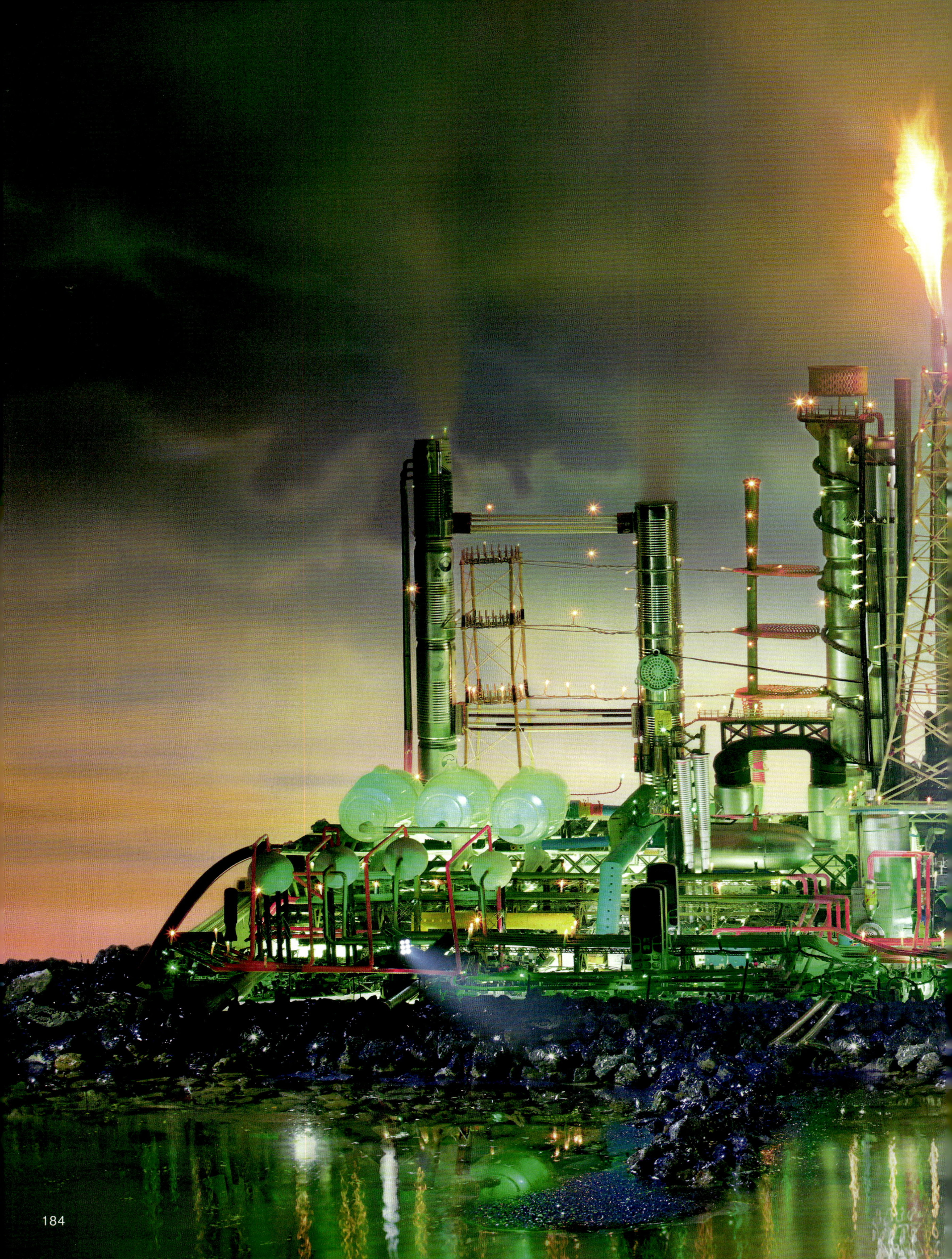

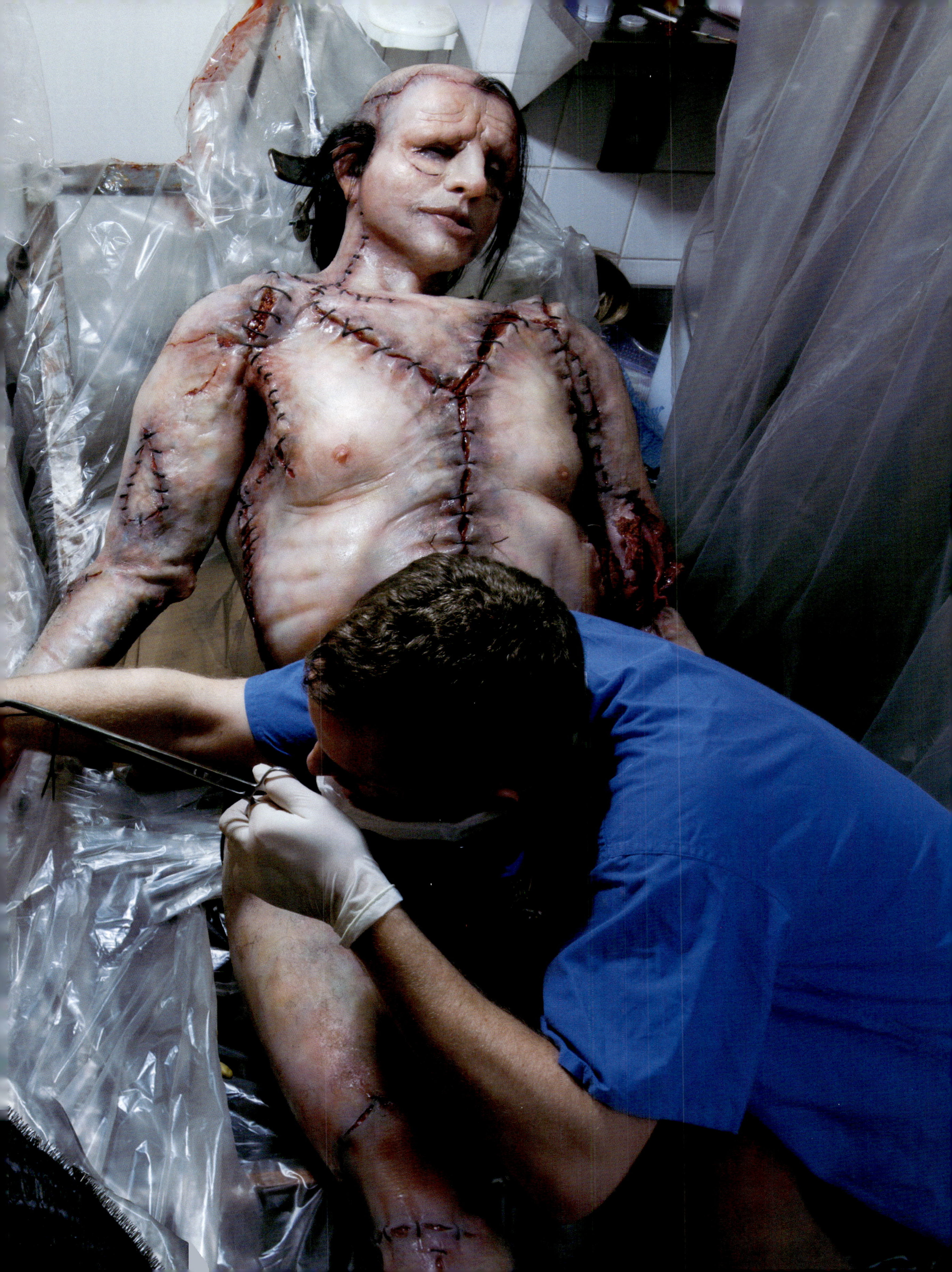

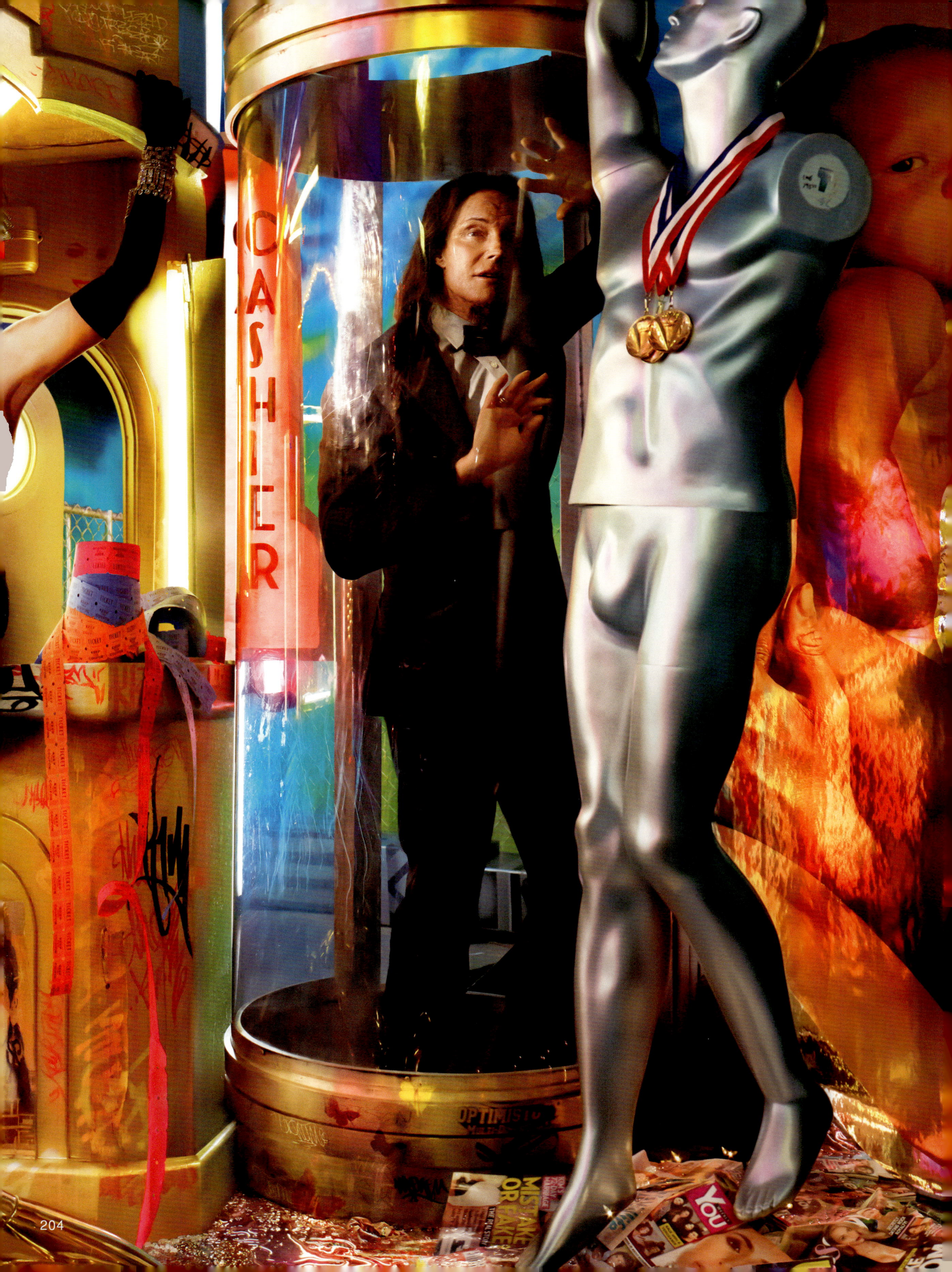
CASHIER
MISTAKE OR FAKE
You

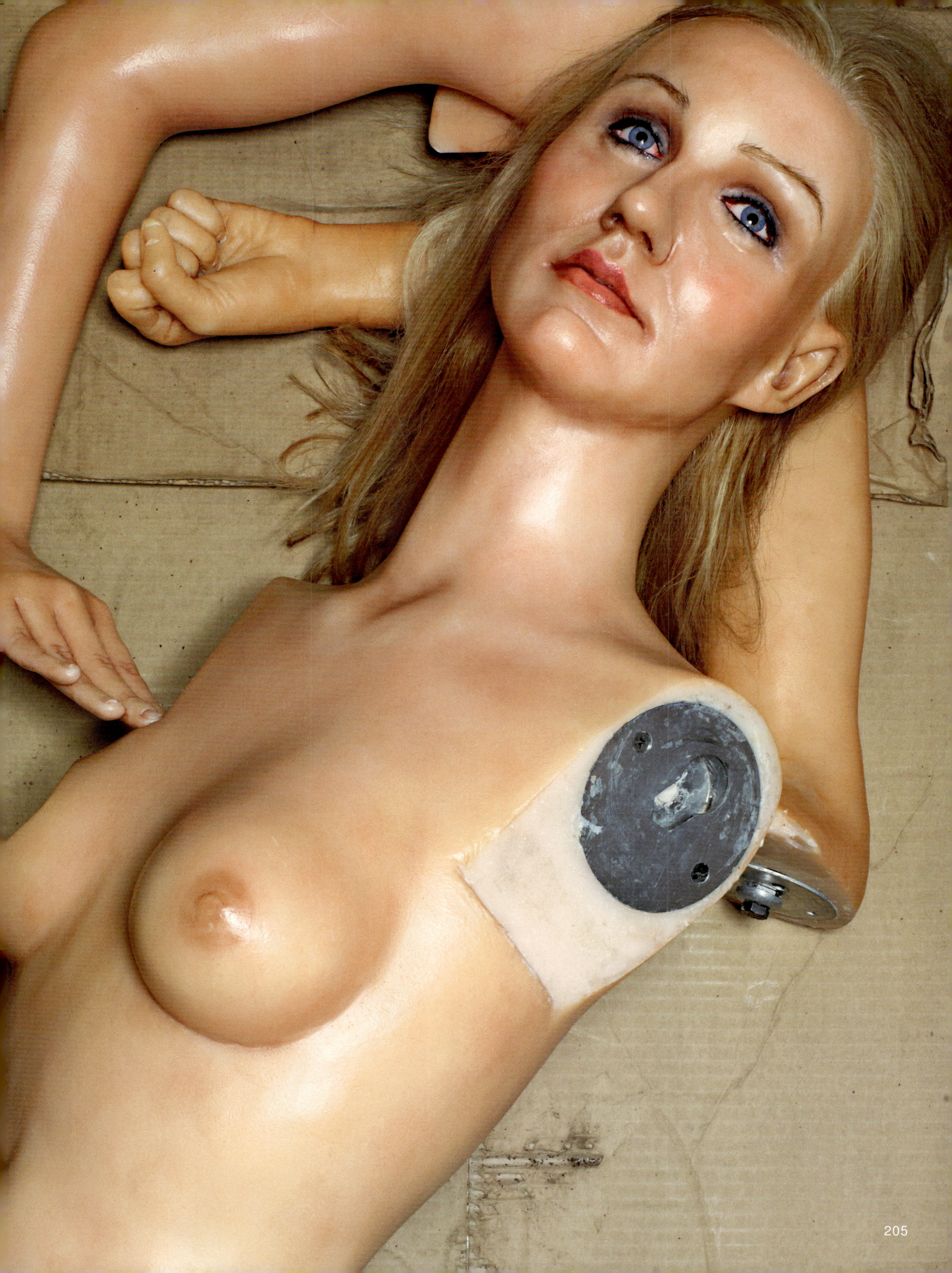

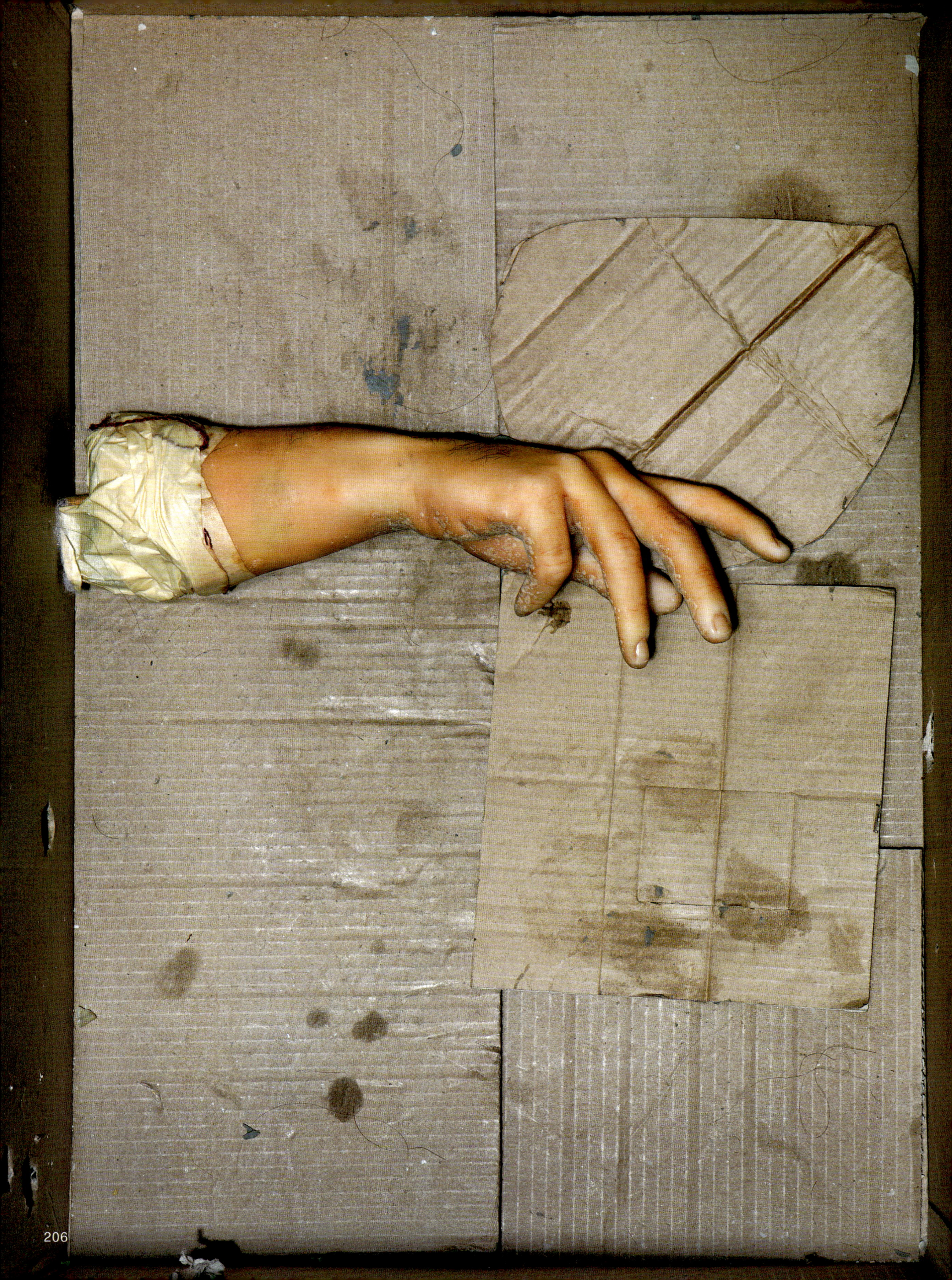

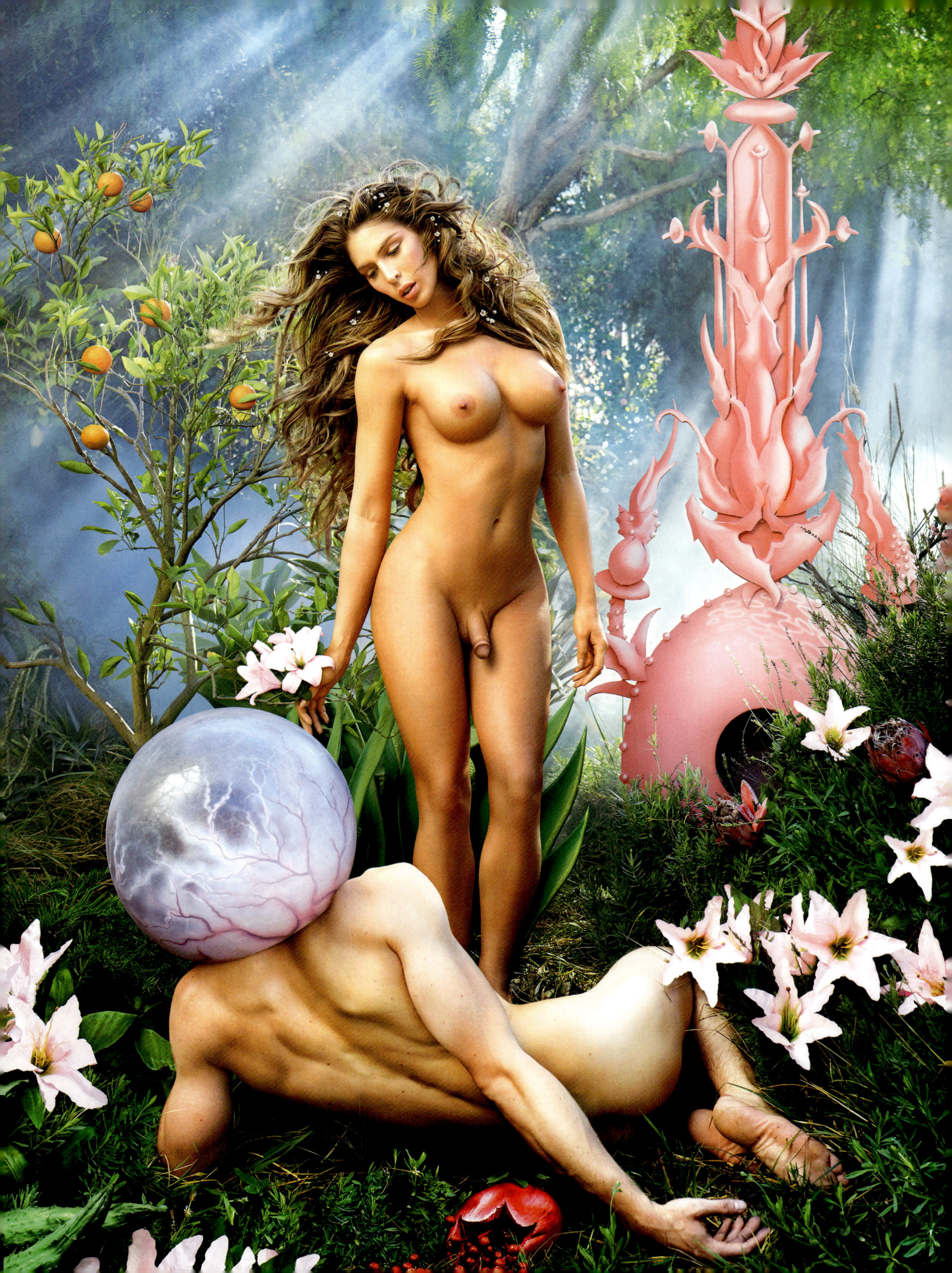

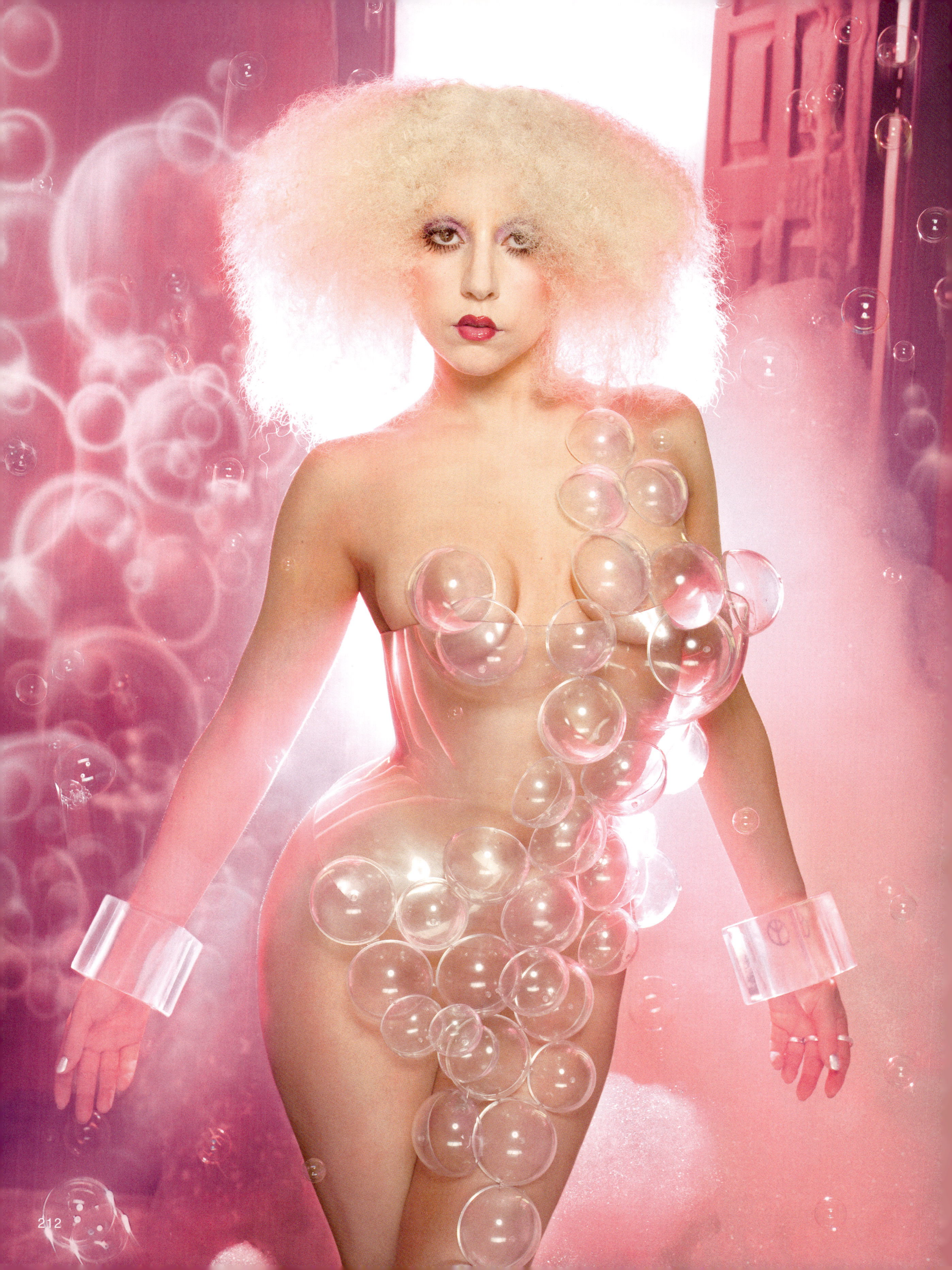

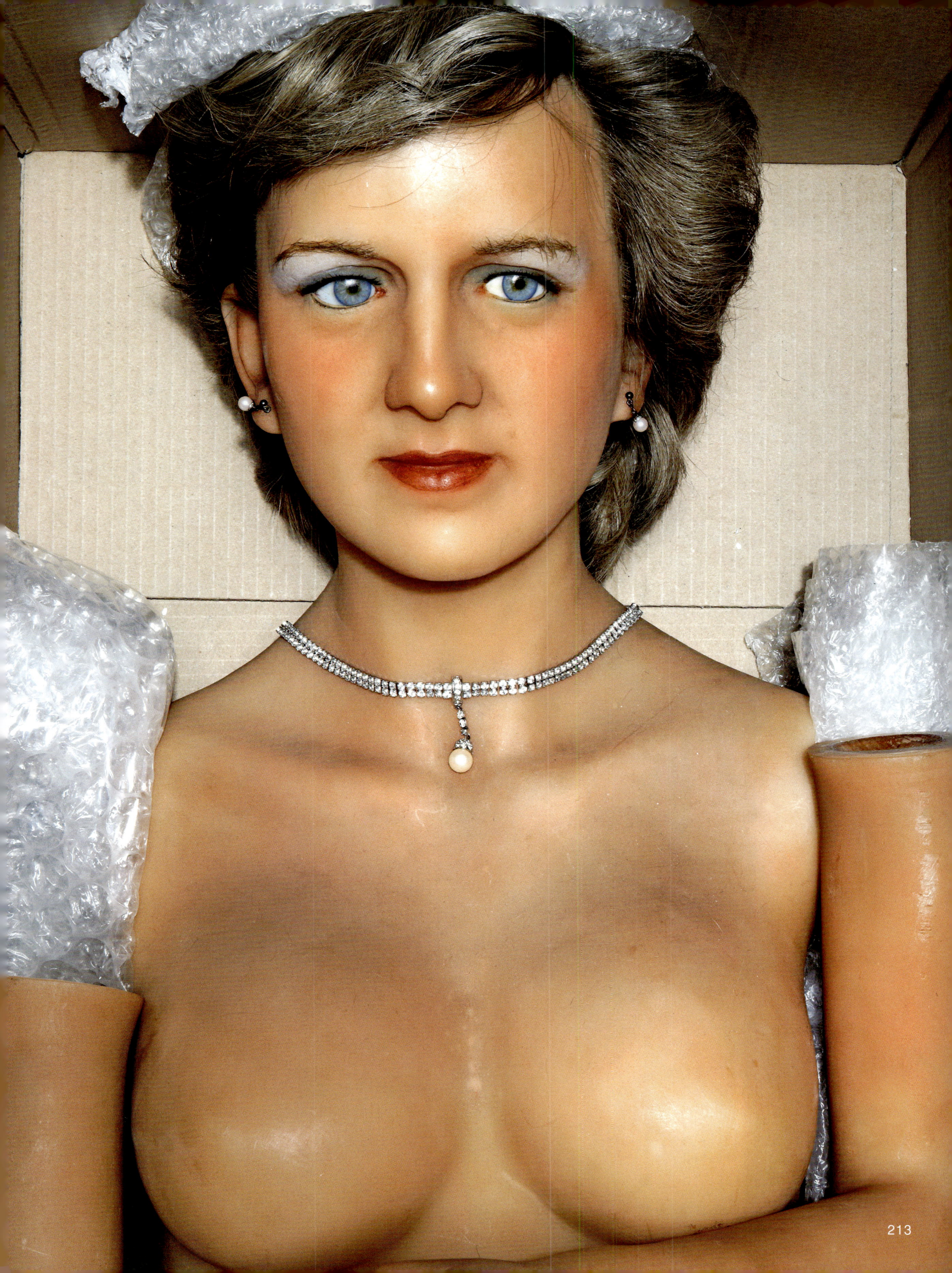

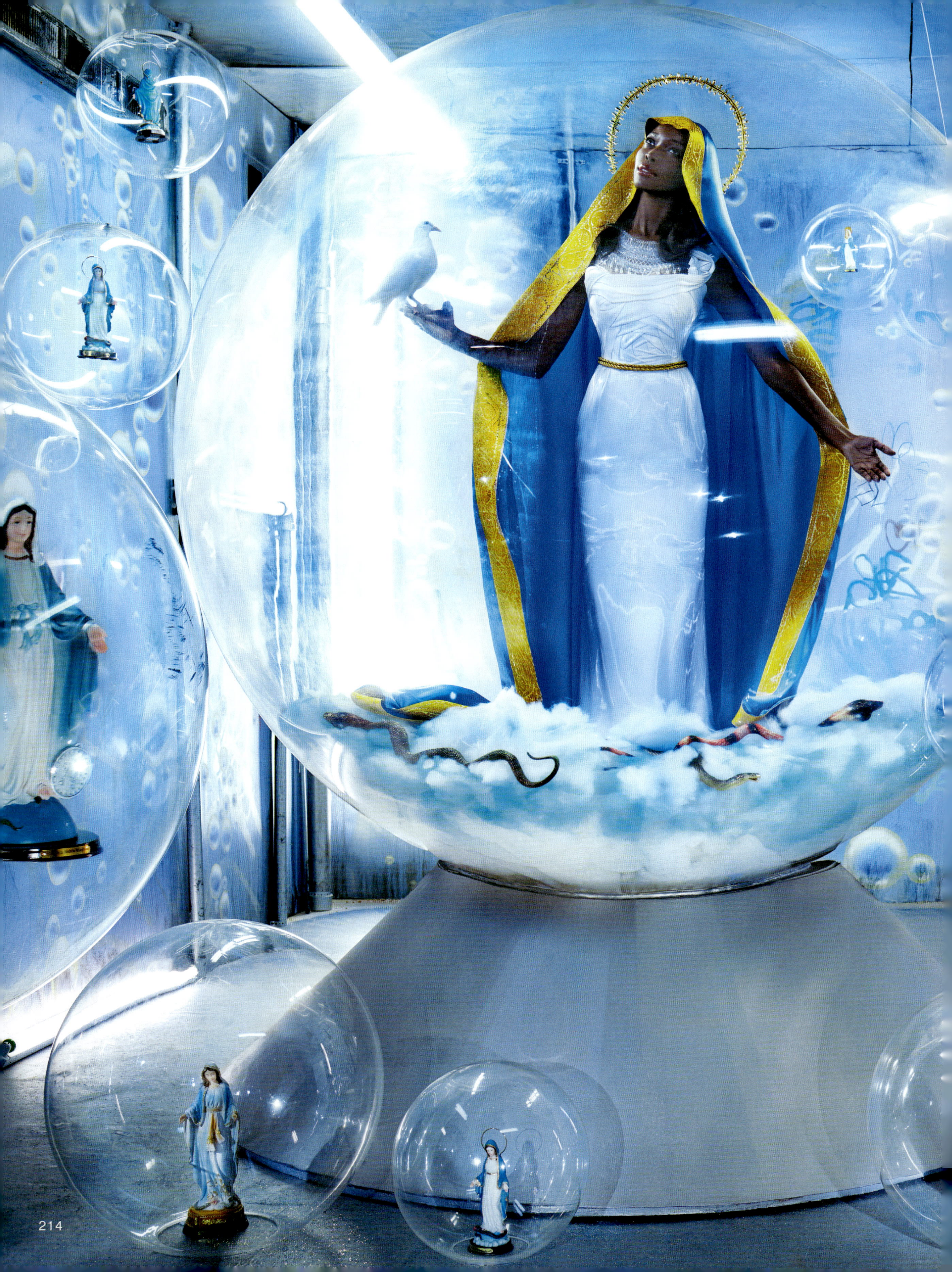

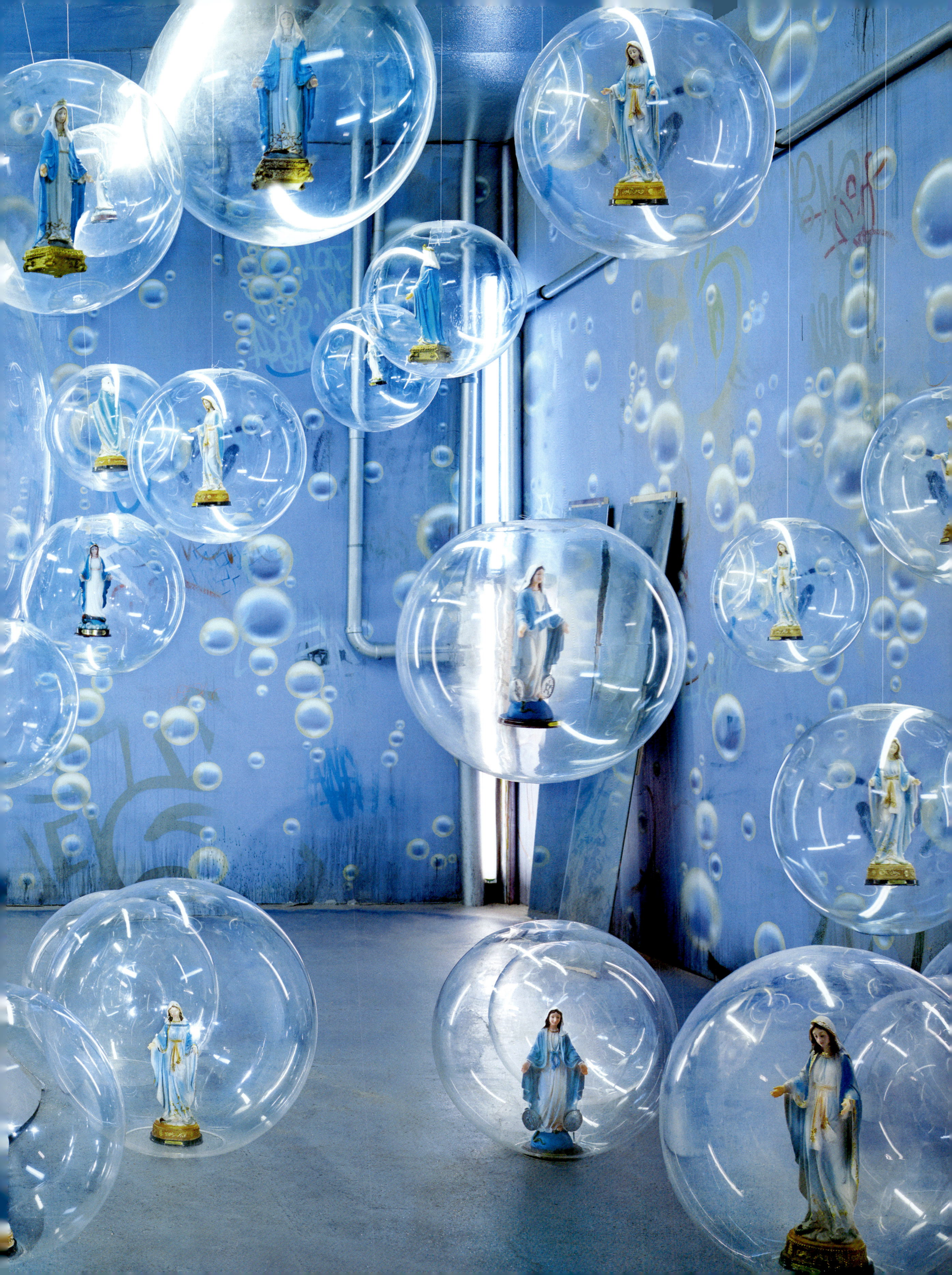

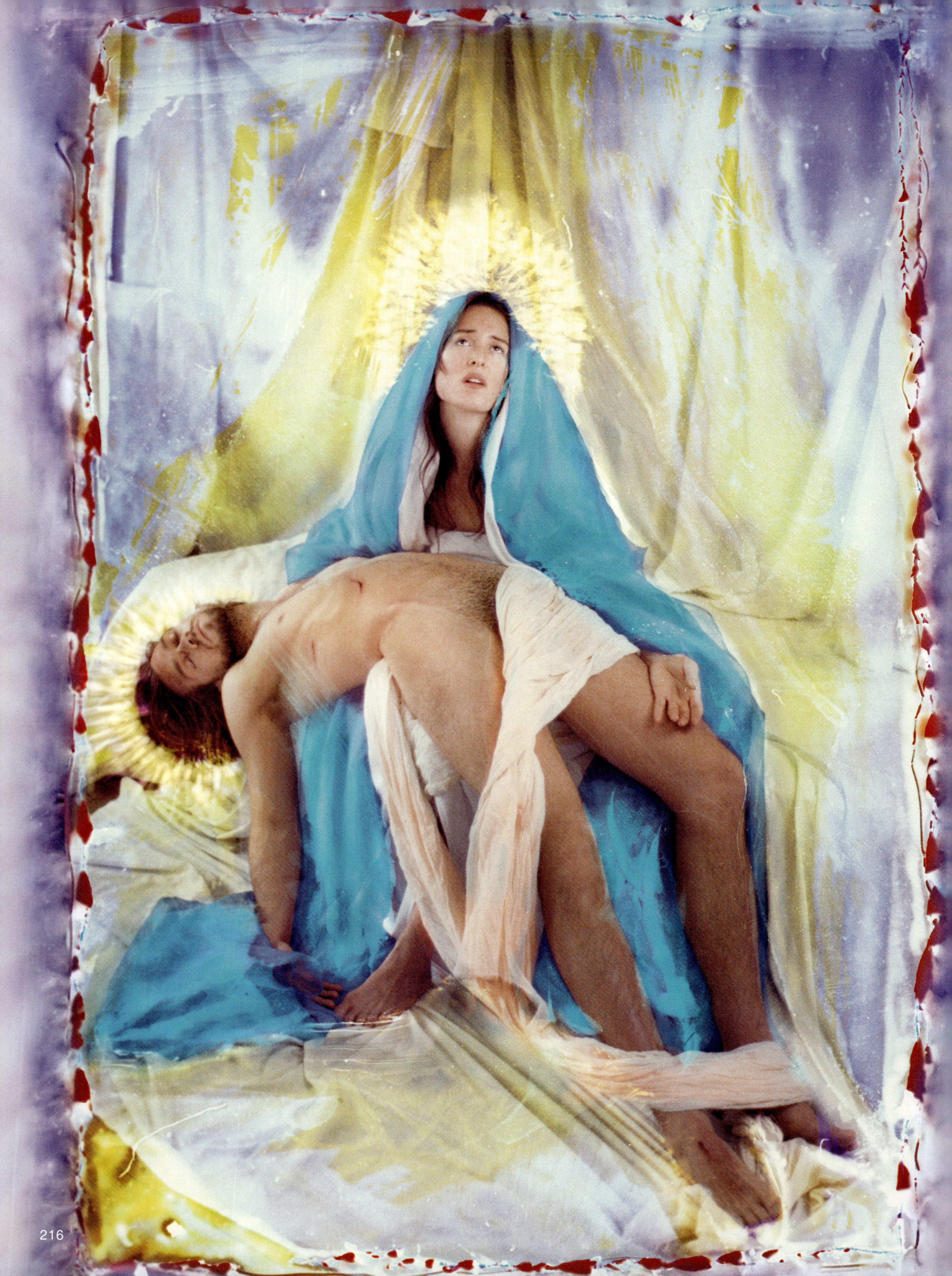

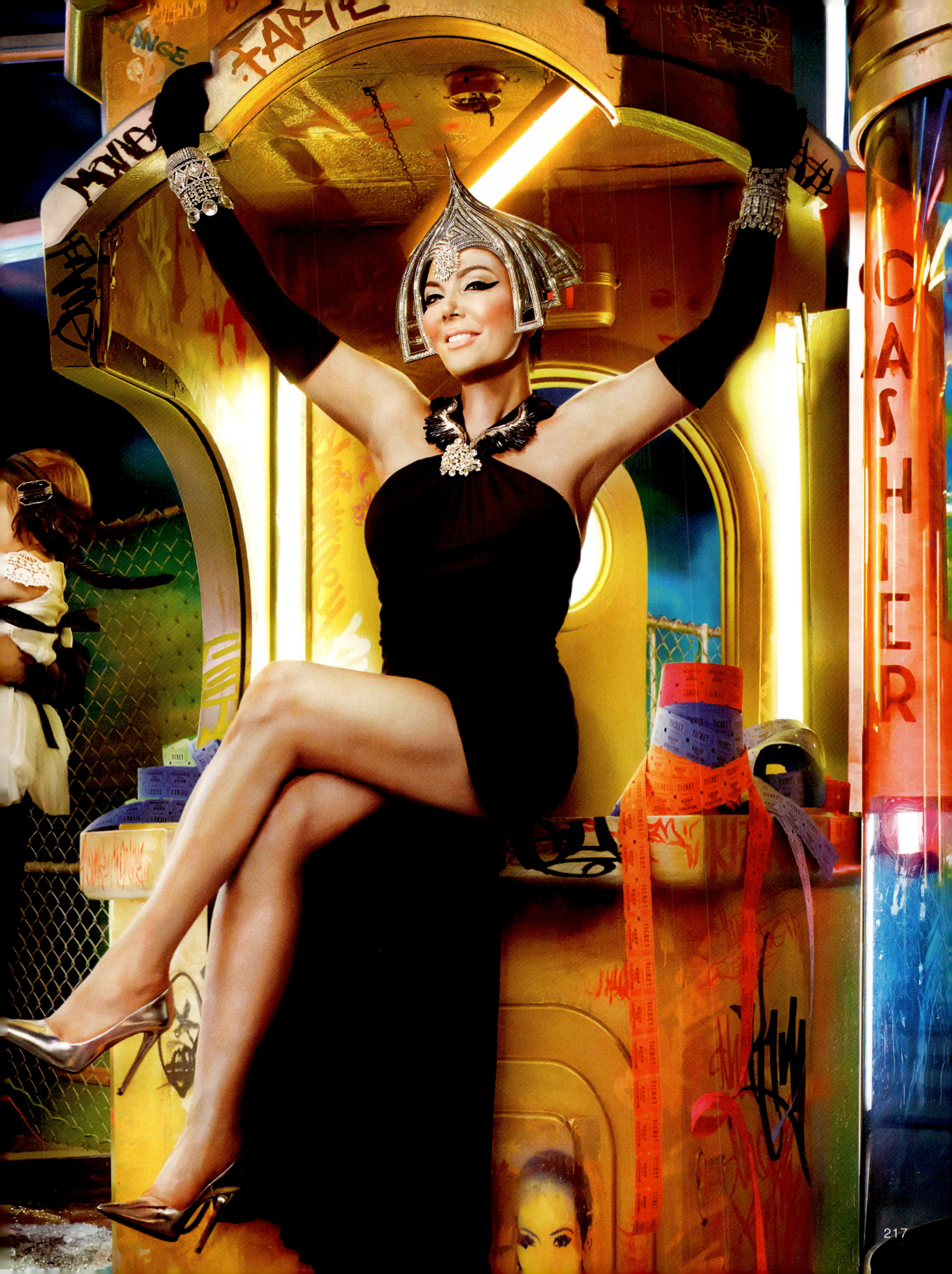
CASHIER

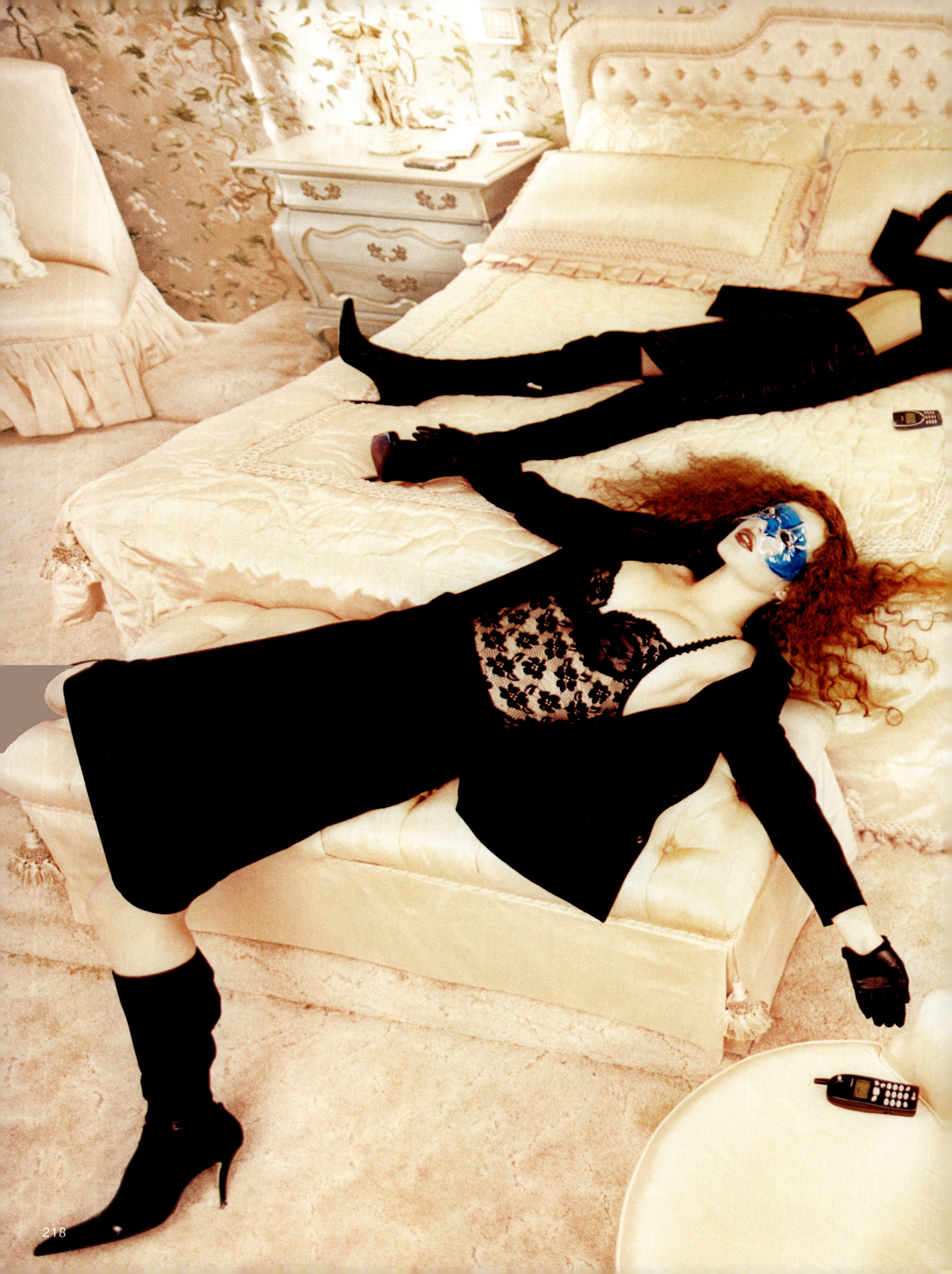

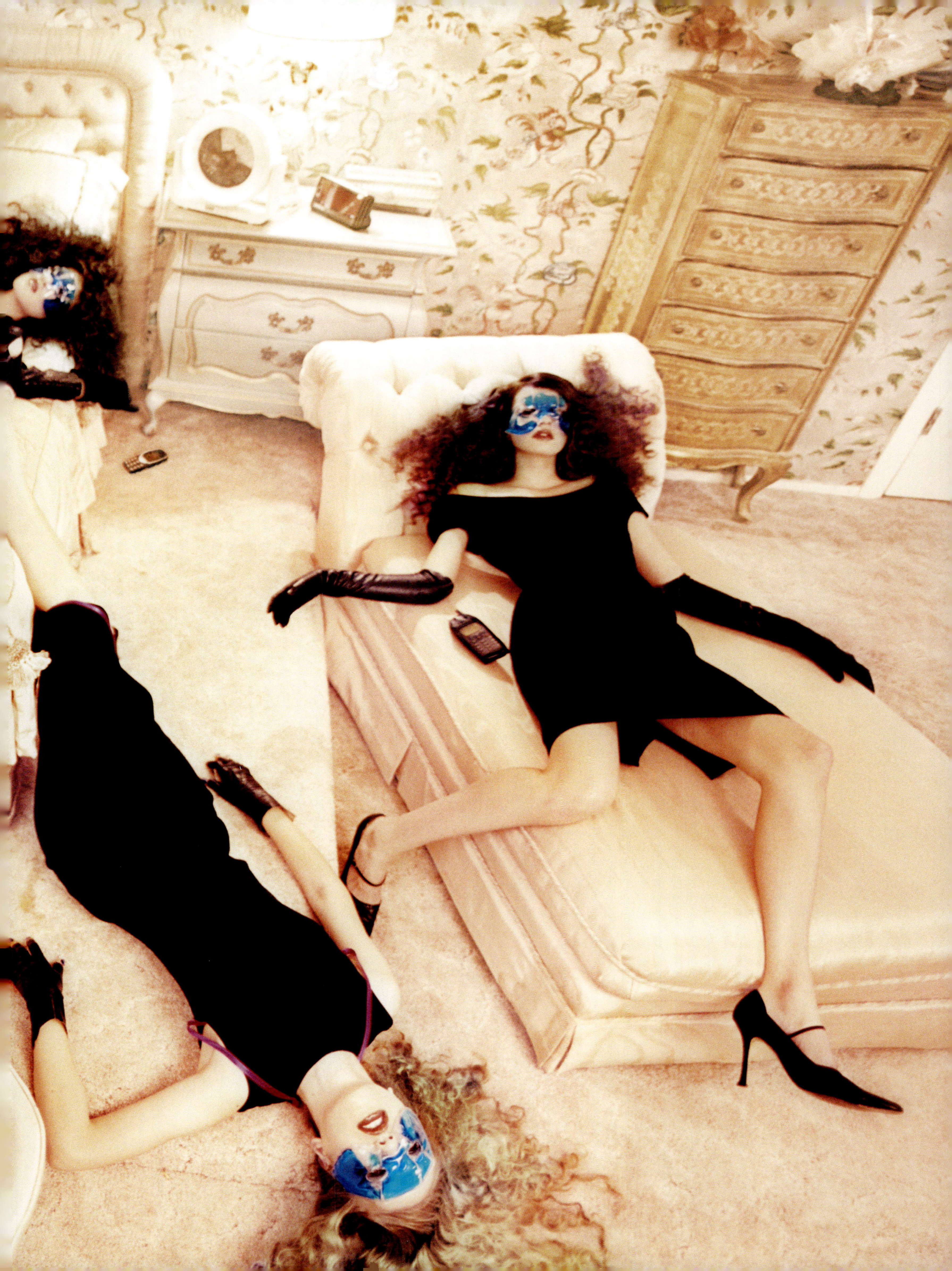

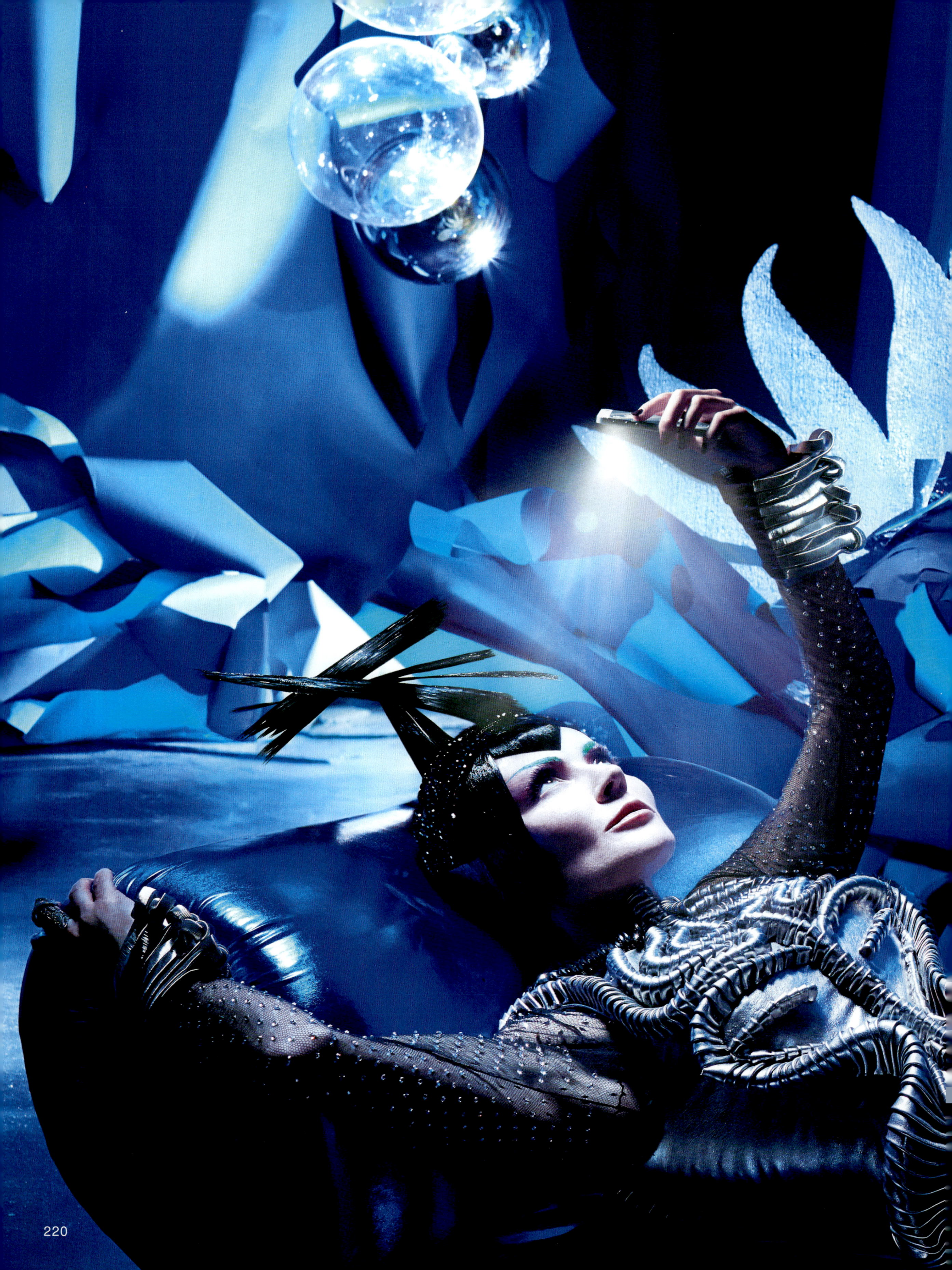

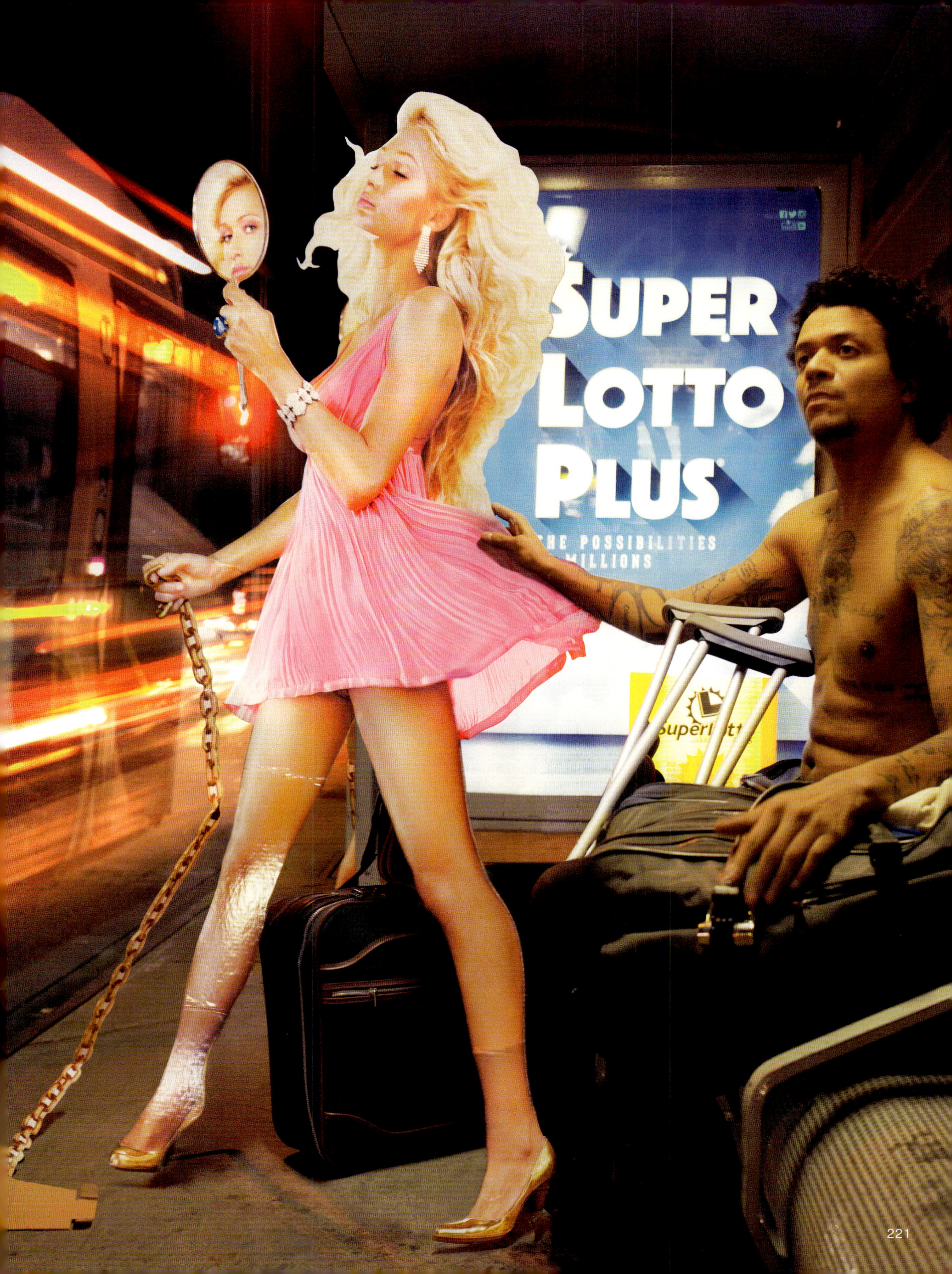
SUPER
LOTTO
PLUS
THE POSSIBILITIES
MILLIONS

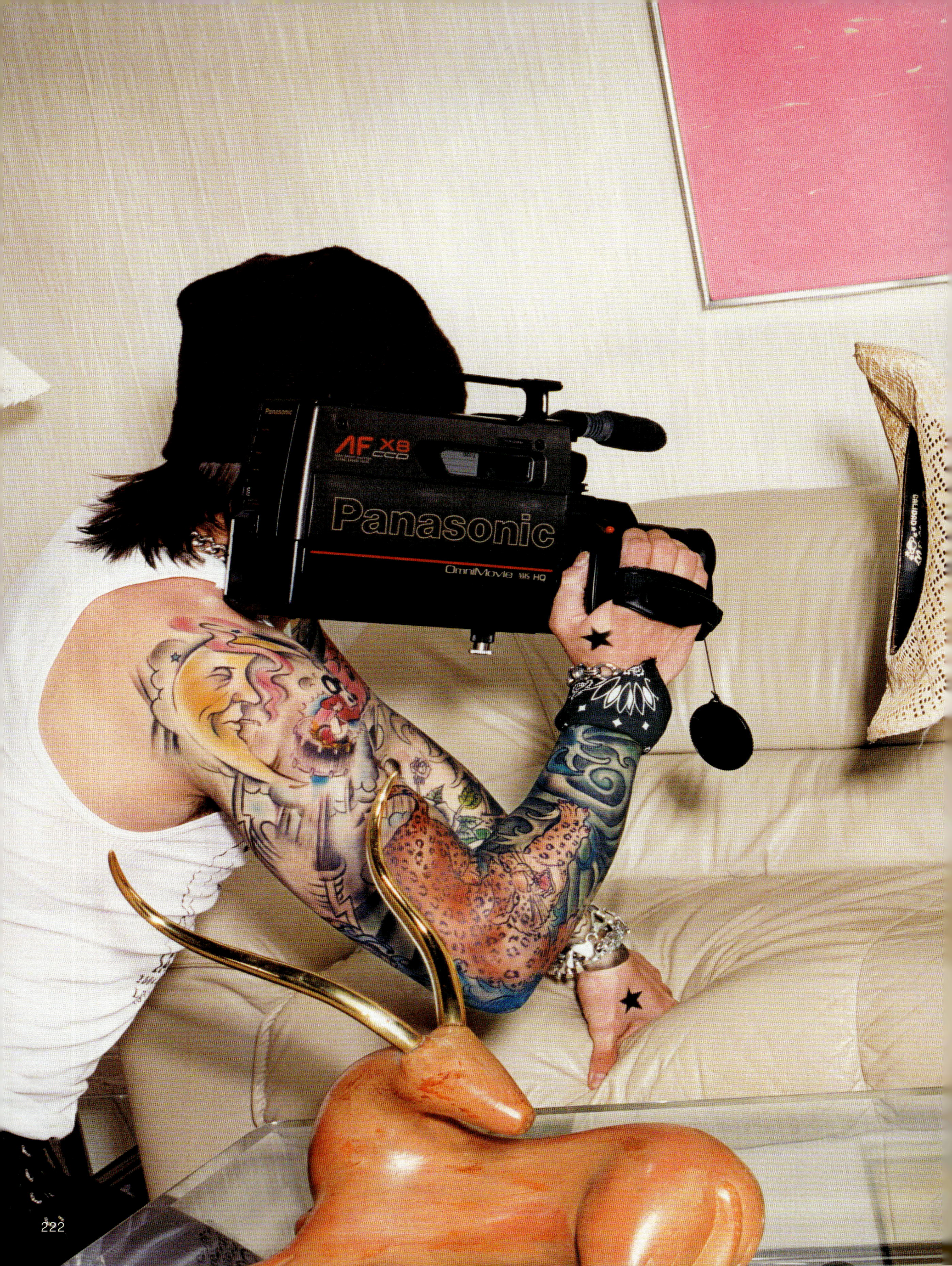
Panasonic
AF X8 CCD
Panasonic
OmniMovie VHS HQ

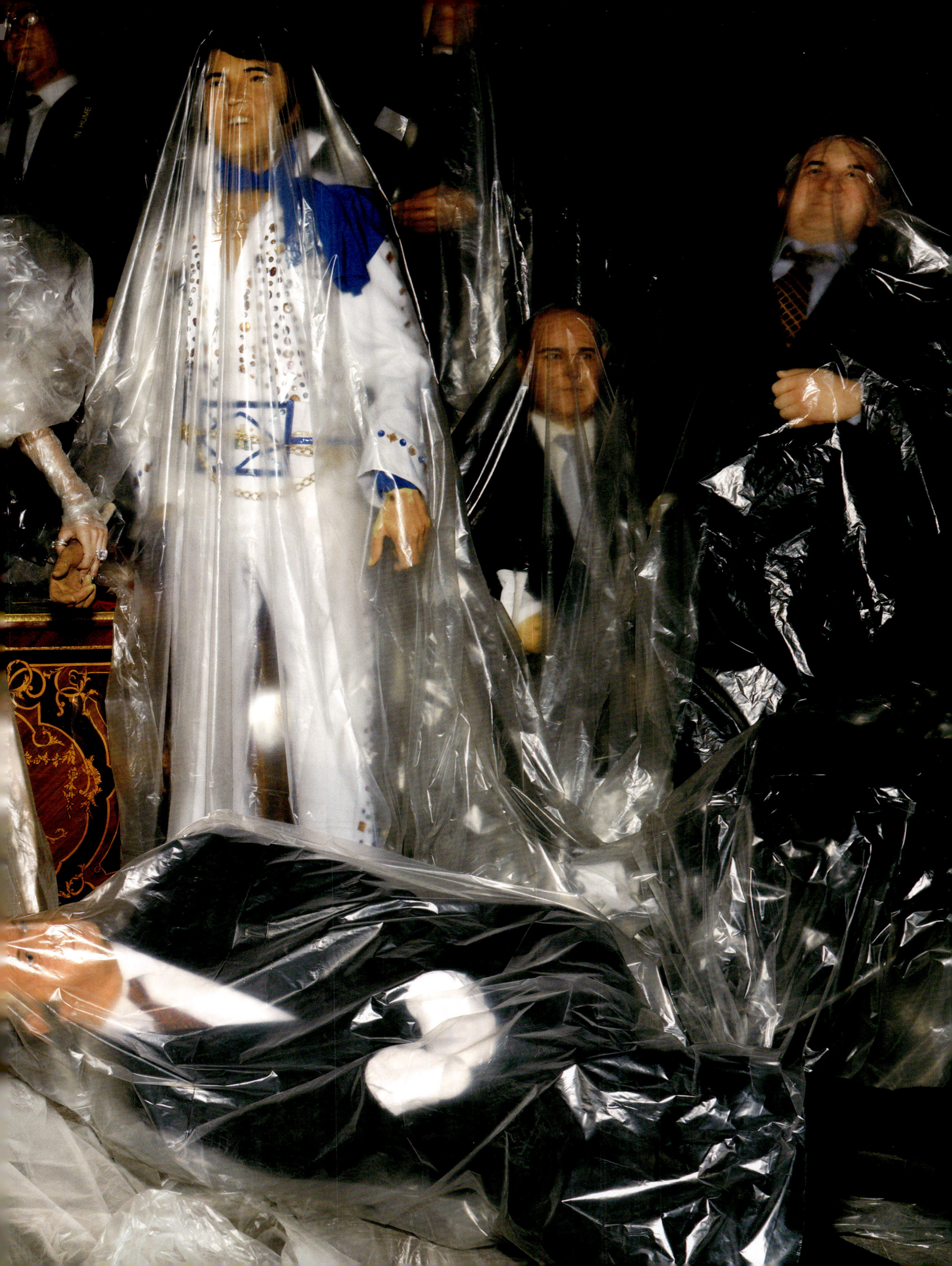

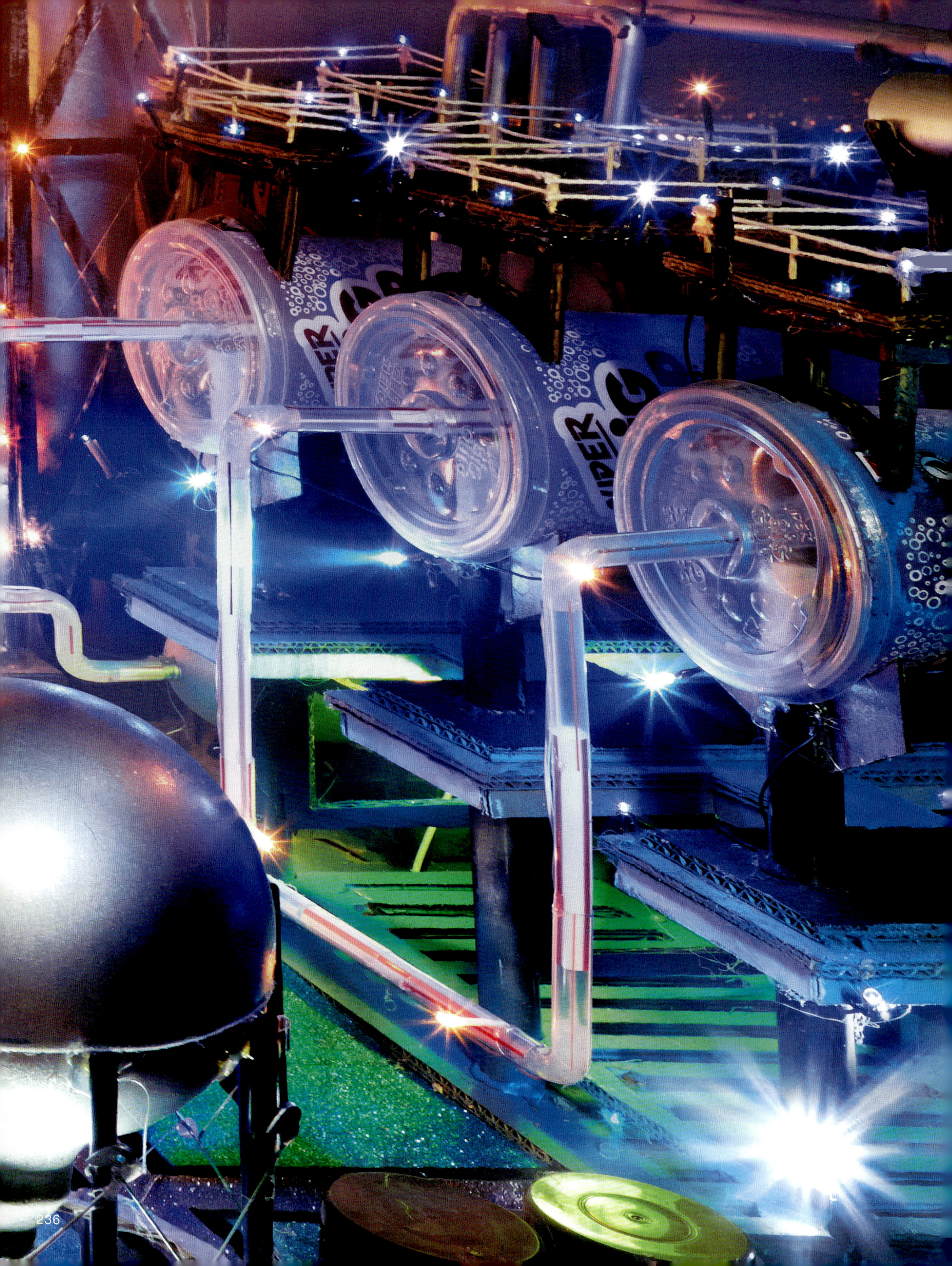

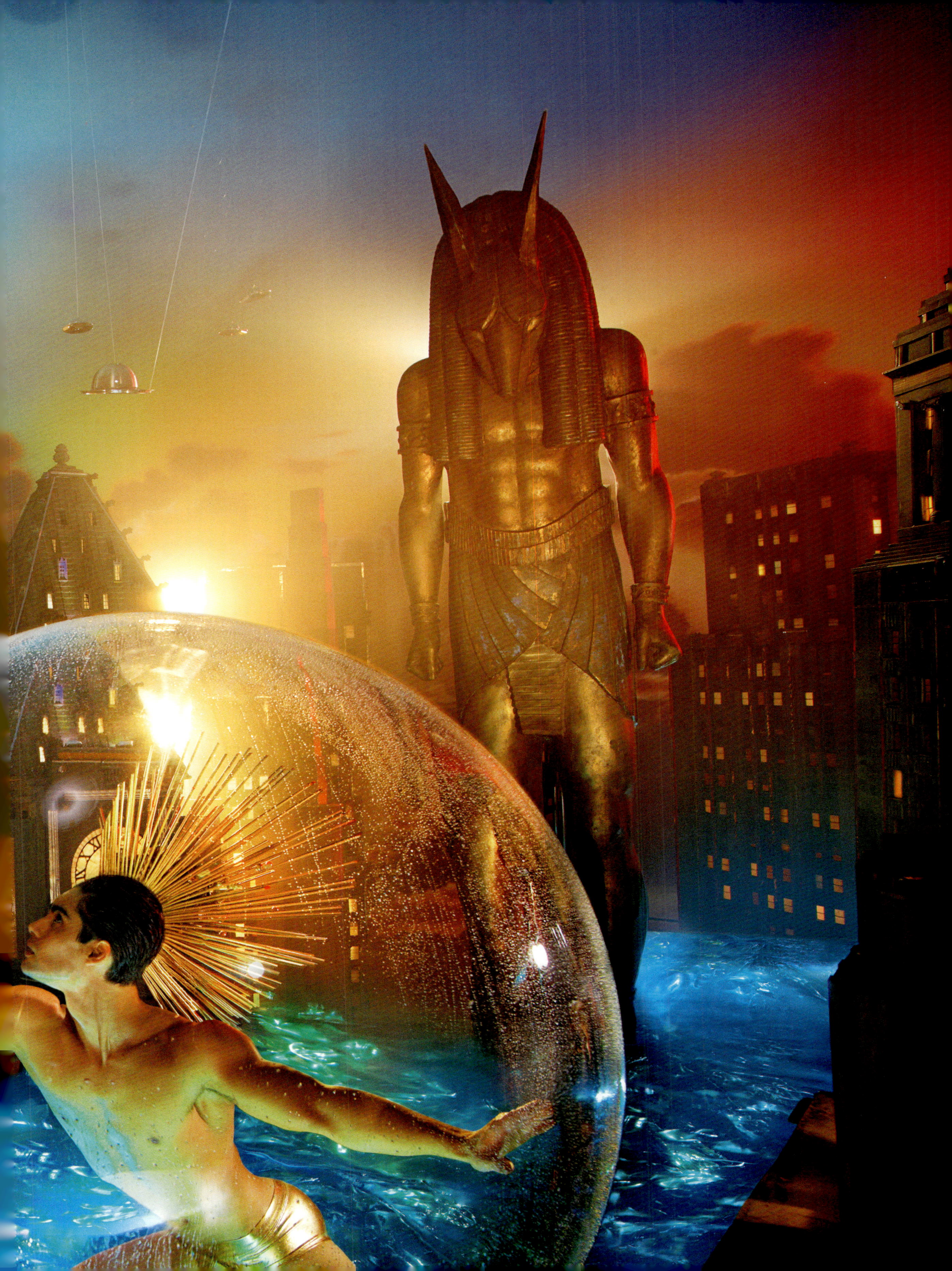

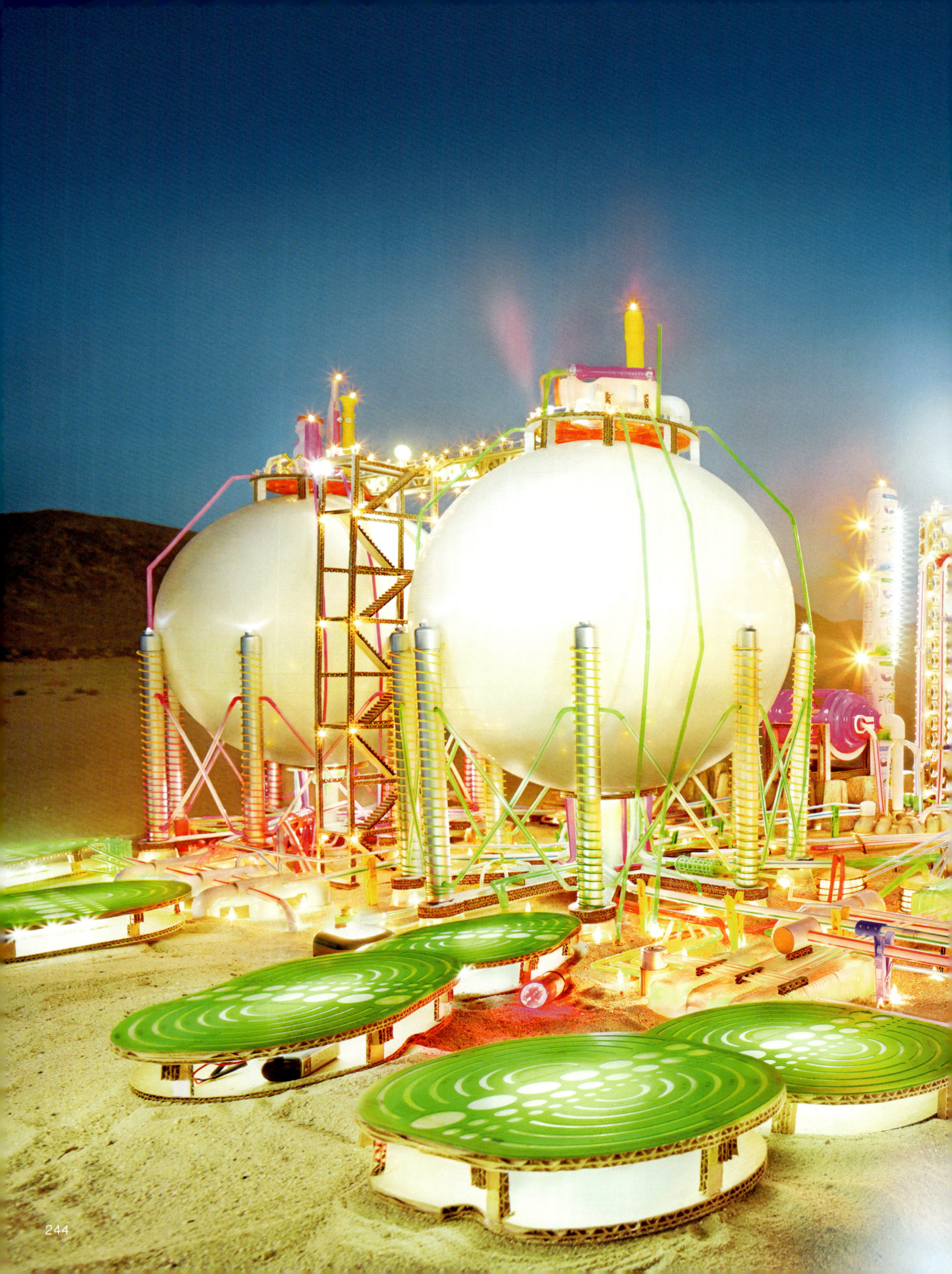

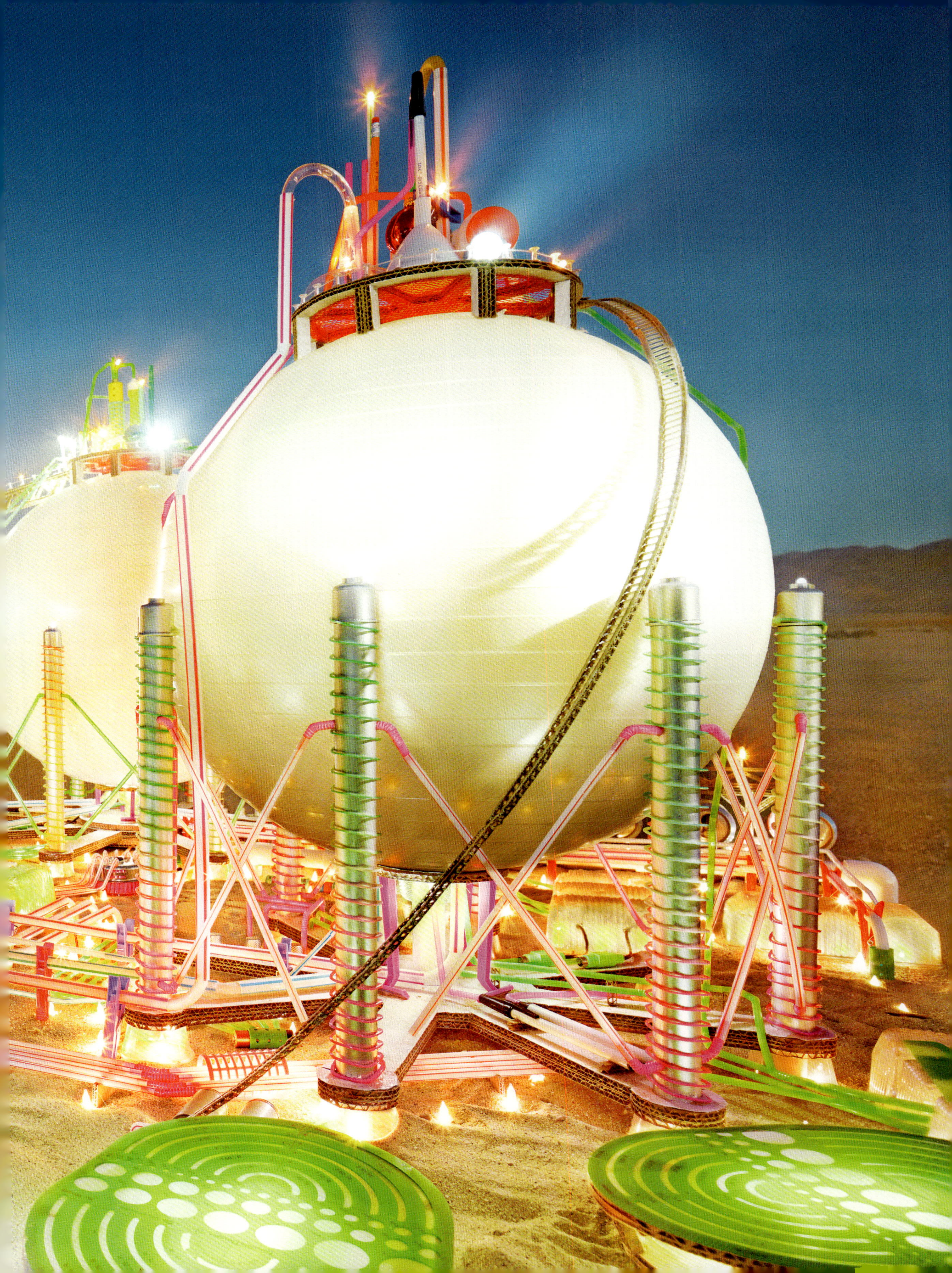

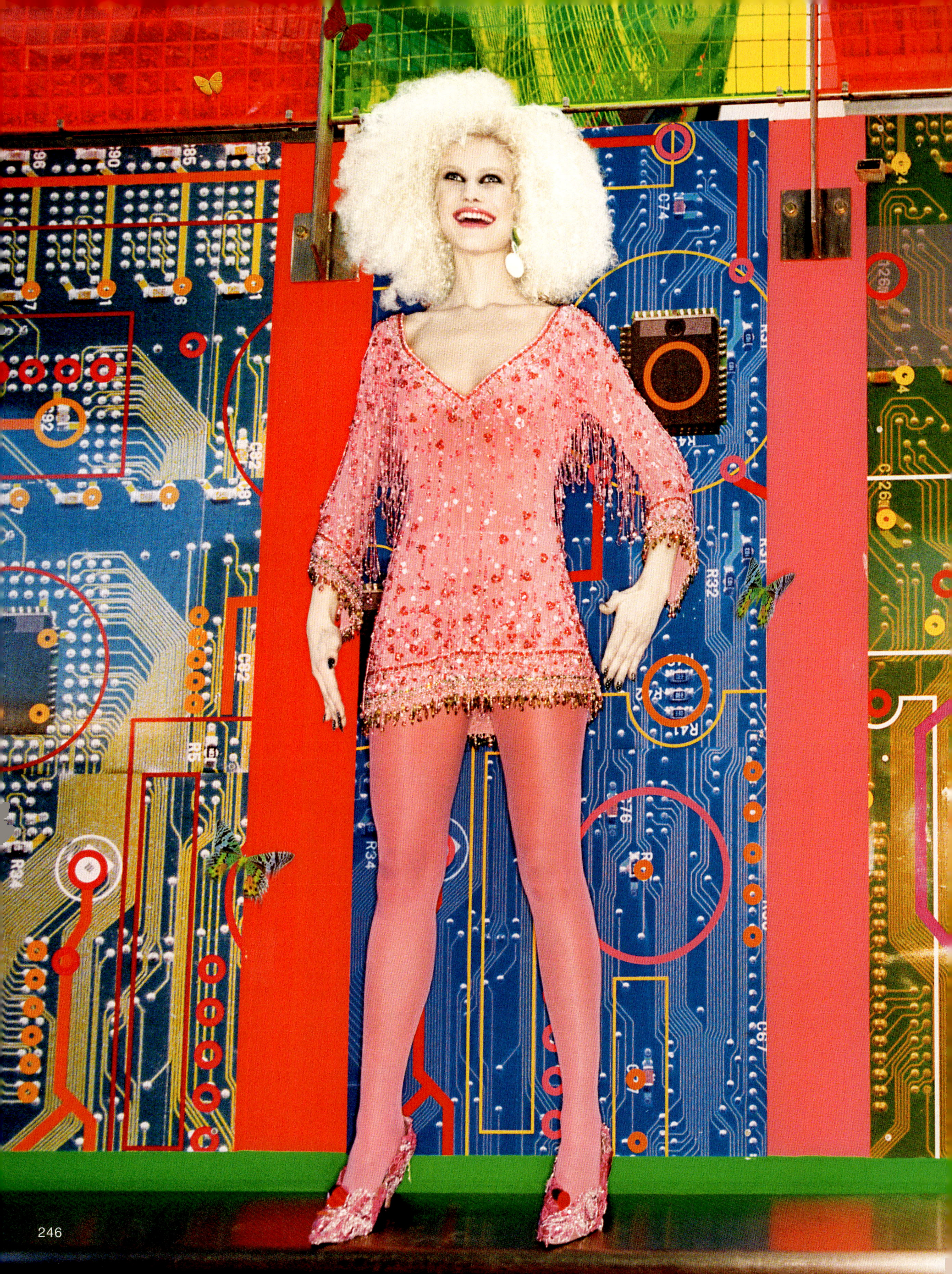

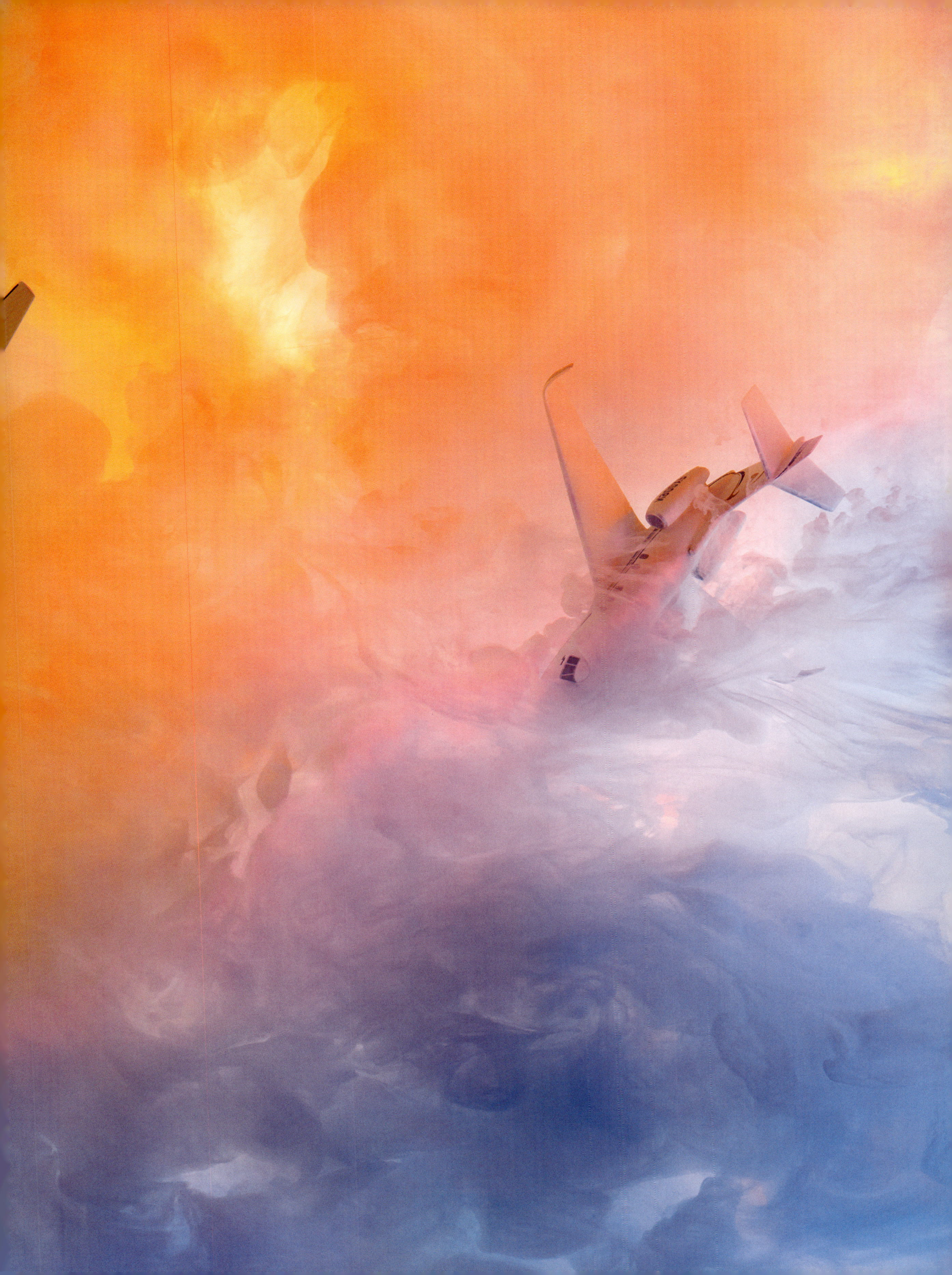

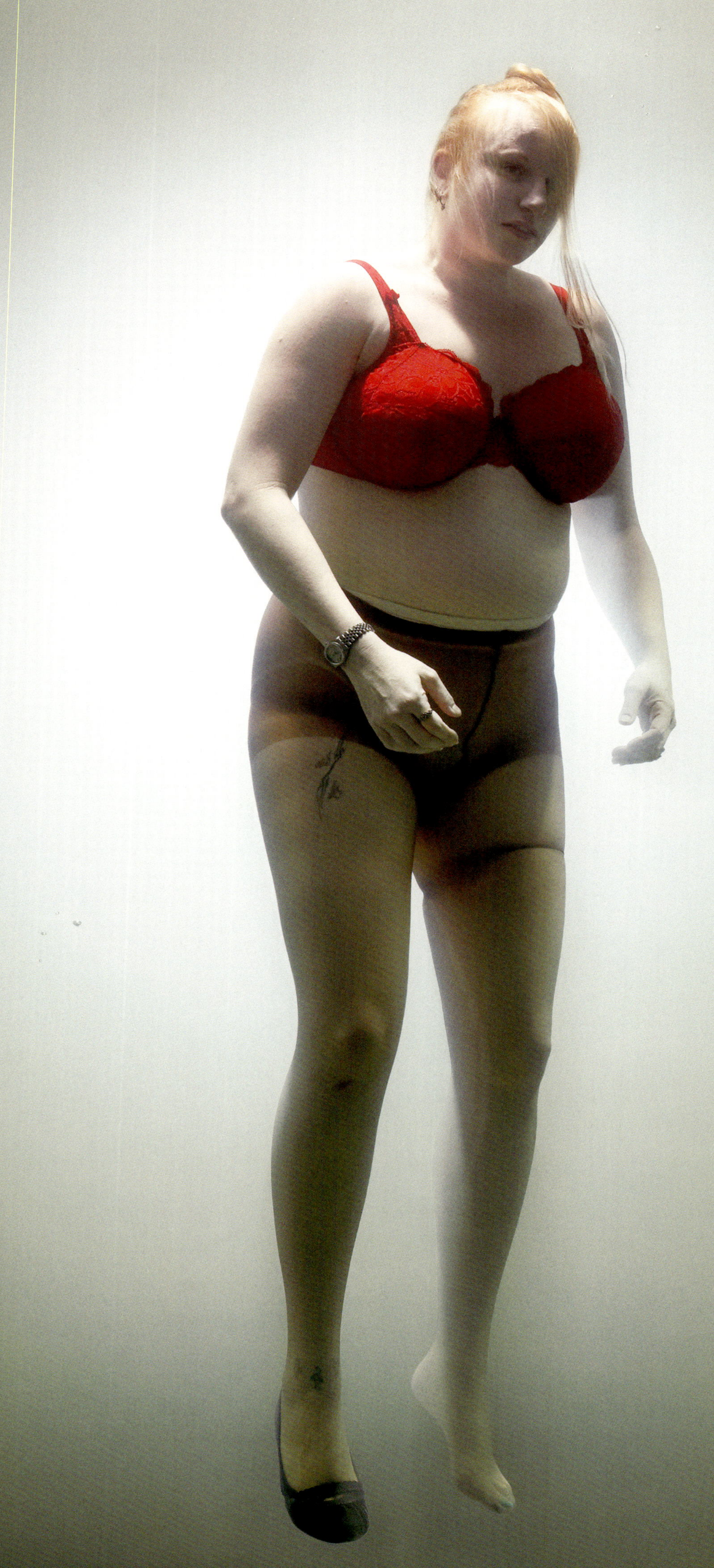

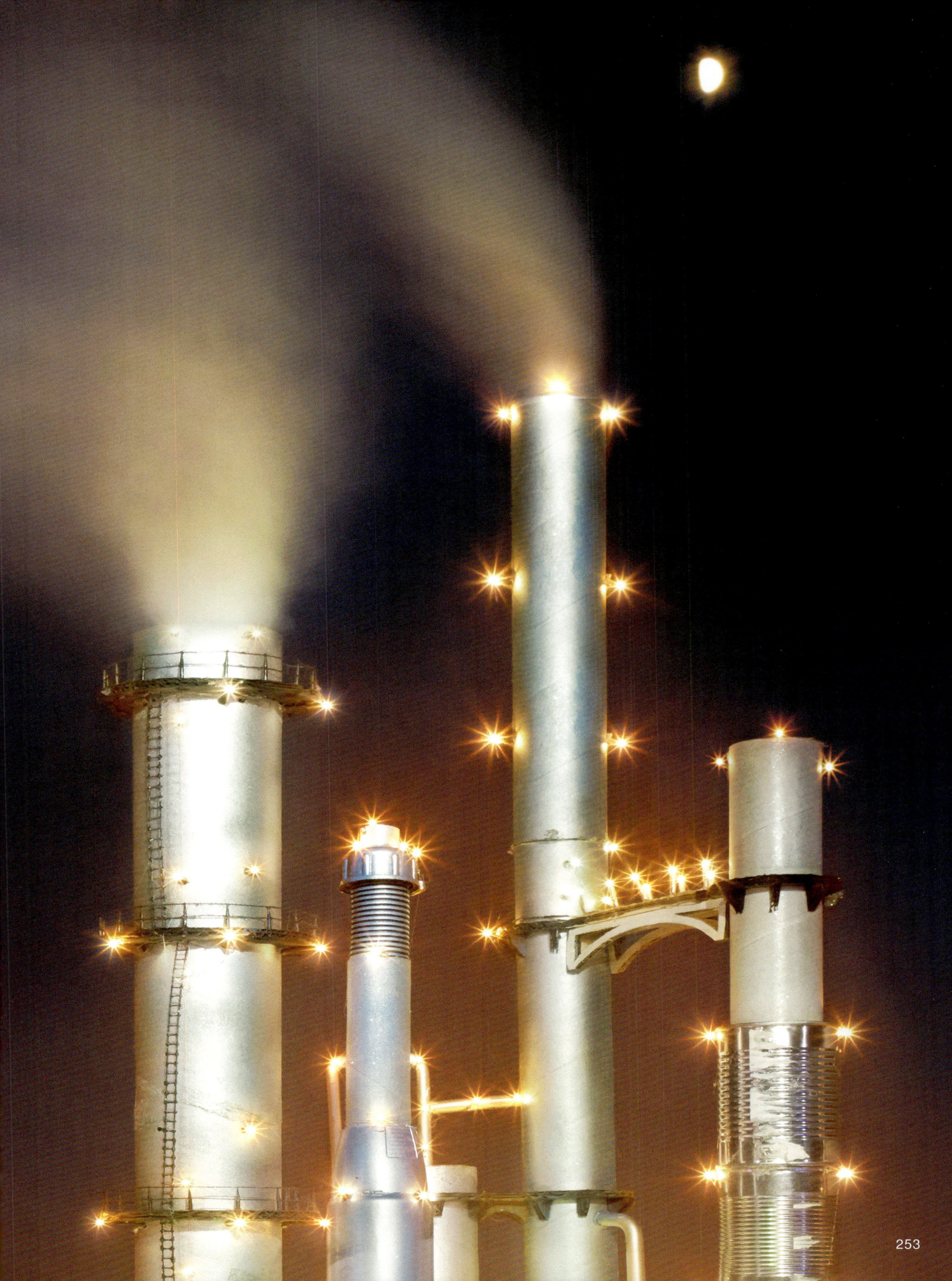

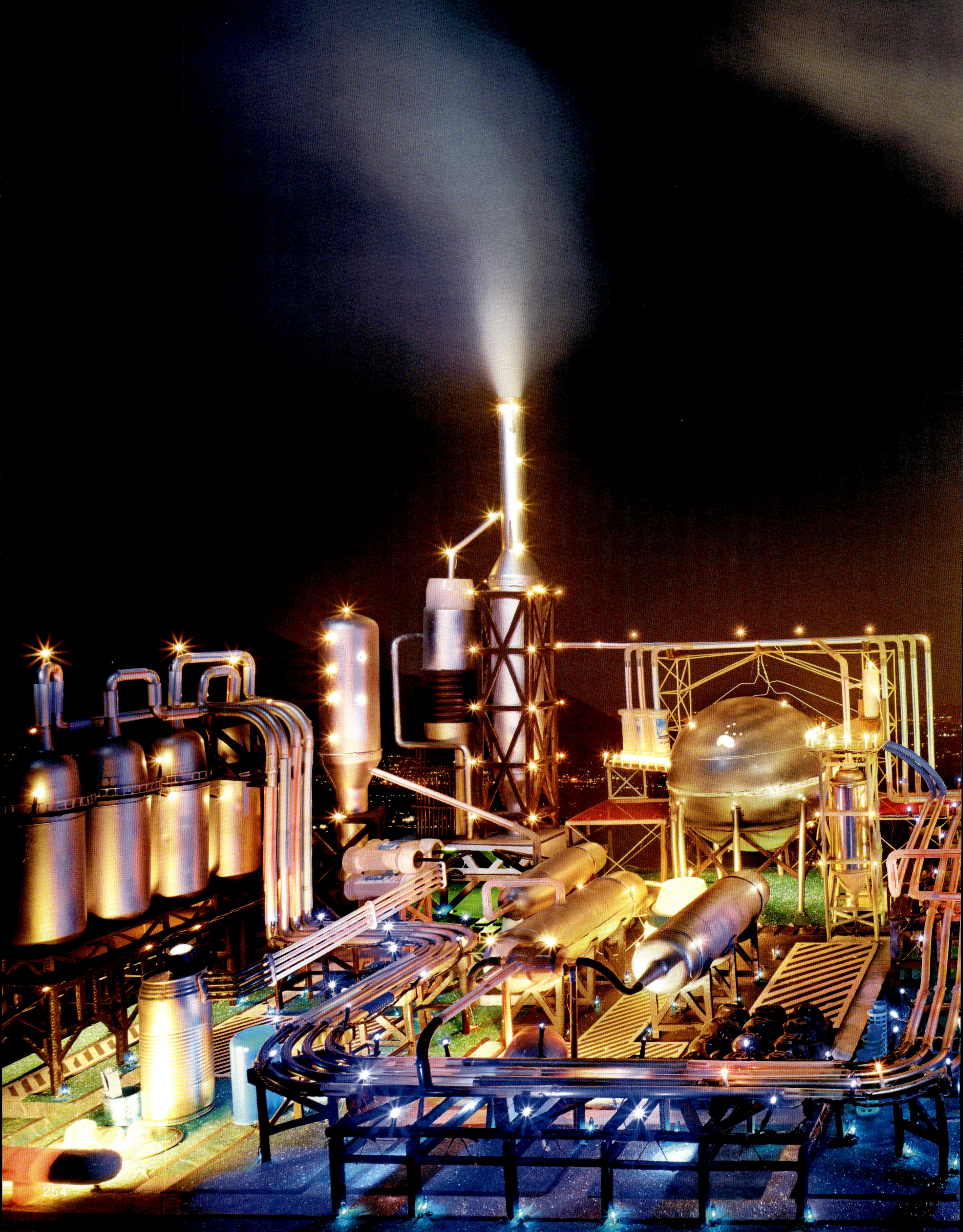

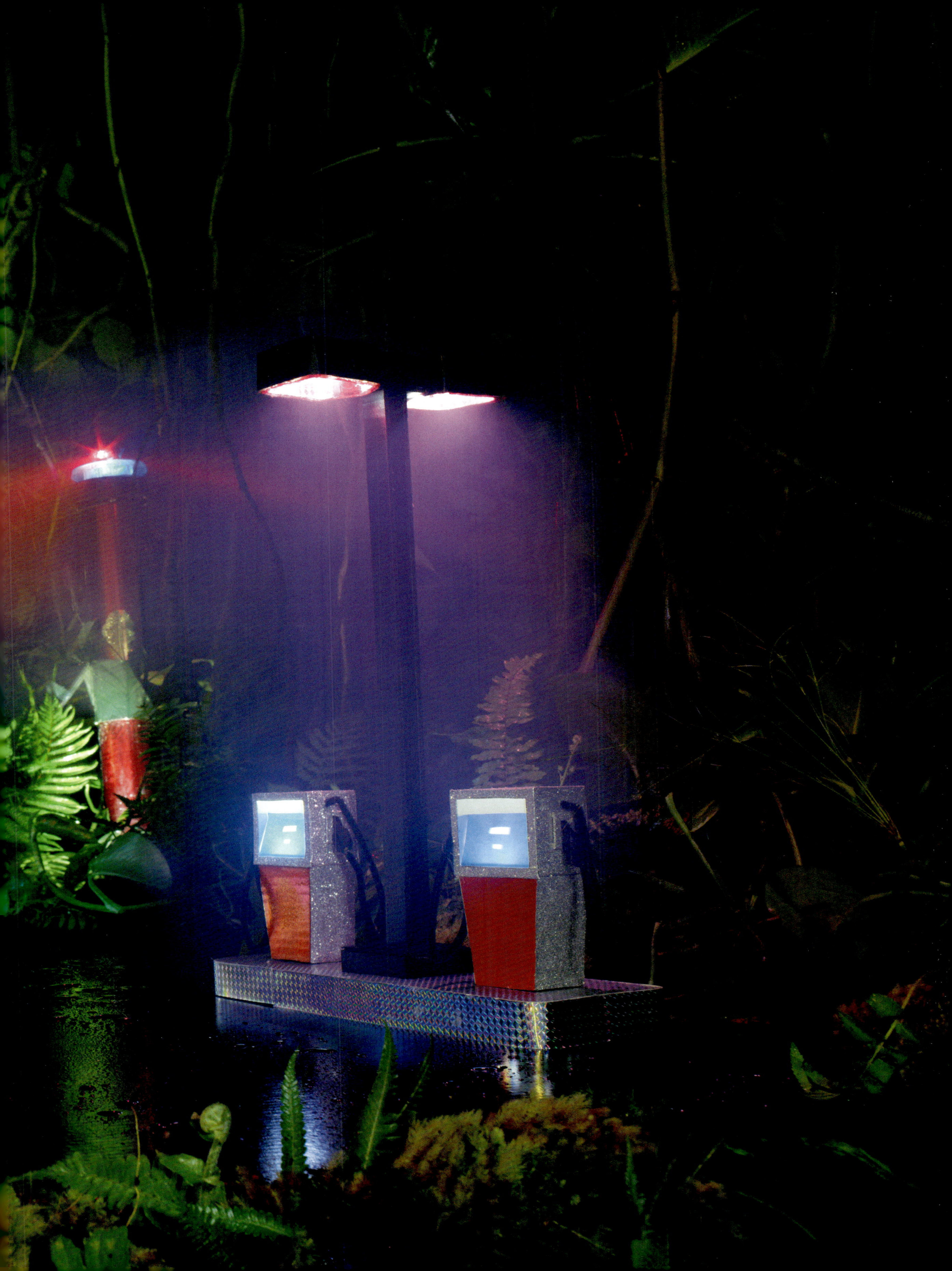

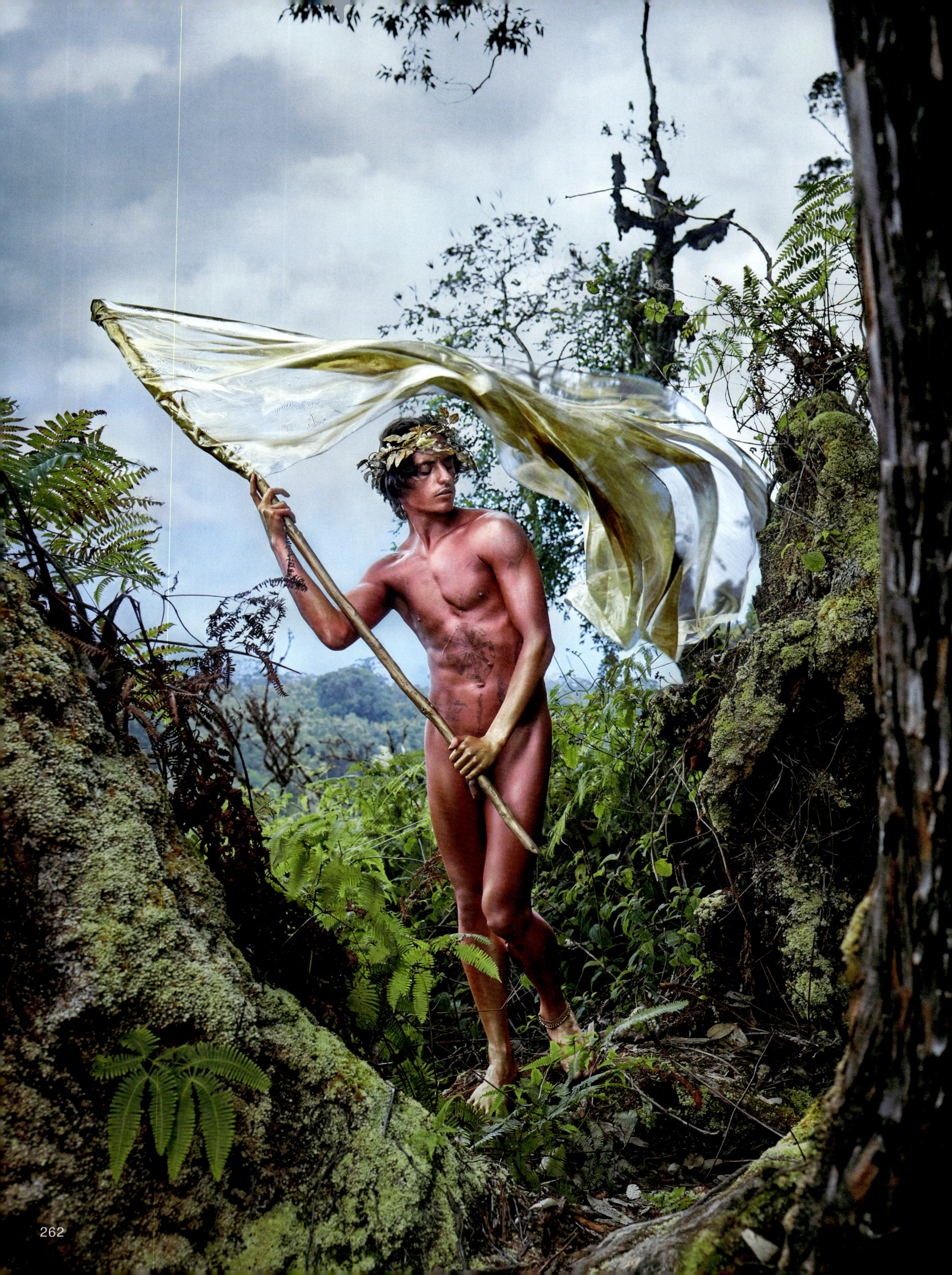

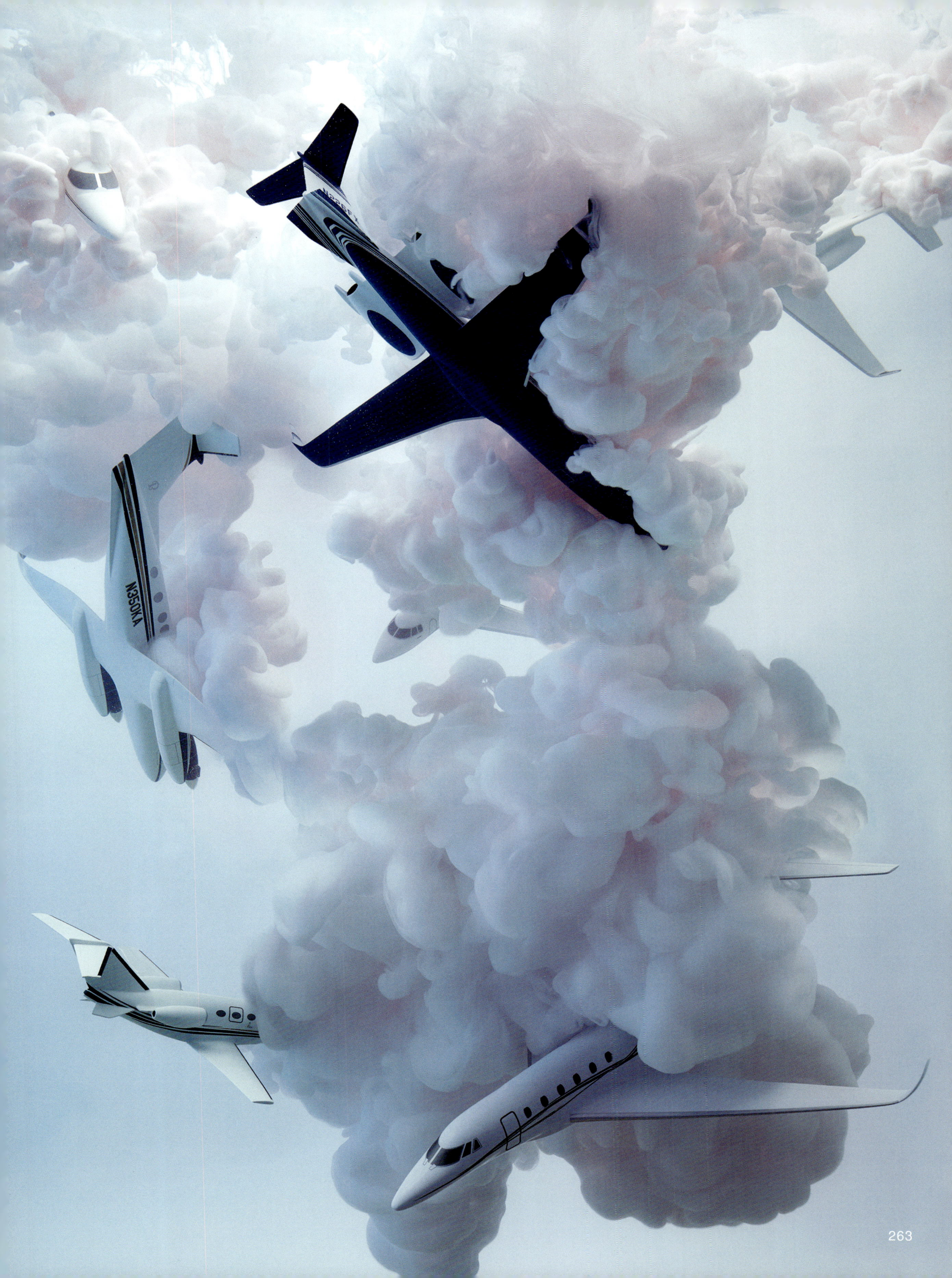
N350KA

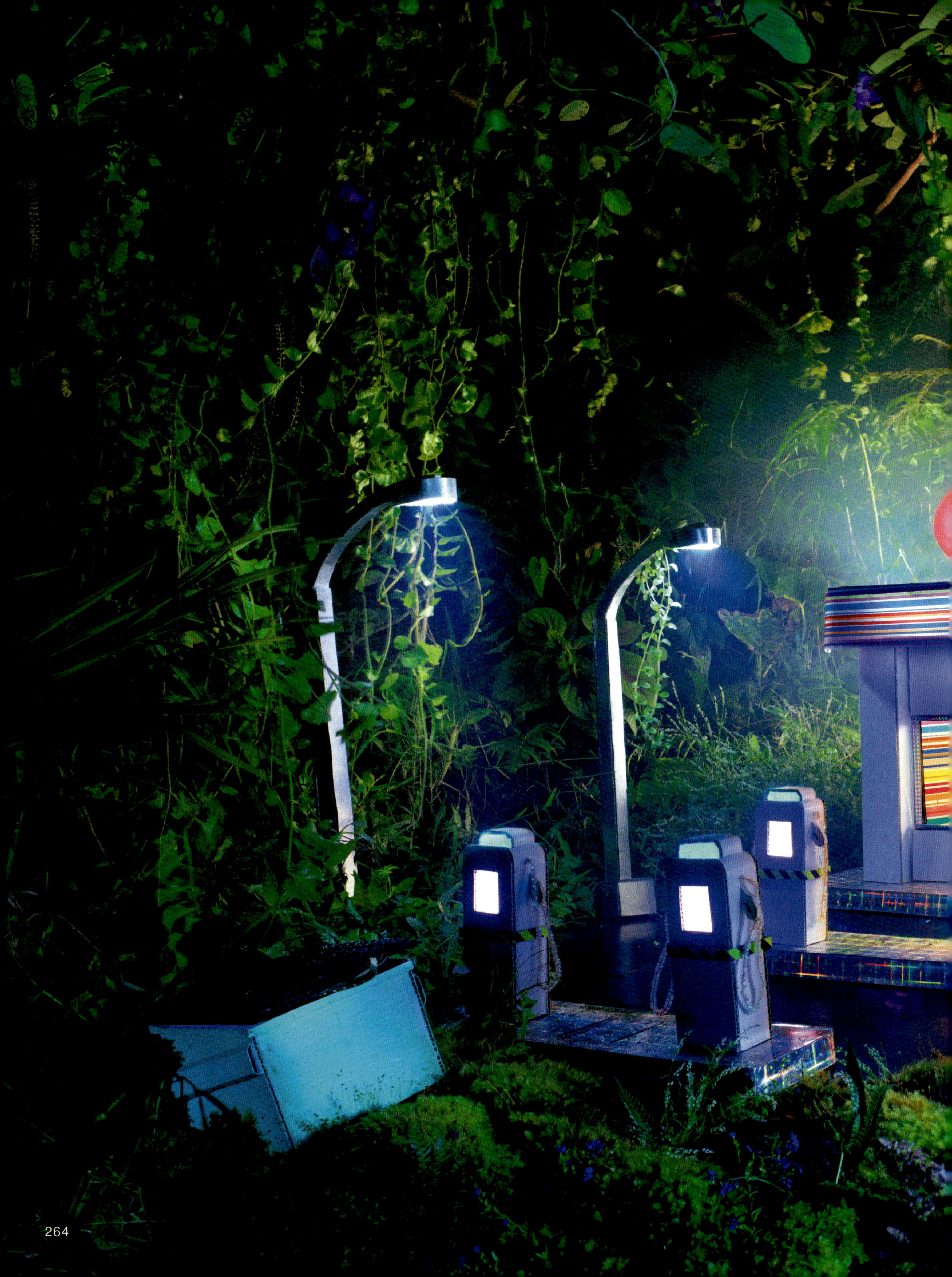

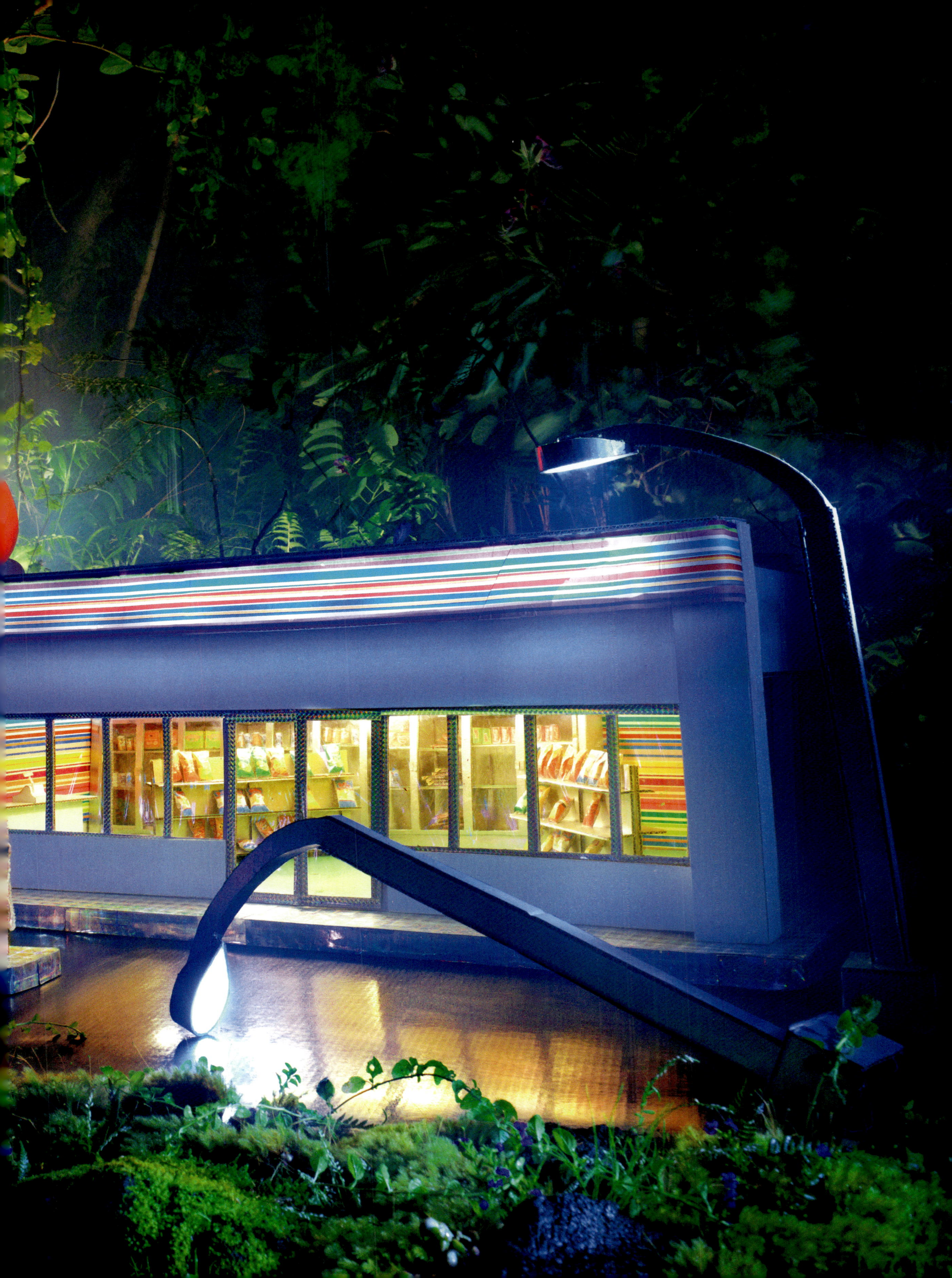

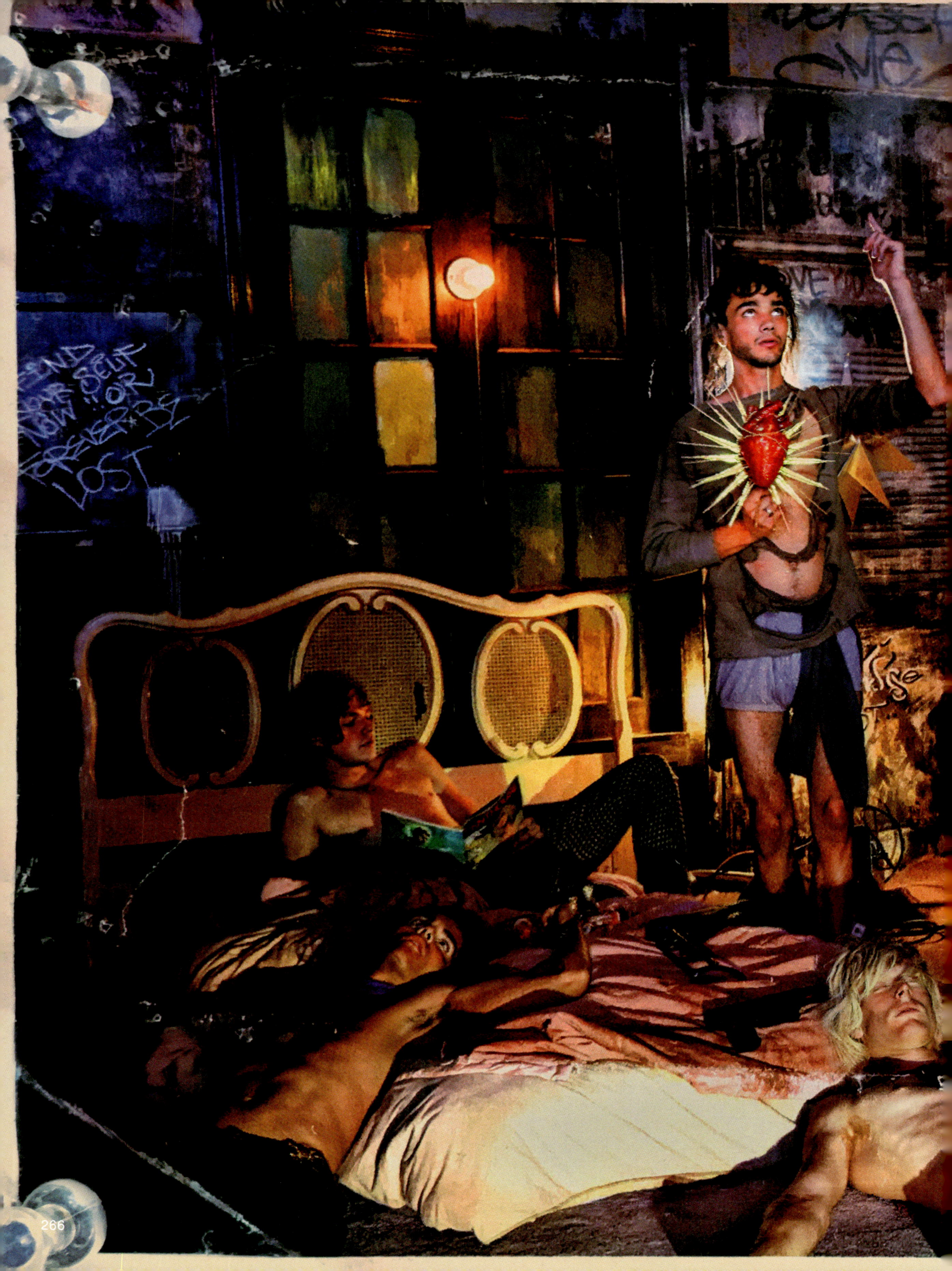
SELF
OR
FOREVER BE
LOST

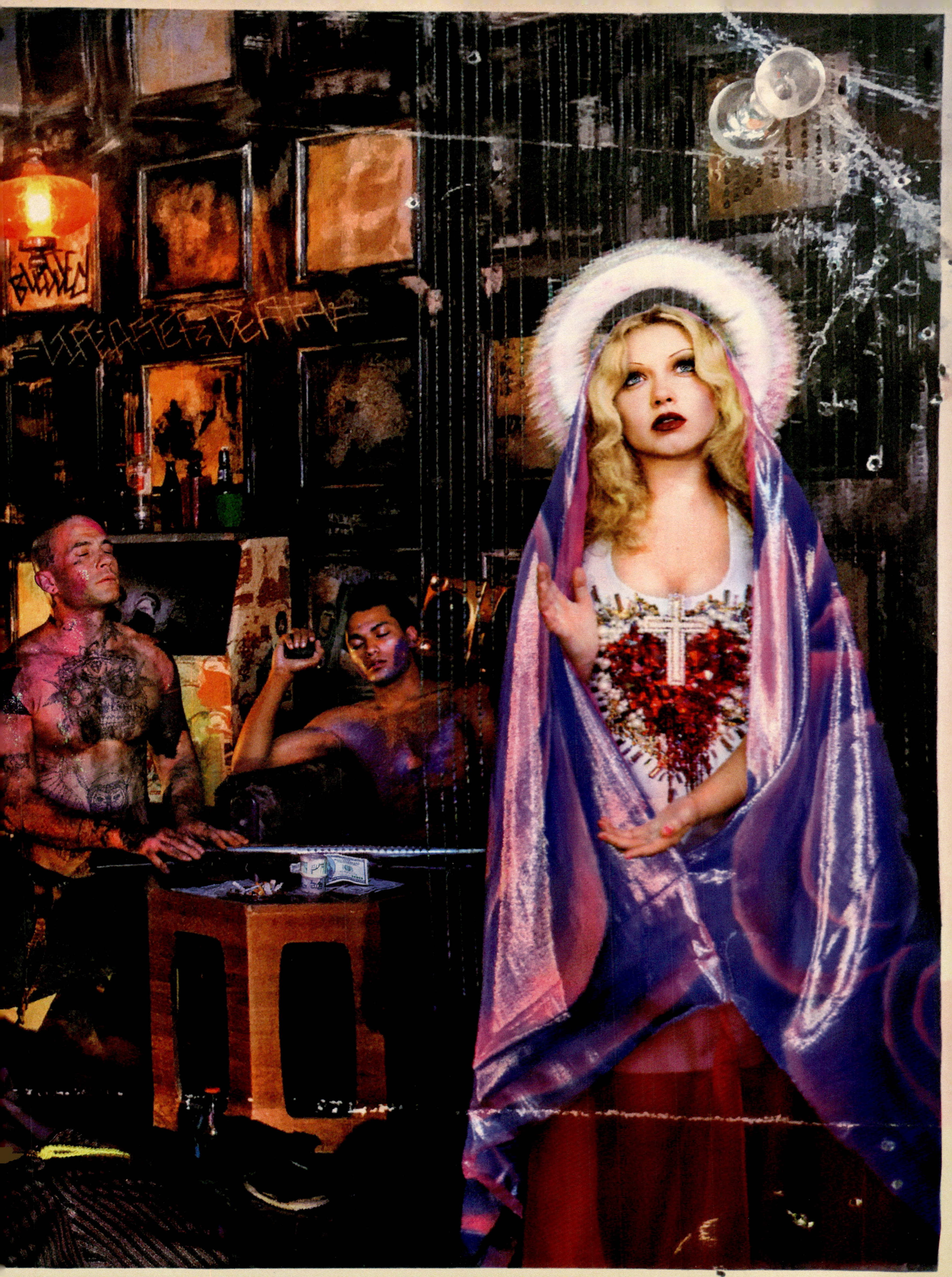

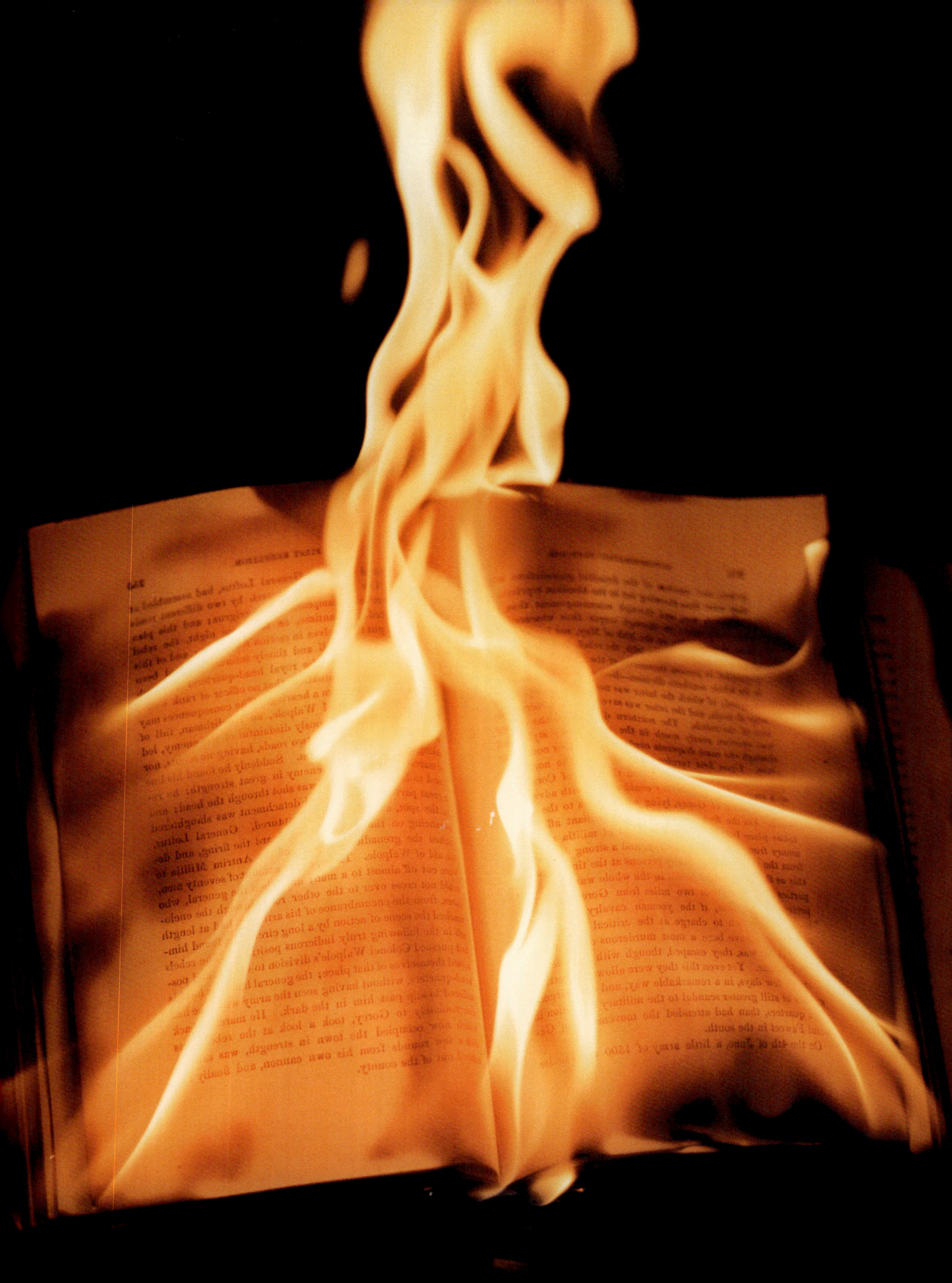

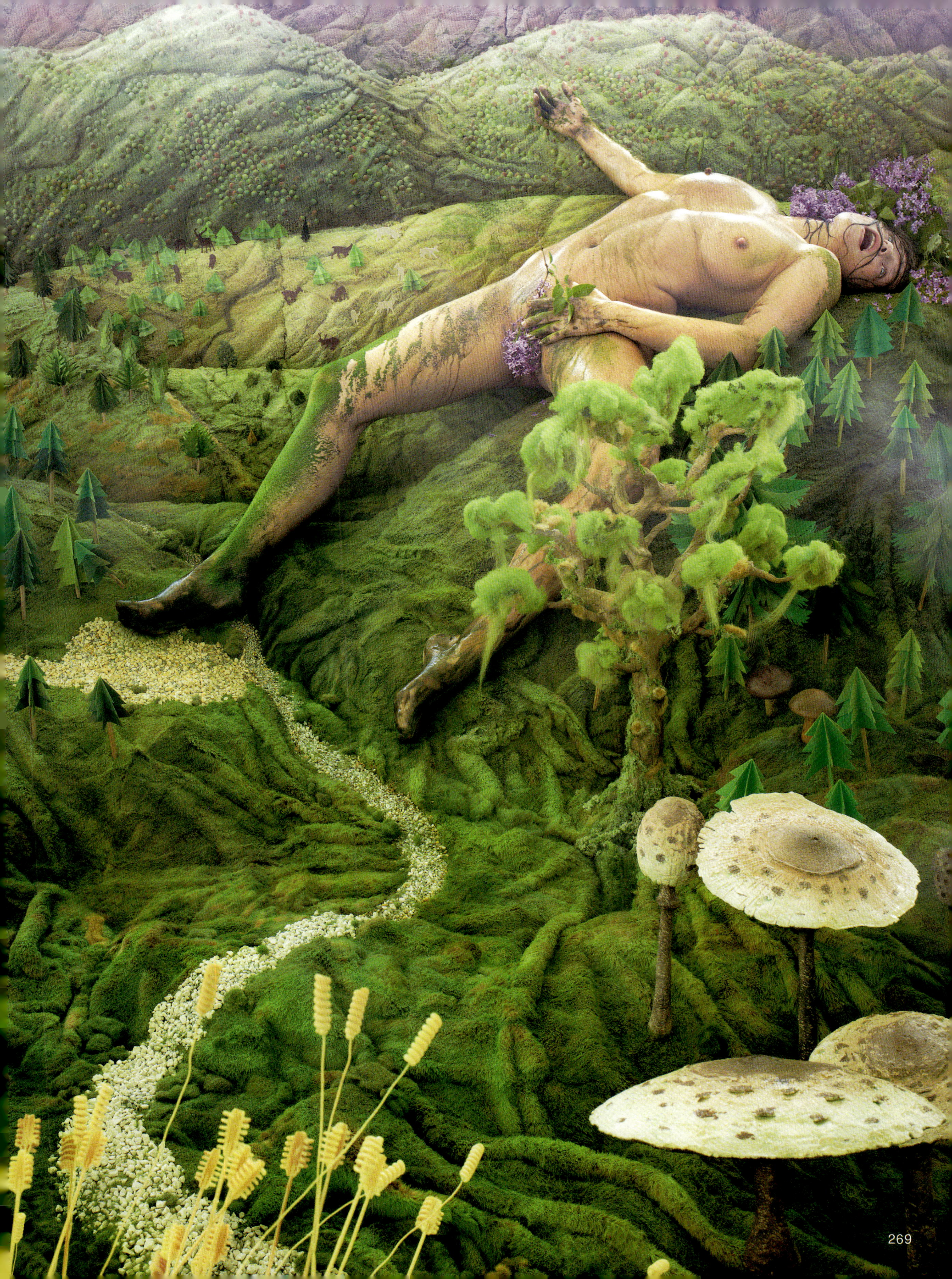

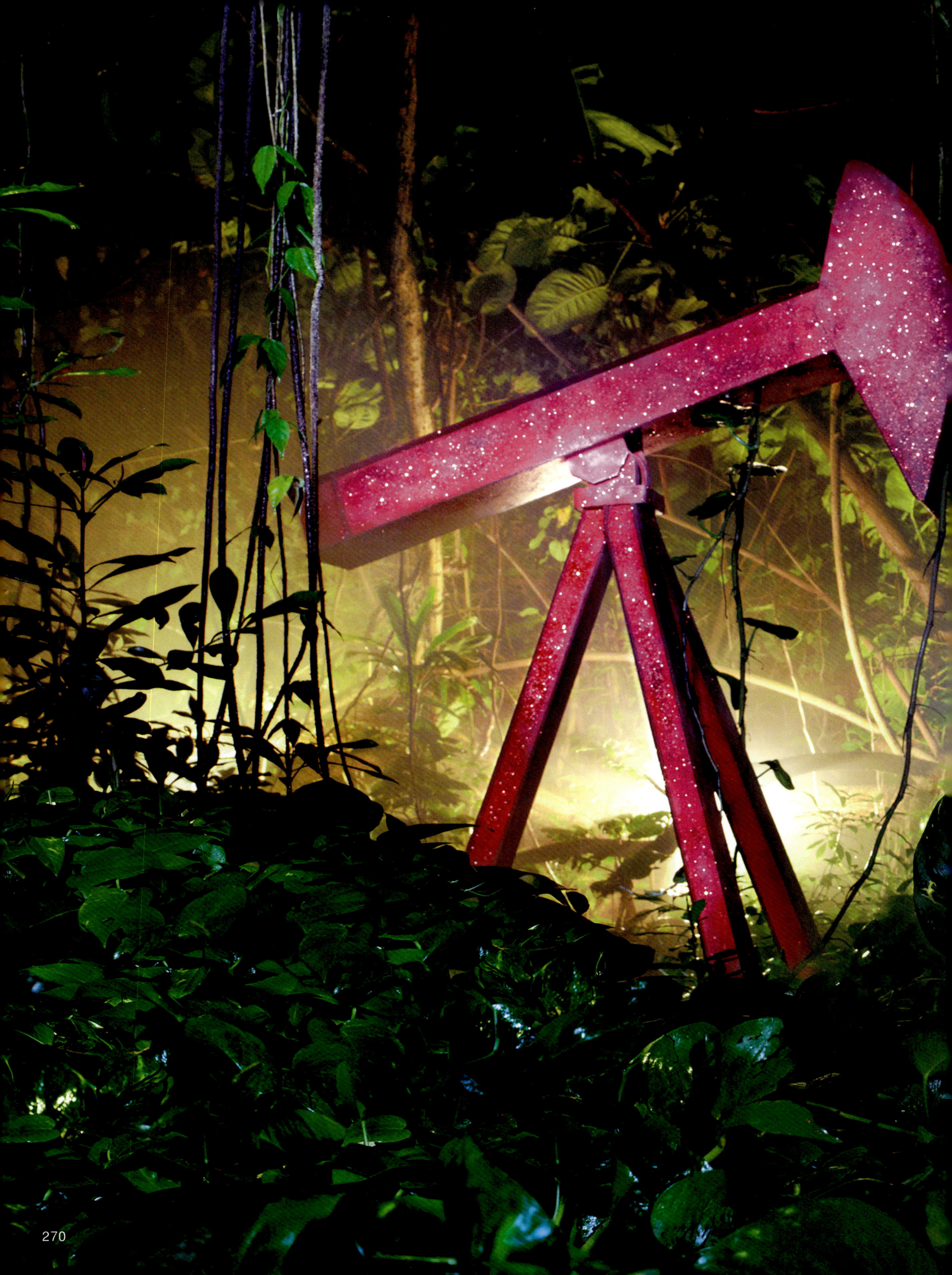

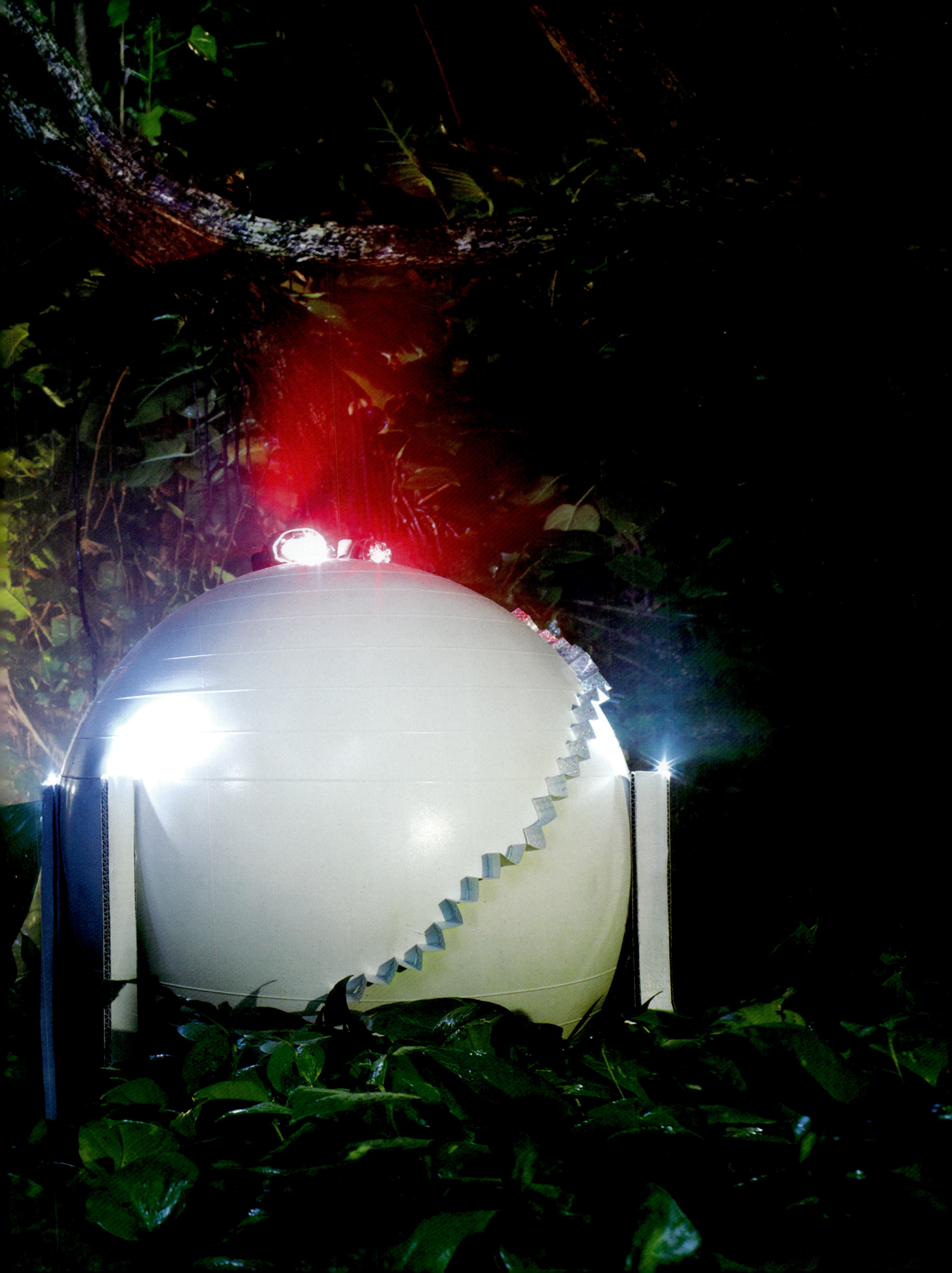

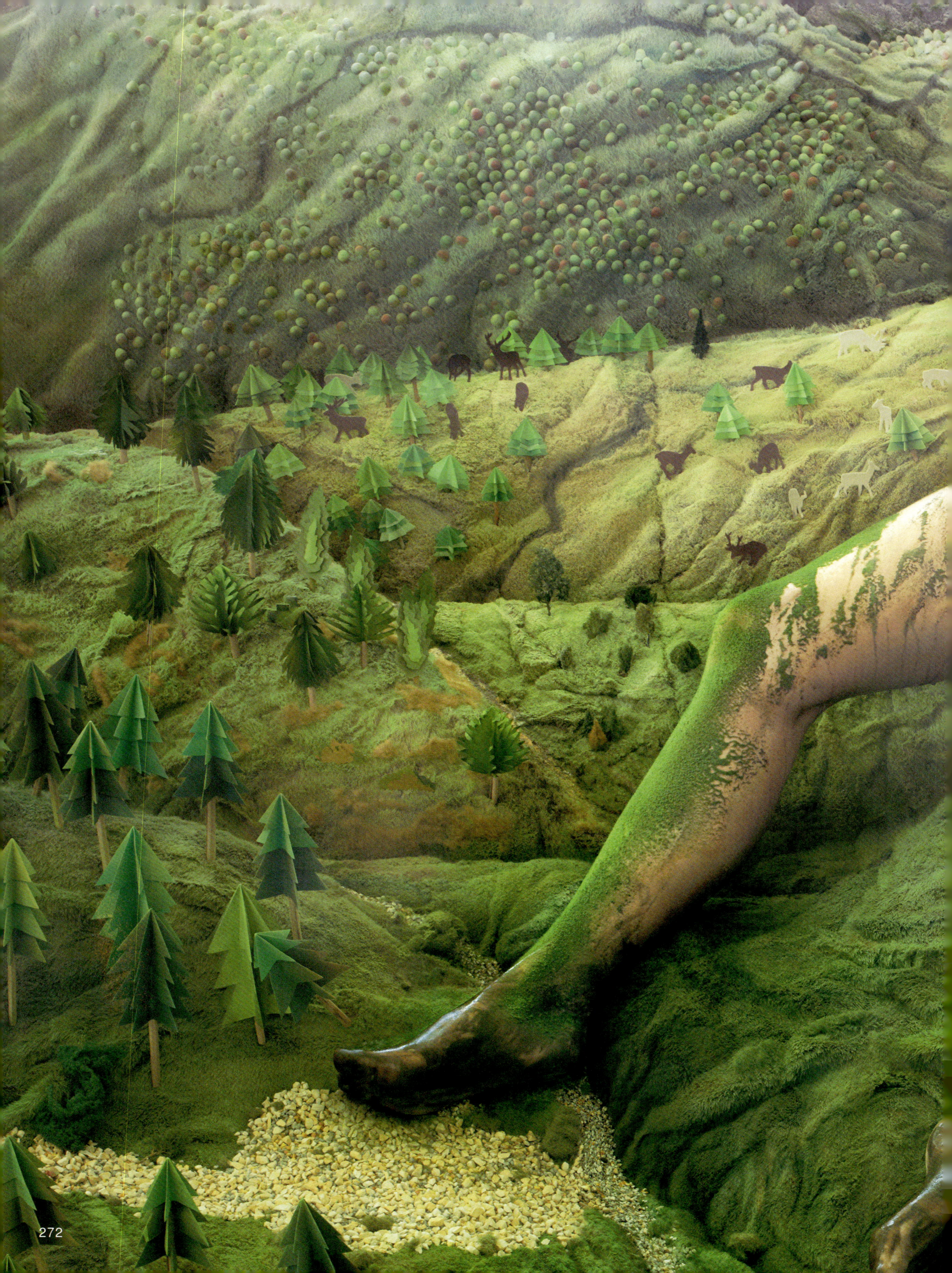

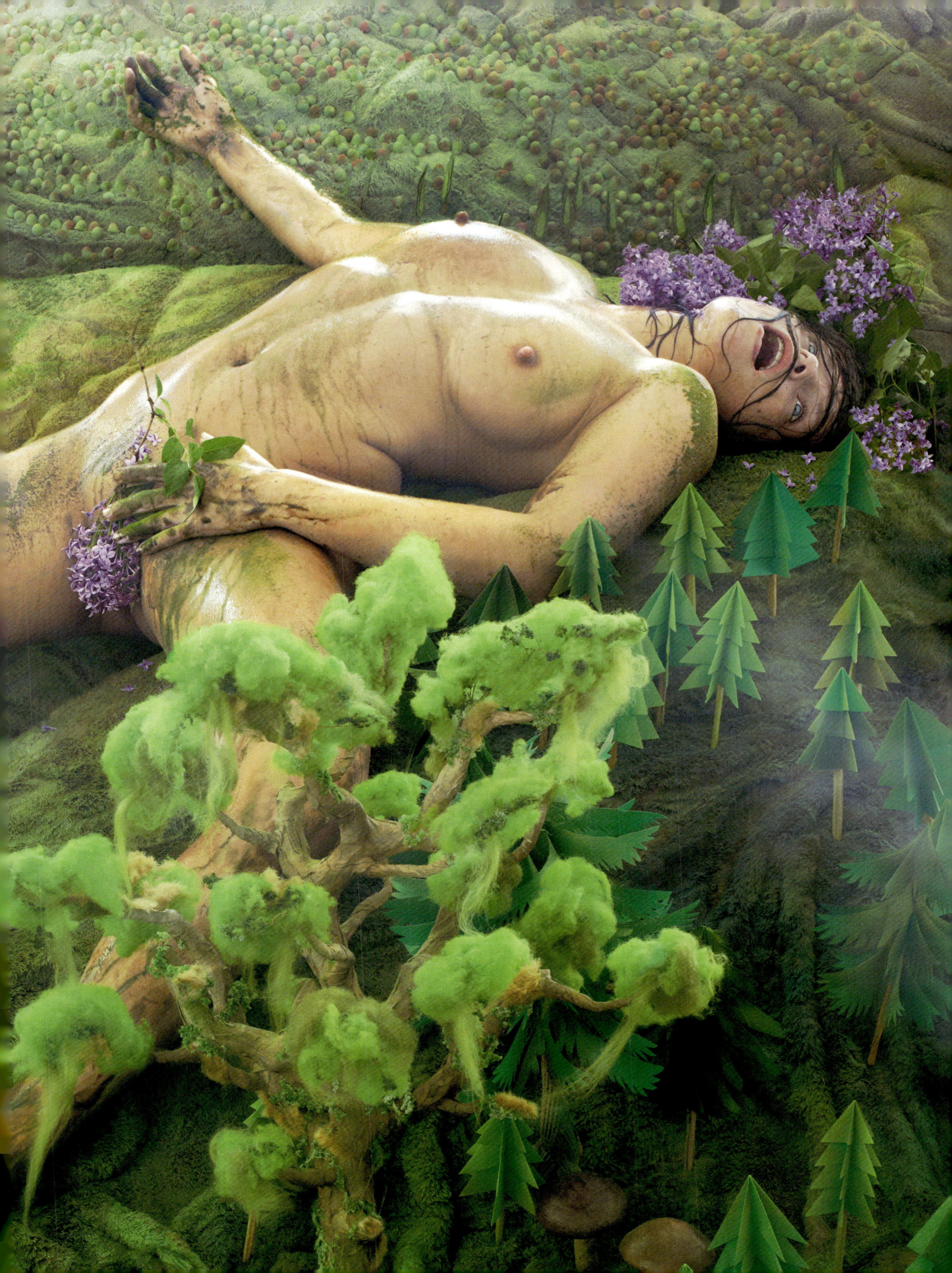

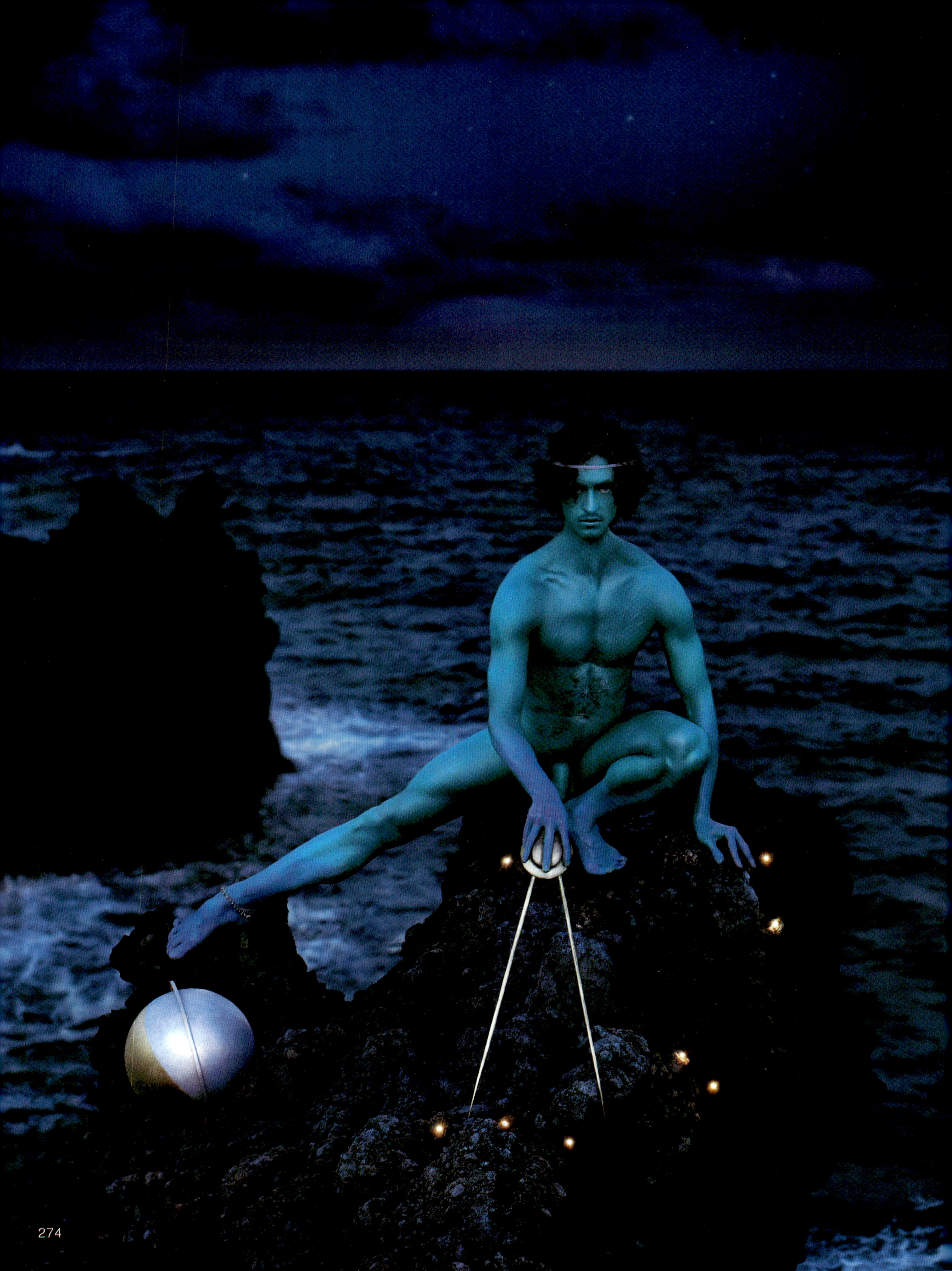

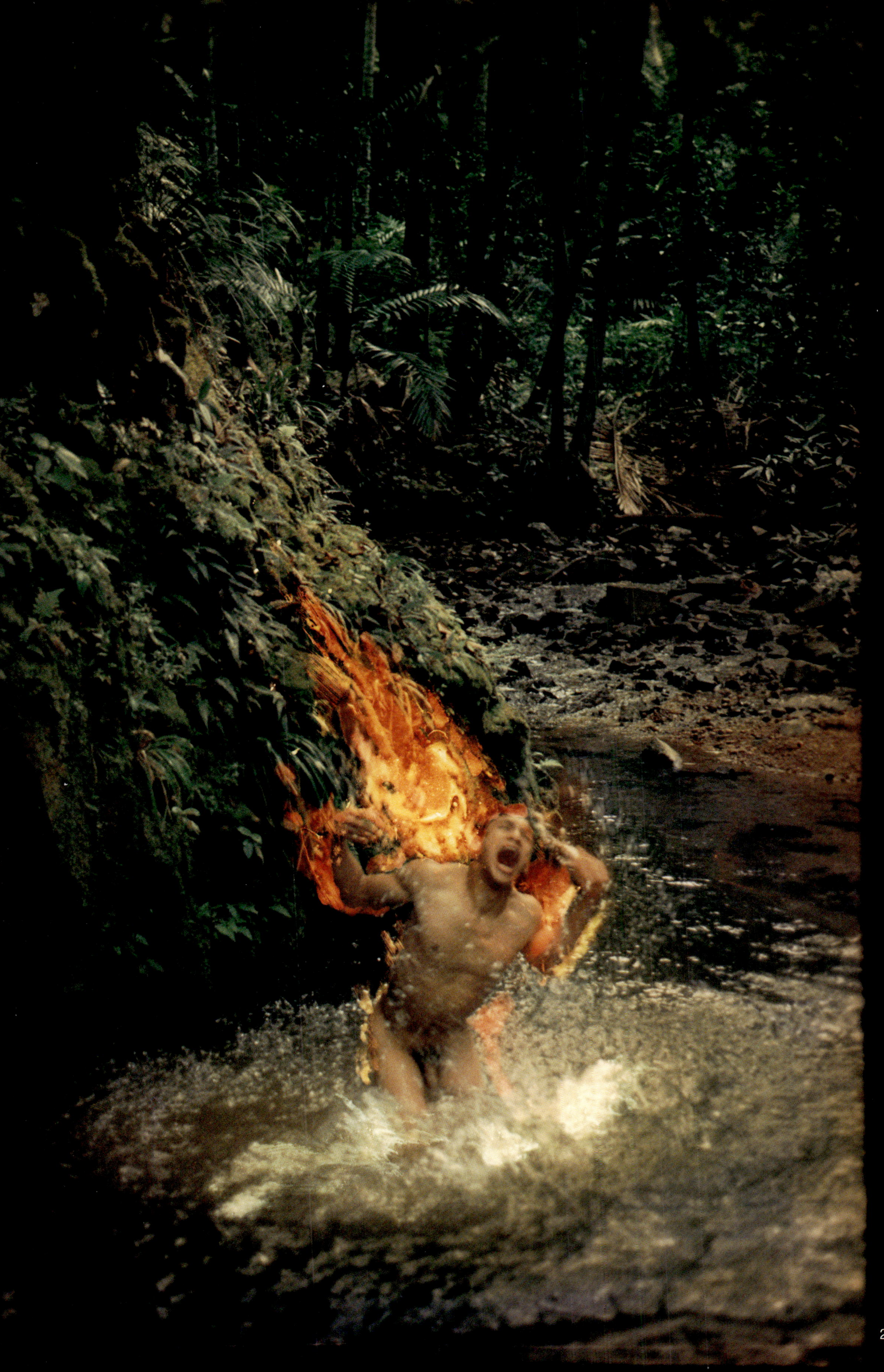

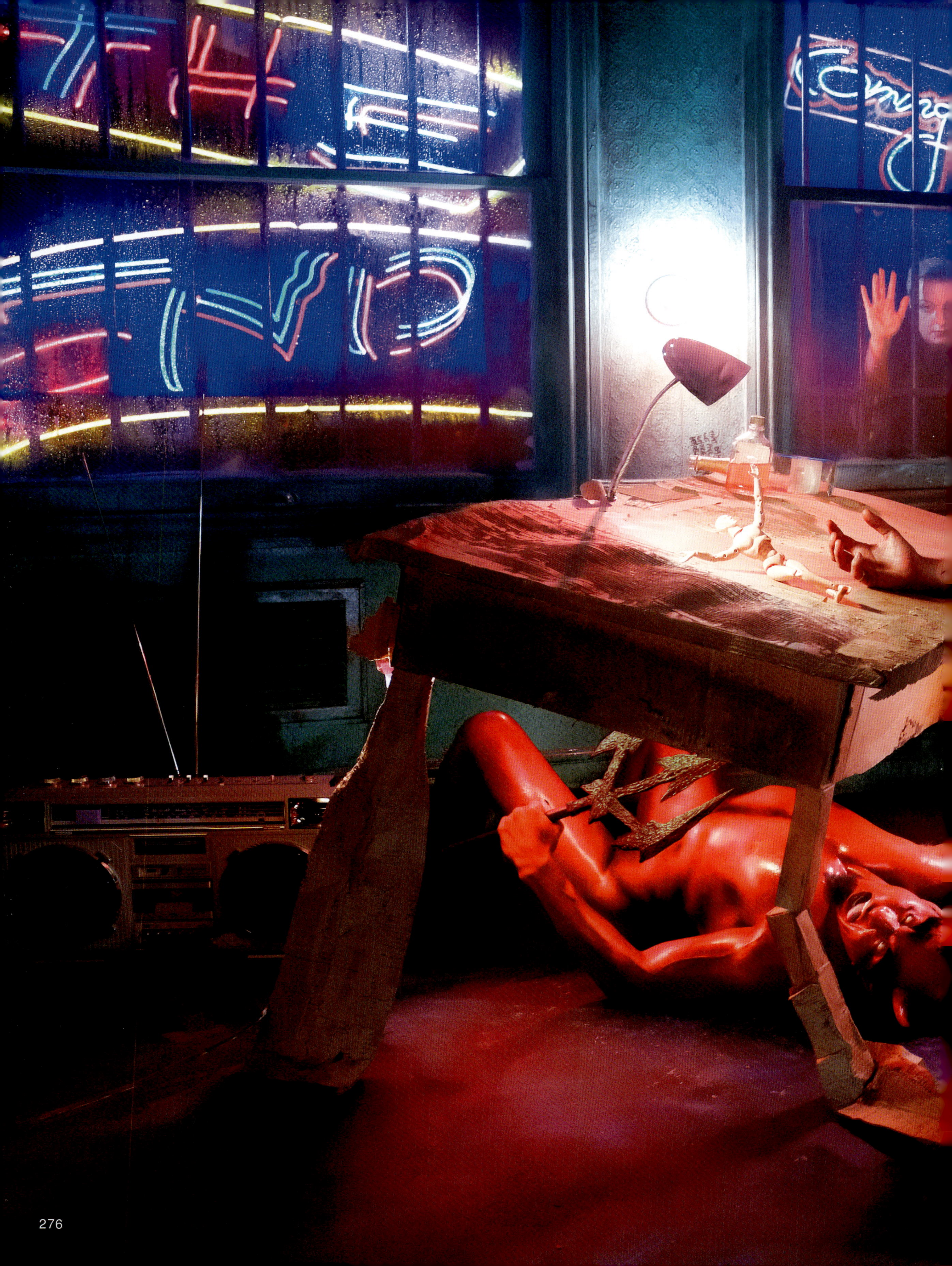

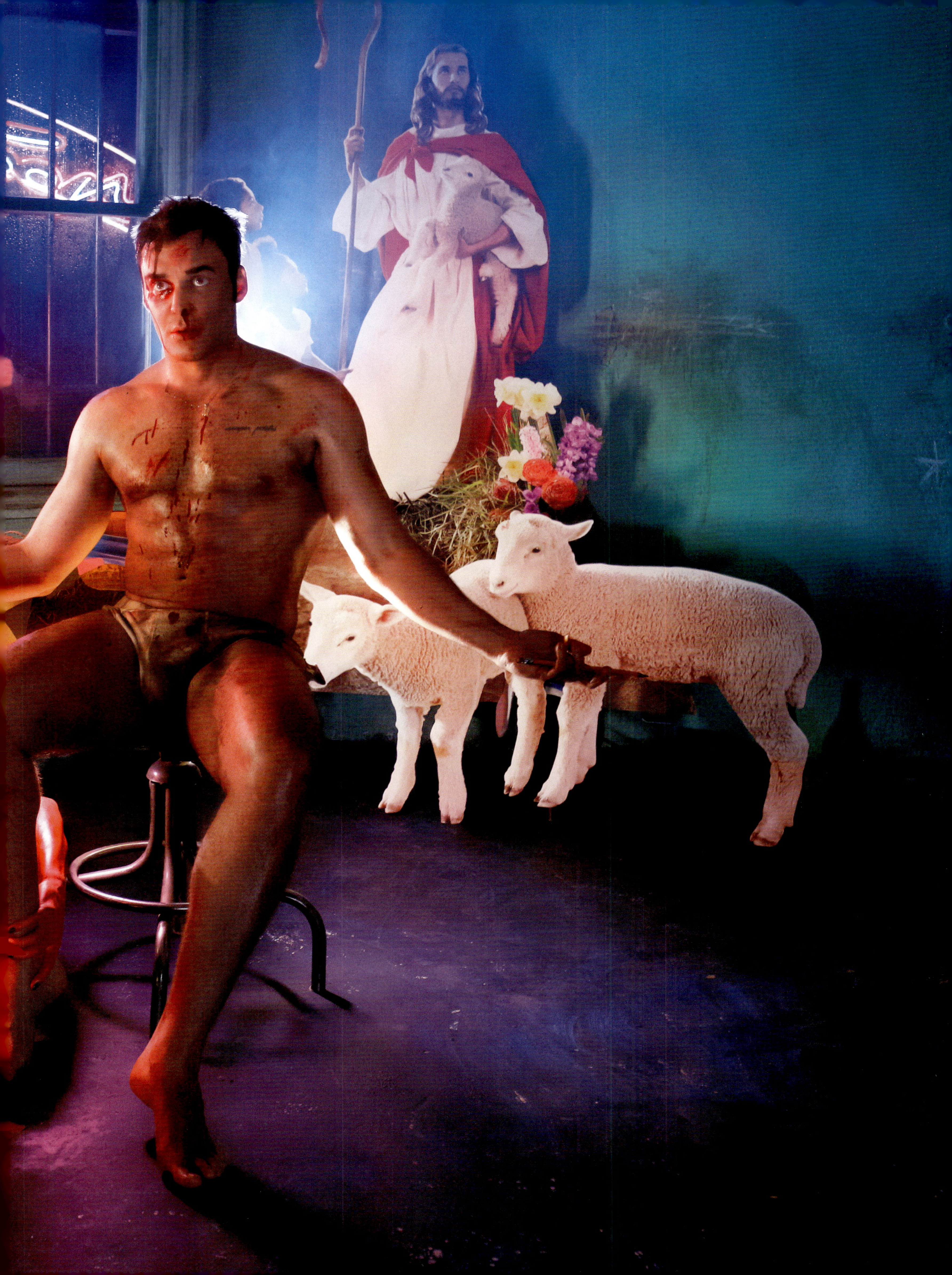

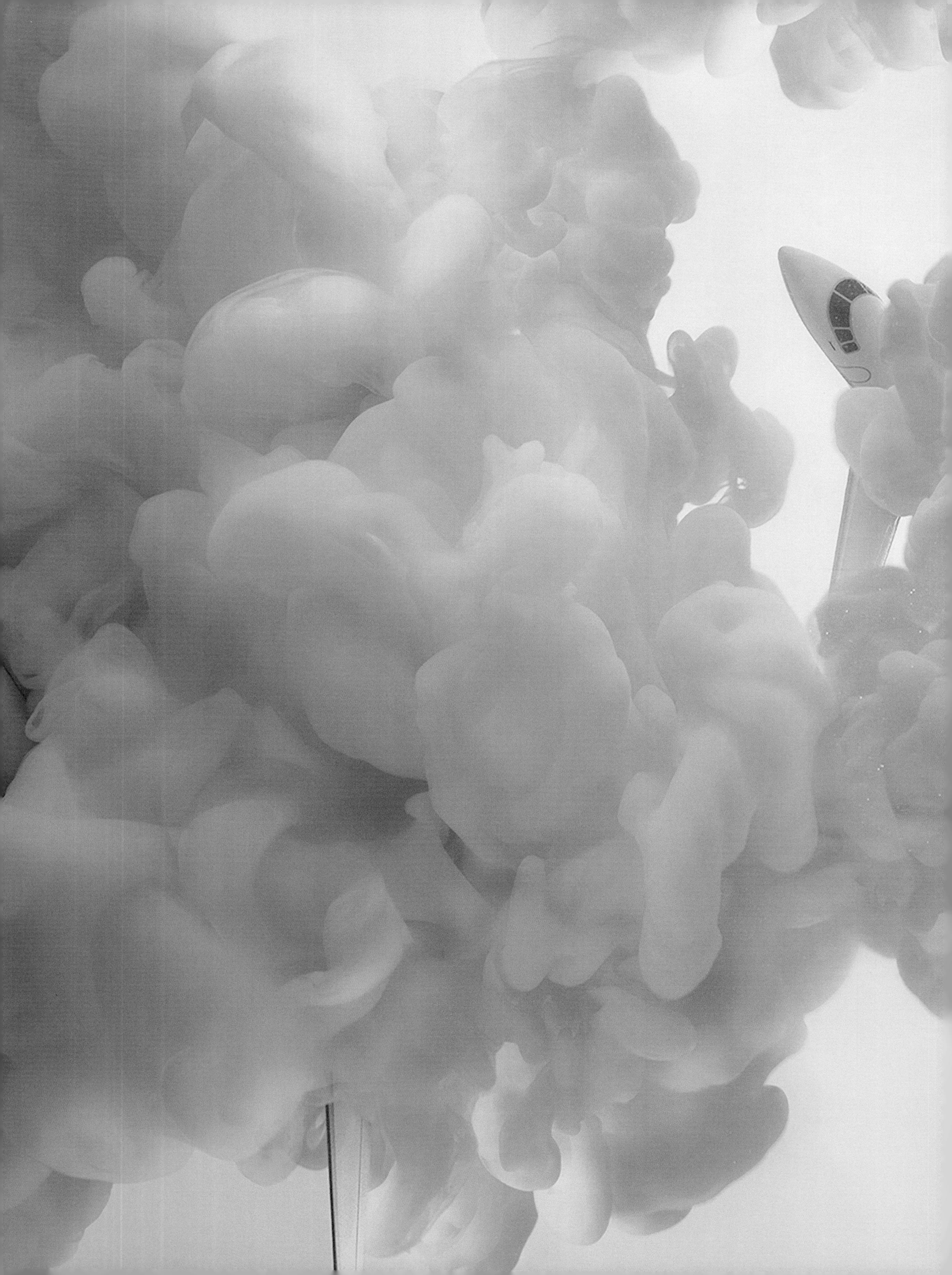

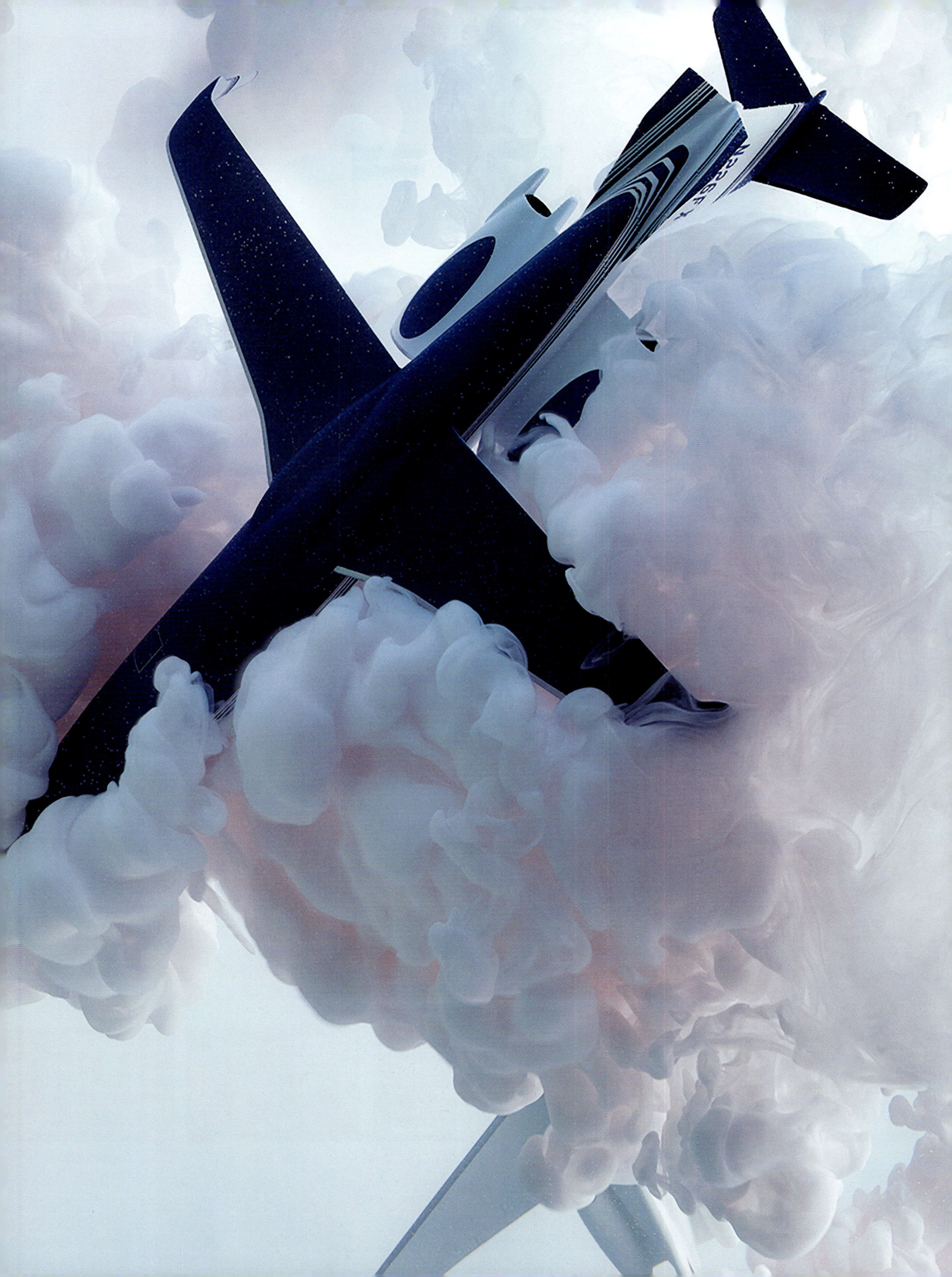

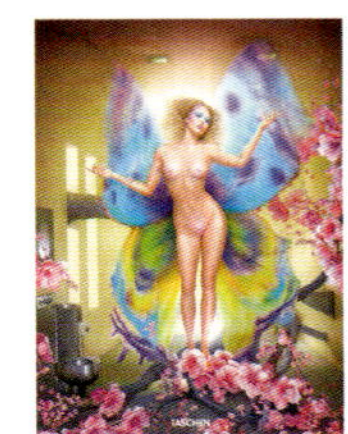

Miley Cyrus
I Walk out of My Prison, 2017

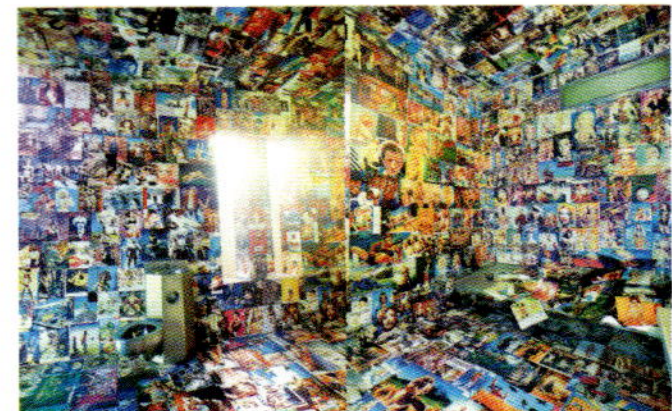

Endpapers I, 2017

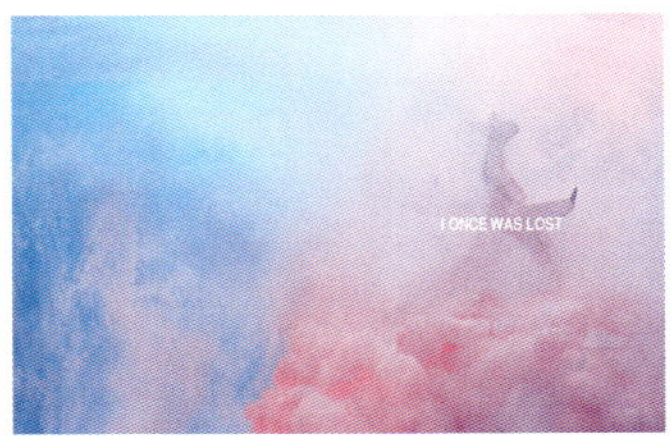

Airistocracy
I Once Was Lost, 2014
Detail

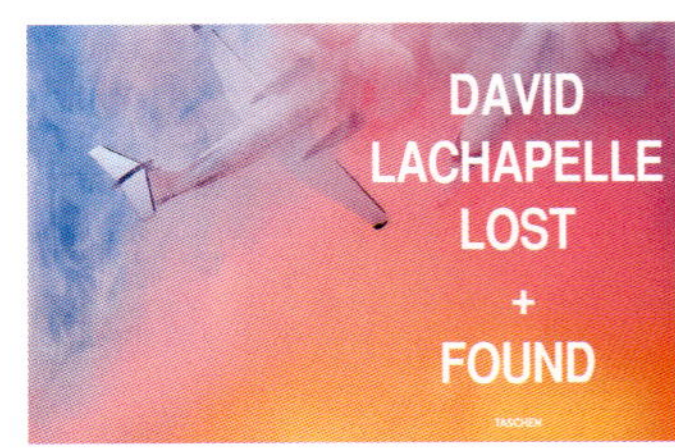

Airistocracy
Lost and Found, 2014
Detail

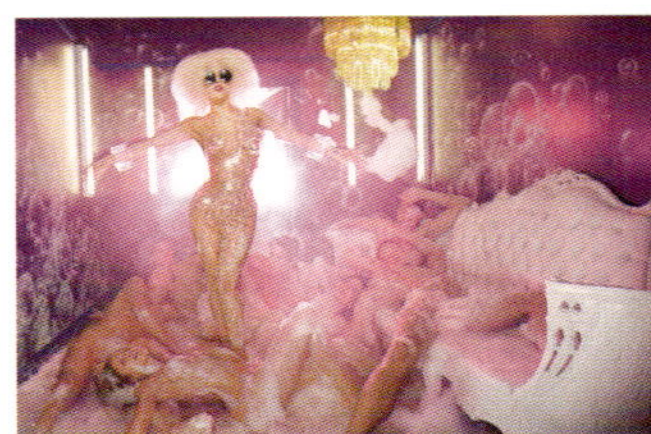

Lady Gaga
Bursting Bubbles, 2009

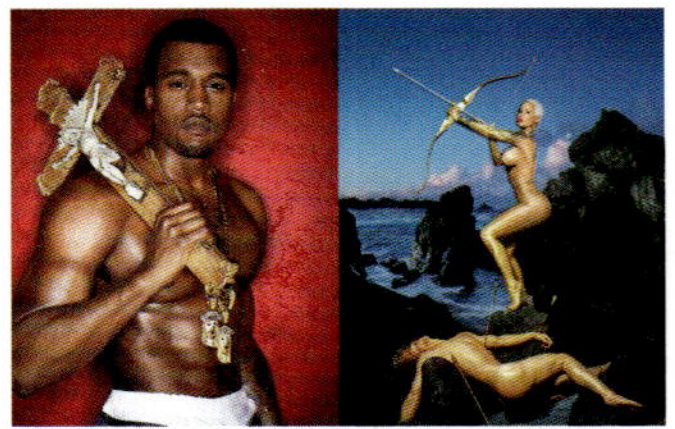

Kanye West
The Cross I Bear, 2006

Amber Rose
I Don't Wear Bows,
I Shoot Them, 2015

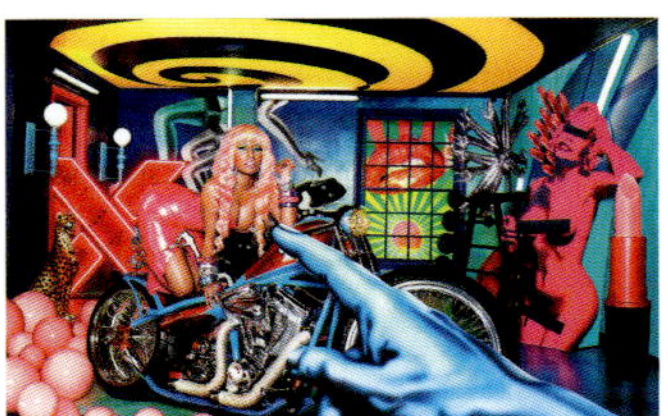

Nicki Minaj
Superbass, 2011

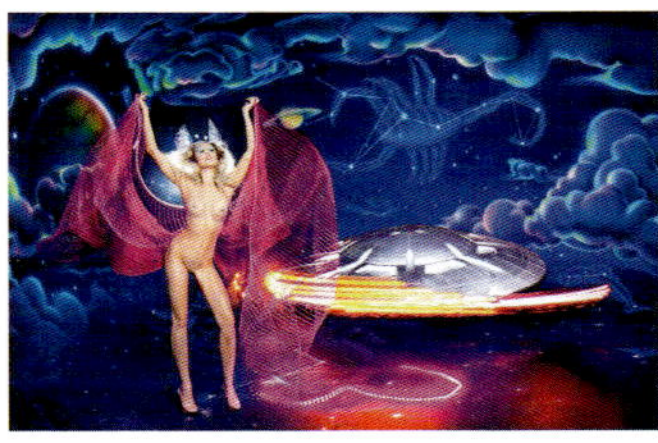

Miley Cyrus
I Look Up and Try to See,
The Stars Are Looking Back
at Me, 2016

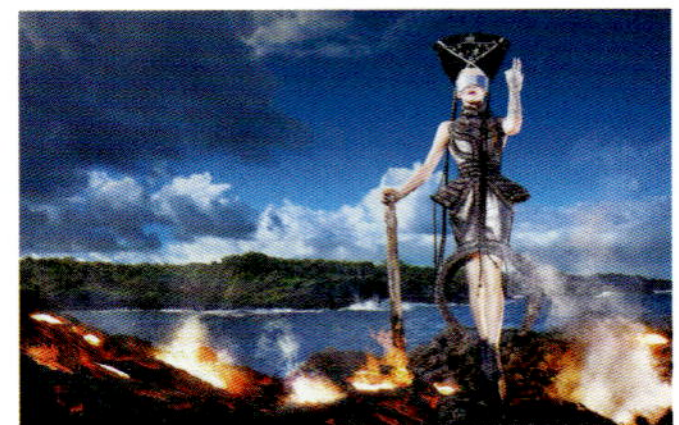

Daphne Guinness, 2012
"My clothes and jewelry became my armor." —Daphne Guinness

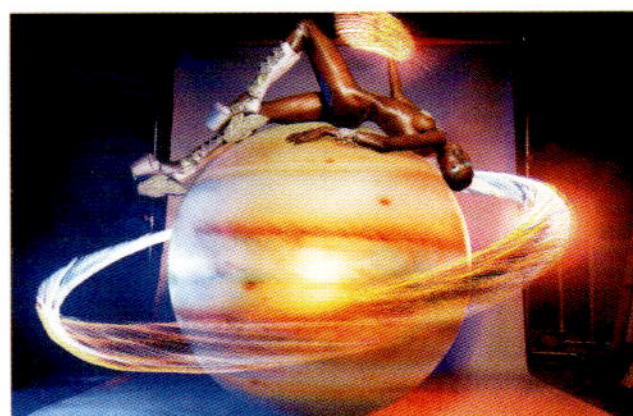

Graceful Planet, 2017

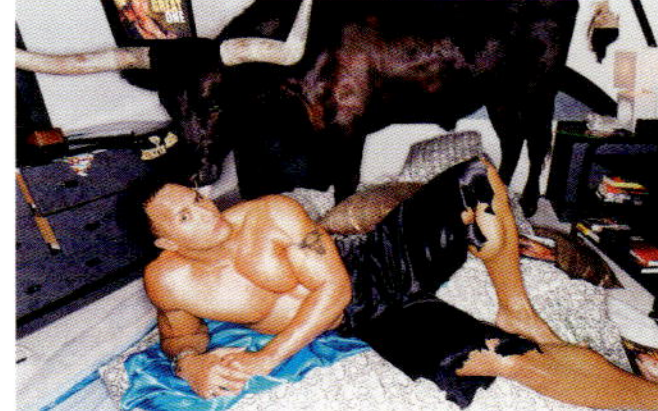

Dwayne Johnson
President Rock, 2001

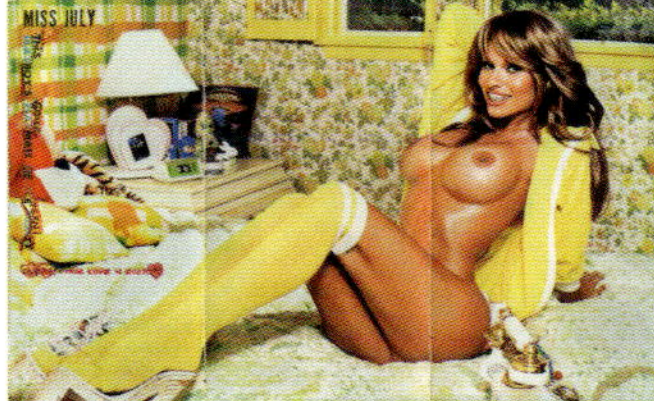

Pamela Anderson
21 Forever, 2000

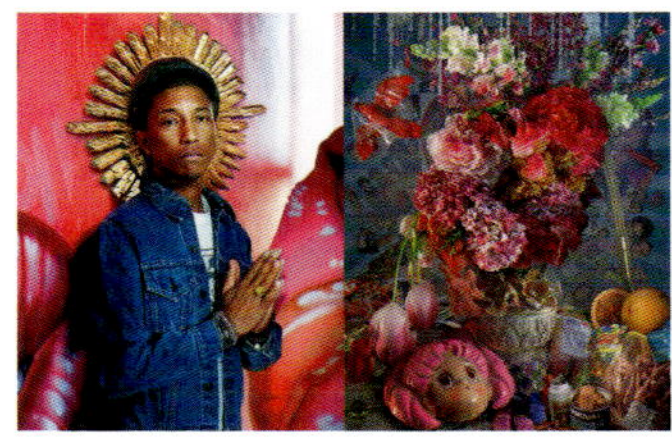

Pharrell Williams
Because I'm Happy, 2016

Earth Laughs in Flowers
Rite of Spring, 2008–2011
Detail

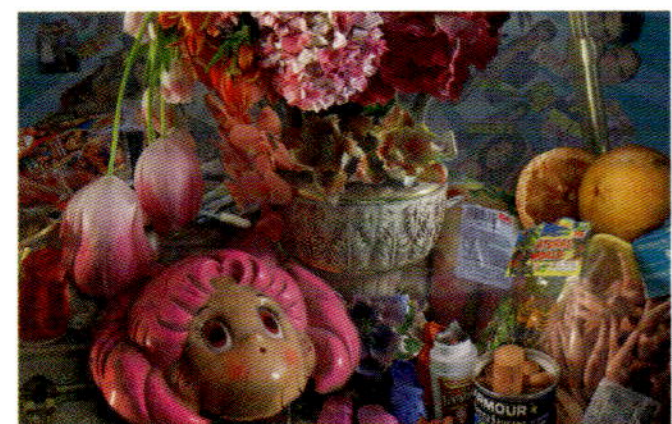

Earth Laughs in Flowers
Rite of Spring, 2008–2011
Detail

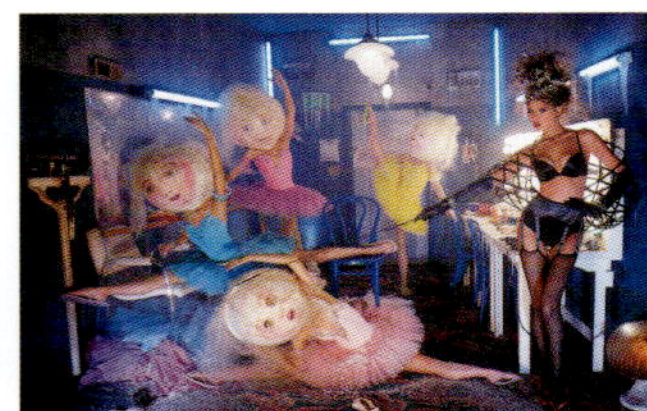

Pointeless, 2011

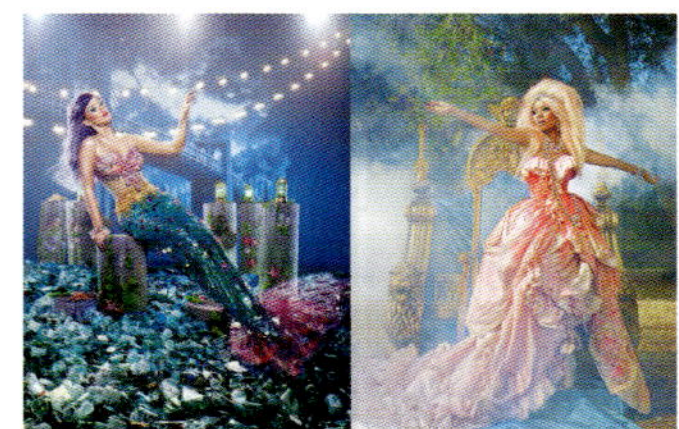

Katy Perry
Siren and the
Synthetic Sea, 2011

Nicki Minaj
Minajesty, 2013

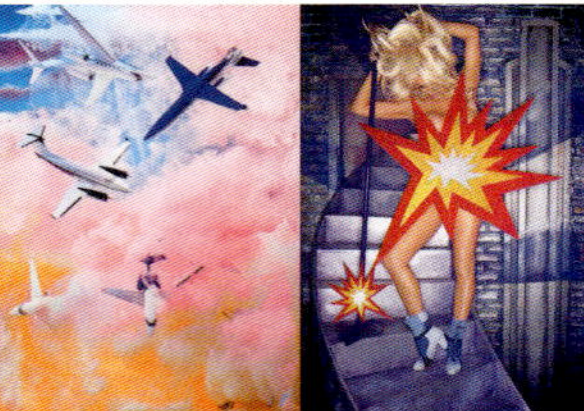

Airistocracy
In Decadence
I Once Reclined, 2014

Pamela Anderson
Mademoiselle
Bombshell, 2016

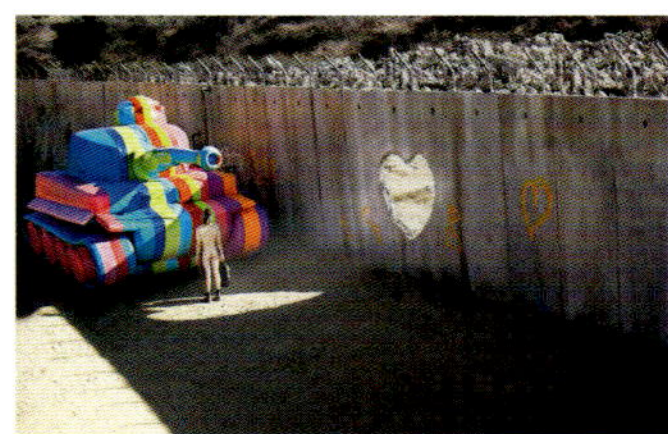

Make Love Not Walls, 2017

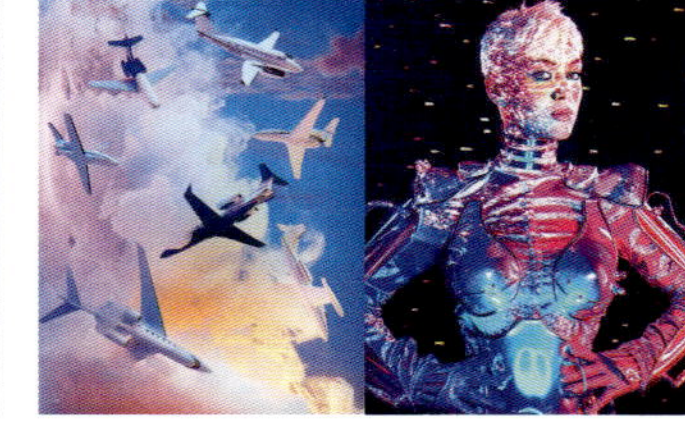

Airistocracy
Mankind's Manic Race, 2014

Katy Perry
Lost in Space, 2017

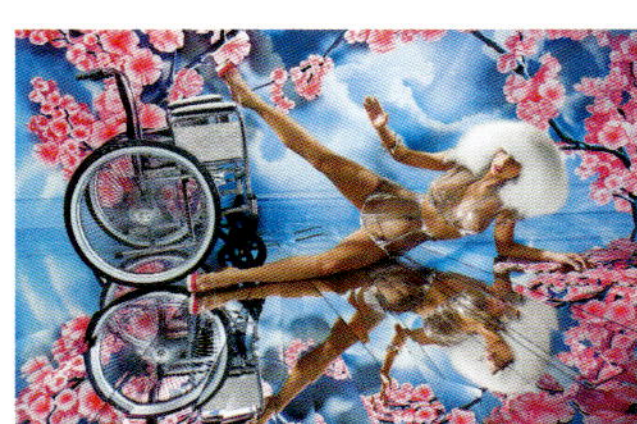

Lady Gaga
Life Alert, 2009

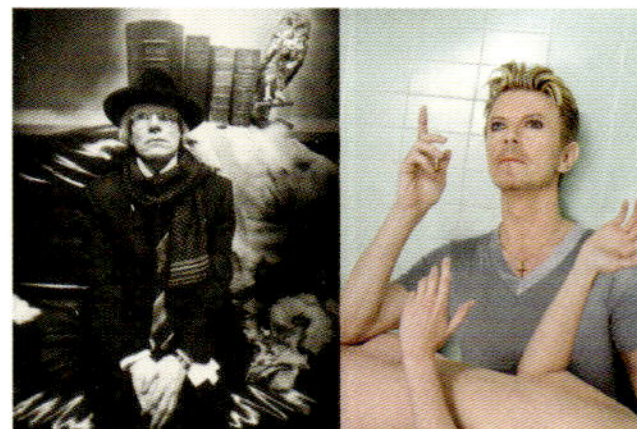

Andy Warhol, 1987
"I'm a deeply superficial person."
—Andy Warhol

David Bowie, 1995
"And the stars look very different today." —David Bowie

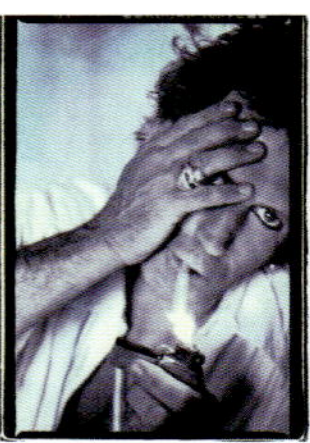

Keith Richards
Lose Your Dreams and You Will
Lose Your Mind, 1992

Sergei Polunin
Dancer, 2016

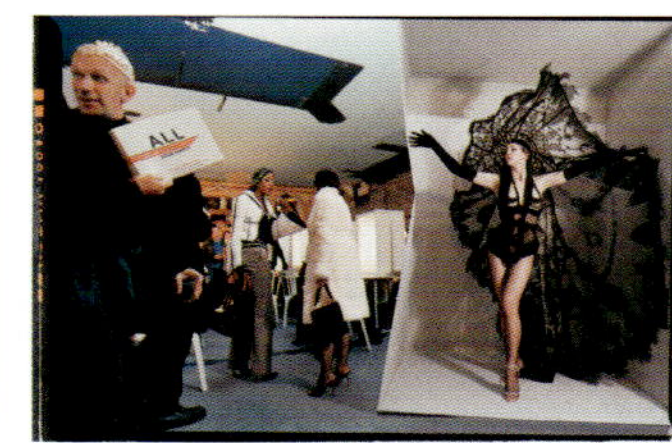

All, 2003

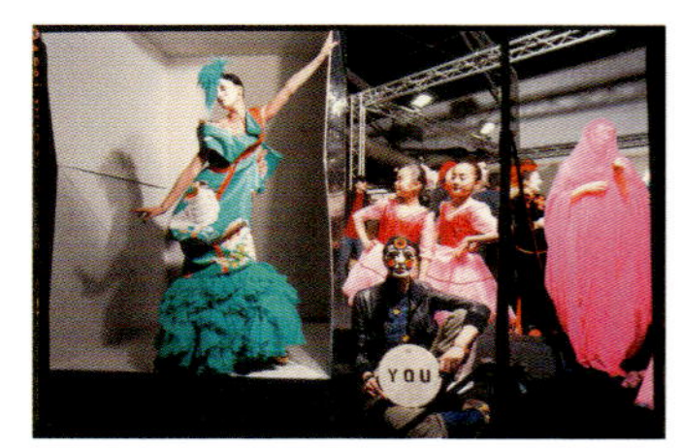

You, 2003

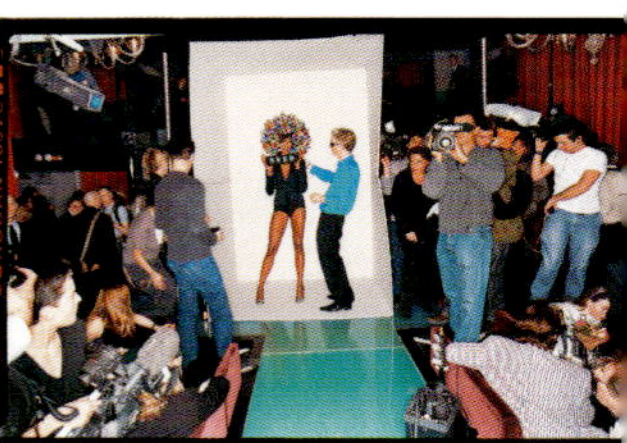

Need, 2003

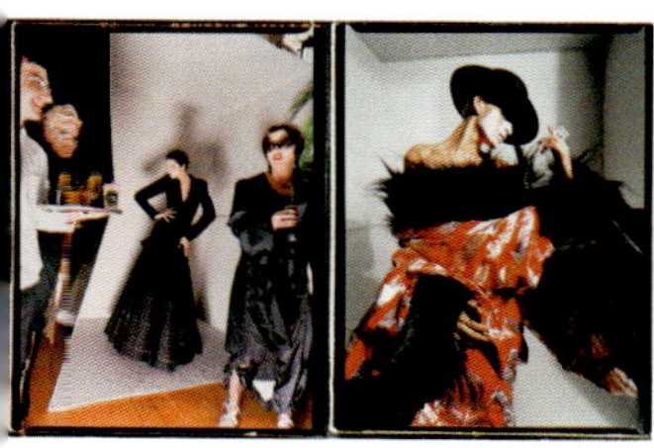

Is, 2003

Love, 2003

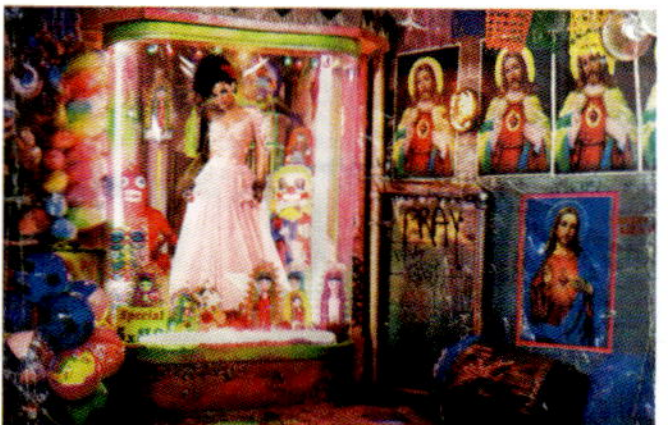

Rihanna
Where Have You Been, 2007

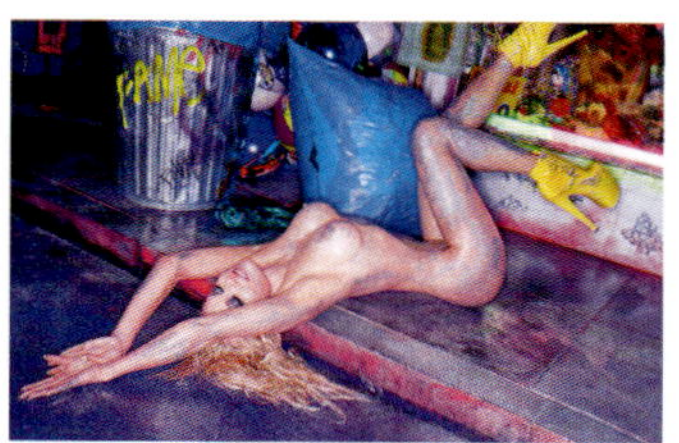

Pamela Anderson
Forget the Pain
Let's Go Insane, 2016

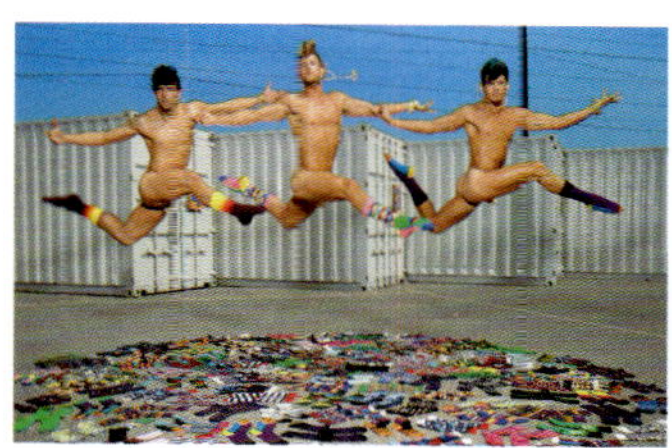

"Youth has no age. Be free."
— Pablo Picasso
2013

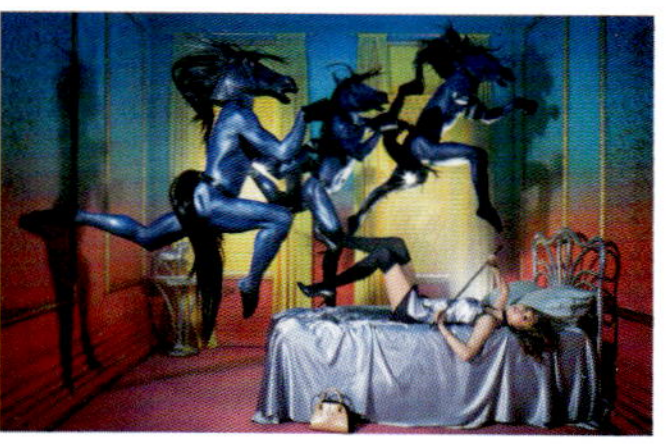

Equestria, 2013

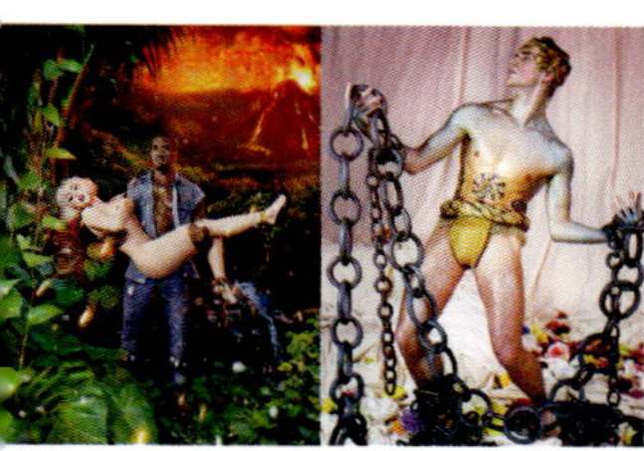

Kanye West, Lady Gaga
Fame Monster, 2009

Sergei Polunin
A Body Can Be Free With a Mind
That Lives Imprisoned, 2017

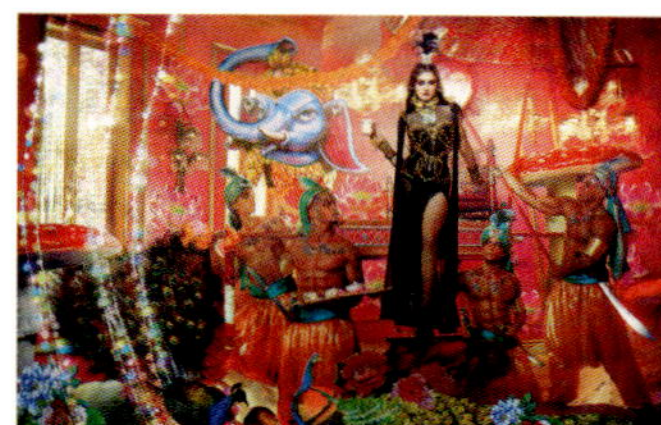

I Was Born Lonely I Guess, 2010

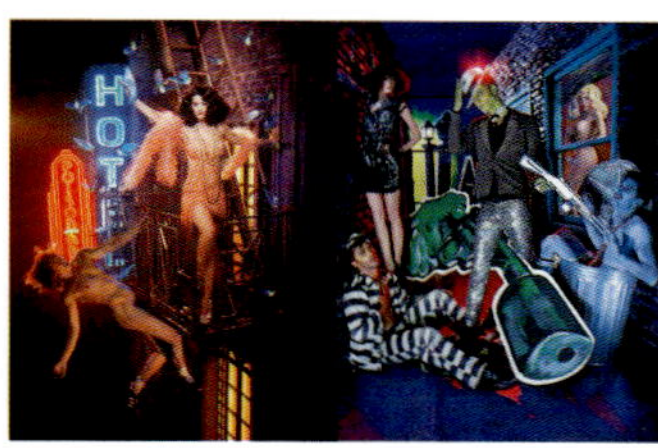

Katy Perry
The Drop of Shame, 2015

Amanda Lepore
Bullets Over Broadway, 2010

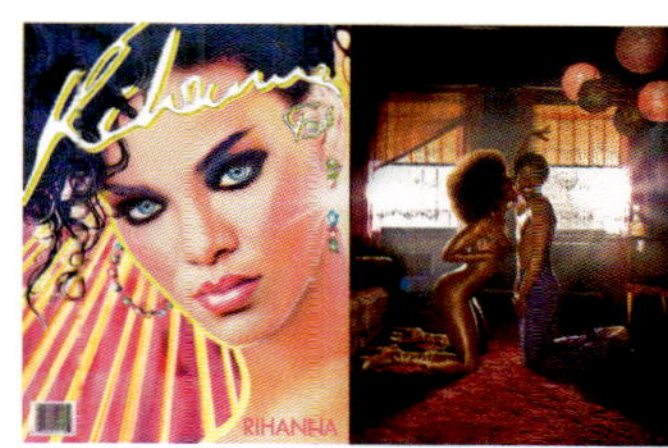

Rihanna, 2013
*"The kind of girl you read about in
the new wave magazines."*
— *Super Freak*,
Alonzo Miller / Rick James

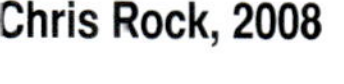

Chris Rock, 2008

Lana Del Rey
Newlyweds, 2017

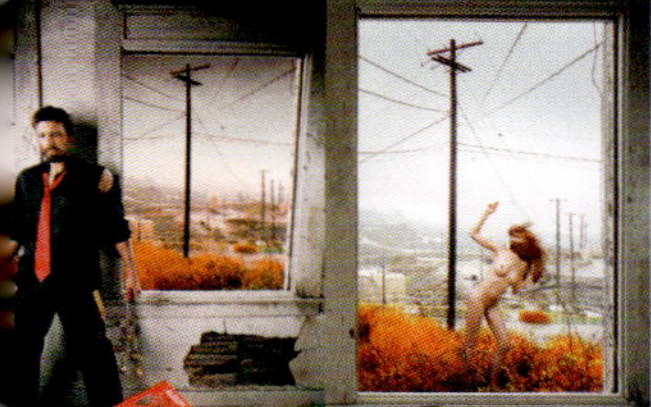

Ben Affleck
Gone Girl, 2004

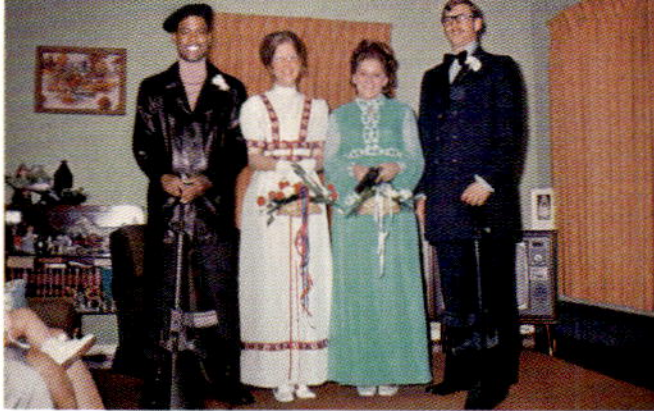

Chris Rock
Gun Control and Casserole, 2008

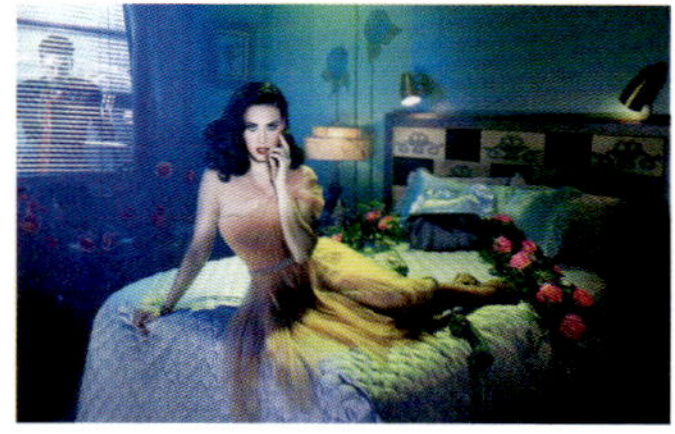

Katy Perry, 2011
*"I have always depended
on the kindness of strangers."*
— Tennessee Williams

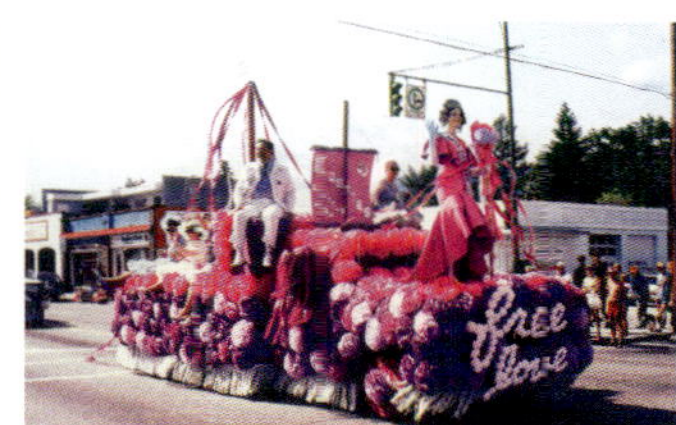

Lana Del Rey
Free Love, 2017

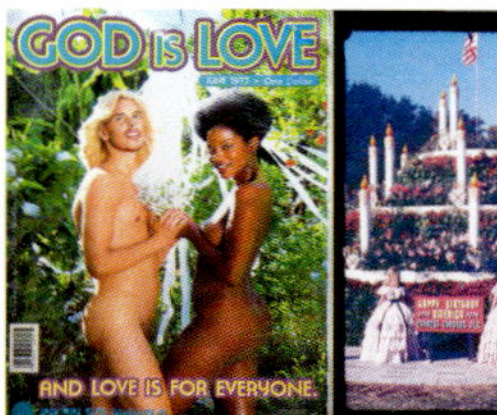

Love Is for Everyone, 2017

Lana Del Rey
Bicentennial Birthday, 2017

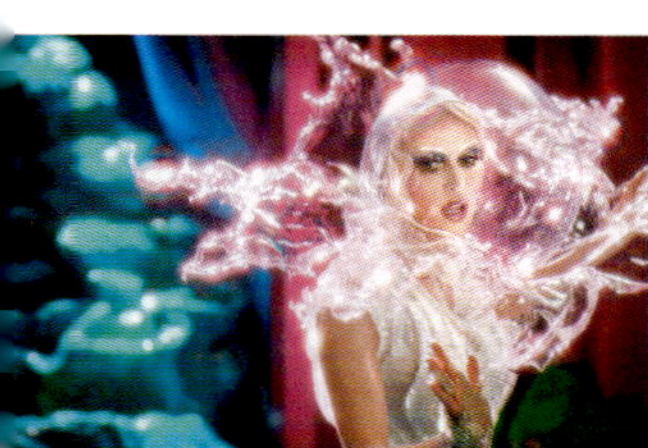

Daphne Guinness
I Feel Like an Alien, 2013

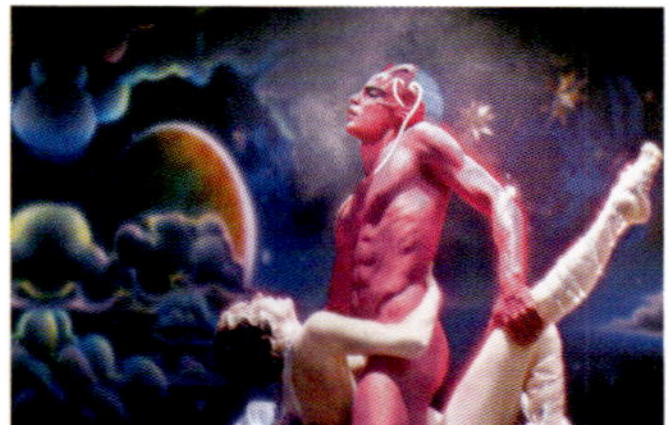

An Evening in Space, 2013

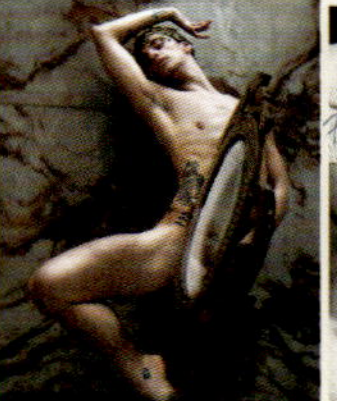

Sergei Polunin
Narcissus, 2017

Eartha Kitt, 1983
*"I'm a dirt person —
I don't trust diamonds and gold."*
— Eartha Kitt

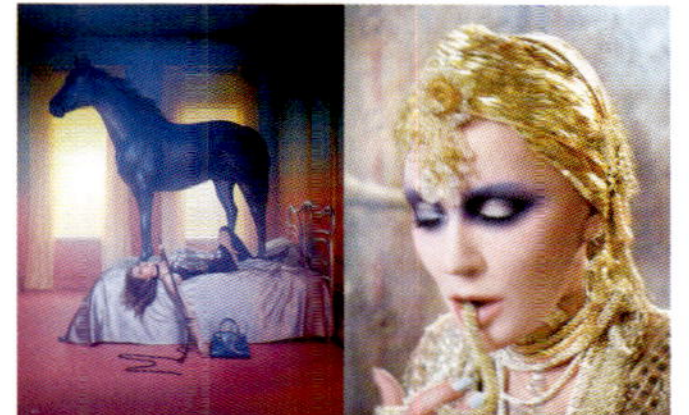

Mounted, 2013

Daphne Guinness
On Gold She Dines, 2013

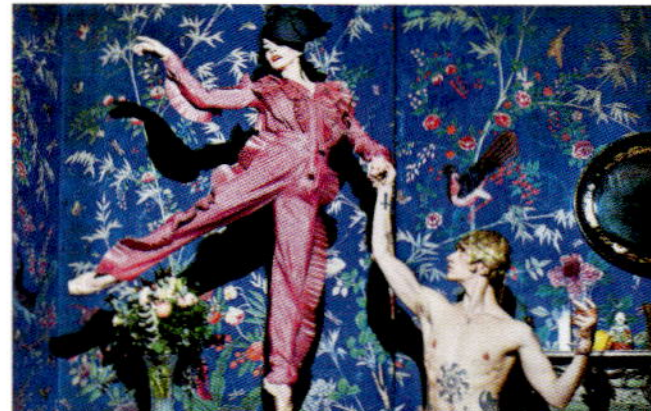

Sergei Polunin, Natalia Osipova
Pas De Deux, 2017

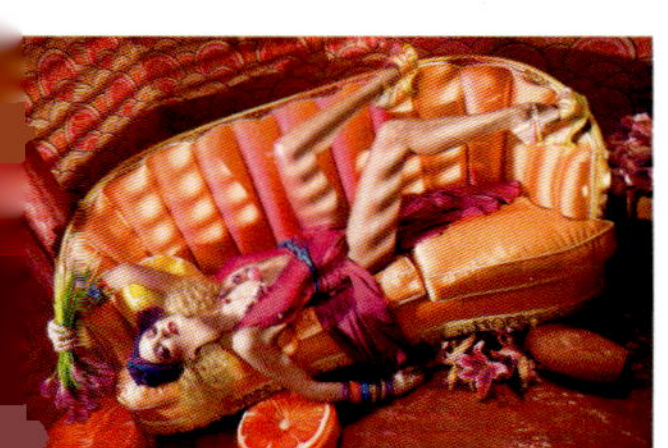

Uma Thurman
Too Glam to Give a Damn, 2011

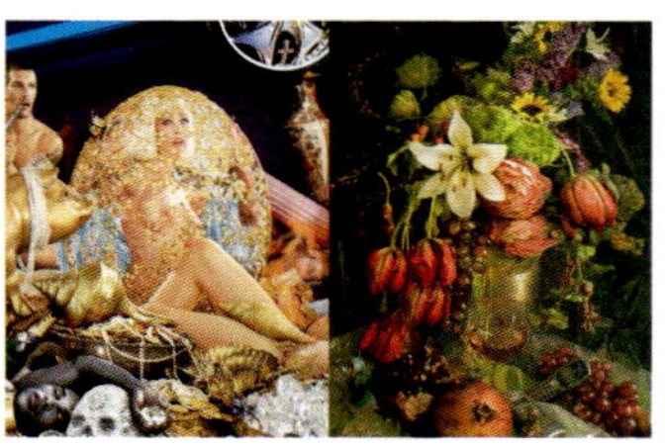

Decadence
The Insufficiency of All Things
Attainable — Gilded Cage, 2007

Earth Laughs in Flowers
Early Fall, 2008–2011

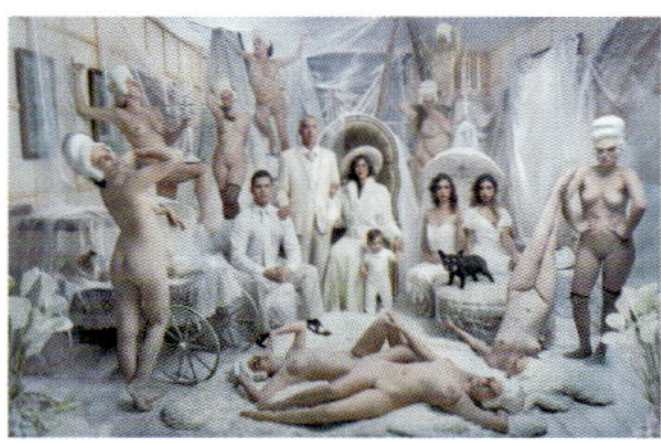

Taschen Family Portrait, 2010

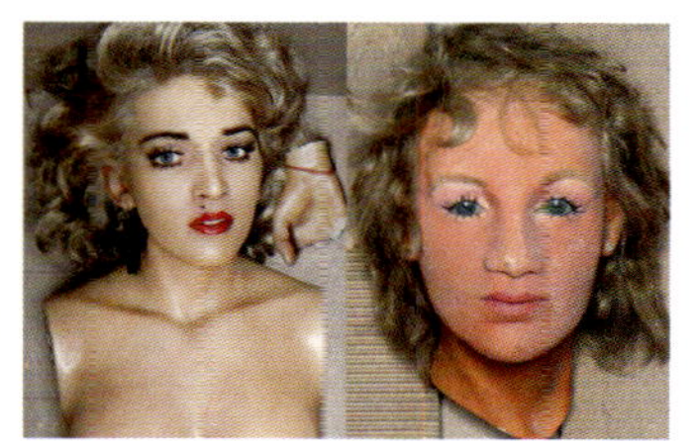

Still Life Series
Madonna
Dietrich
Found wax museum figures,
Dublin, 2009–2012

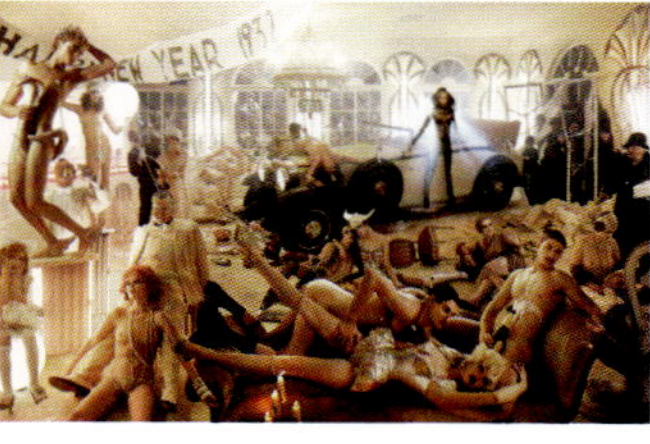

Mankind's Sublime Decline, 2009

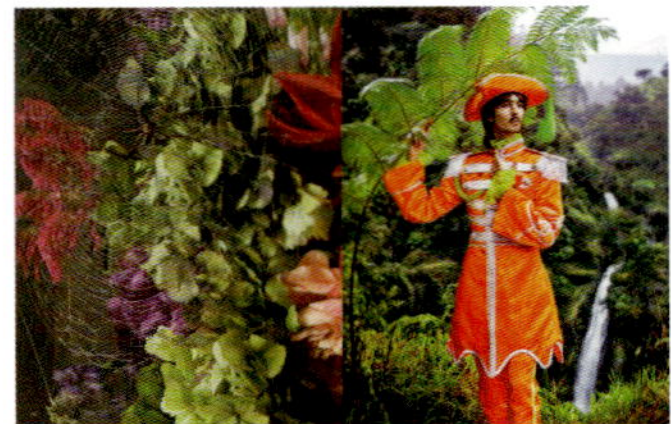

Earth Laughs in Flowers
Risk, 2008–2011
Detail

Within You Without You, 2018

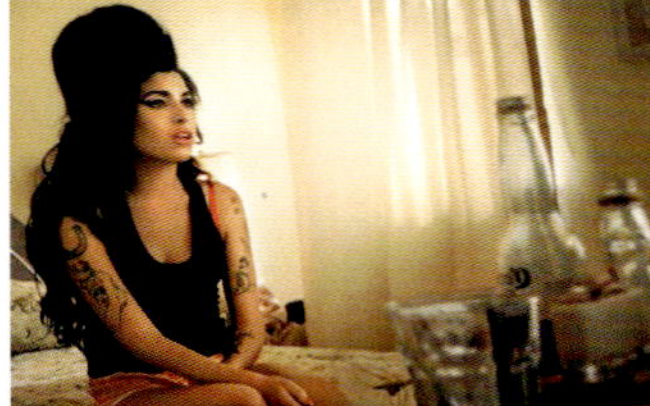

Amy Winehouse
Tears Dry on Their Own, 2007

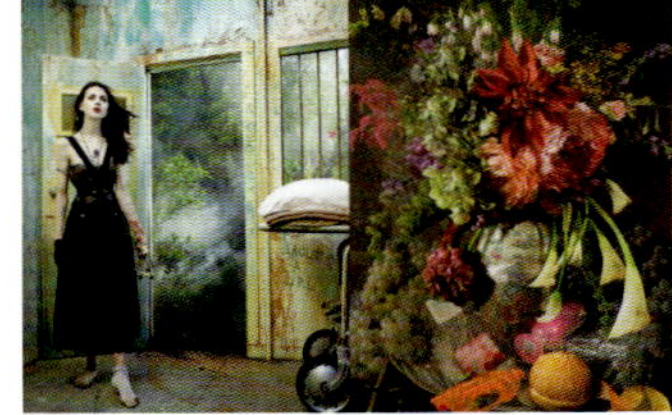

Francis Bean Cobain
About a Girl, 2015

Earth Laughs in Flowers
Risk, 2008–2011

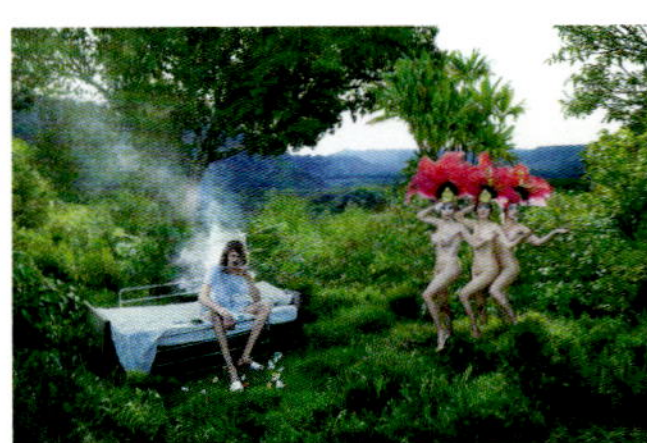

Bellevue, 2009

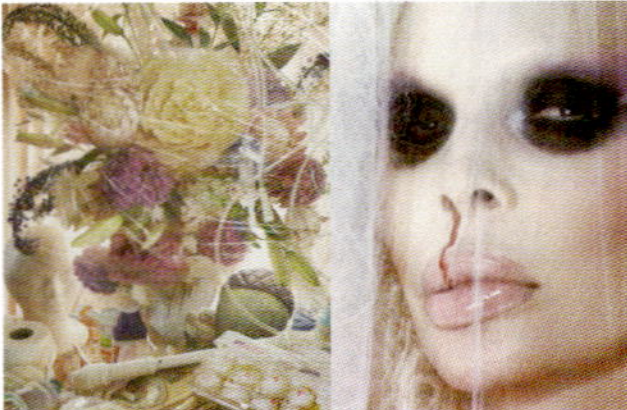

Earth Laughs in Flowers
Deathless, Winter, 2008–2011

Amanda Lepore
Desire, Lust, Fame—Why I Play This Desperate Game, 2011

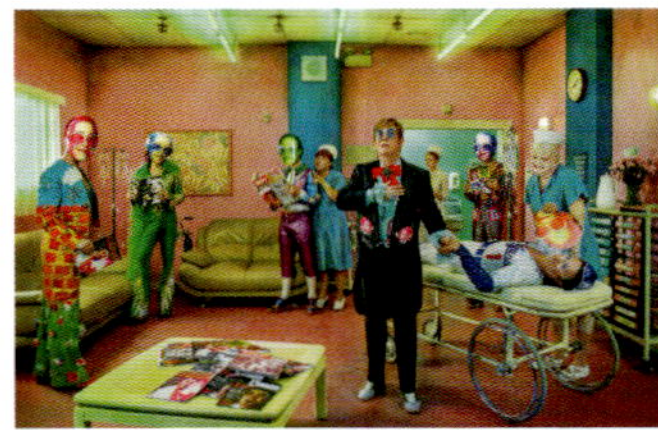

Elton John
Still Standing, 2018

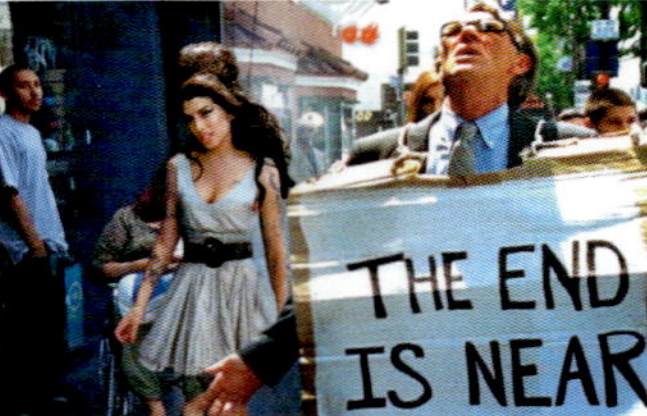

Amy Winehouse
Fallen Friend on the Walk of Stars, 2007

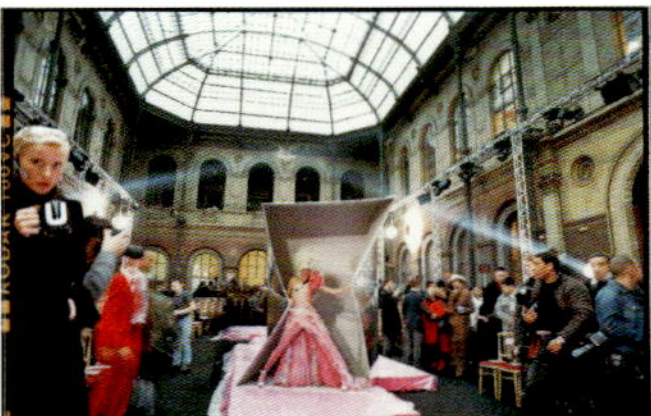

Lies of the Limelight, 2003

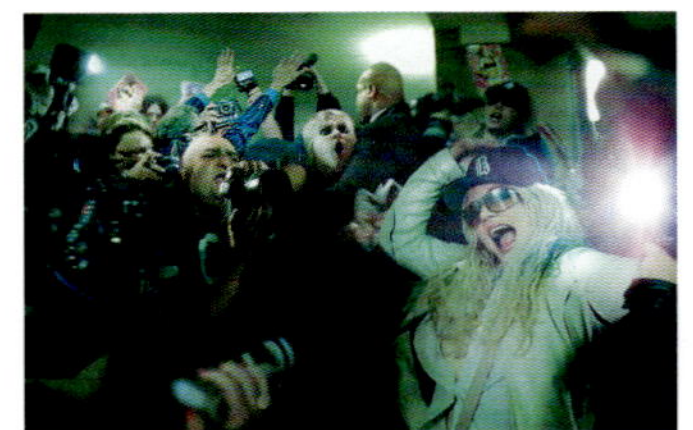

Britney Spears
Toxic Fame, 2003

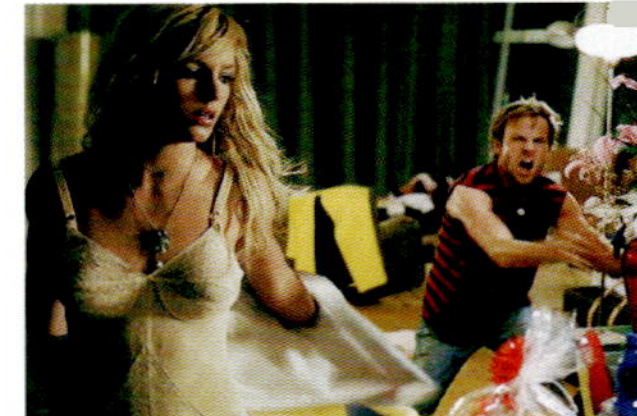

Britney Spears
Hit Me Baby One More Time, 2003

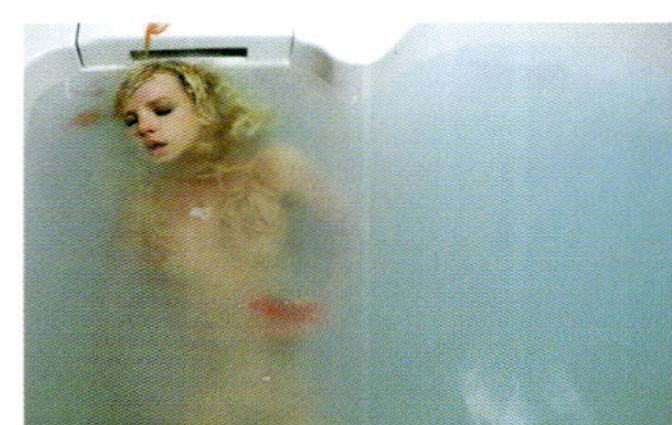

Britney Spears
A World-Famous Singer Drowns in Hotel Bath. Party Goes on as Planned Four Floors Below, 2003

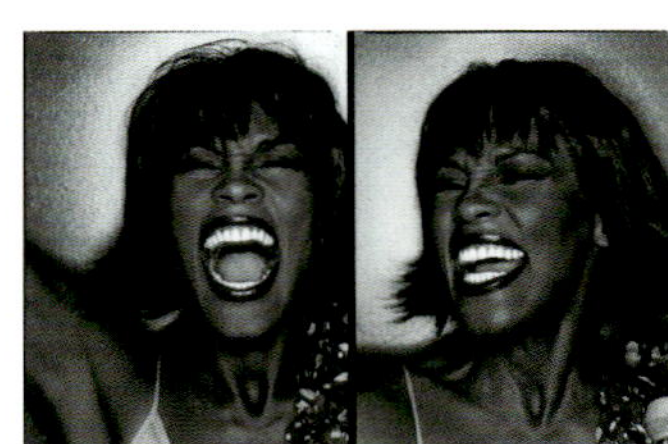

Whitney Houston
And I Will Always Love You, 2000

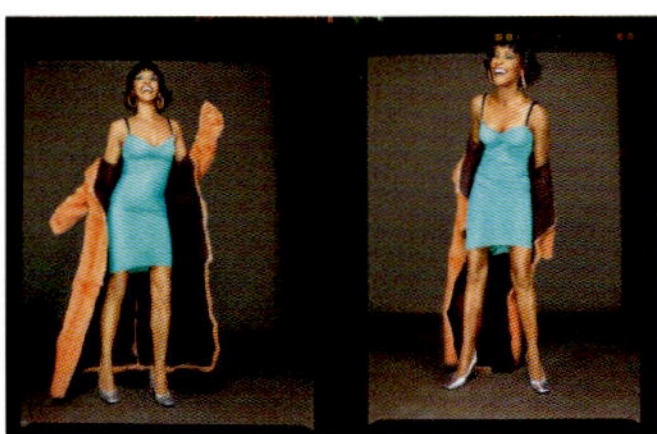

Whitney Houston
Daughter of the New Hope Baptist Church Singing to "Songs in the Key of Life" at 4:00 a.m. NYC, 2000

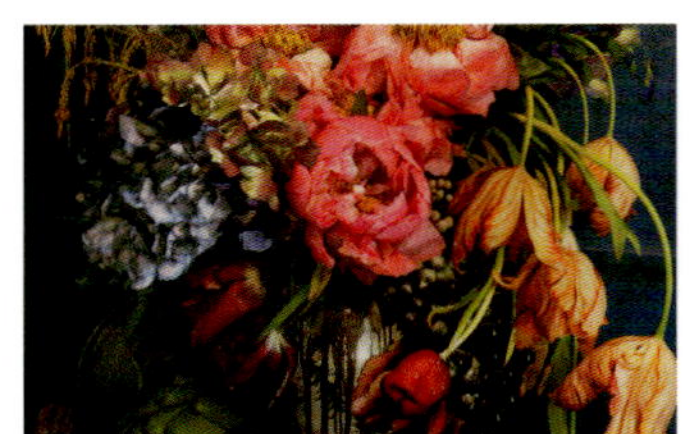

Earth Laughs in Flowers
Wilting Gossip, 2008–2011
Detail

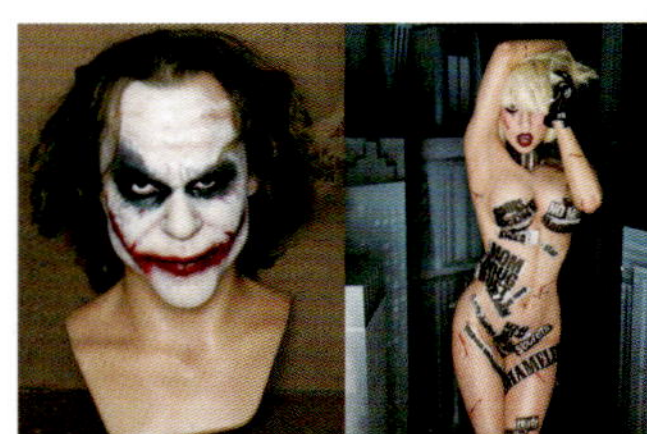

Still Life Series
The Joker
Found wax museum figure, Hollywood, 2009–2012

Lady Gaga
Tabloid Tears, 2009

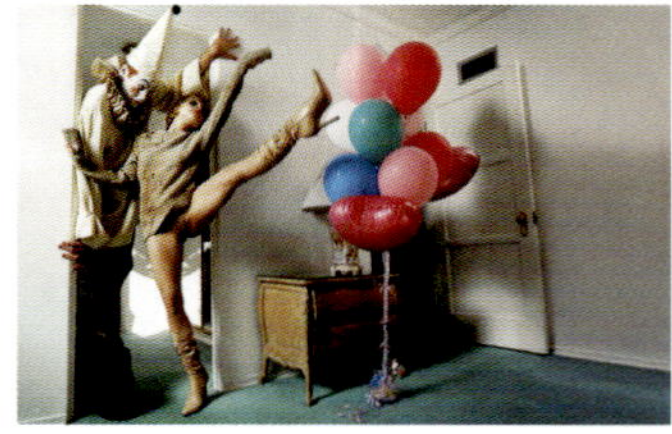

Brittany Murphy, 2000
"A few can touch the magic string and noisy fame is proud to win them; alas for those that never sing but die with all their music in them."
—Oliver Wendell Holmes
(1809–1894)

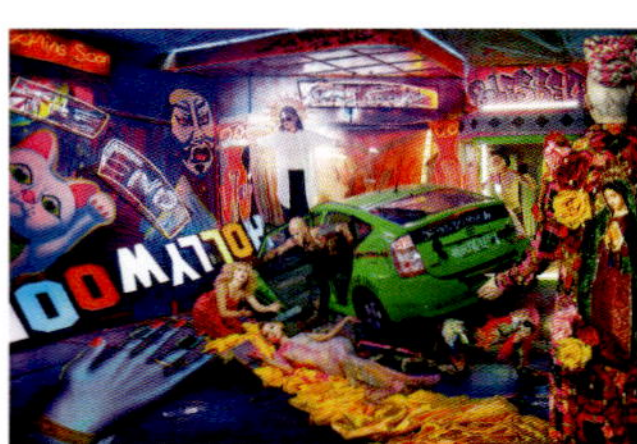

Boulevard of Broken Dreams, 2015

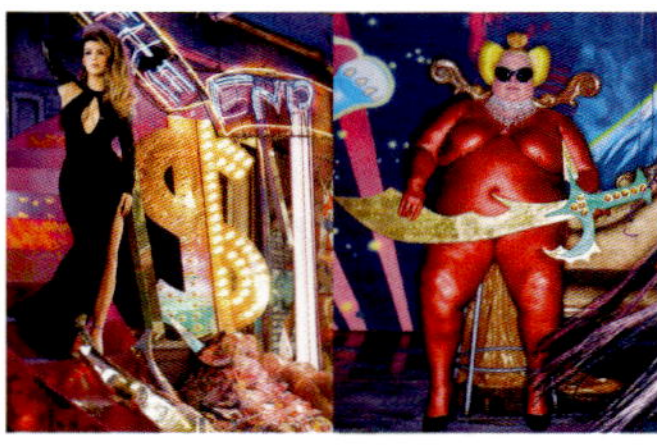

Kim Kardashian
God Has My Back, 2013

The Gate Keeper, 2015

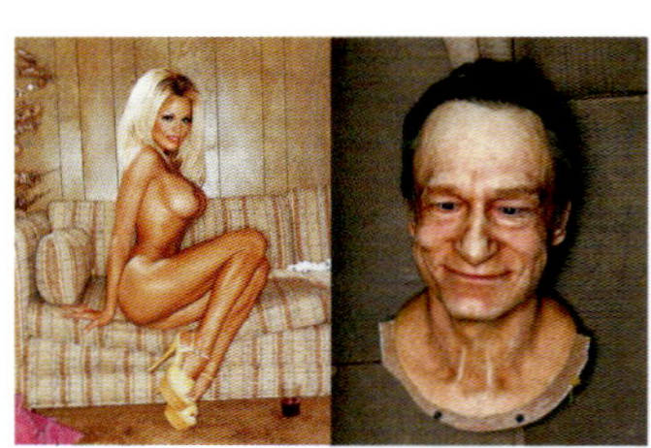
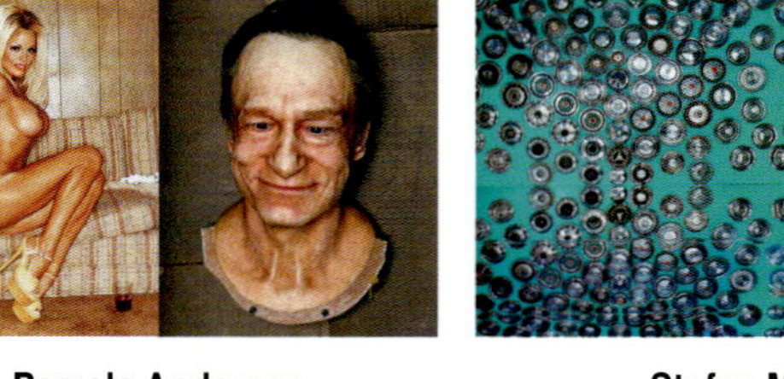

Pamela Anderson
The Whole World Knows Her Face, 2000

Still Life Series
The Gentleman
Found wax museum figure, Hollywood, 2009–2012

Stefan Meier
The Wild Ones, 2017

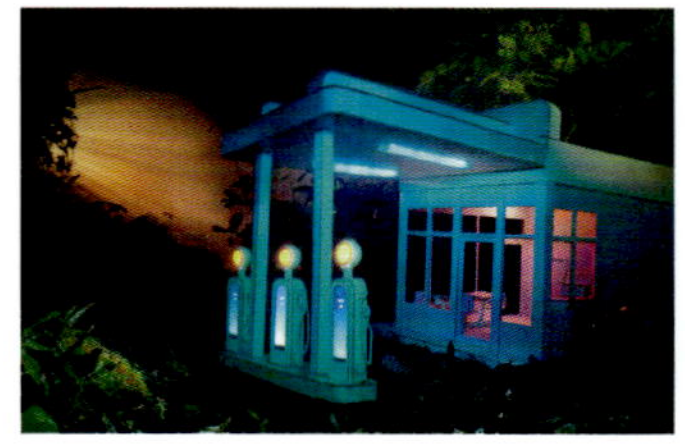

Gas
Quality Oil Quality Service, 2012

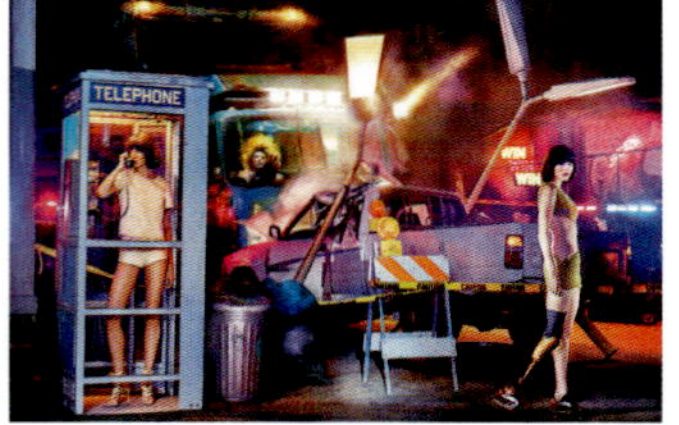

Trick or Street, 2016

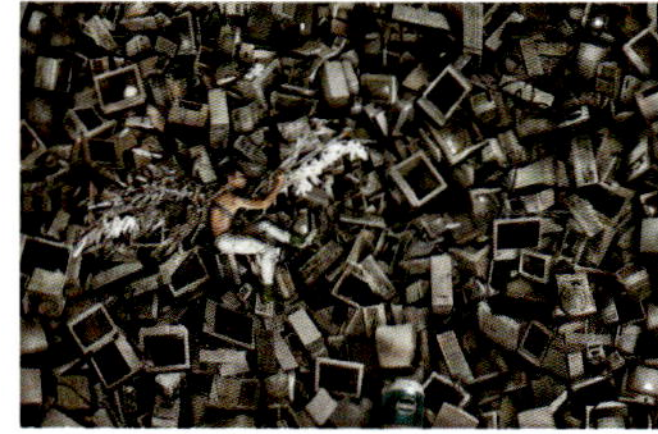

Icarus, 2012

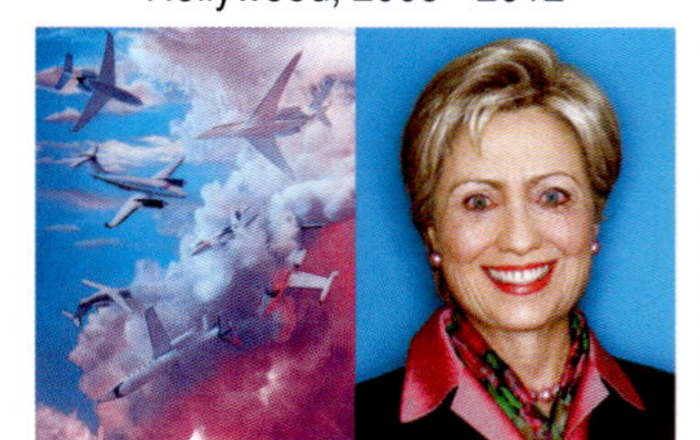

Airistocracy
Missions of Ambition, 2014

Hillary Clinton
Politician's Paradox, 2010

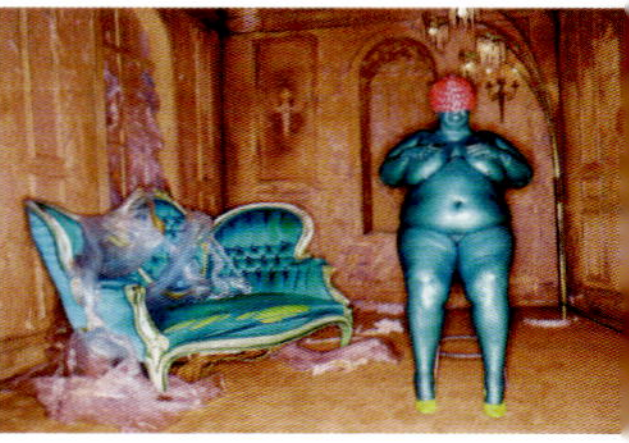

Venus of Willendorf
Hollywood, 2015

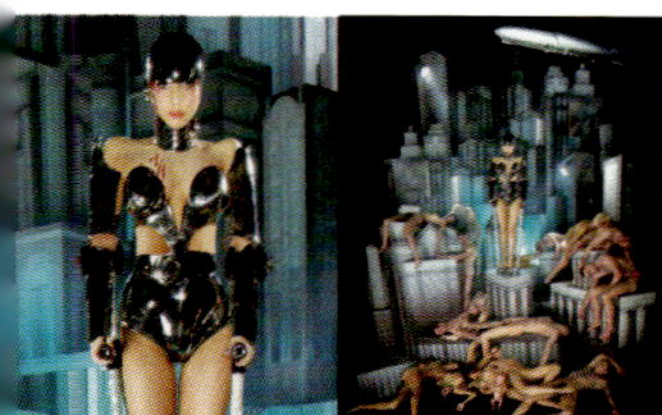

Lady Gaga
Could You Fix Me If I Broke?, 2009

Lady Gaga
I Want Your Disease, 2009

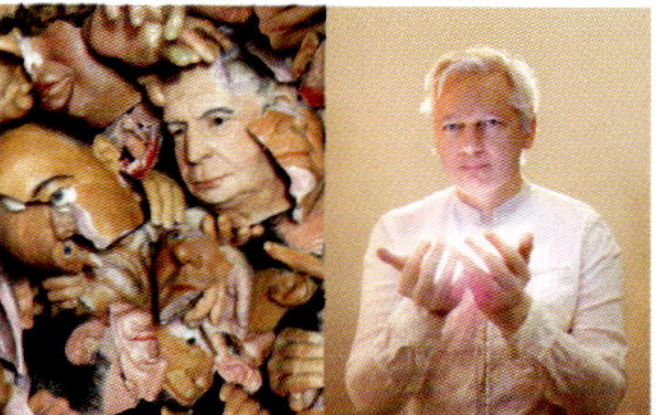

Still Life Series
Busted Politicians
Found wax museum figures, Dublin, 2009–2012

Julian Assange
Wikileaks, 2017

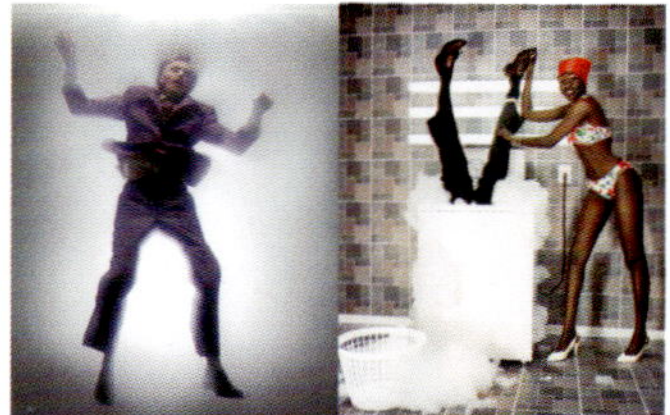

Awakened
Bartholomew, 2007

Drowning Misery, 1998

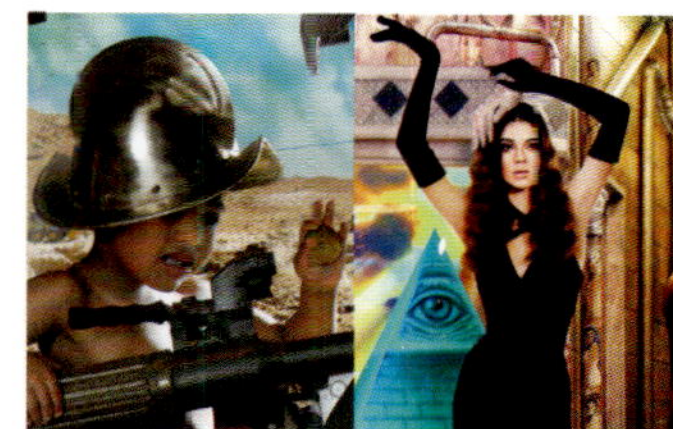

The Rape of Africa, 2009
Detail

Kendall Jenner
We Are The Chosen, 2013

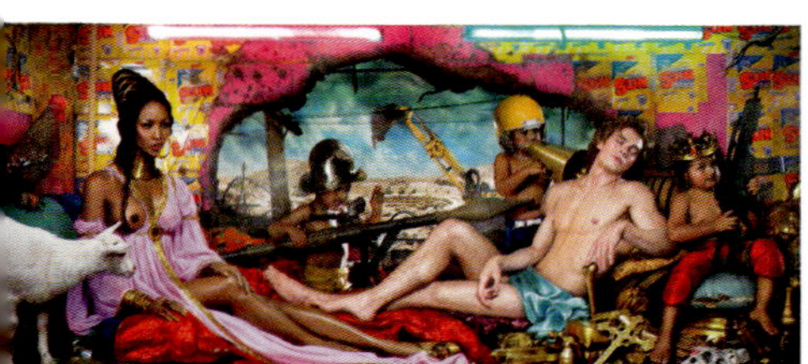

The Rape of Africa, 2009

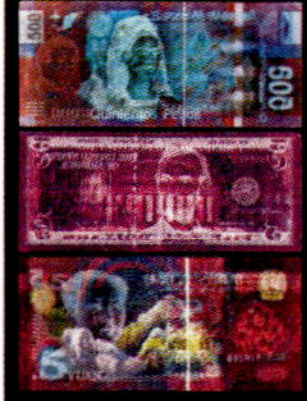

Negative Currency, 1990–2017

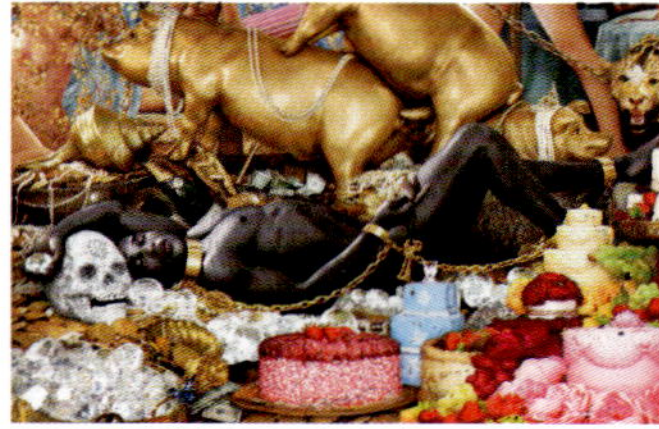

Decadence
The Insufficiency of All Things Attainable
Blood Diamonds and Gold, Lives Of Men Bought And Sold, 2007

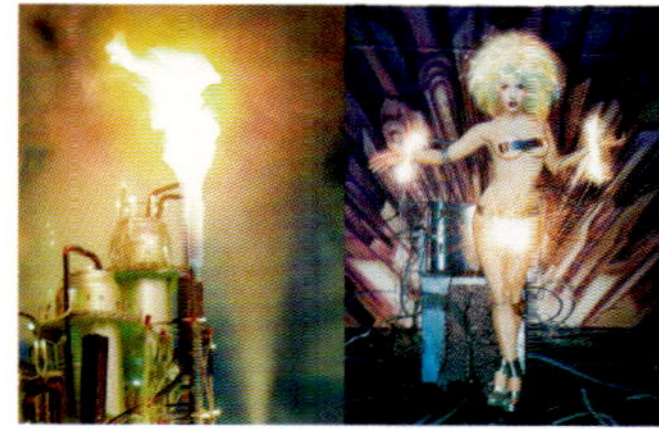

Landscape
Igniting the World, 2013

Lady Gaga
Electric Lady Land, 2009

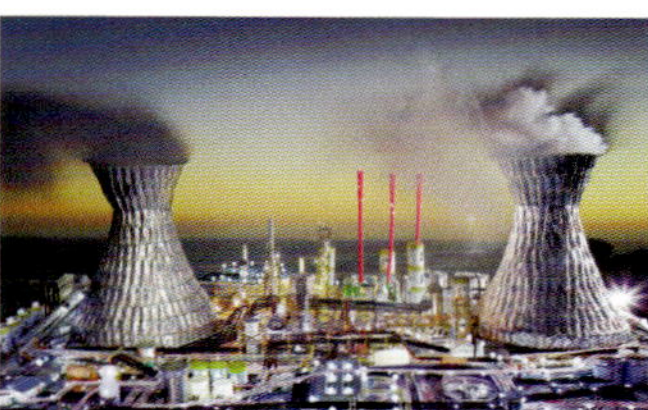

Landscape
Risking Our Lives to Power Yours, 2013

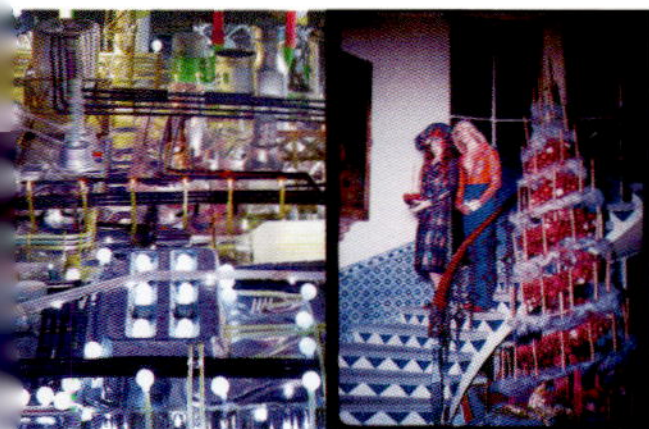

Landscape
Risking Our Lives to Power Yours, 2013
Detail

Lana Del Rey
Holiday, 2017

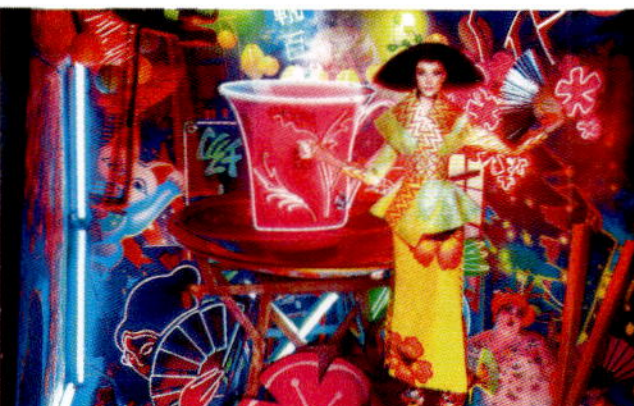

City of Blooming Lights, 2012

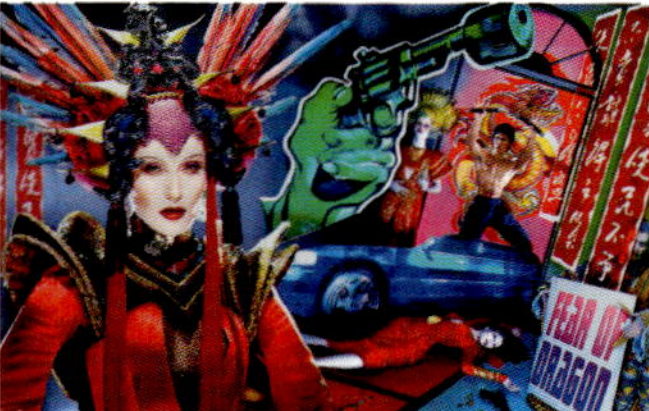

Daphne Guinness
Fear of the Dragon, 2015

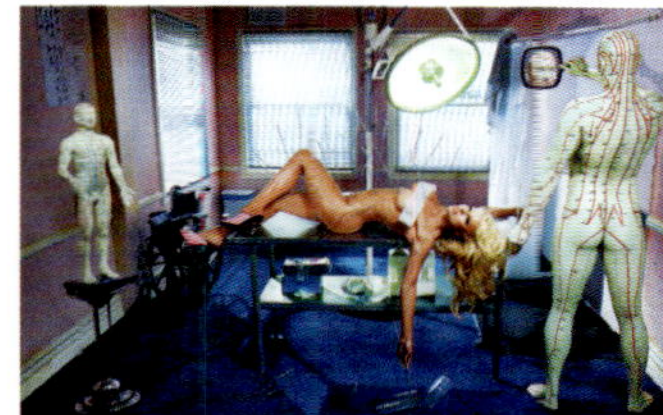

Pamela Anderson
Arrows of Love Lost Puncture My Aching Heart, 2016

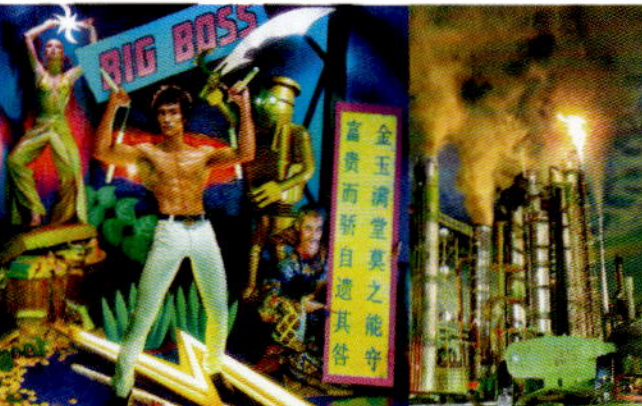

Big Boss, 2015

Landscape
Luminance, Laughter, The Distress, Disaster, 2013

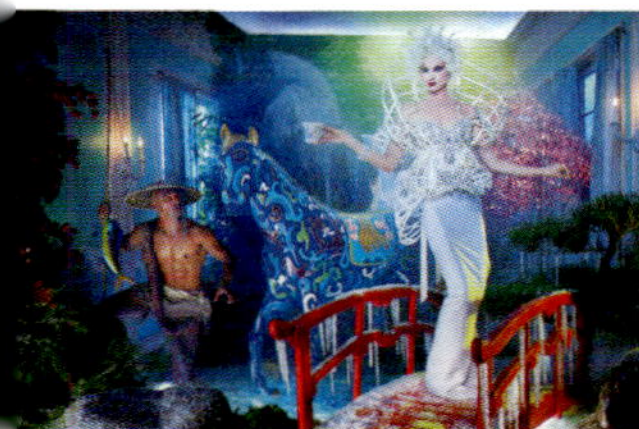

Sometimes It Snows in April, 2012

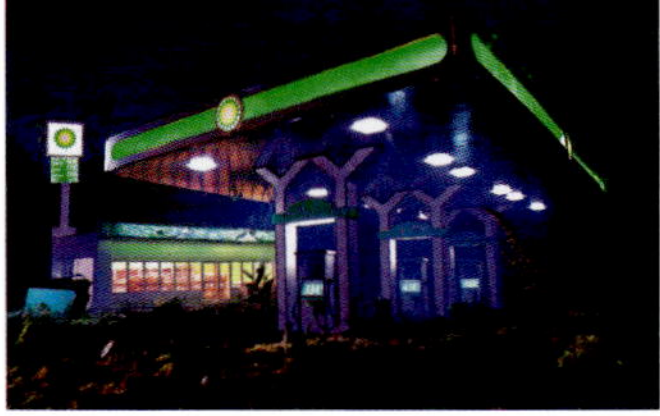

Gas
The World Runs on Us, 2012

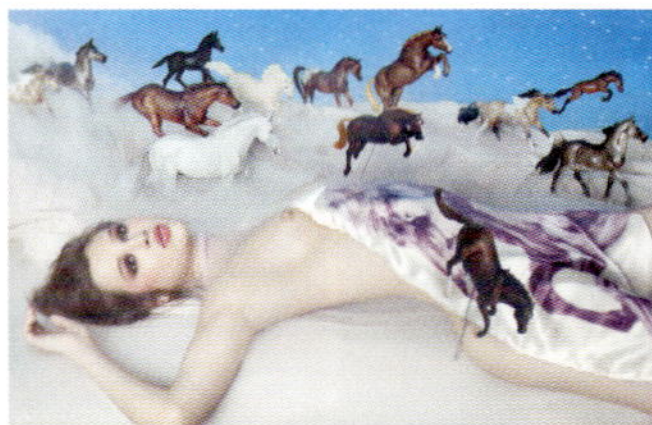

Stampede of A Storm, 2012

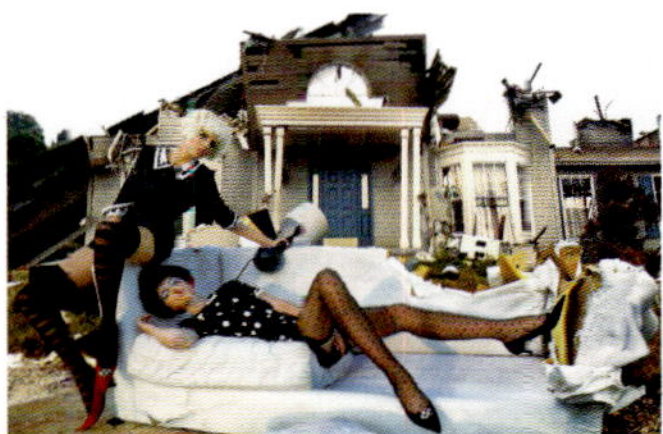

Loss Can Be Good for Us, 2005

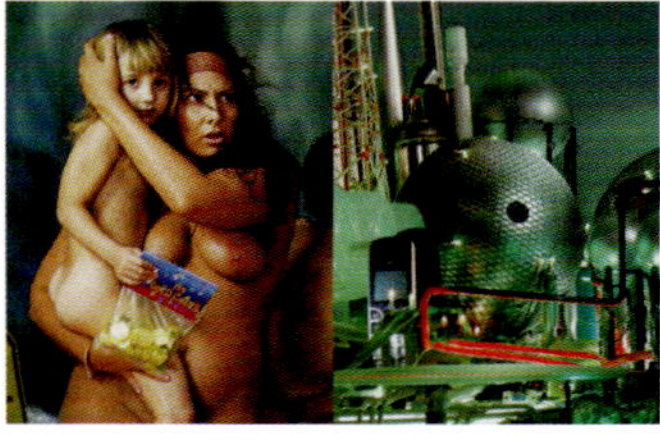

Deluge, 2006
Detail

Landscape
Turmoil, 2013

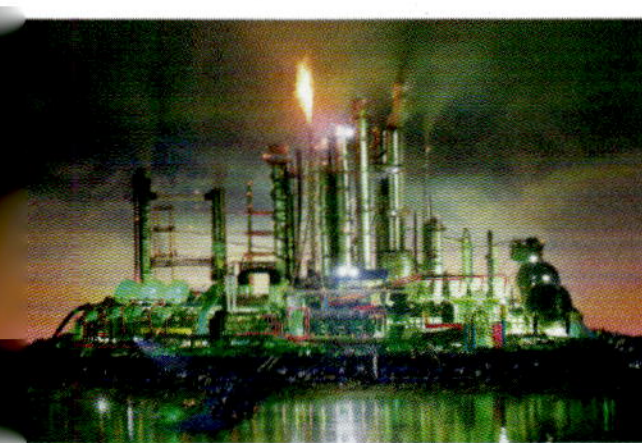

Landscape
Drill Baby Drill, 2013

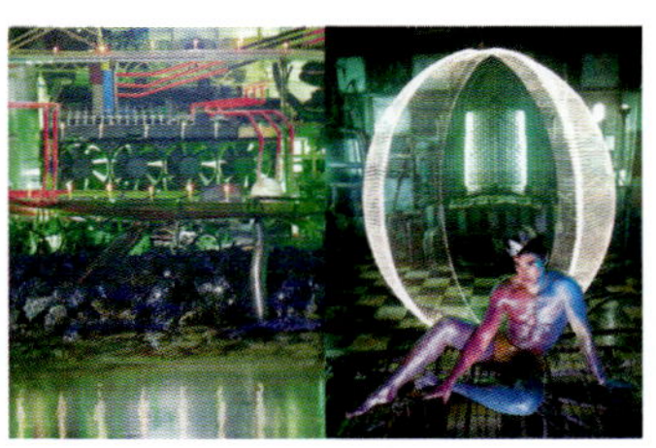

Landscape
Spill Baby Spill, 2013
Detail

David LaChapelle
Quest for Illumination, 2012

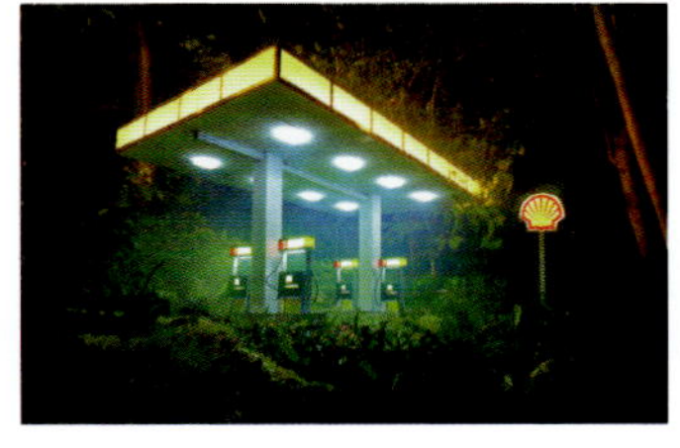

Gas
A Bright Alternative to a Dark Past, 2012

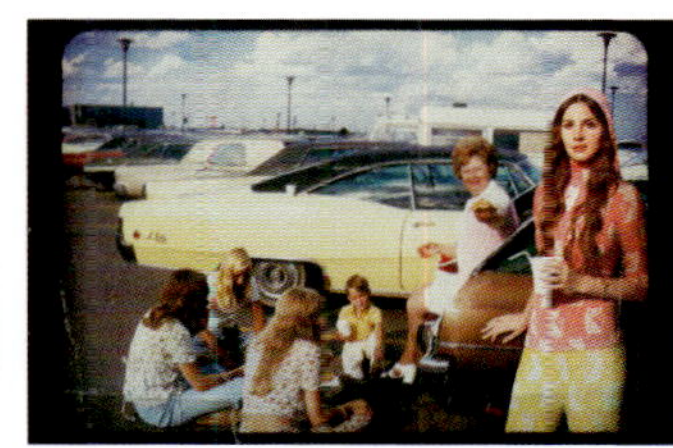

Lana Del Rey
Yesterday Once More, 2017

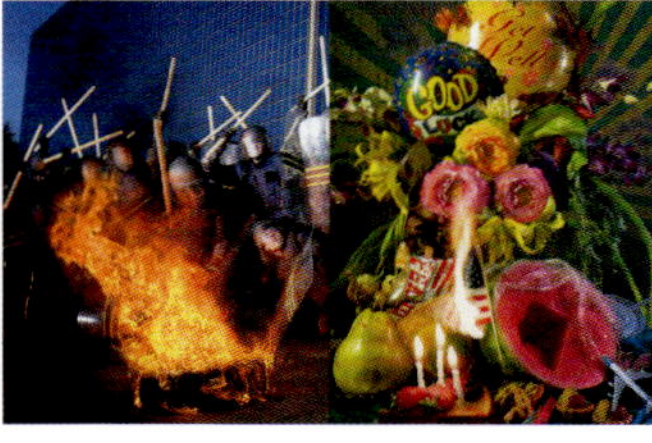

Empires Crumble, 2006

Earth Laughs in Flowers
America, Get Well, Good Luck
2008–2011

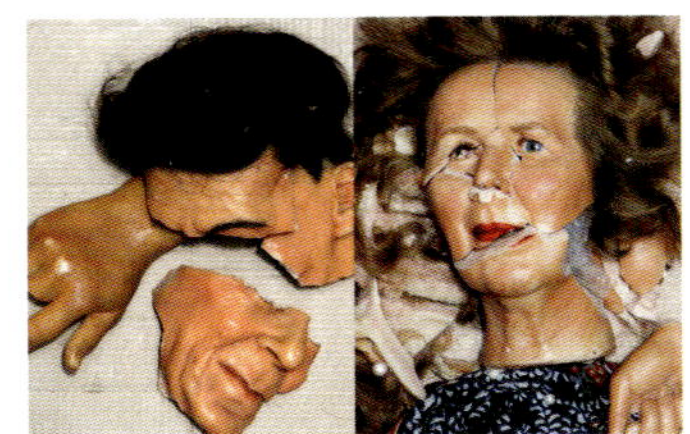

Still Life Series
Ronald Reagan
Margaret Thatcher
Found wax museum figures, Dublin, 2009–2012

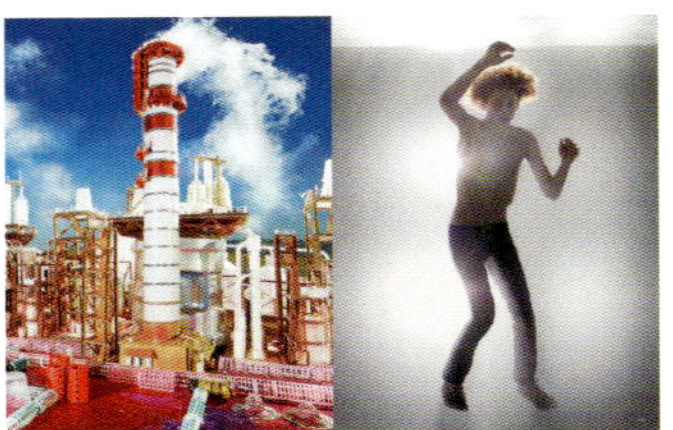

Landscape
I Pledge Allegiance, 2013

Awakened
Abel, 2007

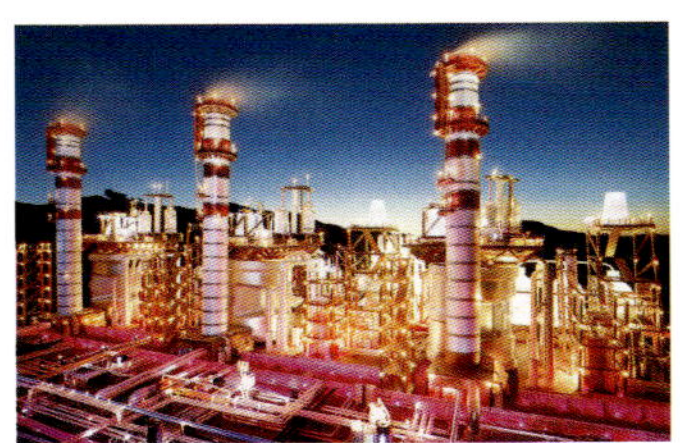

Landscape
Powering Progress, 2013

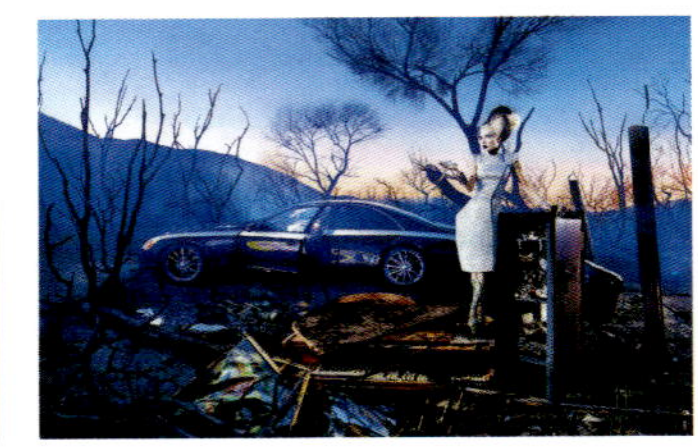

Daphne Guinness
Luxury Class, 2009

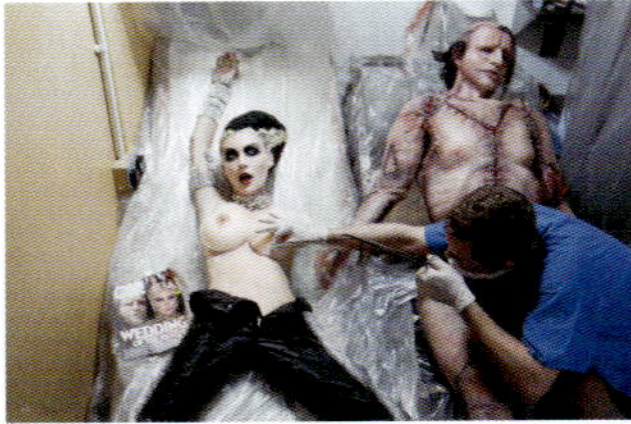

Daphne Guinness
Scar Issue, 2014

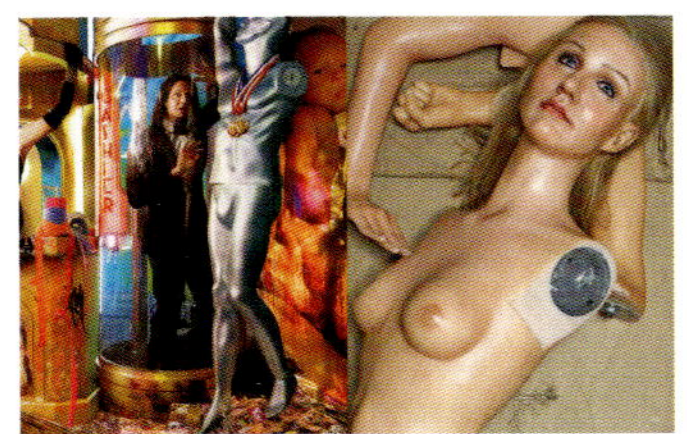

Bruce Jenner
LGBLT MAGA, 2013

Still Life series
Blonde Actress
Wax museum figure, Hollywood, 2009–2012

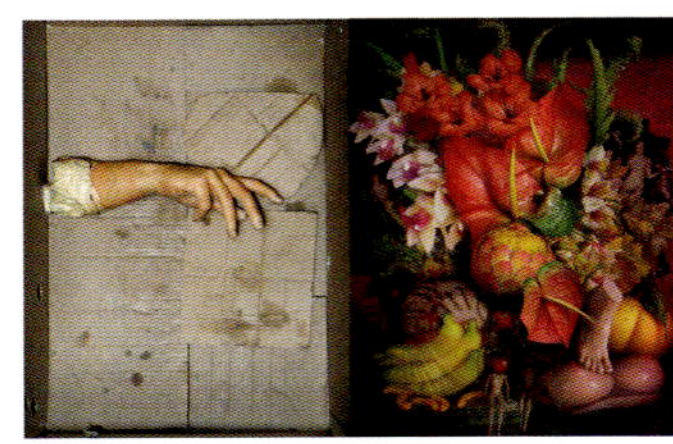

Still Life Series
Creation
Found wax museum figure, Las Vegas, 2009–2012

Earth Laughs in Flowers
We Are More Than Our Parts, 2008–2011

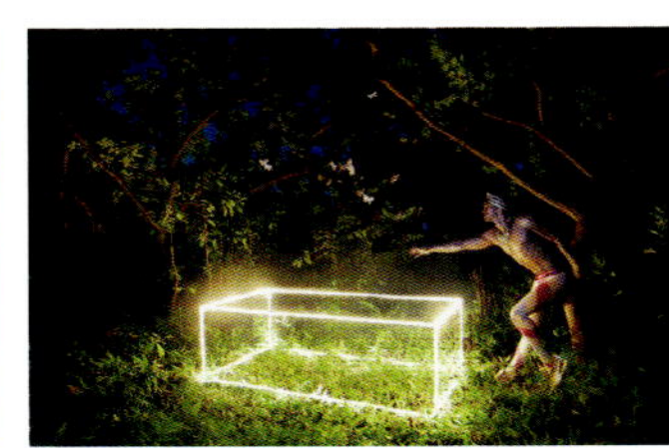

Songs of Loss
and Immortality, 2009

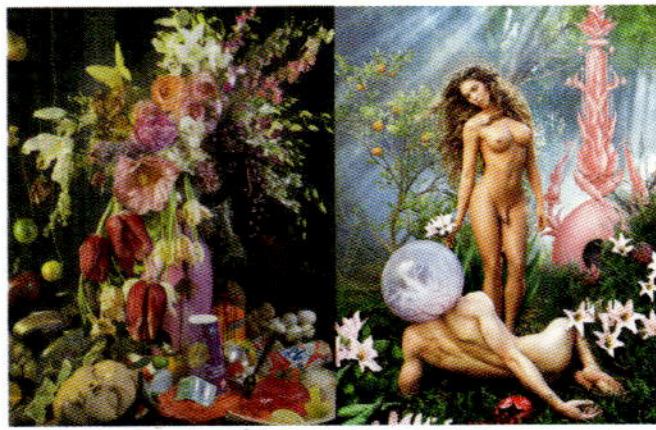

Earth Laughs in Flowers
God Is Not the Author of Confusion, 2008–2011

Carmen Carrera
There Once Was a Garden, 2014

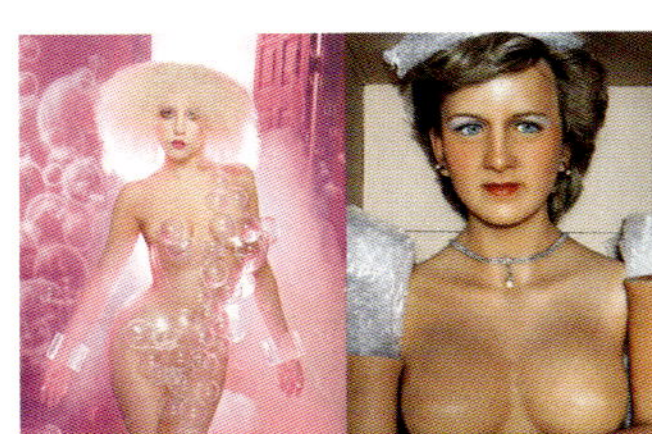

Lady Gaga
Do You Want Love or Do You Want Fame, 2009

Still Life Series
Princess Diana
Found wax museum figure, Dublin, 2009–2012

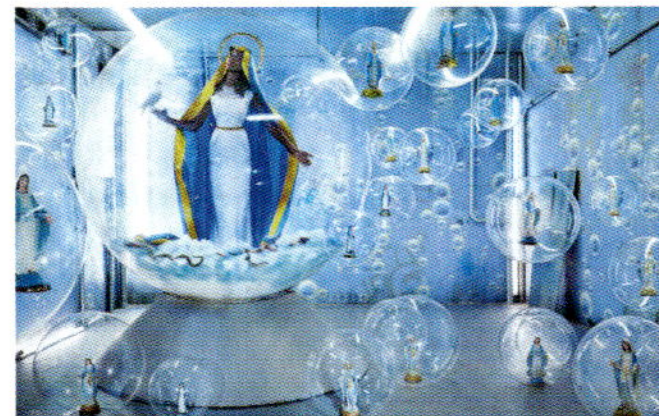

Mother Mary Comes to Me, 2016

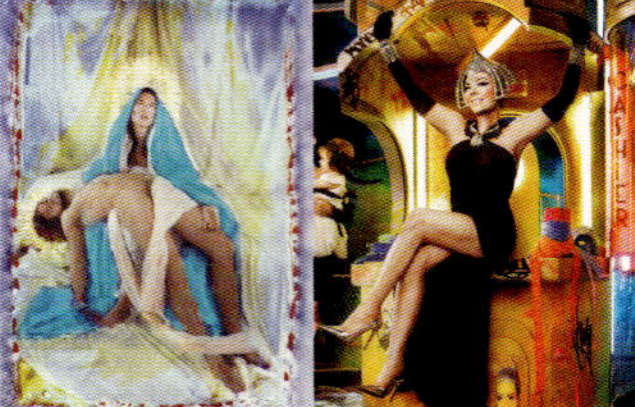

Pieta, 1986

Kris Jenner
Most Famous Mother, 2013

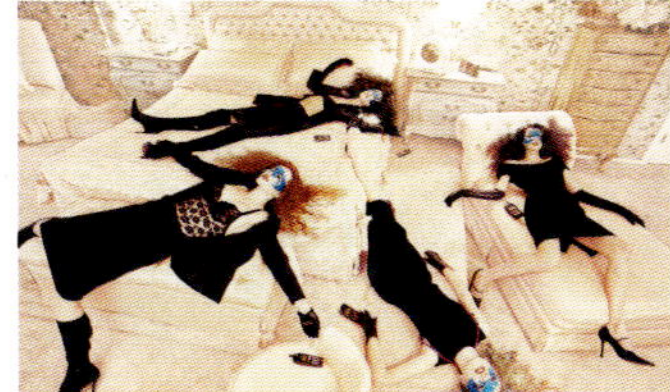

Need 2 Charge
Going 2 Die, 1999

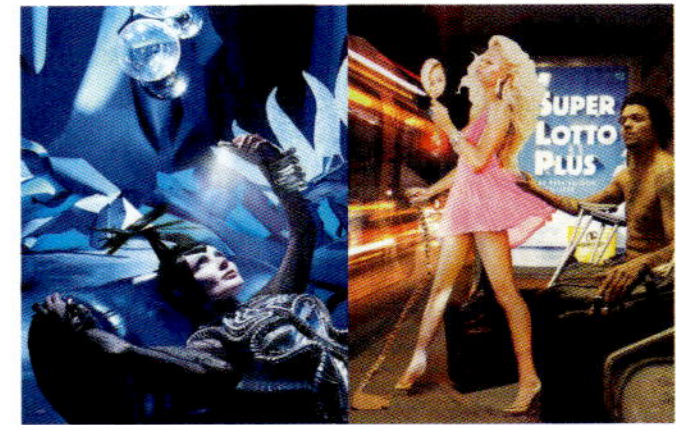

Daphne Guinness
Documentia, 2013

Paris Hilton
It's Not About Me, It's About You, 2007–2017

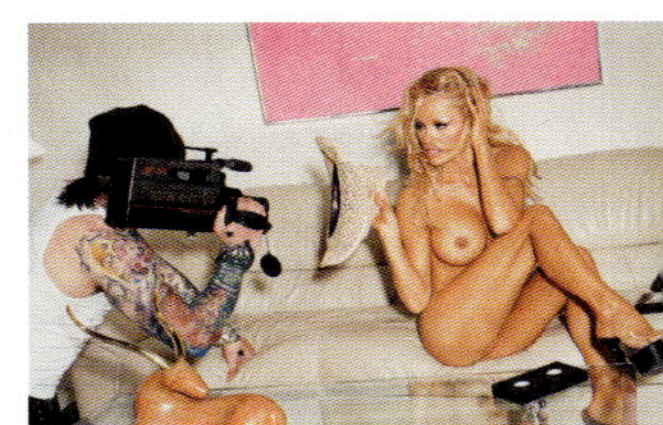

Pamela Anderson
Celeb Sex Tape, 2000

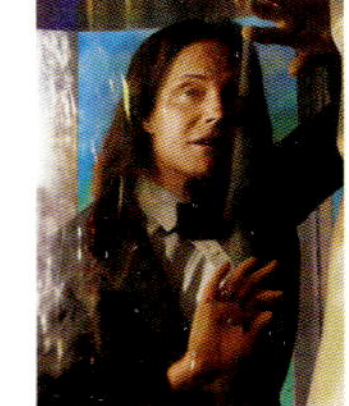

Bruce Jenner
Be All You Can Be, 2013

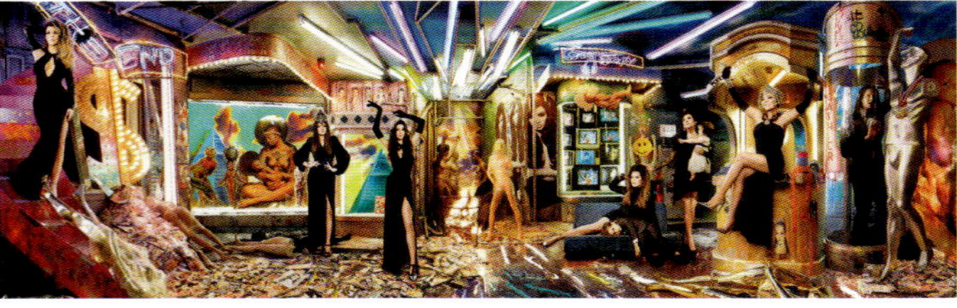

Keeping up With the Kardashians, 2013

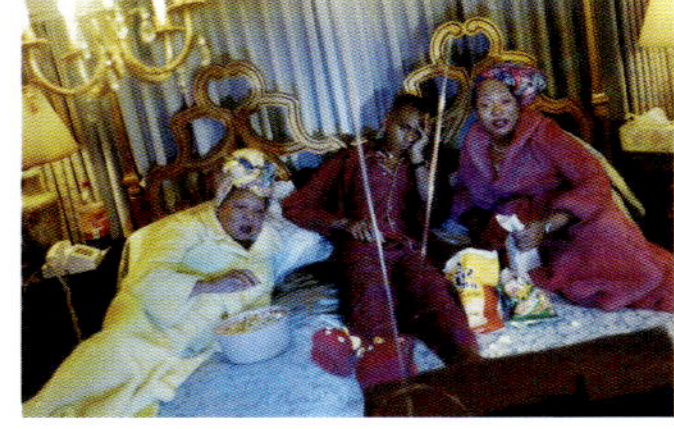

Dave Chappelle With Mom and Grandmother at Home, Washington, D.C.
Stay Tuned, 1993

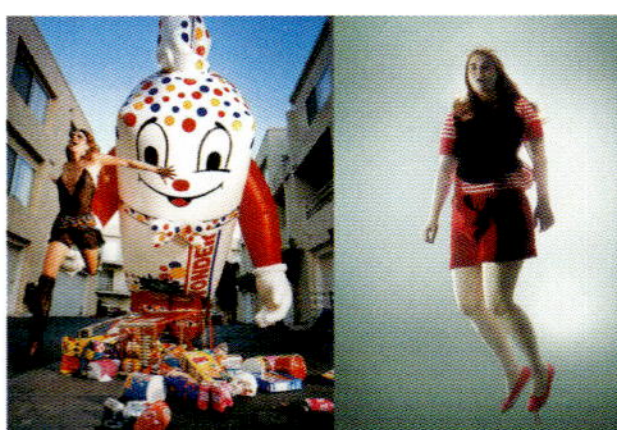

Wonder Bread, 2002

Awakened
Deborah, 2007

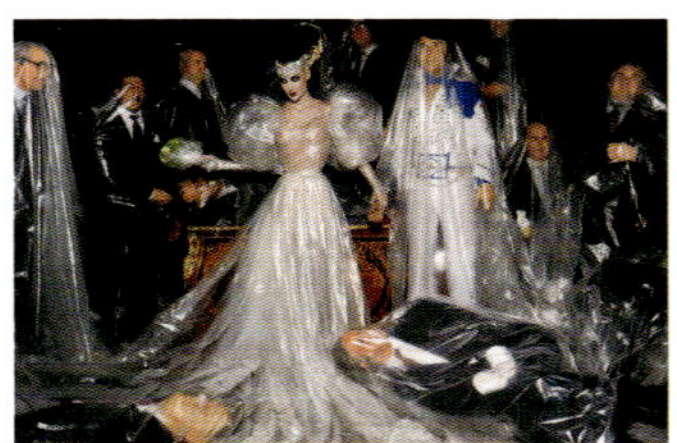

Daphne Guinness
In Sickness and In Health, 2012

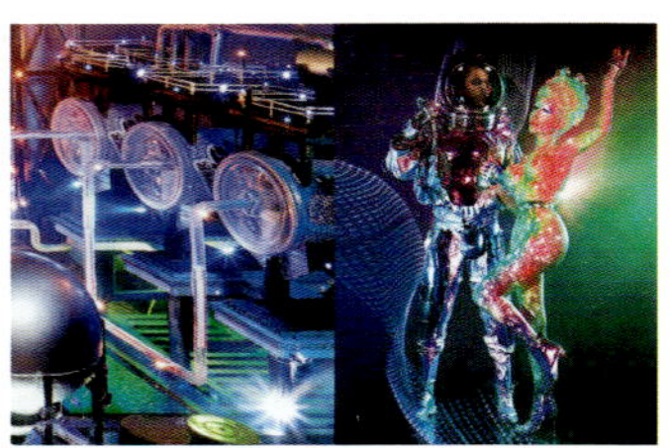

Landscape
Big Gulp, 2013 Detail

Amanda Lepore
This Body, This Face, from Outerspace, 2017

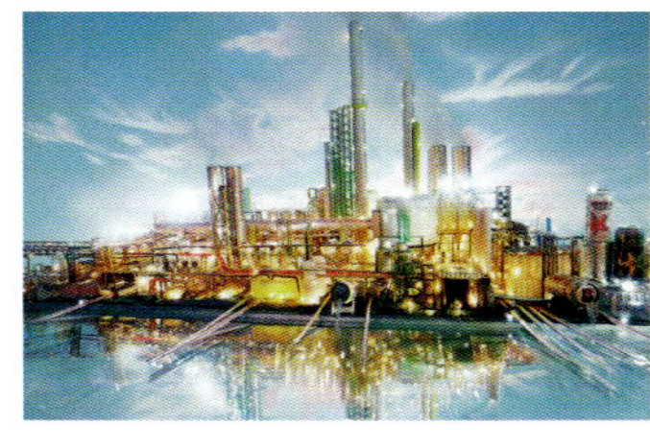

Landscape
By the Dawn's Early Light, 2013

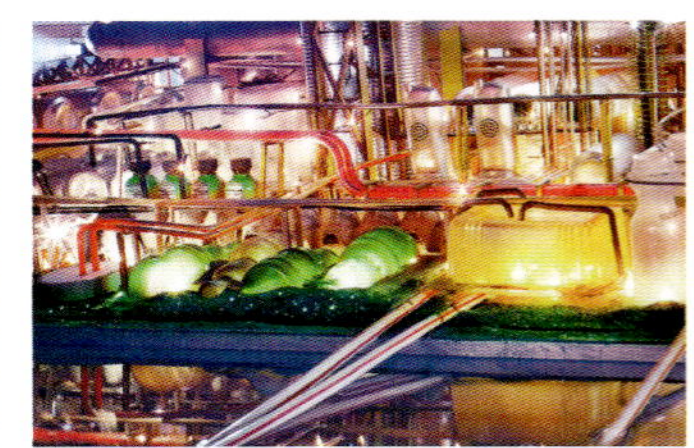

Landscape
Twilight's Last Gleaming, 2013
Detail

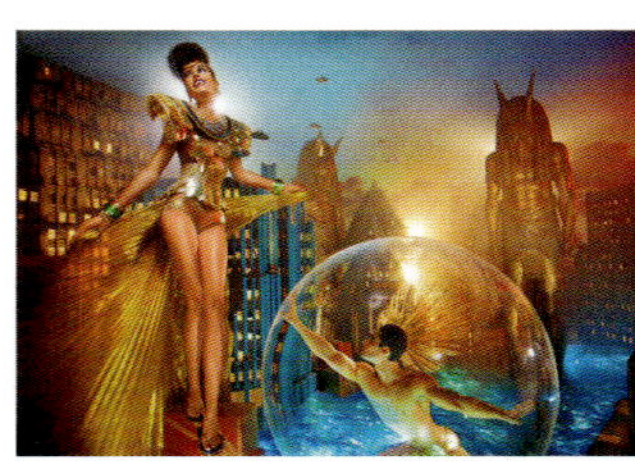

Ancient Aliens, 2012

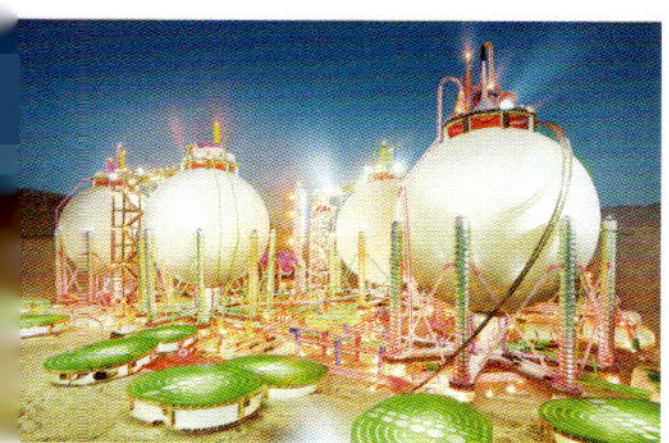

Landscape
Technology Without Apology, 2013

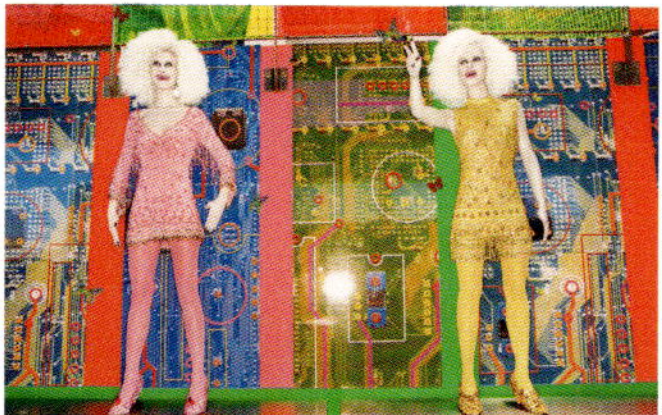

Heard a Rumor From a Tumor—Not All Growth is Good, 2002

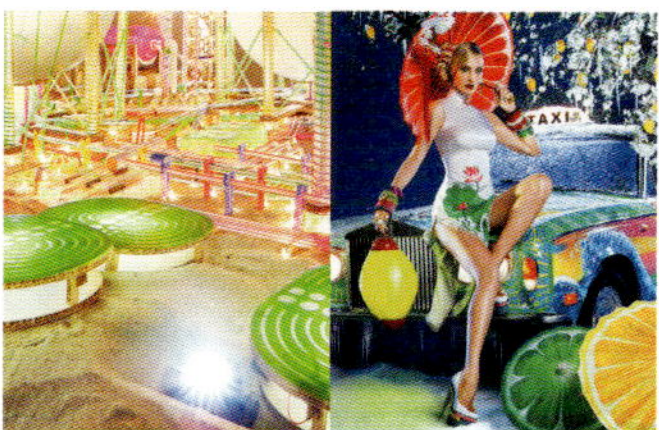

Landscape
Technology Without Apology, 2013
Detail

Uma Thurman
Uma's Uber, 2011

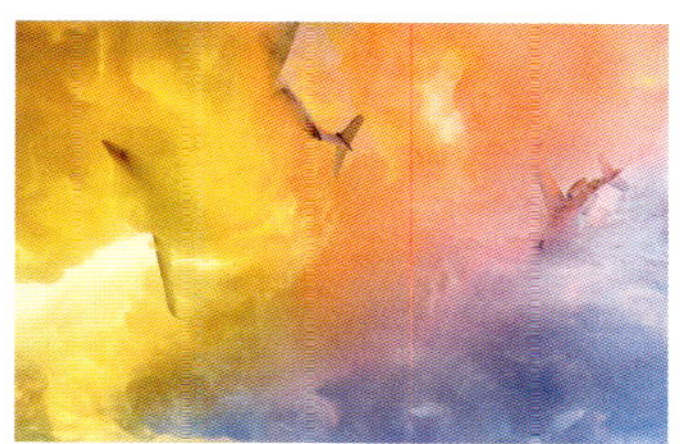

Airistocracy
Lost in the Clouds of Luxury, 2014

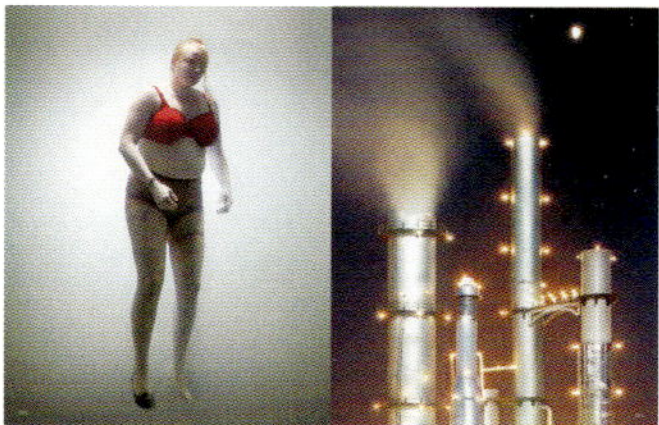

Awakened
Delilah, 2007

Landscape
Twilight, 2013
Detail

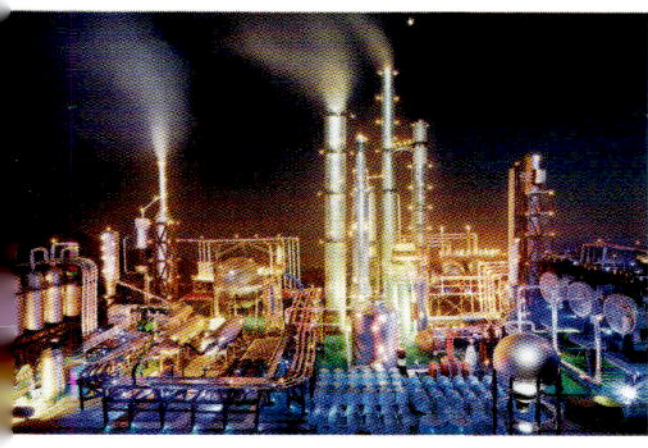

Landscape
Whole World in Our Hands, 2013

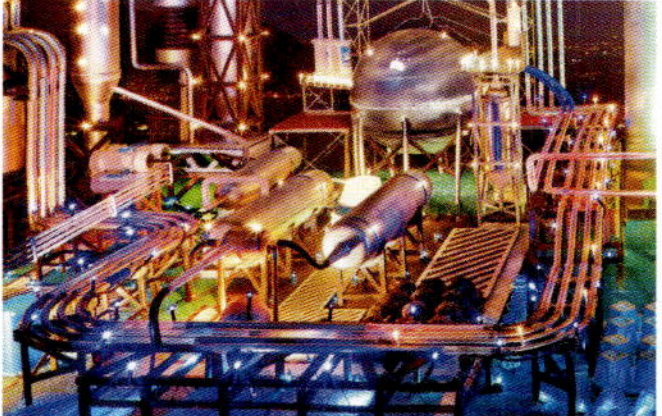

Landscape
Whole World in Our Hands, 2013
Detail

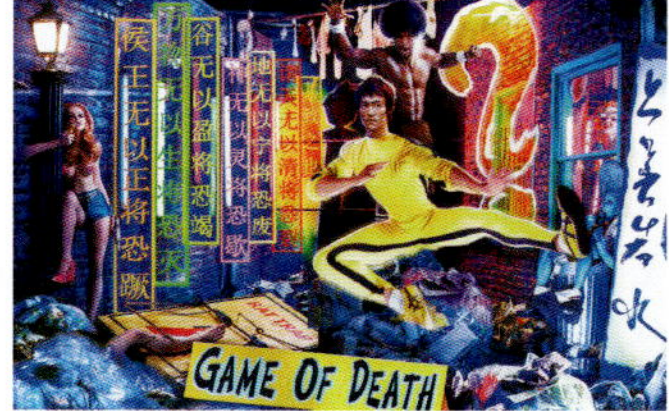

Game of Death, 2010

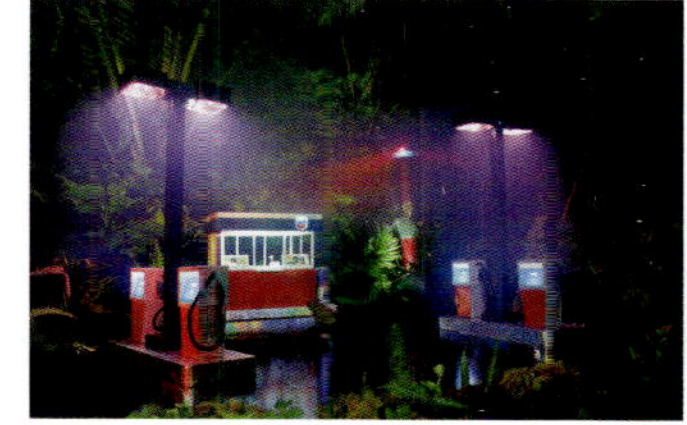

Gas
Proof Through the Night, 2012

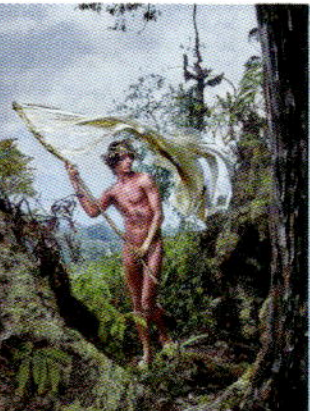

Sergei Polunin
Nature's Glory, 2016

Airistocracy
Fog of Confusion
Private Delusion, 2014

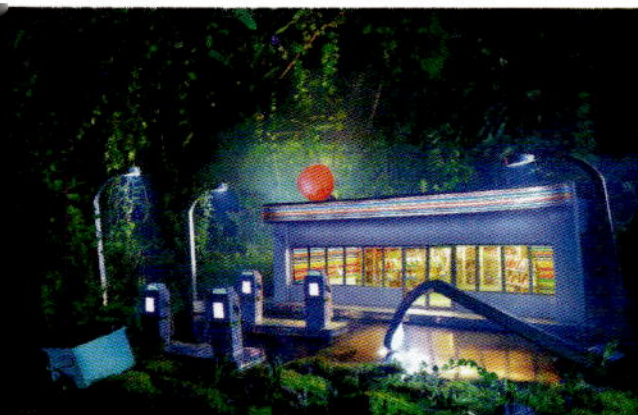

Gas
Amphetamine, 2012

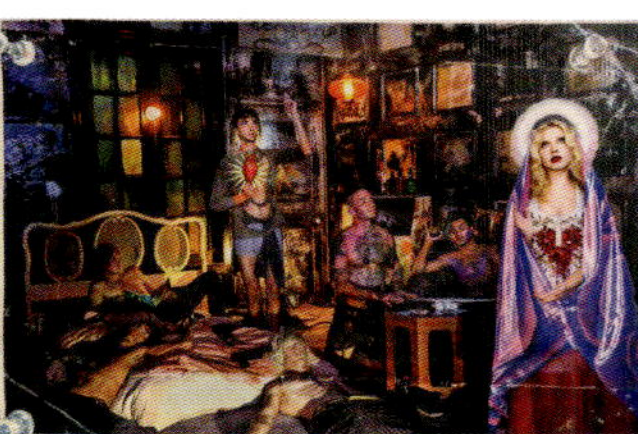

A Prayer For My Friends, 2016

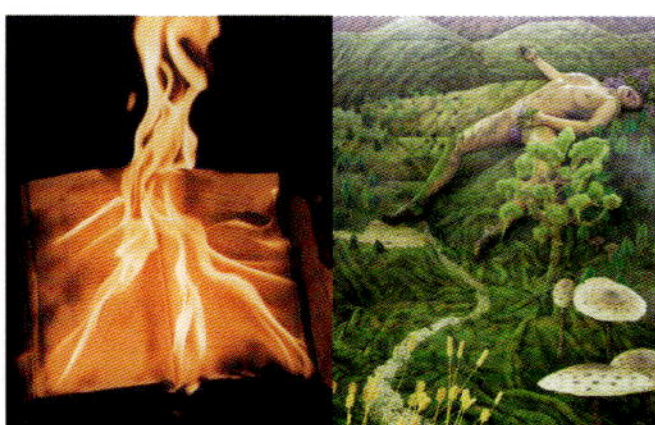

Revelations, 1989

Bleeding Gaia, 2011
"Here lies the body of this world."
—Henry David Thoreau

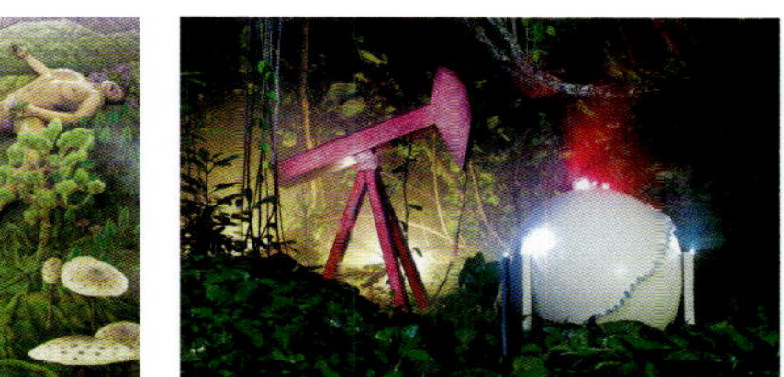

Gas
The Blood of Our Country, 2012

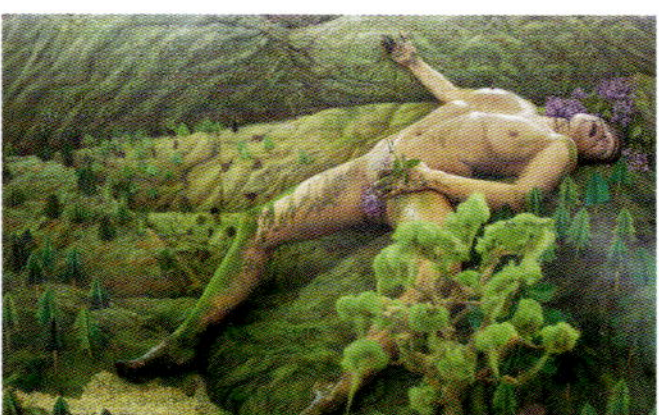

Bleeding Gaia, 2011
Detail

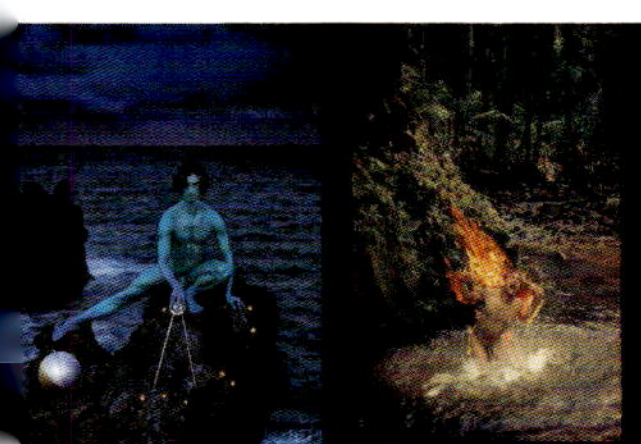

Sergei Polunin
His Kingdom on the Sea, 2017

Scorched Earth, 1988

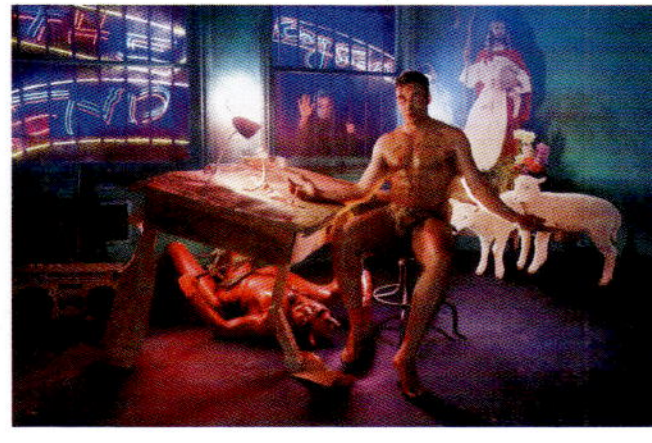

David LaChapelle, 2009
"Every saint has a past, and every sinner has a future."
— Oscar Wilde

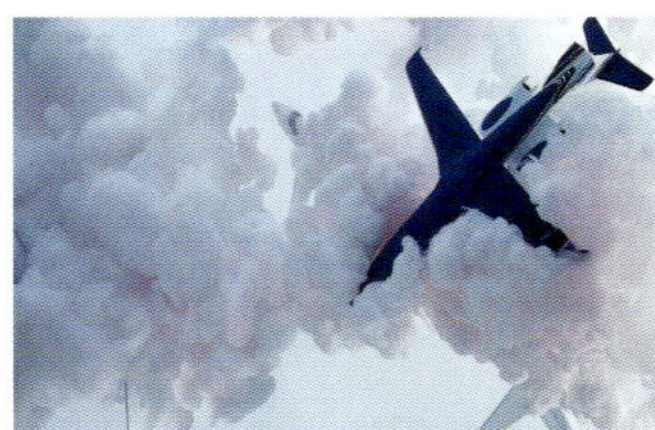

Airistocracy
Fog of Confusion
Private Delusion, 2014

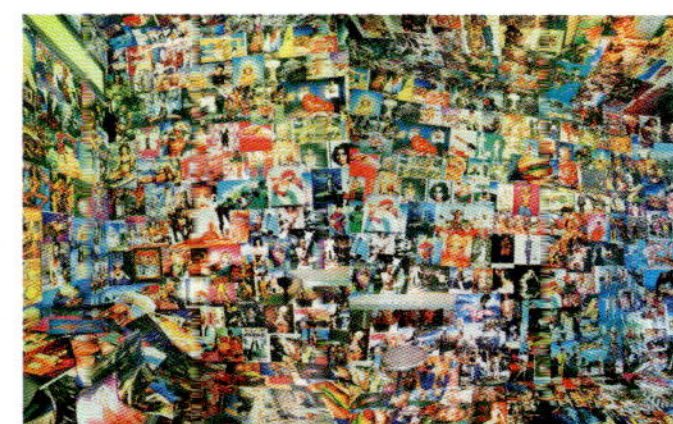

Endpapers II, 2017
The United States has the highest incarceration rate in the world—solitary confinement is considered to be a form of psychological torture. There are more than 80,000 adults and juveniles in solitary confinement across the USA today.

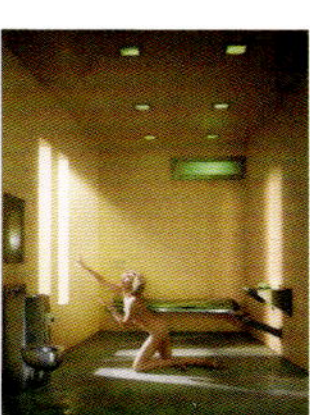

Miley Cyrus
Solitary, 2017

THESE TWO BOOKS, *LOST + FOUND* AND *GOOD NEWS* ARE FOR CHRISTOPHER,
MY DIAMOND IN THE WINDOW.

TO ALL OF THE ARTISTS WHOM I'VE HAD THE PRIVILEGE AND HONOR TO WORK WITH—
ALL OF THE PEOPLE WHO HAVE MADE THESE BOOKS POSSIBLE, BOTH BEHIND THE SCENES,
AND IN FRONT OF THE CAMERA—TO MY FAMILY, SONJA LACHAPELLE, HELGA & PHILLIP LACHAPELLE,
BAMBINI, KUMI, GHRETTA, AND MAMA MAKEUP—MY LOVE AND GRATITUDE.
DAVID LACHAPELLE

A PORTION OF THE AUTHOR'S PROFITS FROM THIS BOOK WILL BE DONATED TO SMILE TRAIN.

EACH AND EVERY TASCHEN BOOK PLANTS A SEED!
TASCHEN IS A CARBON NEUTRAL PUBLISHER. EACH YEAR, WE OFFSET OUR ANNUAL CARBON EMISSIONS WITH CARBON CREDITS AT THE INSTITUTO TERRA, A REFORESTATION PROGRAM IN MINAS GERAIS, BRAZIL, FOUNDED BY LÉLIA AND SEBASTIÃO SALGADO. TO FIND OUT MORE ABOUT THIS ECOLOGICAL PARTNERSHIP, PLEASE CHECK: WWW.TASCHEN.COM/ZEROCARBON

TO STAY INFORMED ABOUT TASCHEN AND OUR UPCOMING TITLES, PLEASE SUBSCRIBE TO OUR FREE MAGAZINE AT WWW.TASCHEN.COM/MAGAZINE, FOLLOW US ON INSTAGRAM AND FACEBOOK, OR EMAIL YOUR QUESTIONS TO CONTACT@TASCHEN.COM.

HOHENZOLLERNRING 53, D-50672 KÖLN
WWW.TASCHEN.COM

EDITED AND DESIGNED BY DAVID LACHAPELLE AND NEMUEL DEPAULA, LOS ANGELES

PRINTED IN ITALY
ISBN 978-3-8365-9964-1

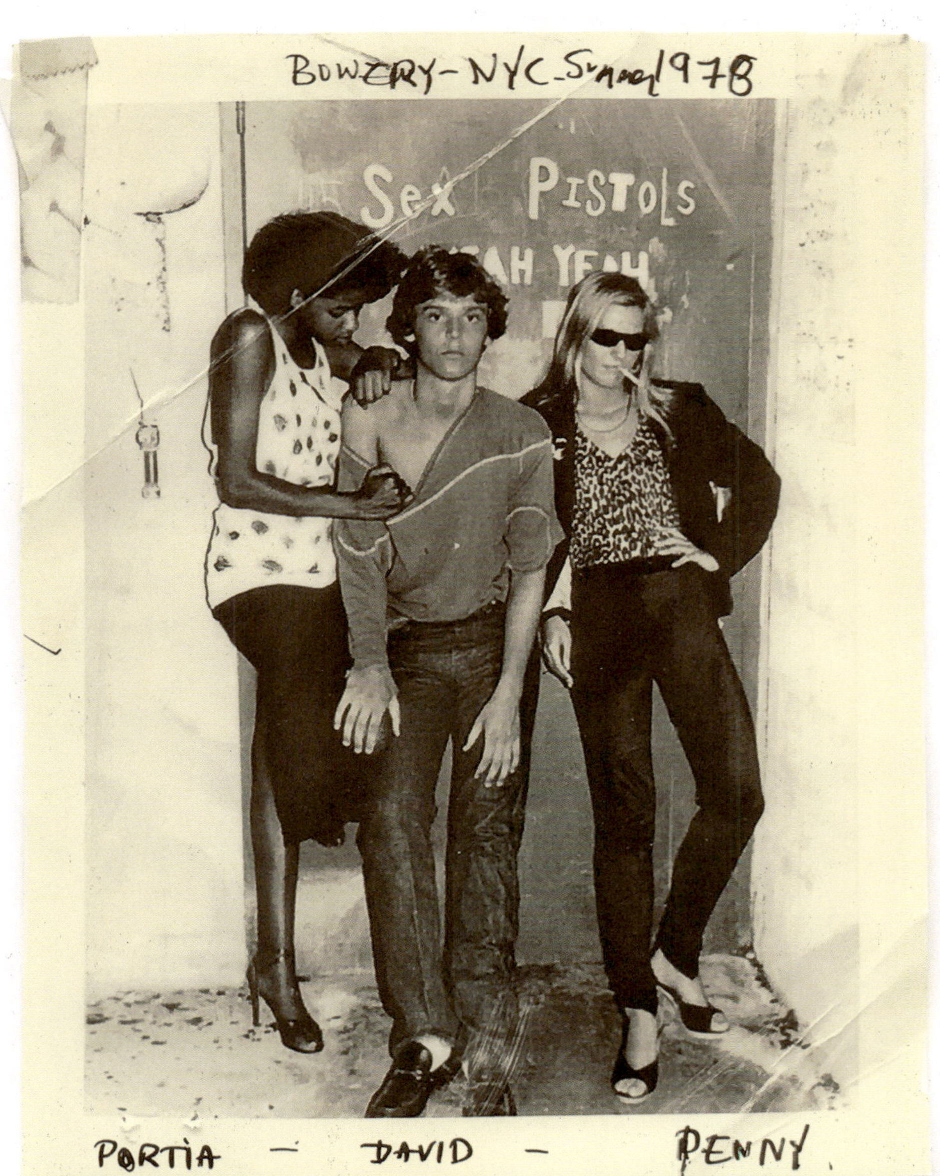
BOWERY - NYC - Summer 1978
Sex PISTOLS
YEAH YEAH
PORTIA - DAVID - PENNY

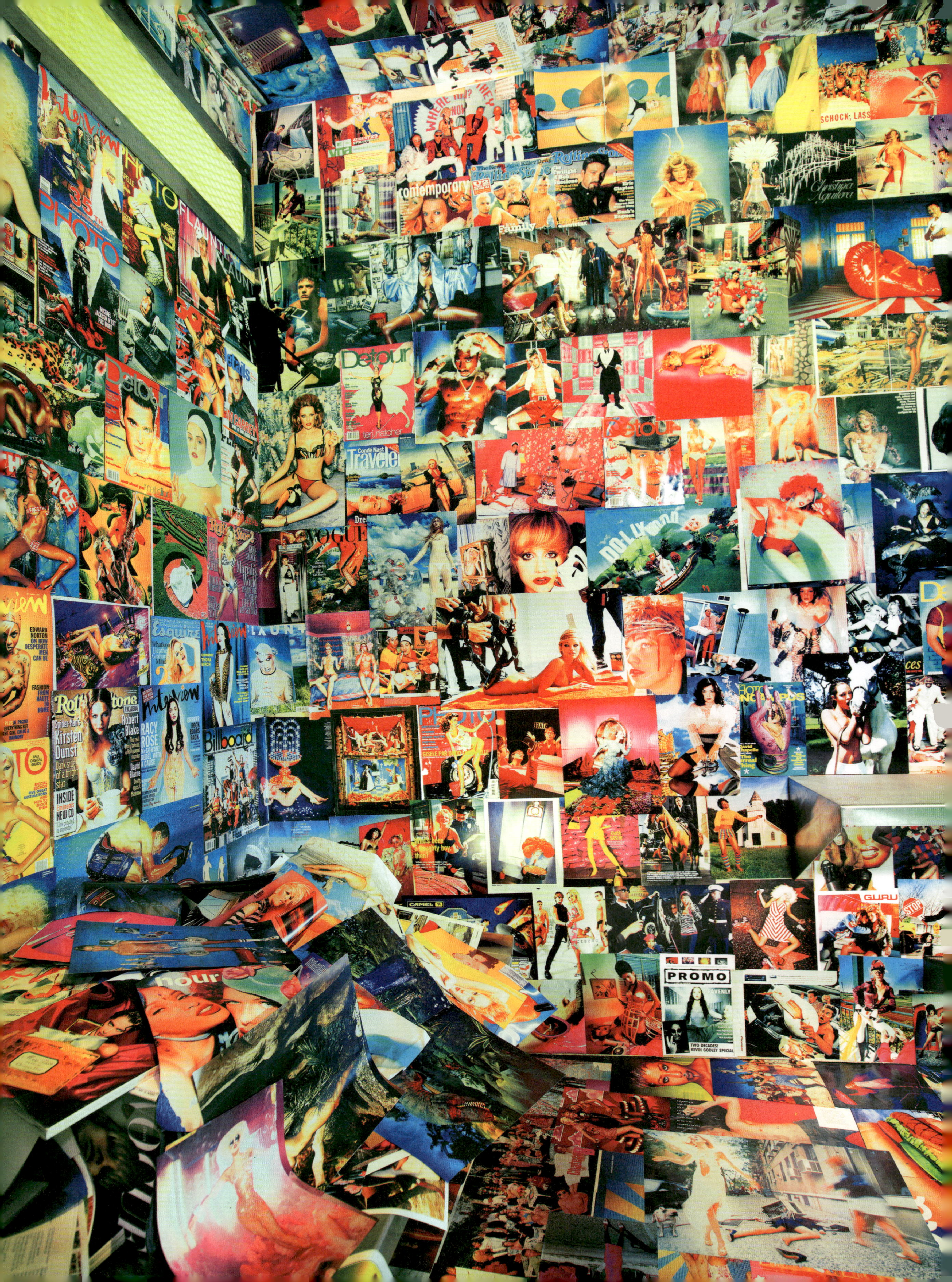

Interview
PHOTO
Detour
teri hatcher
Condé Nast
Traveler
VOGUE
Esquire
Billboard
Kirsten
Dunst
Robert
Blake
RACY
ROSE
EDWARD
NORTON
contemporary
SCHOCK; LASS
Christina Aguilera
CAMEL
GURU
STOP
PROMO
TWO DECADES!
KEVIN GODLEY SPECIAL